BASIC
SOCIOLOGY

BASIC SOCIOLOGY
Structure, Interaction, and Change

Jon M. Shepard
UNIVERSITY OF KENTUCKY

Harper & Row, Publishers
New York, Evanston, San Francisco, London

Sponsoring Editor: Alvin A. Abbott
Special Projects Editor: Claire T. Rubin
Project Editor: Elizabeth Dilernia
Designer: Rita Naughton
Production Supervisor: Stefania J. Taflinska

Basic Sociology: Structure, Interaction, and Change

Library of Congress Cataloging in Publication Data
Shepard, Jon M
   Basic sociology: structure, interaction, and change.
    1. Sociology. I. Title. [DNLM: 1. Sociology.
HM51 S547b 1974]
HM51.S513   301   73-21070
ISBN 0-06-046094-6

To my parents

Contents

Preface

No author sets out to write "just another book"; a sense of purpose and uniqueness is needed. Several sustaining thoughts guided me throughout the writing of *Basic Sociology*. I started on the assumption that sociology—with its perspectives, concepts, and theories—is a vital part of anyone's college education. Sociology is basic to a liberal education because it offers a window on the social forces that affect us all daily. I also faced the fact that the majority of the students enrolled in an introductory sociology course are receiving their first and last exposure to the field. These two ideas led to this question: How can the richness, subtlety, complexity, and abstractness of sociology be communicated to students who come to it without a background for it and who will in all likelihood take no more than one more sociology course? Most introductory texts seem to be written for students who are either majoring in sociology or planning graduate work in the area. Written with professional sociologists (or professionals-to-be) as the unintended but influential audience, these books are too lengthy and too encumbered with excessive detail about historical developments in sociology and specific research studies.

On the basis of these judgments, on the one hand I set out to write a brief and concise text, one that could realistically be covered within a quarter or a semester. On the other hand, I wished to write a thorough and "solid" textbook that would accurately reflect the complexities of sociology, so that those students (majors or nonmajors) taking more advanced sociology courses would have received an adequate background. This desire for both brevity and thoroughness naturally led me to focus on the "basics" of sociology—the most fundamental perspectives, concepts, and theories—and to develop and illustrate them as thoroughly as possible within the confines of space. While students in an introductory sociology course cannot be expected to digest all facets of our burgeoning field, an understanding of its basics is within their reach. My approach is to cover less material thoroughly rather than more, superficially.

Coherence and direction are promoted within each chapter by an introductory statement at the beginning and an overview at the end. For integration across chapters and parts, three major efforts have been made. First, each chapter closes with a preview that leads into the next chapter. Second, several basic (and interrelated) concepts are introduced in the first five chapters, and these concepts are used or assumed throughout the remainder of the book. Third, the entire book is organized around two basic sociological perspectives—the structural and the social-psychological. The distinction between the two perspectives is one that students in an introductory sociology course often miss. Frequently they enter the course with a decided tendency to interpret social life in psychological terms and leave with the same inclination. Organizing a book around both postures has the advantage of making explicit the difference between them, while simultaneously covering material traditionally contained in introductory sociology texts.

One of the psychological difficulties of writing this text came from the constant realization that insufficient formal recognition was being given to the many sociologists whose ideas form the basis and substance of this text. Failure to cite all possible sources was a sacrifice I was willing to make in order to write a more streamlined text. Some, though by no means all, of these intentional oversights are remedied in the list of additional sources and readings that appears at the end of each chapter.

Every author should have an editor. Few are fortunate enough to have Irene Hultman. Her editorial expertise, faith, and encouragement were provided with sustaining and addicting regularity.

I wish to thank the many other persons who helped me complete the book, including Al Abbott, Claire Rubin, Betsy Dilernia, and Myra Schachne of Harper & Row. I also wish to acknowledge Luther Wilson, formerly of Harper & Row, who was instrumental in getting the project off the ground. And how would I have managed without the secretarial skills exercised by Marie Elliott, Linda Holt, Mable Belt, Rosemary Waters, and Sandy Burrows? My friend and colleague, Tom Panko, was a sounding board whose wit and level-headedness will always be appreciated. Finally, thank you, Kay and Jon.

Jon M. Shepard

BASIC SOCIOLOGY

part I

INTRODUCTION

1

Sociological Perspectives

If the world is a stage and its inhabitants are players, it must also be said that the actors generally deliver their lines and act their roles as if they were rehearsed and with a definite flair for mimicry. Yet the action, which sociologists have labeled "social structure," depends not on conscious learning of the appropriate social lines and movements, but in good part on unquestioning acceptance of what we are told and on imitation of what we observe. In one sense, we are puppets responding to tugs on the strings that bind us to essential sets of social relationships. For example, without the sets of social relationships that comprise a family structure, new members of society could not survive to experience the wonders and tragedies of social and psychological development. And yet we are not really puppets, for not only are human beings capable of bucking tradition, they are also active, thinking creatures even when they are conforming. Since both of these qualifications to the puppet analogy are major points in this text, we shall return to them later. For the moment, the important idea is that social relationships are essential for human survival.

We have the luxury of taking for granted most aspects of our social life, because—within a given social structure at a given point in time—human attitudes and behavior tend to be predictable and recurrent. However, the qualifying phrase "within a given social structure at a given point in time" is important; it allows for social change and for differences among subcultures and among societies.

The starting point for sociology, then, is the assumption that social structure—which implies predictability and recurrence in social relationships —is necessary. The premise is that man is a social animal engaged in rather orderly relationships. Sociologists pursue myriad activities in attempts to understand, explain, and predict the often hidden processes that permit successive generations to carry out relatively predictable and orderly lives without having to forge anew the rules for their social relations. Yet because each generation usually is spared the travail of creating new rules and roles by which to conduct their social intercourse, its members fail to ask: Why are things the way the are? How do they change? Sociologists constantly wrestle with these basic questions. Even if you do not plan to become a professional sociologist, it is possible for you to share in the excitement of trying to answer these questions. To be sure, your sharing of the sociological enterprise will, in large part, be a vicarious one; that is, you will be exposed to the answers given by leading sociologists without having sufficient opportunity to seek answers for yourselves. Nevertheless—and this is extremely important—by trying to understand sociological concepts, perspectives, and theories, you will be in a better position to understand and interpret the social orbits in which you have lived and those that you will enter in the future. This point deserves elaboration.

THE USES OF SOCIOLOGY

Why study sociology? To learn more about what it means to be a professional sociologist? To find remedies for the social problems of our times? To satisfy the desire to know that springs from an intrinsic love of ideas? These are perfectly legitimate motivations for pursuing the study of sociology. But there are more immediate and personally relevant reasons. A knowledge of sociology can deepen your understanding of your own life and the settings in which you carry on your social transactions because of the light it throws on the intersection of self, others, and social structure. The remainder of this section will attempt to place this use of sociology in perspective. As a vehicle for illustrating the usefulness of sociology in understanding the interdependence of self and social structure, we will briefly examine the historical origins of the field of sociology.

Sociology in the beginning

A starving man is obsessed with visions of food. Oxygen is uppermost in the mind of a deep-sea diver whose air hose has developed a leak. People in a state of disorder are normally very much concerned about the restoration of predictability and continuity. So it was with man in nineteenth-century Europe. At that time, the social order based on social position, land ownership, church, kinship, community, and autocratic political leadership was being assaulted by new social currents.[1] The social order to which Europeans had become accustomed since the Middle Ages reeled under the new social and economic influences ushered in by the Industrial Revolution and the French Revolution. Philosophers of an earlier age had wondered: How did society emerge? What is the foundation of social order? What is the nature of the human species? But these two cataclysmic processes—industrialism and democracy—so altered the nineteenth-century social order that earlier philosophical questions on the nature of man and society now assumed a moral cast: What is the best type of social order? How can social cohesiveness be restored? On what basis can man be integrated into a meaningful social structure? These questions were natural for intellectuals witnessing the exodus of people from small population centers in rural areas to comparatively massive concentrations in cities, the transition from farming and craft production to factory life, and the emergence of an individualism that severed traditional ties with such social structures as the guild, the community, and the church.

Deprived of the familiar, man began seriously to ask: What's it all about? Rapid social change and its consequences fell heavily on the minds of early sociologists. Men like Auguste Comte, Emile Durkheim, Max Weber, and Herbert Spencer were in the forefront of efforts to probe the depths of social order and social change. It is to this sociological tradition of examining social forces that the sociological imagination can be traced.

Sociological imagination: the interplay of self and society

C. Wright Mills defines the *sociological imagination* as a mentality that sifts information in the quest for understanding the implications of the broader historical canvas for self and others.[2] Thus a significant part of sociology's promise lies in its utility for placing self, others, and society in historical perspective. In one of the most provocative and stimulating treatments of sociology, Mills forcefully calls attention to the relationship between personal situations and social events. Things that trouble us as individuals, notes Mills, are intimately linked with broader societal issues. Consider the following example.

Personal issues were obviously linked with the public issue of whether or not the United States should have waged war in Southeast Asia. At one point there was a dramatic increase in graduate school enrollment in the United States, spurred by young men desiring to avoid the draft. These men extended their schooling because they felt it was preferable to the blisters, boredom, and bullets promised by a tour of duty in Vietnam. Many of those who did go to war had to endure separation from their wives and children; the children, whether permanently or temporarily fatherless, felt the impact of the war, as did the husbandless wives. The link between these personal troubles and the public issue of the merits of the war is obvious. What is not so obvious are the structural causes of the pursuit of this or any other military victory. The point here is, who profits from war? It is to the political, economic, and military structures that we must look for the answer. When nations make war, whether on a moral or immoral basis, forces are unleashed that create complex situations for individuals.

However, most people find it difficult to grasp the interplay between public issues and their own lives. Those who can see the relationship between distant, impersonal events and intimate, psychological phenomena, those who can make the intellectual transition between social structure and self, are heir to the classic sociological legacy of Comte, Spencer, Durkheim, Weber, and others—the quality of sociological imagination. This quality of mind permits one, for example, to read the newspaper with a better understanding of both the broad perspective and the personal impact of the information it contains. A news item on somebody's opposition to social welfare can be viewed not solely as an indication of man's inhumanity to man, but as an expression of the American value of individualism and its subsidiary tenet of self-help—a value that impels many persons to voice seemingly heartless sentiments toward the poor. With this window on the social world, the thoughts, feelings, and actions of self and others become more comprehensible.

Sociological imagination: the debunking theme

Because sociology's task is to reveal the nature of social life, it has a tendency to challenge what most people assume to be eternal verities.[3] What the population takes for unassailable truth chiseled in stone may, under examination, prove to be fiction. In addition to unmasking discrepancies between established views and what is really happening, sociology casts social life in relative terms. Ways of thinking, feeling, and acting are presented as mere alternatives from a wider set of possibilities. This aspect of the sociological imagination, then, involves penetrating official interpretations of social structure in order to see what is behind them.

The innocent myths surrounding Santa Claus and the stork are outgrown early, when a first-grader shatters a friend with the news that there is no Santa Claus and supplies some shocking details on how babies are really made. The rather high level of political awareness among contemporary American youth has brought to public attention what sociologists have known for a long time: Decisions regarding the use of political power are not always made by persons in official positions but by big-money manipulators in the background. Countless other social myths are consciously or unconsciously held throughout the life cycle. It is the sociologists' task to question the veracity of these beliefs. For example, research has challenged the widely held tenet that the value of property inevitably declines when Blacks move into a neighborhood.

Sociological imagination: intellectual liberation

Implicit in the recognition of the interplay of self and society and the sociological imagination is the promise of intellectual liberation. Understanding the interplay between self and society and discovering the truth behind social myths free people to share in a personal way Somerset Maugham's wisdom that "tradition is a guide and not a jailer."

Robert Bierstedt[4] expanded on the liberating function of sociology for the college students who take only an introductory course and have no intention of pursuing sociology as an occupation. As with other liberal arts courses of study, even a brief encounter with sociology allows the human mind to transcend the narrow confines of personal experience. Through sociology, the student makes discoveries about the value systems of societies very different from his own and may come to understand how such a practice as the sacrificial murder of infants, bizarre in the extreme to him, is expected behavior and therefore a normal dimension of social life in some other societies. To understand this is to understand a great deal, and the liberating perspective it gives can subsequently be applied to aspects of your own social environment.

Although we have highlighted the personal benefits of sociology—i.e., the sociological imagination can promote understanding of the interplay between self and society, it can encourage the habit of peering behind the facades of social structure, and it can be intellectually liberating—paradoxically enough, sociology never takes the individual as an object of investigation. The remainder of this chapter is devoted to an elaboration of sociology's unique focus, a focus that always remains above the level of the individual.

STRUCTURAL AND SOCIAL-PSYCHOLOGICAL PERSPECTIVES

Long before the idea of a field of study called sociology germinated in Auguste Comte's mind, philosophers hotly debated this question: Which is real, the individual or social structure? Echoes of that ageless debate can still be heard in sociological circles. Various schools of thought have attempted to answer the question: What should be studied in order to understand, explain, and predict social structure?

One answer to this question, providing the basic theme of this text, is that two perspectives—the structural and the social-psychological—are central to the understanding of sociology. The *structural perspective* holds that principles of social structure can be discovered through the analysis of

Thomas Hopker, Woodfin Camp & Associates

social structure itself, without reference to individuals. This viewpoint represents sociology's uniqueness in relation to other social sciences. Yet it is impossible adequately to portray the domain of sociology without reference to the *social-psychological perspective*, which focuses on the interplay among persons in the social structures within which they act out their lives. Some aspects of sociological interest are best viewed in strictly structural terms; others are best approached from an exclusively social-psychological perspective. Still other areas are more clearly understood by a combination of the two perspectives. Both perspectives contribute to the understanding of social life; therefore, throughout this text, the two will be distinguished.

The structural perspective

Emile Durkheim, the French sociologist, advanced the structural perspective as sociology's unique focus.[5] Whereas most sociologists prior to Durkheim's time believed that only the individual was suitable for sociological scrutiny, Durkheim argued that both the individual and the social structure in which he exists are abstract units and, of the two, social structure is the more suitable for sociological study. Let psychologists study man at the individual level, he contended, while sociologists pursue the investigation of social phenomena at the social structural level.

Why, Durkheim asked, do we not attempt to explain human life by reference to the individual hydrogen, oxygen, carbon, and nitrogen atoms that comprise a living body cell? Why do we accept the idea that the synthesis of these elements forms something unique (a living cell) that is not reducible to any single element? Why do we attribute the characteristics of water to the combination of hydrogen and oxygen rather than to either separately? In making the case for the extrication of sociology from psychology, Durkheim held that, like physical substances, social structure is not reducible to its individual parts. According to this perspective, social structure is external to individuals and is not merely a product of the addition of individual attitudes and behavior. Just as the properties of ice do not exist apart from the synthesis of the correct proportions of hydrogen and oxygen at a particular temperature, social structure is a unique phenomenon that cannot be explained by consideration of its separate elements. In Durkheim, then, we find the earliest brief for sociology as the science that deals with social life without reference to psychological factors.

How can this be? Is it really possible to consider social structure as something that is external to individuals, that exists independently of its appearance in individuals, and that influences the attitudes and behavior of persons? Some illustrations will demonstrate the validity of the structural perspective. There are two ways to view the structural perspective. In the first instance, social structure exists in spite of conflict between the ideas of individuals and the ideas dominant in the social structure. In the second view, there is no conflict between the individual and social structure. Thus the structural perspective encompasses conflict and integration, both of which are inevitable in social life. As an example of the first view (conflict), hypothetical figures regarding the frequency of marijuana smoking are presented.

• CONFLICT BETWEEN THE INDIVIDUAL AND THE SOCIAL STRUCTURE. While Durkheim originated this uniquely sociological perspective, Peter Blau deserves credit for its further development. Blau attempted to formalize Durkheim's thesis that, while social structure could not exist if not for the minds of individuals, social structure is external to persons taken singly.[6] The impact of social structure can be seen in instances where the ways persons think, feel, or act are counter to their personal predispositions. When persons act, think, or feel in a manner that conforms to prevailing ideas in a social structure, and yet is contrary to their personal ideas, a *structural effect* has been operative.

Consider Table 1.1, which contains hypothetical figures on attitudes and behavior with reference to marijuana-smoking. For the sake of illustration, suppose two groups of college students have been surveyed on drug use. Members of each group, it must be assumed, are in frequent and close contact with other members of their group. On the basis of survey results, the majority of the members of Group A have been shown to express favorable attitudes toward marijuana. The majority of Group B members, in contrast, indicated unfavorable attitudes toward the drug and its use. This means that a minority of Group A members indicated unfavorable feelings while a minority of Group B members may be characterized as positively inclined toward the smoking of marijuana.

TABLE 1.1 Hypothetical illustration of a structural effect

	GROUP IDEAS REGARDING MARIJUANA-SMOKING			
	Group A: Favorable		Group B: Unfavorable	
	INDIVIDUAL IDEAS REGARDING MARIJUANA-SMOKING			
Extent of marijuana-smoking over past year	Group A: Favorable (1)	Unfavorable (2)	Group B: Favorable (3)	Unfavorable (4)
Often	80%	60%	10%	10%
Seldom	10	30	30	10
Never	10	10	60	80
Total	100%	100%	100%	100%

Table 1.1 shows each group's reaction to marijuana-smoking as well as responses to a question designed to determine the frequency with which individuals in each of the four subgroups have actually smoked the drug during the past year.

From a psychological viewpoint, it would not be surprising to find that a high percentage of persons who are members of a group supportive of this sort of drug use and are also personally inclined toward marijuana-smoking have smoked the drug frequently within the past year. Note the hypothetical percentages in column (1) of Table 1.1. Similarly, it is consistent from a psychological perspective for a lack of marijuana use to prevail among persons in an unfavorable group who are also personally negatively disposed [see column (4) of Table 1.1]. In both columns (1) and (4), group ideas are consistent with individual ideas.

However, a structural effect would have been demonstrated if individuals who belong to a group favorable to marijuana-smoking but who are personally opposed to it have actually smoked the drug over the last year. Similarly, a structural effect would be operative if members of a group unsupportive of marijuana-smoking have not smoked marijuana much over the preceding year, in spite of their personal feelings that this use of the drug is appropriate. Examine columns (2) and (3) of Table 1.1.

Reasoning according to the structural perspective, we could conclude that these findings, if valid, illustrate the overriding effect of external social structure on the behavior of its members. The effect is overriding and external because behavior is channeled in a direction inconsistent with individual predispositions. Such an effect is possible partly because conformity to prevailing group pressures allows persons to avoid guilt feelings raised by deviation and partly because social approval is preferable to criticism from others.

The marijuana example emphasizes the overriding influence of the social structure on the individual even when the orientations of the two are in conflict. There is the simpler category in which individual members' definitions of the proper ways of thinking, acting, and feeling are not at odds with those of the social structure.

• LACK OF CONFLICT BETWEEN THE INDIVIDUAL AND THE SOCIAL STRUCTURE. In the fictitious case of marijuana-smoking, the structural perspective was illustrated for that part of the social world in which social structure prevails over the individual even when personal predispositions are in conflict with it. This principle helps to explain the predictability and recurrence found in social life. As noted in the opening pages, much of our social life is taken for granted. If this tends to be true when the ideas of individuals and those prevailing in their social structure are inconsistent, it is almost invariably true for that larger portion of social life in which persons have accepted the ideas prevalent in a social structure.

In the following example, suicide is used to illustrate the structural perspective in instances where individual and social structural conflict is not involved. This example is particularly enlightening because self-destructive behavior is often attributed to psychological factors.

Why do people kill themselves? Or, more consistent with Durkheim's frame of reference, why does the suicide rate vary from place to place? In his classic study, *Suicide*, Durkheim attempted to lay to rest the commonly held explanations for the taking of one's life.[7] He punched a good many holes in such popular explanations for suicide as climate, insanity, and heredity. Although willing to concede that, all other conditions being equal, an alcoholic or depressed person is more likely to end it all than a psychologically healthy person, Durkheim found the underlying causes of suicide to reside in the nature of social life itself. That is, while psychological characteristics may make some individuals more likely to commit suicide, until we locate in social life the conditions that trigger this final act, we are without an explanation for variations in the suicide rate.

From careful scrutiny of variations in suicide rates among different types of people, Durkheim derived a series of separate findings for which he formulated one encompassing explanation. Why would single persons commit suicide with greater frequency than do married persons? Why is the suicide rate lower among Jews and Catholics than among Protestants? Why does the incidence of suicide climb during periods of political instability and decline in eras of political tranquility? To these and other apparently unconnected questions, Durkheim found a unifying answer: The degree of social integration or cohesiveness is the explanatory factor underlying variations in suicide rates among societies and different kinds of people.

Durkheim developed a schema outlining three types of suicide, each of which was related to the degree of social cohesiveness within any given social structure. It was not a simple one-way schema. A high suicide rate could result either from excessive social integration or from a lack of social cohesion. For example, *altruistic suicide* is said to occur when persons are so committed to the social structure to which they belong that the sacrifice of oneself for the structure's welfare is an acceptable personal choice. If the structure is benefited by one's death, then it becomes a moral duty to serve it by self-inflicted death. A Japanese samurai who would rather fall on both swords than face disgrace, or a soldier who accepts certain death while saving comrades in battle are excellent illustrations of altruistic suicide.

If a strong moral commitment to a social structure makes suicide a reasonable alternative, a relative lack of social integration can produce the same result. Higher rates of *egoistic suicide*, contended Durkheim, are associated with a social structure that fails to provide social anchorages for its members; bonds between the structure and its members are so loose that the involvement of self in the pursuit of larger ideals is difficult. If the social structure fails to provide reasons for living, individuals may use some pretext for escaping the burden of a meaningless, purposeless existence.

Durkheim also associated *anomic suicide* with the absence of individual-social structural bonds; however, anomic suicide was thought by Durkheim to be the result of sudden shifts toward personal or societal disorganization. A precipitous change in circumstances, such as occurs in the transition from married life to widowhood, might result in anomic suicide. The epidemic of ledge-jumping that swept America when the stock market crashed in 1929 falls into this category. True to Durkheim's line of reasoning, even in the case of anomic suicide, personal disorganization is linked to its social antecedents. The portion of the suicide rate attributable to the loss of values and norms would presumably be greater in a social structure suffering from the shocks of frequent and rapid social change. Table 1.2 presents the social antecedents of each of the three types of suicide, along with representative findings from Durkheim's *Suicide* reflecting each type.

Durkheim's study of suicide illustrates that what seems to be an extremely individual and personal act can be traced to social roots. This is not to say that suicide cannot be investigated from a psychological viewpoint, but in constructing the case for sociology as a unique discipline, Durkheim forcefully showed the possibility of explaining and forecasting human behavior without resorting to psychological factors. While psychological characteristics, he asserted, predispose some persons more than others toward certain kinds of behavior, the forces actually precipitating

TABLE 1.2 Durkheim's three types of suicide

TYPE OF SUICIDE	ANTECEDENT	SAMPLE FINDINGS FROM **SUICIDE**
Altruistic	Commitment to welfare of social structure	High rate of suicide among military
		High rate of suicide among the old and the sick
Egoistic	Lack of structure-defined reasons for living	Higher suicide rate among Protestants than among either Catholics or Jews
		Increase in suicide rate with higher educational level
Anomic	Sudden shifts toward personal or social disorganization	Increase of suicide rate during economic crises
		High suicide rate among the divorced and separated

SOURCE: Adapted from Emile Durkheim, **Suicide**, trans. by John A. Spaulding and George Simpson (New York: Free Press, 1951).

that behavior are to be found in the nature of social structure itself; hence, we arrive at the structural perspective.

This presentation of the structural perspective has been lengthy because of the need to overcome the natural tendency to reduce social phenomena to the psychological level of analysis. We have, however, run the risk of overstatement regarding the extent to which sociology actually excludes *any* focus on the behavior of individuals. It did not escape Durkheim that social structure requires the presence of individuals, just as individuals cannot exist without social structure. In spite of this recognition, the structural perspective legitimately de-emphasizes the individual side of the picture in order to center on certain aspects of social life that might otherwise be ignored. It is now necessary, however, to take a more balanced position by introducing the social-psychological perspective.

The social-psychological perspective

Central to the social-psychological perspective is the idea that social structure and individuals exist only in relationship to each other; that is, social psychology concentrates on individuals within the context of their social environment and on the social structure produced by the interaction of its members. This emphasis on the interaction of individuals within social contexts adds an indispensable sociological perspective.

Less effort will be expended on the social-psychological perspective at this point because of the rather detailed attention devoted to it in later chapters. It would, however, be unfair not to add some depth to your understanding of this perspective at this early stage. A few words are needed in order to crystalize in your mind the sense in which social psychology is interested in the "individual."

Of critical importance is the understanding that the social-psychological perspective does not take the individual per se as an appropriate unit of analysis. Rather, the individual's behavior is viewed in the context of his position within a particular social structure and in the context of the pattern of social relationships that flows from his interaction with other individuals in the structure. Let us consider the practice of knife-fighting by street gangs. From a social-psychological perspective a sociologist might attempt to explain participation in this "sport" through reference to individual needs, motives, and aspirations. A street-gang leader, for example, may feel he must fight either a member of his own gang who is challenging his position or the leader of another gang in order to validate periodically his right to leadership. Or it may be important for each gang member to fight occasionally if he is to establish or reaffirm his "manhood."

As implied in the foregoing example, from the social-psychological perspective it is not the individual per se that is of importance but the parts he acts out as a member of a social structure. Politicians are expected to compromise with others to achieve their goals, businessmen are expected to interact with others with a constant eye on the profit sheet, and ministers are not expected to seduce their parishioners. In turn, we have expectations for our own behavior. We see nothing inappropriate in asking a politician for a favor; we know that wariness is in order when an "Honest John" delivers his pitch on that low-mileage, one-owner car at a giveaway price; we believe that ministers should be above temptation.

It should be clear by now that the closest sociology comes to the individual is in the context of his social interaction with others. In short, sociologists do not ever take the individual himself as a unit of study.

• AN ILLUSTRATION OF THE STRUCTURAL AND SOCIAL-PSYCHOLOGICAL PERSPECTIVES. In closing this section it will be helpful to consider the structural and social-psychological perspectives within the context of a common example. Let us pursue another illustration on drug use. What factors are predictive of variations in the use of so-called hard drugs such as heroin and cocaine? From the structural perspective, it could be predicted that hard drug use will vary with the social class level. Specifically, hard drug consumption might be expected to be lower within the middle and upper classes and higher within the lower class—and particularly prevalent in males between the ages of 16 and 25.

At the social-psychological level, on the other hand, it could be predicted that it is the social class of one's friends, not social class as such, that contributes to variations in hard drug use.

Which of these two interpretations is valid? Can we, consistent with the structural perspective, predict variation in hard drug consumption by knowledge of social status alone? If so, a social phenomenon will have been explained without reference to the personalities, needs, and motivations of individuals. Or, in line with the social-psychological perspective, can we best predict variation in hard drug use from information regarding the social status of an individual's friends? If the latter interpretation is closer to reality, the following argument can be made: The effects of social structure on persons are mediated through interaction with other individuals; that is, individuals consume hard drugs to varying degrees as a result of personal relationships with others within a social structure.

Just as in the case of Durkheim's study of suicide, which of the two interpretations would be upheld in actual research is, in the present context, irrelevant. If the structural and social-psychological perspectives have been clearly distinguished, the paramount purpose of the section will have been accomplished. As explained earlier, a grasp of these two perspectives is vital because the bulk of this text rests on their distinction.

Sociology and the individual

The place of the individual in the sociological enterprise is important enough to risk a restatement of what may already be obvious from reading this section on the structural and social-psychological perspectives. To say that the individual as an object of study is inappropriate within the structural perspective is to restate the evident. But what about the social-psychological perspective? How is the individual incorporated into this angle of sociological vision? The answer is simple and bears repeating: It is not the individual per se that is of importance but the parts he acts out as a member of a social structure.

Finally, while sociology does not consider the individual per se as an appropriate unit of study, the structural and social-psychological perspectives are central to grasping intersections between one's own biography and society, to unmasking social myths, and thereby achieving some measure of intellectual liberation.

OVERVIEW AND PREVIEW

Two basic starting points have been developed. First, personal uses of sociological imagination were discussed. Paramount among the uses of sociology are: (1) comprehension of the interplay between self and social structure; (2) ability to look behind the facades of social structure; and (3) intellectual liberation. Intellectual liberation is a use of sociology implied both in the debunking motif and in understanding the interplay between self and society.

Second, sociology's unique focus on nonindividual phenomena was elaborated by distinguishing between the structural and social-psychological perspectives. Central to the structural perspective is the assumption that one aspect of social structure can be understood only by reference to other aspects of social structure. Social structure in this view cannot be reduced to the level of individuals. Illustrations of the structural perspective were given for those instances where individual and social structural conflict is present and for social situations where individual and social structural conflict is not prominent.

Nor does the social-psychological perspective take the individual, as such, as an object of study. Rather, individuals are examined in the context of their positions within a social structure in terms of the network of social relationships that are generated through social interaction with other persons. So, at neither the structural nor social-psychological levels of analysis is the individual per se considered to be an appropriate unit of sociological analysis. Yet these two perspectives are indispensable tools for the individual in capitalizing on the three uses of the sociological imagination discussed in the first part of this chapter.

In Chapter 2, sociology is defined as the scientific study of social structure. The concepts central to the idea of social structure are defined, interrelated, and illustrated. Finally, two nonsociocultural factors (biological heritage and geographic environment) are assessed in terms of their impact on social structure.

REFERENCES

1. This theme is fully developed in Robert A. Nisbet, *The Sociological Tradition* (New York: Basic Books, 1966).
2. C. Wright Mills, *The Sociological Imagination* (New York: Oxford University Press, 1956).
3. The debunking theme is developed in Peter L. Berger, *Invitation to Sociology: A Humanistic Perspective* (Garden City, N.Y.: Doubleday, 1963), pp. 30–53.
4. Robert Bierstedt, "Sociology and General Education," in Charles H. Page, ed., *Sociology and Contemporary Education* (New York: Random House, 1963), pp. 40–55.
5. Emile Durkheim, *The Rules of Sociological Method*, trans. by Sarah A. Solovay and John H. Mueller and edited by Sir George E. G. Catlin (Chicago: University of Chicago Press, 1938), especially pp. xlvii–xlix, lii.
6. Peter M. Blau, "Structural Effects," *American Sociological Review*, 25 (April 1960), 178–193.
7. Emile Durkheim, *Suicide*, trans. by John A. Spaulding and George Simpson (New York: Free Press, 1951).

ADDITIONAL SOURCES AND READINGS

Berger, Peter L. "Sociology and Freedom," *The American Sociologist*, 6 (February 1971), 1–5.
Blumer, Herbert. *Symbolic Interactionism: Perspective and Method* (Englewood Cliffs, N.J.: Prentice-Hall, 1969).
Bolton, Charles D. "Is Sociology a Behavioral Science?" *Pacific Sociological Review*, 6 (Spring 1963), 3–9.
Goffman, Erving W. *Interaction Ritual* (Garden City, N.Y.: Doubleday, 1967).
Homans, George C. "Bringing Men Back In," *American Sociological Review*, 29 (December 1964), 809–818.

Horowitz, Irving Louis, ed. *The New Sociology: Essays in Social Science and Social Theory in Honor of C. Wright Mills* (New York: Oxford University Press, 1964).

Warriner, Charles K. "Groups Are Real: A Reaffirmation," *American Sociological Review*, 21 (October 1956), 549–554.

2

Key Concepts

Chapter 1 should have provided you with some reason for studying sociology, together with a sense of sociology's unique focus. Sociological concepts are no different in function from those of mathematics, literature, or engineering; they refer to things or relationships among things. Such concepts are building blocks in the sociological language—a language at the vital center of the study of the emergence, stability, and change in social structure—and therefore are useful for categorization and generalization. Sociological concepts are not dictated by the inherent nature of social phenomena or their relationships. They are merely means for isolating aspects of social structure that must be mentally separable from other facets of infinitely larger and more complex social events. Like all language forms, then, sociology chooses to focus on selected aspects of "reality" while leaving others untouched. In this sense sociological concepts are no more or less arbitrary than those of any discipline.

This chapter will offer answers to three questions: (1) If sociology is the scientific study of social structure, just what is social structure? (2) What are the major concepts with which sociologists push forward their quest for understanding, explaining, and predicting social structure? (3) What is the impact of culture, biological heritage, and geographic environment on social structure?

BASIC CONCEPTS

What is social structure?

In this section you will be given a definition of sociology that, in turn, entails a series of concepts whose interrelationships are as complex as they are central to understanding sociology. Although many more concepts will

be encountered, those described here are singularly important in the acquisition of sociological perspectives and knowledge. Be patient and proceed deliberately.

Sociology is the scientific study of social structure. Sociology starts with
the basic assumptions of regularity and predictability in social life; thus
it is appropriate that a definition of social structure contain these elements.
More importantly, the concept of social structure is based on additional
concepts that provide a framework for explaining the order and continuity
evidenced in our interaction with others. *Social structure* is an interrelated
set of social relationships based on man-made patterns for thinking, feeling,
and behaving.

To understand this mind-boggling definition of social structure at this
point would cancel the need for several later chapters. This introduction to
social structure and to the additional concepts its definition entails is meant
only to sensitize you to the terms and to show the interrelationships among
these concepts that are central to the study of sociology. To that end, several concepts will be defined, interrelated, and then illustrated. Keep in
mind the unlikelihood of full comprehension and the absolute necessity
for gaining, if only by memorization, the beginnings of a working familiarity
with the meaning of these concepts and their interrelationships. Study the
definitions of these concepts in Table 2.1 and then read the following
description of their interrelationships.

Interrelationships among key concepts

Interrelationships among the concepts central to social structure are depicted in Figure 2.1. Since separate chapters will be devoted to culture and
social structure, together with the other concepts contained in this graphic
presentation, this introductory note will be of the "thighbone connected
to the hipbone" variety.

• CULTURE. The term *culture* refers to all man-made patterns for feeling,
thinking, and behaving that are socially transmitted to an entire society or to
segments of the society. A subunit within a society, whose patterns for
thinking, feeling, and behaving are different in certain respects from the
larger society, is termed a *subculture*. Thus, we can speak of American
culture but also recognize the drug subculture or the subculture of poverty.
Culture may be either material or nonmaterial. *Material aspects of culture*
are tangible products of human creation, of which technology is an im-

TABLE 2.1 Basic sociological concepts

CULTURE CONCEPTS

CULTURE: Man-made patterns for thinking, feeling, and behaving that are socially transmitted to an entire society or to segments of the society.

MATERIAL CULTURE: Tangible products of human creation (for example, a space ship).

NONMATERIAL CULTURE: Intangible products of human creation (for example, the prohibition against murder).

SUBCULTURE: Patterns for thinking, feeling, and behaving subscribed to by identifiable societal subunits that in certain important respects are different from the larger society.

SOCIAL VALUES: General cultural principles embodying standards for thinking, feeling, and behaving that evoke deep emotional commitment.

NORMS: Rules for thinking, feeling, and behaving.

MORES:· Norms that are considered essential to social well-being (for example, the prohibition against bastardy).

FOLKWAYS: Norms that are important but considered to be less significant for social welfare than mores (for example, the presence of love between spouses).

LAWS: Norms that are formally defined, recorded, and enforced by public authority. Many mores and folkways are eventually expressed in legal code.

SOCIAL STRUCTURE CONCEPTS

SOCIAL POSITION:,   A location within a system of social relationships (e.g., mother, father, son, daughter within the family).

ROLE PRESCRIPTIONS: Culturally defined rights and duties expected of all persons occupying a particular social position. Although listed as a social structure concept, role prescriptions are actually part of culture.

ROLE BEHAVIOR: The manner in which role prescriptions are actually executed by a holder of a social position.

ROLE EXPECTATIONS: The repertoire of behavior expected for oneself and anticipated from others within the context of interrelated social positions.

SOCIAL INTERACTION: Exchange of social influence in which the actions of one person affect the behavior of another person, whose reactions in turn affect the first person, and so on. This is the process by which role behavior occurs.

EPISODIC SOCIAL RELATIONSHIP: A pattern of social interaction, either of short duration (customer-clerk) or of infrequent occurrence (nurse-patient).

CONTINUOUS SOCIAL RELATIONSHIP: A pattern of social interaction that is conducted on a relatively constant basis (father-son).

portant part. Examples of material culture range from moon rockets to "the Pill." *Nonmaterial aspects of culture* are intangible human creations, such as values and norms.

Values are broad cultural principles embodying standards for thinking, feeling, and behaving that evoke deep emotional commitment. Yet values are very general principles and do not specify acceptable kinds of thinking, feeling, and behaving. Consequently, more specific rules must be developed, called *norms*—rules for acceptable thought, sentiment, and behavior that are based on cultural values. They pertain to expected behavior from members of social units.

"Slippage" between the statement of a value and the development of norms based on that value partially accounts for the wide variations in belief, thought, and behavior that appear among persons and subunits that hold the same value. Consider the value of honesty. Among white men on

CULTURE ———————————— SOCIAL STRUCTURE

Nonmaterial culture Material culture   Social positions–Role prescriptions

Values ←——————→ Technology   Role expectations

Norms   Role behavior
  Mores
  Folkways
  Laws

                                 Social interaction

              Episodic social   Continuous social
              relationships   relationships

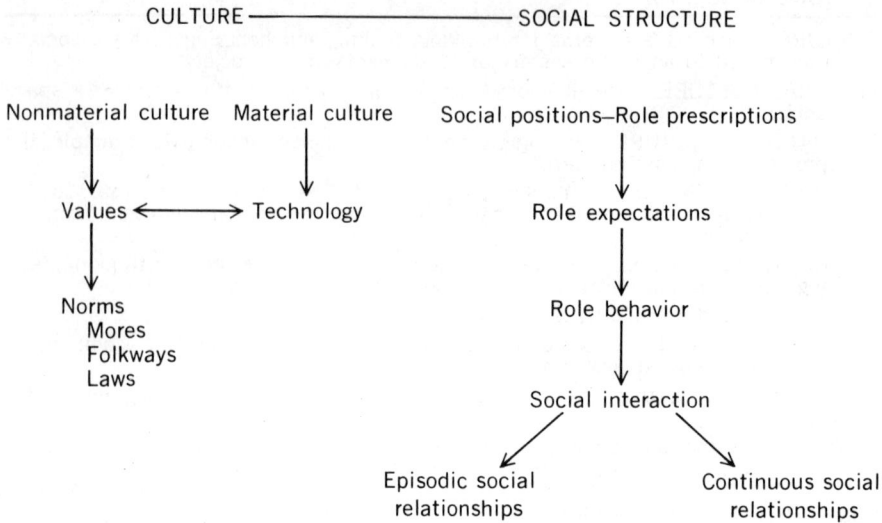

Figure 2.1   Interrelationships of key sociological concepts

the American frontier, horse-stealing was considered a serious enough breach of honesty to merit hanging. Among Indians at that time, however, stealing horses was not a breach of honesty but a means of fulfilling their values of bravery and cunning. Hanging Indians for horse-stealing gave the "white eyes" a feeling of justice done in response to what they regarded as gross dishonesty. Yet in other matters, Indians had good reason to hate the white man for his string of broken promises. Both peoples shared the *value* of honesty, but they held quite different *norms* of honesty.

Norms whose violation is severely sanctioned because of their perceived centrality to social well-being are labeled *mores*. Examples of mores in American society are the prohibition against illegitimate birth and the traditional ways of showing respect for the flag. On the other hand, there are norms, called *folkways*, that are considered less significant for social welfare and include such things as the expectation that love will exist between husband and wife and that fathers will spend time with their children. *Laws* are norms that are formally defined and recorded and that are enforced by public authority. Many mores and folkways are eventually expressed in legal code.

• SOCIAL STRUCTURE. As illustrated in Figure 2.1, social structure is composed of the pattern of social interaction and social relationships made possible by social positions, role prescriptions, role expectations, and role behavior. *Social positions* are locations in a system of social relationships that have culturally defined rights and duties associated with them. These rights and duties, called *role prescriptions*, are actually part of culture; they are listed under "social structure," however, because they cannot be meaningfully defined when divorced from the concept of social position. Within a family, the social position of daughter is related to other positions such as father, mother, and brother. Daughters are aware of the behavior expected of them in relation to persons in other social positions within the family. *Role expectations* are the repertoire of behavior anticipated from oneself and from others within the context of interrelated social positions. *Role behavior* refers to the actual behavior resulting from an attempt to fulfill the culturally defined role prescriptions attached to a given social position. Sons and daughters generally defer to parental authority in cases of disagreement; professors try to appear learned; and politicians act as if each of their decisions were heavily influenced by their constituents.

Social interaction is a feedback process of action and reaction; the actions of one person affect the actions of another, whose reactions in turn affect the first person—and on it goes. When fists fly in a barroom brawl, it is safe to assume that a gradual escalation of insult, counterinsult, and challenge had preceded the fight. Although most social interaction is considerably less negative and violent in nature, the process of reciprocal influence based on mutual expectations remains the same.

Of most interest to sociologists is the type of social interaction that occurs when the occupants of interrelated social positions behave toward each other on the basis of their mutual understanding of their reciprocal rights and duties. Social interaction is the process that makes role behavior possible. Patterns of social interaction related to social positions may be brief, infrequent, or continuous. *Episodic social relationships* are patterns of social interaction that are either of short duration (customer–clerk) or of infrequent occurrence (hospital nurse–patient). Patterns of social interaction engaged in on a constant basis (father–son) are called *continuous social relationships*.

In summary, aspects of *culture* are used to define the role prescriptions attached to social positions. As a result of mutually shared expectations, persons and groups can interact with each other. Interactions grounded in common understanding produce interrelated sets of social relationships that sociologists term *social structure*.

A closing note on the difference between culture and social structure is of first-order importance. Culture encompasses abstract patterns for feeling, thinking, and behaving that supply content and direction to *concrete* social activity, which sociologists label social structure.* To illustrate, take the concrete act of two male friends greeting each other after a period of

---

*Of course, material aspects of culture would be concrete rather than abstract. Consistent with sociological convention, this text will place primary emphasis on nonmaterial culture.

separation. Behavior in such a situation varies according to cultural designs. In the United States, if the two men embraced and kissed, observers might look askance; but in other cultures, if the two men did not kiss each other on both cheeks, such an omission would indicate deviant behavior. Concrete behavior is heavily influenced by cultural designs.

Note the avoidance of any statement that social structure is *determined* by culture. It is incorrect to regard social structure as culturally determined because cultural designs provide only the blueprints for thought and action. As a fuller discussion later in the text will reveal, individuals and societal subunits fashion their own variations on cultural themes. A Frenchman can kiss a male friend on the cheeks with or without sexual passion; beliefs regarding the definition and virtue of "hard work" vary among religious, ethnic, and regional subunits within a society.

The province of sociology, then, is the sociocultural phenomenon called social structure. Formally defined, social structure is an interrelated set of social relationships based on man-made patterns for thinking, feeling, and behaving. Although it is necessary to act as if social structure and culture are separable, they actually appear together. Culture cannot be enacted without social interaction, and social structure exists only when expectations have been culturally defined. A class and the university of which it is a part require persons to interact in patterned ways. University authorities and students must know what to expect of each other, and these expectations are culturally defined. That this is so is best seen when expectations change. It once seemed appropriate for university officials to act as parental substitutes, but in many universities and colleges, the philosophy of *in loco parentis* has suffered an irreparable assault in the past decade from the point of view of those who attended college prior to the mid-1960s. Freedom to choose a member of either sex to share one's university-owned bed is a startling example of how cultural norms change over time.

The key concepts just discussed can be used without reference to any particular real social situation, but they are intended, of course, to extend knowledge, understanding, and prediction of ongoing social life. Thus, it will be helpful to close this section with a specific illustration. The "wino" subculture on almost any skid row contains all the aspects of social structure with which you have just been showered.[1]

• AN ILLUSTRATION OF BASIC CONCEPTS. The wino subculture is a subculture because, despite its apparent deviance, it shares in the larger American culture. In American culture there is a strong emphasis on independence and self-support. Similarly, in the wino subculture there is a norm against becoming dependent on the church-related missions that offer shelter, soup, and salvation.

Becoming a "mission stiff," a frowned-upon condition, is a folkway. Mission dependency is not desirable but does not threaten existence. There are other folkways. Talking about one's troubles only burdens other winos, who already have a full share of troubles. A certain level of cleanliness is valued: If one becomes too dirty, he is unable to panhandle and thereby becomes a liability to his associates.

The obligation to share wine and money with other winos is one of the important mores in the wino social structure. Severe condemnation is reserved for "chiselers"—those who take wine and money from others but do not reciprocate when they can. Why? Because sharing is a matter of survival. The earning power of winos is low. Since begging is their only source of income and since they suffer frequent bouts of ill health, winos are forced to depend on each other.

The above are examples of some cultural dimensions of the wino subculture. What about the social structural dimensions? Social interaction is guided by cultural norms such as those just noted. Other norms are crystallized into rights and duties associated with social positions. Consider the social positions of "promoter" and "runner" in the wino world. The primary role prescription of the promoter is to beg money for wine; a runner is supposed to purchase a supply of wine after money has been appropriated. Choosing colleagues to occupy these positions and to fulfill the attached role prescriptions must be done with great care. An excessively dirty or drunk promoter or runner is police bait. An unscrupulous runner may "head south" with the fruit of the vineyard. In the latter case, role behavior would be at odds with the role prescription.

Sociological concepts, by their very nature, are abstract, as are concepts in any field of study. Yet the major function of abstract concepts is to help us understand, explain, and predict events in the real world. Sociological concepts must be applied to particular social structures, as in the present discussion of the wino subculture and in discussions in later chapters of this text. But first, some attention is given to two noncultural influences on social structure.

NONCULTURAL INFLUENCES ON SOCIAL STRUCTURE

From the portrait of social structure that has so far been drawn, any impression that culture completely determines social structure is a correct perception; it is, nevertheless, only partially true. Although they remain for the most part silent partners in the sociological enterprise, noncultural factors contribute to variations and uniformities in social structure across time and space. Diversity and similarity in social structure in different historical periods and in various locales is at least *conditioned* by a host of

Algimantas Kezys, DPI

noncultural forces. Two such forces, biological heritage and geographic (physical) environment, will receive attention in this section.

Biological heritage refers to those physical traits passed across generations from parents to children. Biological determinists maintain that variations and similarities in social structure are accounted for by inherited characteristics. Those aspects of the human environment that are not the product of human activity constitute man's *geographic environment*. Most prominent in sociological consideration are mineral, plant, and animal resources, climate, and terrain. Geographic determinists place the natural environment at the center of causation in the study of social structure. As you will see, both geographic and biological determinism are not newly conceived concepts.

Biological heritage

According to Aristotle, existing forms of government are a natural product of their subjects' biological heritage: Some peoples are born to enjoy the freedom of democracy while others are predestined either to slavery or autocracy. The ancients had no corner on biological determinism. For example, Hitler's ambition to conquer the world had deep roots in the philosophy of racial superiority penned by Nietzsche, Joseph Arthur de Gobineau, and Houston Stewart Chamberlain. Cesare Lombroso built a reputation on the premise that criminality could be predicted from physical traits; persons with bushy eyebrows or extraordinarily hairy bodies would not wish to be subject to a system of law based on Lombroso's classification.

One traditional view of biological determination is that woman is man's weaker counterpart. Today there are many voices that decry the myth of feminine inferiority and contend, sometimes stridently, that the "weaker sex" is an appellation more descriptive of the male than the female animal. In brief, theories of biological determinism range from explanations of the rise and fall of entire civilizations to explanations of such specific behaviors as criminality and differential occupational assignment based on sex.

Geographic environment

Writers from Hippocrates to Chamberlain have attributed differences among civilizations to geographic environment. Aristotle believed that the Greeks possessed both the mental acuity of southern peoples and the energy of those in northern climates. Being neither of the North nor of the South, he reasoned, Greeks were not handicapped by the dullness of people in cold climates or by the lethargy of those in hot climates. Their temperate climatic conditions, Aristotle believed, endowed the Greeks with that combination of mental and physical traits that destined them to superiority.

Similarly, the French philosopher Montesquieu located societal differences in natural causes. Why do free men live in cold climates while people in southern climates are prone to bondage? Montesquieu's answer was that cold weather invigorates the mind and body to heights of bravery, patience, and endurance, whereas heat saps strength and courage, leaving effeminacy in its wake.

Others have attempted to explain social structure by reference to terrain and natural resources, but no theory based on geographic determinism has successfully weathered the onslaught of accumulated evidence. If natural environment accounts for social life, why have similar societies developed under quite different geographic conditions and dissimilar societies emerged under comparable natural environments? Why have certain civilizations flowered and wilted with no alterations in climate, terrain, and physical resources? And why have some peoples developed more advanced civilizations in particular geographic environments where others had not?

An obvious implication of all this is that neither biological heritage nor geographic environment, separately or conjointly, constitutes a sufficient explanation of variations in social structure. Such a conclusion raises an appropriate question: Do inherited characteristics and geographic features play *any* part in the creation and change of social structure?

Intersection of social life, heredity, and geography

Culture and social structure are influenced by biological heritage and geographic environment. These influences, however, consist only in imposing very wide boundaries around man's creative efforts and achievements. Biological and geographic factors condition culture and social structure by *limiting human options.*

Let us consider the biological side first. Although there are advocates of a unisexual society, our very existence depends on the continuation of, and fraternization between, the only two sexes we have. The short supply of sex variations places a limit on the number of marital arrangements that can be socially created. Although a third sex might well interject some useful and even interesting facets to family life, we can empirically observe only these marital relationships: female-male (monogamy), females-male (polygyny), female-males (polyandry), females-males (group). Of course, the existence of even this small number of marital variations illustrates a degree of freedom from biological determinism. However, while societies may contain male-male and female-female unions, their adoption as a widespread familial form would probably generate incredibly severe social, biological, and psychological strains.

Geographic environment also operates to limit human social and cultural alternatives. Without such physical resources as water, oil, and various metal ores, the Industrial Revolution would have remained only the fantasy of some prehistoric visionaries, crudely imprinted on cave walls, never to be discovered by an archeological team on a government-sponsored "dig." Yet, as noted earlier, the theory of geographic determinism cannot withstand the evidence that vastly different societies have appeared and disappeared on the same physical landscape.

Human flexibility and the unique capacity of humans for mastering their environment are paramount reasons why social life is not a mere reflection of biology and geography. On the matter of human flexibility, Eskimos traditionally fashioned their houses of snow. In contrast, their neighbors, under the same climatic conditions, created their homes from animal hide and wood, ignorant of the advantages of igloo construction. Testimony to man's capacity for environmental control is the fact that the wing span of the modern 747 jet airplane exceeds the distance of the Wright brothers' first flight. Man was able, in only a few years, to extend phenomenally his mastery of gravity, a force that had defied him for centuries.

Effects of existing social structure

Still another reason why humans can and do enjoy considerable independence from their genes and natural settings lies in the fact that biology and geography are filtered through *existing* culture and social structure. A certain level of social and cultural advancement must precede utilization of existing natural resources. Prior to the Industrial Revolution the discovery of oil in the Middle East (assuming, of course, the presence of sufficient knowledge and technology for tapping underground reservoirs) would have meant nothing compared to the discovery or creation of a water supply in that area. The value assigned to a physical resource or a biological characteristic is determined primarily by the existing culture and social structure into which it is introduced. In some societies, fat is beautiful, and the skinniness worshiped by the "Pepsi generation" is associated with sickness or death.

The existence of arguments for black inferiority offers a further illustration of the manner in which a noncultural factor works through existing social structure and culture. According to Arnold Rose, America's reverence for liberty and equality clashed mightily with the reality of the slave system.[2] Consequently, several myths were created in order to reconcile and retain these contradictory elements. It became desirable to fashion a justification for the systematic subjugation of a race within an allegedly democratic society: Black inferiority was a natural choice. Racial superiority, then, while a false belief, meshed well with the social structure and culture of America and other countries that found slaves to be an economic asset. In this context whether or not racial differences in intelligence actually do exist is irrelevant.[3] What does matter is that biological differences (in this case, skin color) are refracted by, filtered through, and elaborated on by certain cultural tenets.

Although a rather lengthy elaboration on the place of biological and geographic determinism was necessary for a clear understanding of the concept, the conclusion can be succinctly stated. Neither biological heritage nor natural environment *determines* the level and type of social structure and culture. Social structures are quite variable while biological heritage and natural environment tend to be constant, and it is not possible to explain something that changes with something that does not. However, noncultural factors do *condition* social structure by providing opportunities and limitations with which we must grapple in the creation, maintenance, and alteration of our social life. The ways in which these opportunities and limitations are handled depend heavily on the existing level and type of social structure in which they appear. Thus, while biological inheritance and the geographic environment should not be ignored, they cannot be considered as explanations for social structure.

OVERVIEW AND PREVIEW

This chapter attempted to present in a brief yet systematic form the most basic sociological concepts. Social structure, the central focus of sociology, is an interrelated set of social relationships based on man-made patterns for thinking, feeling, and behaving. These man-made patterns for thinking, feeling, and behaving are culture. The major cultural concepts are values and norms. Social structure is formed through social relationships that are patterns of social interaction. These patterns of social interaction are based on role prescriptions attached to social positions that, when acted out, constitute role behavior.

Two noncultural factors that affect social structure—biological heritage and geographic environment—were placed in perspective. While these noncultural factors limit and condition social structure, it is primarily to culture that we must look in order to understand, explain, and predict variations in social structure.

Part I has been designed to provide a basic understanding of sociological perspectives and concepts. In Part II the concepts of culture and social structure will be elaborated. Chapter 3 notes the diversity of culture, explores further the meaning of culture and outlines its distinctive characteristics, and goes on to discuss dimensions that comprise the content of culture: the cognitive dimension, the material dimension, and the normative dimension. The normative dimension is emphasized by placing folkways, mores, and laws within the context of social control mechanisms intended to promote conformity to norms.

REFERENCES

1. For a more detailed description of a wino subculture, see Joan K. Jackson and Ralph Connor, "The Skid Row Alcoholic," *Quarterly Journal of Studies on Alcohol*, 14 (September 1953), especially 471–479.
2. Arnold M. Rose, "History with a Present Meaning. The Negro in America," *Commentary*, 24 (December 1957), 542–546.
3. To paraphrase Sergeant Preston in reverse, this case may not be closed. In 1969 Arthur Jensen, an educational psychologist, created a raging controversy by taking the side of inherited racial differences in intelligence. Although clearly a minority report, Jensen's arguments should not be summarily dismissed. See Arthur Jensen, "How Much Can We Boost IQ and Scholastic Achievement?" *Harvard Education Review*, 39 (Winter 1969), 1–123. Not unexpectedly, Jensen has had no problem in attracting interest to his ideas. For a detailed rebuttal, see Arthur L. Stinchcombe, "Environment: The Cumulation of Effects Is Yet to Be Understood," *Harvard Education Review*, 39 (Summer 1969), 511–522. Other findings challenging inherited social superiority are cited in Otto Klineberg, "Race Differences: The Present Position of the Problem," *International Social Science Bulletin*, 2 (1950), 460–466; and "Statement on Race and Intelligence," *Journal of Social Issues*, 25 (Summer 1969), 1–3.

ADDITIONAL SOURCES AND READINGS

Bertrand, Alvin L. *Social Organization: A General Systems and Role Theory Perspective* (Philadelphia: F. A. Davis, 1972).

Bierstedt, Robert A. *The Social Order* (New York: McGraw-Hill, 1970).

Coleman, James R., et al. *Equality of Educational Opportunity* (Washington, D.C.: U.S. Department of Health, Education, and Welfare, 1966).

Myrdal, Gunnar. *An American Dilemma* (New York: Harper & Row, 1944).

Olsen, Marvin E. *The Process of Social Organization* (New York: Holt, Rinehart and Winston, 1968).

Theodorson, George A., and Achilles G. Theodorson. *Mordern Dictionary of Sociology* (New York: T. Y. Crowell, 1969).

Williams, Robin M., Jr., *American Society: A Sociological Interpretation*, 3rd ed. (New York: Knopf, 1970).

part II

COMPONENTS OF SOCIAL STRUCTURE

{3}

The Nature of Culture

Maggie was in the kitchenette washing dishes. She uttered a cry of delight, gave her hands a quick wipe, and ran to Guido. "Oh darling, you've come!" she said exultantly. "I knew you'd stick by me!"

"What?" said Guido, blinking in bewilderment. "Stick by you? What have you done?"

"Only my duty, dear," she replied and kissed him soundly. "Oh, I'm so glad you're here to help me fight this thing!"

Guido took her shoulders and gently disentangled himself. "Maggie baby, I've been on a train from New Mexico for the last four days. Would you mind filling me in?"

"That's right. You couldn't know about it."

"About what?"

"I've been fired from my job."

"Fired? From the school? For what?"

"For trying to let a little light into the darkness!" declared Maggie, lifting a fist. "For trying to clean out the ignorance and sickness of centuries!"

"Could you be a little more specific?"

"I gave," said Maggie, "a talk on sex."

Guido's jaw plopped open. "To the second grade?" he whispered in horror.

"Of course."

"ARE YOU OUT OF YOUR GODDAM MIND?" shrieked Guido.

Max Shulman, **Rally Round the Flag, Boys** (Garden City, N.Y.: Doubleday, 1954), pp. 18–19.

THE DIVERSITY OF CULTURE

In the passage above, if Maggie is not out of her mind, she is, to Guido's assaulted senses, considerably out of bounds. Guido's visceral detectors have flooded his brain with the message that his very own Maggie is attempting to unlock the mysteries of sex to tender and yet unready minds. Visions of second-graders holding orgies during recess must have been running through

Guido's mind. Yet in other societies, consciously designed sex education precedes by a wide margin the bathroom wall as the initial source of sexual revelations. Indeed, even within American society today, a more enlightened view is taken of early sex education, particularly by college-educated parents. Still, Guido's horror could serve to illustrate that notwithstanding the changing American pattern regarding sex education in the school, heated opposition can still be generated on the matter.

Patterns for thinking, feeling, and behaving vary from society to society. Yet the diversity does not stop here. Even within societies, there are social structures whose cultural patterns are either different in certain respects from those of the larger society or are in direct contradiction to certain important aspects of the broader culture. Furthermore, even within social structures that are different from, or in conflict with, the larger society, the expression of culture is conditioned by such factors as age, sex, and social class.

Such is the diversity of human social life. How can it be explained? Why do some peoples refuse to eat pork while the sensibilities of others make room for grasshoppers and rat meat? Just as the diversity in cuisine cannot be explained by inherited differences in alimentary tracts, other aspects of social life cannot be accounted for in terms of biological variations. People the world over are too much a part of the biological family of man to permit an instinctual explanation for the observed divergence in human behavior.

Guido's response to Maggie's crusade for the sexual enlightenment of second-graders was described above as a visceral one. Actually, Guido's explosion was ignited not by an intestinal spark but by a cultural one. While most human behavior is learned, this learning process is so effective that ways of thinking, feeling, and behaving often seem to originate deep within us. Nevertheless, variations in human behavior can, for the most part, be traced to cultural differences that are exhibited by members of a social structure as a result of the learning process.

Since patterns for thinking, feeling, and behaving are man-made, what accounts for the divergence of patterns among and within societies? Chapter 2 introduced you to the idea of culture and its subconcepts. In this chapter you will learn more about culture, the concept that anthropologists and sociologists have developed in their efforts to make sense out of the diversity of social life.

Culture was defined in Chapter 2 as man-made patterns for thinking, feeling, and behaving that are socially transmitted to an entire society or to segments of the society. Several crucial characteristics of culture, each of which will be discussed separately, are either stated or implied in the above sociological definition. These characteristics are:

1. *Culture is a human creation*—it is man-made.
2. *Culture is transmitted socially*—it is learned.
3. *Culture is abstract*—it consists of *patterns* for thinking, feeling, and behaving.
4. *Culture is structured*—it consists of *organized* patterns for thinking, feeling, and behaving.
5. *Culture may be differentially shared*—cultural patterns may be socially transmitted to members of an entire society or to members of segments of that society.

CHARACTERISTICS OF CULTURE

Culture as a human creation

A central point of Chapter 2 was that biological heritage and geographic environment influence social structure and culture by limiting the options available to man. Yet in that same context it was also stated that man's flexibility and unique capacity for environmental mastery enable him to rise above biological and geographical boundaries in the creation and enactment of cultural patterns.

From this portrait it sounds as if man is the lord of nature, unleashing at will his innate creative talents on all fronts in a never-ending conquest of life. The reality is much less romantic and flattering, for the human species has no alternative but to fashion cultural patterns. Why? Because, by raw biological nature, man is undoubtedly one of the most helpless creatures in the animal kingdom. After a minimal amount of care and with no instruction, a young eagle will soar, scan the terrain, and give hot and deadly pursuit to a scurrying rabbit. Ants and bees assume their positions and perform their functions with the same untutored and unerring touch. In fact, most of the behavior of insects and lower animals is instinctual.

An *instinct* is a biologically inherited pattern of behavior that unfailingly appears among members of a particular species under appropriate environmental conditions. Birds do not walk south for the winter, salmon do not fly upstream, and lions do not prefer ferns to fresh meat. Nor do they have to experiment in order to discover what is appropriate behavior for each of them. They are programmed for action by their instincts. Thus they enjoy an advantage over man: They need not (and as will be noted shortly, they cannot) devise patterns for thinking, feeling, and behaving that must be socially transmitted to new members of the flock, school, or pride.

Human infants, by contrast, cannot go very far on the basis of their biological heritage. Their repertoire is limited to such reflexes as breathing, sucking, and eliminating. Human beings come no closer than this to instinc-

United Nations

tual behavior.[1] This leaves the human infant at a distinct disadvantage. Lacking innate solutions to such problems of survival as protection from heat and cold, and without built-in patterns for thinking, feeling, and behaving, the human species is *forced* into the creation of culture. Man parlays nature's short shrift into an infinite variety of conquests over his biological heritage and geographic environment. He is able to do so partly because the very absence of inherited behavioral patterns and solutions to environmental problems leaves him with considerable flexibility and adaptability. The most significant reason underlying the human species' unique capacity for creating culture lies in its facility for the development and use of language. But before turning to the importance of language in the creation and transmission of culture, the second characteristic of culture—that it is learned— deserves some amplification.

Social transmission of culture

While each of us is not a blueblood or a Boston Brahmin, nevertheless from the sociological perspective we are "cultured." Because culture is learned, to be human is to possess culture. A central implication of this is that most of the behavior and other characteristics we consider human have a cultural rather than a biological origin. Consider reactions to physical pain. Mark Zborowski, while recognizing that physiological factors such as intensity, duration, and quality condition responses to pain, emphasizes the role of culture in the pain experience.[2] Jews and Italians, according to Zborowski's findings, manifest similar responses to pain: Members of both cultures feel free to talk, complain, moan, groan, and cry about their pain. In contrast, "Old American" patients tend to be more restrained. Almost like uninvolved observers, they attempt clinically to report the nature, location, and duration of pain. Crying and related overt expressions tend to be reserved for periods of solitude. Zborowski provides a cultural explanation for these variations in response to pain—children reared in "Old American" homes are taught not to cry when hurt, not to be "sissies," not to run to mother, and to fight back. Conversely, Jewish and Italian parents (particularly mothers) express a great deal of concern and emotion over injuries to their children. As a result, Jews and Italians learn to pay attention to their pains and to be expressive about them, while persons from "Old American" homes tend to ignore or minimize their discomforts.

Culture, in short, is learned. The process by which culture is transmitted from generation to generation is called *socialization*, a concept implicit in Zborowski's explanation for differences in response to pain. It is necessary to recognize that much of what we consider "normal" or "natural" is not really so in an ultimate sense. It is widely believed in our society that girls are "naturally" made of "sugar and spice, and everything nice" and that boys are a distillation of "snips and snails and puppy dogs' tails." In fact, we are social heirs to cultural patterns that lead us to channel the activities of girls so that playing with dolls and having tea parties seems a natural preference to acting out roles of dominance and leadership, which boys learn through pretending to be quarterbacks, soldiers, cowboys, and astronauts. It is no more natural, however, for men to strive for leadership or to be economically competitive than it is for women. Judging from the hostility generated in some men and women by the women's liberation movement, one would think that those engaged in the movement are trying to thwart the natural dictates of the sexes.

Yet it is well to qualify any impression that culturally achieved nature operates to the exclusion of man's biological nature. To err on the side of cultural determinism is as one-sided as to account for human behavior by strictly biological explanations. The two factors are intertwined. Cultural variation is limited by human biology. In no culture do men have babies, and all cultures must contain designs for child rearing. At the same time, culture channels the biological capabilities of man. Humans have the capacity for love. However, awareness of this fact does not allow us to predict the precise ways in which different groups of people express this potentiality. Being one of several husbands to one woman, or vice versa, may be hotly defended as the most natural form of marriage by people of one culture, while monogamous unions are equally sanctified by persons of another culture.

Culture, then, is the social heritage of man. This heritage was created by previous generations and must be learned by the newest members of society. Both the creation of culture and its subsequent transmission as social heritage depend heavily on the human species' unique capacity for the development and use of arbitrary symbols, the most significant of which is language.[3]

• LANGUAGE AND CULTURE. In Lewis Carroll's *Through the Looking Glass*, Humpty Dumpty says to Alice with some finality, "When I use a word, it means just what I choose it to mean—neither more nor less." So it is with symbols—they are indications for things that are determined by those who create and use them. Symbols range from physical objects to sounds, smells, and tastes. The meaning of a symbol is not dictated by the physical characteristics of the thing for which it stands. There is nothing intrinsically laudatory about the sound created when hands are clapped. While applause warms the heart of an entertainer, politician, or professor in America, in other cultures this same physical act symbolizes severe disapproval. Of course, after meaning has been assigned to an event such as hand-clapping, and a person learns to associate the event with approval or disapproval, then the appropriate meaning seems as if it were an inherent property of the event itself. Figure 3.1 graphically illustrates the variety of meaning that can be attached to a single symbol.

Because man is the only animal capable of the arbitrary assignment of meanings (*symbolization*), he is the only animal capable of creating and perpetuating a cultural heritage. Lower animals can learn new things—apes can discover the utility of sticks for getting ants from trees, and dogs can be taught to heel—but only man can arbitrarily assign meaning to objects, events, or sense experiences and then communicate these meanings to others. Let us consider the specifics of the link between culture and the system of symbols known as language.

Language promotes the development as well as the transmission and perpetuation of culture. Symbolization allows humans to transcend time and space. Apes have been observed in the act of inventing and using tools. This knowledge may also be passed on to other apes. Yet, "Planet of the Apes" notwithstanding, the higher primates have never evolved a culture. This is partly because they are not capable of creating symbols that would permit them to abstract beyond a concrete situation at a particular point in time. Problem-solving among apes is tied to the present, both in terms of time and location. They cannot elaborate on experience gained in one situation in order to solve a more complex problem in another. An ape, for example, although he might have discovered the usefulness of a long stick in probing an ant colony, cannot abstract from that discovery and proceed to the crea-

Whereas to Winston Churchill this symbol meant Allied victory over the Axis—

Whereas to Jane Fonda this symbol means "peace in Vietnam"—

To Spartacus and four of his comrades in revolt it was an order for five more beers.

Figure 3.1 The arbitrary nature of symbols

tion of a ladder. Apes cannot build on the abstract concept of distance that is involved in both behaviors. Thus the experiences of apes are said to be discontinuous; each generation is forced to learn by personal experience and participation within the context of concrete situations. Not so with man. Via symbolization, man can continue problem-solving thought processes far beyond his own actual experiences. The Wright brothers' victory over gravity did not spring from their personal attempts to fly from a hilltop with a complex arrangement of feathers. Rather, they fashioned their airplane in accordance with known aerodynamic principles, which had been cumulating for some time prior to Kitty Hawk. Continuity achieved through symbolization allows man to fashion cultural patterns.

Just as in the creation of culture, the key factor in the transmission and perpetuation of culture is man's unique ability to assign arbitrary meanings. How can an ape transmit to his offspring the knowledge that dipping food into the salty ocean adds to its flavor? An ape has no symbols for dipping, food, salty, ocean, or flavor. Only by demonstration can the knowledge be transmitted. Only by personally observing another ape dipping food into the ocean and then mimicking the action can a young ape discover the value of adding salt. If this is true for something as practical as seasoning food, you can appreciate the absence of more abstract concepts such as semantics, sanity, or satanism.

Armed with the arsenal of symbols called language, man can transmit to others his experiences, ideas, and knowledge—his culture. Children are verbally taught things prior to any actual experience on their part. Although it may take some time and repetition, a child can be taught the dangers of fire and heights without being burned or toppling from stairs. The same transmittal process applies to cultural patterns such as exhibiting patriotism, consuming food, or staying awake in church.

In summary, symbolization liberates man from the confines of time and space so that he can create culture. And it is by virtue of symbolization that cultural patterns can be transmitted across generations. Because of these two processes, culture accumulates. Through written and verbal symbols, man can preserve past creations pretty much at will. Your generation does not have to invent the automobile—it is your heritage from past generations, including the generation that discovered the mechanical advantage of the wheel. So, not only does culture accumulate, it *cumulates* as well—creations at one point in time may be combined with later creations in order to form yet another creation. This is the process of *invention*. By the principle of cumulation, each human generation is potentially more advanced than the preceding one because it can take advantage of past culture and add to it. In this way, the base of culture is broadened with each generation. Let us avoid for the present the specific question of man's "progress" and the broader area of cultural change and move on to the abstract nature of culture.

Culture as an abstraction

ARCHIE: Let me ask you something, buddy boy. Suppose you came home some fine day and find your wife's throat has been cut . . . you mean to say you wouldn't be itching to fry that guy?

MIKE: No, what's the use of that?

ARCHIE: You see the kind of guy you married? A fiend comes in and kills you and this jellyfish won't lift a finger to help.

MIKE: If I did kill the murderer, would it bring Gloria back?

ARCHIE: No, but it wouldn't send her further away neither!

MIKE: Archie, an eye for an eye isn't the answer. The problem rests with society.

ARCHIE: So it's society's fault again, eh? Are you gonna tell me that society came in here and murdered Gloria?

EDITH: We don't even know any Society People.[4]

Archie Bunker recognizes a reification when he sees one. In Archie's mind it "don't take no college education" to know that a knife-wielding murderer, not society, would have done Gloria in. The *reification fallacy* is the mistake committed when an abstraction (such as Mike's use of the term society) is thought of as having material substance. It is not culture (or society) that eats, speaks, loves, or murders young girls; people do these things. Culture, in a word, is an abstraction. It is not directly observable, but it is inferred from the behavior of persons. Gravity is no less a force because of its invisibility. Its properties were observed by men who labeled it "gravity." Some such force must exist (by whatever name), otherwise interference with the law of inertia would play as much havoc with us as it does with astronauts who, for example, have no luck controlling uncontained liquids in outer space where the force of gravity, as man on earth measures it, exerts less pull than it does on earth. One way we know this is by observation of behavior—consider the giant steps taken on the moon by astronauts or the enviable distance that astronaut Alan Shepard belted golf balls while standing on the moon's surface.

So it is with culture. Culture is no less an operating force because it is not available to the senses except by tasting, seeing, hearing, touching, or smelling aspects of it through concrete social behavior. We know culture exists by discerning patterns of thinking, feeling, and behaving that are exhibited among people. Because such patterns exist, because behavior is predictable and recurrent, we can infer with assurance the existence and operation of culture. If, for example, we observed that members of Archie's society shared his aversion to the hypothetical fate of his daughter, then we could conclude that a cultural pattern prohibiting the murder of daughters is operative. Should we discover that Archie and his friends felt the same way about their wives, then we would infer the presence of a broader pattern, perhaps one prohibiting the murder of all females. If we observed that Archie's concern did not extend to his son-in-law, Mike, then we would be on the trail of yet another cultural pattern. So when you encounter a phrase such as "culture is passed from generation to generation," keep in mind that what is transmitted intergenerationally is an abstraction that can be inferred only from behavior. Abstract cultural elements are activated by and transformed through social interaction among persons and within social structures.

The tendency to reify—to attribute concreteness to abstract things—can be minimized but not completely avoided. In fact, as long as it is recognized as reification, this tendency is quite useful. Abstraction—which often involves reification—is central to sociology because it allows the analysis of sociocultural phenomena without reference to concrete persons. However, when the proposition that Catholics "have" higher social cohesion than do Protestants is taken too literally, the fallacy of reification can create difficulties. Catholics may *exhibit* higher social cohesion in episodes of social interaction; this is as close as they come to "having" it.

Finally, while it is people who eat, speak, love, and murder, it is as part of a sociocultural unit that they do so in certain ways and at specified times. The source of this regulation lies in cultural patterns that have been socially transmitted and learned. Cultural patterns exist prior to persons and they exist beyond them. People come and go, but culture goes on and on. Culture in this sense is also "external" to persons. It is the existence of cultural patterns as forces channeling thought, feelings, and behavior that contributes to the legitimacy of the structural perspective. The fact that culture is structured or organized is also important in this respect.

The structure of culture

A key idea in the formal definition of culture is "pattern." This idea undergirds the discussion of culture as an abstraction in that cultural patterns are *guidelines* for thinking, feeling, and behaving; they are expressed through concrete behavior but they are not themselves concrete. Pattern also implies structure or organization.

Ruth Benedict, an anthropologist, gives the following account of the words of Ramon, a chief of the Digger Indians in California: "In the beginning, God gave to every people a cup, a cup of clay, and from this cup they drank their life."[5] By "cup" this Digger chief meant the fabric of life that anthropologists like Ruth Benedict call culture. This man felt keenly the structure of culture, the wholeness of culture, even though he did not intellectually understand it as Ruth Benedict did. The fabric of culture was, in his mind, stitched together with meaning now lost, for Ramon went on: "They all dipped in the water, but their cups were different. Our cup is broken now. It has passed away."

Benedict makes it clear that the chief was not lamenting the physical extinction of his people. It was the fabric of his people's way of life—their patterns for thinking, feeling, and behaving—that had in his mind suffered irreparable fragmentation. The loss of some patterns and the addition of some new ones had ruined the cultural symmetry that had been theirs.

Of course, the structure of culture is more integrated and its splintering more apparent in small isolated societies such as that of the Digger Indians. In large, complex societies, the structure of culture is not only more difficult to discern, it is less complete.

Differential sharing of culture

Because of the abstract nature of culture, it can exist and be transmitted only if it is shared by persons who belong to an identifiable social structure. Social structures may range from a total society to such "total" institutions as prisons or mental asylums and to delinquent gangs. Whatever the nature of the social structure, its members subscribe to a complex of cultural patterns and bring social pressures to bear on members who violate this system of cultural patterns.

Some cultural patterns are transmitted to most members of a society, and some cultural patterns are shared only by particular segments of the society. Moreover, the sharing of culture is a matter of degree. Sharing of cultural patterns within a society or within a social structure in a society may be nearly complete, or differences in the degree of sharing among societal sub-units may border on distinctions as fine as a razor's edge or on distinctions so vast that no connecting bridges can be imagined.

The sharing of culture is a complicated phenomenon. Americans may be said to share a common language. A comparison of the American brand of English with French, Russian, or Spanish supports this belief. Yet, the sharing of language among Americans is not complete. A narcotics agent would interpret as innocent a middle-aged person's remark to the effect that he intended to cut the grass, but the same statement overheard in the campus grill from the lips of a long-haired, army-coated "freak" might elicit quite a different interpretation from the same narc. In sum, to say that persons share a cultural pattern does not mean that they share it uniformly.

There is no absolute standard for determining whether cultural patterns are shared by members of a particular social structure or only by a segment of that structure. Sociologists employ the concepts of subculture and contraculture to aid them in making distinctions regarding the extent of the sharing of cultural patterns. A *subculture* refers to cultural patterns that are in some ways different from those of the larger culture. A social structure in which certain important patterns for thinking, feeling, and behaving conflict with the larger culture may be said to possess a *contraculture*. These two concepts will be discussed in the next chapter.

THE CONTENT OF CULTURE

The content of culture—beliefs, knowledge, norms, values, and material objects—may be classified into three primary dimensions: cognitive, material, and normative.

The cognitive dimension

All human beings share in the process of cognition: They all think, feel, recognize, recall things from the past, and project into the real and fantasied future. *Cognition* is the process that enables humans to comprehend and to relate to their surroundings. Basic to any person's organized conception of his environment are his beliefs. Ideas that are accepted by persons as representing reality, as being true, are *beliefs*. Beliefs may or may not actually be true, but to their subscribers they portray reality. The extent of verification for cultural beliefs covers a wide range. Some beliefs are held because of habit, tradition, or appeal to an authority when, in fact, they are false. Other beliefs that rest on habit, tradition, or an authoritative source are based on sufficient critical observation to be considered true.

The material dimension

Nonmaterial culture, under which the cognitive and normative dimensions of culture are classified, refers to intangible products of human creation. Tangible or concrete products of human creation are labeled *material cul-*

ture. To be consistent with the idea that culture is not actual behavior but an abstraction that is inferred from the observation of behavior, it must be concluded that material culture is not culture at all. On the other hand, we cannot simply ignore art, buildings, bridges, typewriters, and motor vehicles. Rather, we must view man's tangible creations within the context of the meanings that have been assigned to them through symbolization. While concrete objects as such are not part of culture, the techniques for their construction, the uses to which they are put, and the value placed on them are cultural.

Consider newspaper and pepper as physical objects. Of course, each of these things has various meanings for you. Can you think of a use for them in combination? Some people have used them together in a highly practical, if irritating, manner. "Nettling" is a part of the childbirth process that has been instituted and used by some midwives. An old medical doctor tells the story of his first encounter with nettling in this way:

> The ink of my medical license was hardly dry, and as I was soon to find out, my ears would not be dry for some time. I had never delivered a baby on my own and faced my maiden voyage with some fear.
>
> Upon entering Mrs. Williamson's house, I found a local midwife and several neighbors busily at work preparing for the delivery. My fear caused me to move rather slowly and my happiness over my reprieve prompted me to tell the women that they were doing just fine and to proceed without my services.
>
> Having gotten myself off the hook, I watched the ladies with a fascination that soon turned to horror.
>
> At the height of Mrs. Williamson's labor pains, one of the neighbors rolled a piece of newspaper into a funnel shape. Holding the bottom end of the cone she poured a liberal amount of pepper into it. Her next move was to insert the sharp end of the cone into Mrs. Williamson's nose. With the cone in its "proper" place, the neighbor inhaled deeply and blew the pepper from the cone into the inner recesses of Mrs. Williamson's nose.
>
> Suddenly alert, Mrs. Williamson's eyes widened as her senses rebelled against the pepper. With a mighty sneeze, I was introduced to nettling. The violence of that sneeze reverberated through her body to force the baby from her womb in a skittering flight across the bed. An appropriately positioned assistant fielded the baby in midflight and only minor details of Orville's rite of birth remained.[6]

Before the doctor's introduction to nettling, this particular combination of the physical objects of newspaper and pepper had no meaning for him. And, until nettling was devised, this combination was without meaning for anyone, even though the component physical objects existed.

Material objects may have various meanings in different societies, or even in different social structures within a single society. All corny movies aside, to a people unfamiliar with modern civilization, a 747 jet airliner may very well represent a giant bird sent from the gods. Within American society, the back seat of an automobile does not mean the same thing to all people—to a wealthy lady it is the proper place to sit while being chauffeured, to a child it is a place to romp, and to some college students it may represent an inexpensive substitute for a local motel.

In brief, it is the meanings assigned by man to physical objects, not the physical objects themselves, that are properly termed cultural. The tangible products of human creation become part of man's cultural heritage when the meanings regarding their construction, use, and value are socially transmitted and learned.

The normative dimension

At a minimum, long periods of order and stability in human behavior are required for the continued existence of a social structure. As noted in Chapter 1, the starting point for sociology is that social structure—with implied predictability and recurrence in social interaction—is necessary. The *normative dimension* of culture is of critical importance in promoting recurrence and predictability in human interaction; this explains the emphasis in Chapter 2 on norms, folkways, mores, laws, and values as concepts central to an understanding of culture. Of greater significance is the degree of integration of the cognitive, material, and normative dimensions, for without a high degree of integration a social structure could not exist. However, much of the recurrence and predictability in human feeling, thought, and behavior is made possible by two aspects of the normative dimension—norms themselves (which are crucial for order and stability), and the enforcement of these norms. Adherence to norms is fostered through both childhood and adult *socialization*, the process whereby culture is socially transmitted; and through *sanctioning*, or behavior designed to ensure conformity to norms. The subject of socialization will be treated later, but sanctioning will be briefly discussed in the present context.

Norms and sanctions

Norms are rules for thinking, feeling, and behaving that have been adopted, transmitted, and practiced by members of a social structure. The cognitive dimension of culture differentiates the true from the false; the normative dimension delineates the "dos" and the "don'ts." William Graham Sumner, the sociologist who originated the concepts of folkways and mores, wrote that anything can be made to seem acceptable, if the society has devised norms to support that thing. During the Middle Ages, for example, legal proceedings were truly "trials" for the accused. "Good" men during this era, with little or no compunction and with full social and legal approval, participated in the tortures that were a regular feature of the civil proceedings.[7]

As an example closer to our time, a hanging in the 1800s was a social occasion—a time to go to town, mingle with friends and enemies, and eat. And it was only in 1972 that the Supreme Court of the United States ruled that under certain conditions capital punishment constitutes "cruel and inhuman punishment." The grotesque physical side of capital punishment has not changed much over the last century in America, but norms have. In fact, capital punishment had not been inflicted for several years prior to the 1972 Supreme Court ruling. Nevertheless, since norms are used to define morality, capital punishment may once again become common practice in the United States.

The capital punishment issue offers an excellent illustration of the existence of conflicting norms within a social structure. Many Americans consider the abolition of capital punishment a grave error; they feel that such leniency only opens wider the floodgates of crime. Folkways may conflict with other folkways, mores may be inconsistent with other mores, folkways may clash with mores, and both folkways and mores may be in contradiction to certain laws.

Figure 3.2 shows the interconnection between the sanctioning aspect of the normative dimension and the norms themselves. In this figure, mores, folkways, and laws are placed in a four-celled matrix cross-classifying the strength of a sanction (ranging from light to heavy) and the type of social control (informal or formal). It is more difficult to distinguish degrees in strength of sanctions than it is to differentiate formal from informal sanctions.

Formal sanctions reside in the hands of appointed or elected representatives of the social structure. Formal sanctions rest on established procedures and written codes, and are more intimately involved with legal norms. Formal sanctions, then, are codified and administered by officials. But reality is not as clear-cut as Figure 3.2 might indicate. As you will see, there is some shading of mores into the formal sanctions side.

Informal sanctions are expressions of reward or punishment by one or more social structure members for either an unusual fulfillment of a norm (saving someone's life) or a violation of a norm (beating a dog). Such positive or negative sanctions may be expressed by a smile or a disapproving look, or they may assume a more physical form such as a handshake or a karate chop to the Adam's apple.

It should be noted that whether sanctions are formal or informal, they may be either positive (rewarding) or negative (punishing). Formal and informal sanctions are the two factors in Figure 3.2 by which the three types of norms can be classified. The following discussion describes each of the types of norms within the framework of this cross-classification.

STRENGTH
OF
SANCTION

TYPE OF SOCIAL CONTROL

Informal

Formal

	Informal	Formal
Light	Folkways	Laws
Heavy	Mores	Laws

Figure 3.2 Types of norms classified by type of social control and strength of social sanction

• FOLKWAYS. As you know from Chapter 2, norms may be classified into three general types—folkways, mores, and laws. *Folkways* are norms that define customary ways of thinking, feeling, and behaving. While they are invested with meaning, they usually do not have a moral coloration. A family may eat two meals a day or four, a man and a woman may marry for love or money, and tea may be preferred to coffee. Folkways are traditional customs created with little conscious thought and unreflectively accepted and adhered to by new generations. Because this type of norm is not considered essential to social welfare, the violation or fulfillment of folkways is greeted with light sanction and with mechanisms of informal social control (see Figure 3.2). Parades are not scheduled and bands do not play when professors come to class dressed in tie and suit, although deans and university presidents may feel an inner glow that at times overflows into complimentary statements about their faculties. Similarly, nonverbal displeasure and verbal criticism may be directed at university faculty members who adopt the more informal attire of Levis and tieless shirts. But as long as these violators of the informal dress code fulfill their teaching and research responsibilities, they are not likely to be subjected to punishment beyond light, informal expressions of criticism or ridicule.

• MORES. Mores have a more conscious origin than folkways. *Mores* are norms that have been defined as central to the well-being of a social structure. As such, their preservation is a matter of great concern to members of the social structure. Thus the violation of mores evokes heavy social punishment, while their fulfillment brings significant social approval. Consider for a moment the question of illegitimate births. Mores against bastardy exist because it is perceived as disruptive of family and social life. Yet mechanisms of social control directed against parents of illegitimate children have not been completely formalized into laws; that is, such parents are not sought out and prosecuted by public officials, as are burglars, for example. Nevertheless, social control is exercised informally through strong societal disapproval. Father- or Mother-of-the-Year awards would not be given to persons who were known to have illegitimate children. Such positive sanctions are reserved for upholders of the prohibition against bastardy. Similarly, Mother's and Father's Day are not intended as celebrations for those who violate this norm. Cruelty toward illegitimate children is another reflection of the strong social disapproval of bastardy.

• LAWS. Unlike folkways and mores, laws are consciously created. *Laws* are formally defined and recorded norms whose enforcement is carried out by public authorities. Depending on the offense, sanctions may be light or heavy. Lifting a carton of cigarettes from a store potentially bears a considerably lighter penalty than being busted for possessing or smoking marijuana, or for stealing in order to buy the marijuana.

The strength of sanctions for identical infractions of the law varies from one social structure to another as well as from one time to another within the same social unit. Sanctions for illegal drug activity are stiffer in many countries than they are in the United States, and even within the United States sanctions differ from state to state. And, like alcohol before it, marijuana may someday be an over-the-counter item in America.

Most formal sanctions are negative in the sense that they do not reward the recipient of the sanction. There are, however, formal sanctions that are positive and rewarding. Some bounty-hunters in the old American West made a reasonable living from collecting rewards placed on the heads of outlaws. Soldiers—both dead and alive—are given medals for service to their country. And official titles ranging from "Lord" in England to "Kentucky Colonel" in the Bluegrass State are positive formal sanctions.

As was stated earlier, a certain degree of overlap exists between mores and laws, because laws often represent the formalization of mores. (That this is not always the case is evidenced by the fact that the violation of some laws, for example, those related to traffic, is not heavily sanctioned.) The overlap between mores and laws is illustrated well in the case of bastardy. Public officials have little or no recourse against the father of an illegitimate child unless the mother is willing to initiate action. If the mother does initiate legal proceedings, it is the legal duty of appropriate public officials to redress the situation. If a jury has decided that the accused man is the child's biological father, compensation takes the form of monetary support geared to the needs of the child and the mother, and to the ability of the father to pay. Refusal to make such compensation on the part of the father leaves him open to a jail sentence for contempt of court. In brief, the proscription against bastardy may or may not be enforced via formal sanctions as determined by legal codes.

It is also true that laws do not always reflect current mores. Laws often remain on the books long after the mores of the social structure have changed. So-called blue laws that prevent the selling and purchasing of certain goods and services on Sunday are out of step with the contemporary American scene; in recent years, such laws have either been rejected by, or are under assault in, many states. There are other laws such as the prohibition against kissing in public that are still legally valid but are seldom if ever enforced (see Figure 3.3).

OVERVIEW AND PREVIEW

The fact that different social structures have radically divergent orientations toward the same area of human activity was used to illustrate the diversity of culture. Behind the idea of the diversity of culture is the point that variations in social life can be largely attributed to cultural factors. Culture was defined as man-made patterns for thinking, feeling, and behaving that are socially transmitted to an entire social structure or to segments of the structure. From this definition, five characteristics of culture were derived: (1) Culture is a human creation; (2) culture is transmitted socially; (3) culture is an abstraction; (4) culture is structured; and (5) culture may be differentially shared.

The content of culture is comprised of cognitive, material, and norma-

• Any person who appears on any highway, or upon the street of any city that has no police protection, when clothed only in ordinary bathing garb, shall be fined not less than five dollars nor more than twenty-five dollars.
• Any person who commits fornication or adultery shall be fined not less than twenty dollars nor more than fifty dollars.
• Any person who shall publish or distribute for sale any book, pamphlet or magazine consisting of narrative material in pictorial form, colored or uncolored, and commonly known as comic books, the content of which is devoted to or principally made up of pictures or accounts of methods of crime, terror, physical torture, brutality or illicit sex, shall, upon conviction, be fined not more than one thousand dollars or imprisoned not more than one year, or both.

Figure 3.3   Illustrations of outmoded state laws that remain legally valid
SOURCE: Kentucky Revised Statutes 436.140; 436.070; 436.550.

tive dimensions. While integration of the three dimensions is necessary for social structure, the normative dimension is the most important for explaining the predictability and recurrence in social life. Folkways, mores, and laws were elaborated in terms of socially distributed rewards and penalties designed to minimize deviation from norms. These socially distributed rewards and penalties are called sanctions. Both the strength of sanctions (light versus heavy) and the type of social control (informal versus formal) were brought to bear on the discussion of folkways, mores, and laws.

This chapter has focused on the nature of culture and the content of culture. Chapter 4 deals with the structure of culture. The idea of the structure of culture is pursued by exploring the cultural diversity that exists within any particular society and among various societies. Ethnocentrism and cultural relativism, the next topics of discussion, are seen as results of cultural diversity. If cultural diversity within and among societies exists, so does a certain degree of cultural similarity. Chapter 4 closes on this note.

REFERENCES

1. At least until quite recently, social scientists have rejected any connection between human behavior and instincts. For a readable account of what may be a new emphasis on the biological side of man, you may wish to read Tom Alexander, "Psychologists Are Rediscovering the Mind," *Fortune*, 82 (November 1970), 108ff.
2. Mark Zborowski, *People in Pain* (San Francisco: Josey-Bass, 1969).
3. Excellent elaborations on the relationship between language and culture may be found in Leslie A. White, "The Symbol: The Origin and Basis of Human Behavior," in Leslie A. White, *The Science of Culture*, 2nd ed. (New York: Farrar, Straus & Giroux, 1969), pp. 22–39; and Kingsley Davis, *Human Society* (New York: Macmillan, 1949), pp. 39–45.
4. *The Wit and Wisdom of Archie Bunker* (New York: Popular Library, 1972), pp. 90–91.
5. Ruth Benedict, *Patterns of Culture* (New York: Mentor, 1946), pp. 33–34.
6. This account is a liberal reconstruction of a story told at every opportunity by my wife's grandfather, the late John C. Hall, M.D.
7. Summer introduced the terms folkways and mores in *Folkways* (Boston: Ginn, 1906). This example is cited on page 522 of his book.

ADDITIONAL SOURCES AND READINGS

Beals, Ralph J., and Harry Hoijer. *An Introduction to Anthropology*, 3rd ed. (New York: Macmillan, 1965).
Benedict, Ruth. *Patterns of Culture* (New York: Mentor, 1946).
Hoijer, Harry. "The Relation of Language to Culture," in A. L. Kroeber, ed., *Anthropology Today* (Chicago: University of Chicago Press, 1953), pp. 554–573.
Kluckhohn, Clyde. *Mirror for Man* (Greenwich, Conn.: Fawcett, 1957).

Kluckhohn, Clyde, and William H. Kelley. "The Concept of Culture," in Ralph Linton, ed., *The Science of Man in the World Crisis* (New York: Columbia University Press, 1945), pp. 78–105.

Kroeber, A. L., and Clyde Kluckhohn. *Culture: A Critical Review of Concepts and Definitions* (New York: Random House, 1971).

Linton, Ralph. *The Study of Man* (New York: Appleton, 1936).

Mazur, Allan, and Leon S. Robertson. *Biology and Social Behavior* (New York: Free Press, 1972).

Williams, Robin M., Jr. *American Society: A Sociological Interpretation*, 3rd ed. (New York: Knopf, 1970).

The Diversity of Culture

"I have made inquiries among other [Eskimo] women and it seems that some white men are very fond of laughing* with the women of the Men. They even give them beautiful presents afterward. Also to their husbands."

"Maybe that's what he wants," Ernenek said, beaming again all over. "Make yourself beautiful."

Tittering, Asiak let her hair down, rolled up her sleeves and dunked her arms into the urine tub, passing her fingers through her hair till it was smooth and shiny. Mirroring herself in the tub, with the spine of a fish she combed her hair and rearranged it. Then she scooped up a handful of blubber from the lamp, where it was near-melted from the flame, rubbed it into her face, and sat down on the couch beside the white man who had followed her antics with a puzzled eye. He backed up with a face of fright and she moved up to him, offering her grin and blushing.

"Don't be embarrassed," Ernenek smirked at him. "A husband is taking the children for a little walk." Then, remembering that the guest didn't know the language of the Men, he signaled with his hands that he was leaving.

At this the white man flung himself to the ground and tried to run the gauntlet. But Ernenek, eyes blazing, grabbed him by the seat of his pants as he wiggled through the tunnel and tossed him back onto the couch while Asiak, utterly mortified, burst into tears.

"Son of a tailless bitch and a toothless walrus!" Ernenek thundered at his cringing guest. "How dare you so insult a man?" He picked him up again and dashed him repeatedly against the wall, till the explorer's head grew limp and his skull made a dismal thud against the wall, leaving a blotch of blood on the ice; only then did he drop him, saying:

"Let this be a lesson to you!"

The white man was never again going to insult anyone's wife. The white man was dead. Blood and brainy matter were seeping from his cracked skull, soiling the hides.

*Having sexual intercourse.

"Now see what you have done," Asiak said, still sniffing, while the crying children clung to her pants.

"Somebody didn't intend to kill him," Ernenek said, opening his arms disconsolately.

Hans Ruesch, **Top of the World** (New York: Pocket Books, Inc., 1959), pp. 65–66. (Originally published by Harper & Row.)

Contrast Ernenek's attitude toward sex with that of Max Shulman's Guido cited in the introduction to Chapter 3. If Ernenek was willing to give his wife away sexually to another and was so angered by the refusal of the offer that he murdered his "ungracious" guest, Guido seemed willing to give Maggie away permanently merely because she had dared to discuss sex in the classroom. Cultural diversity is clearly depicted in the contrast of these two excerpts from literature.

In the passage from *Top of the World*, another important aspect of culture can be inferred—its structure. That culture is structured, or organized, should be obvious from the definition of social structure as any interrelated set of social relationships. Chapter 5 will deal with the intersection between culture and social structure, but first it is necessary to consider the structure of culture apart from its manifestation in actual behavior. In the real world, culture and social structure are conjoined, but each of the two components can, for the sake of clarity, be analytically disengaged. Remember, this separation of culture from social structure is not always possible, and when such a separation is made, it is only an abstraction.

In the present chapter, two aspects of the structure of culture will be considered. First, culture is structured in that its cognitive, material, and normative dimensions are variously connected via complex interrelationships. Second, culture is structured by virtue of the nature of its *distribution* —the degree to which aspects of culture are shared—both within societies and across societies. As many of the illustrations offered thus far indicate, societies can display vast cultural differences. Further, the existence of subcultures and contracultures means that cultural differences abound even within a particular society. Although cultural variations across and within societies are numerous, at the same time cultural similarities exist that tend to bind each society together and that provide for some degree of sharing across societies. These two topics—interrelationships among the cognitive, material, and normative dimensions of culture, and societal diversity and similarity due to variations in the degree of cultural sharing—occupy the bulk of this chapter. Also of relevance are the concepts of ethnocentrism and cultural relativism.

INTERRELATIONSHIPS AMONG THE DIMENSIONS OF CULTURE

In the passage from *Top of the World*, the cognitive, material, and normative dimensions of culture are interconnected. In instructing Asiak to make herself beautiful for the white visitor, Ernenek was acting on the belief (cognitive dimension of culture) that his guest wished to make love to her. Sharing his belief, Asiak made herself "appealing" to the stranger by applying urine to her hair, combing it with a fish spine, and rubbing blubber on her face (material dimension of culture). The white man's apparent revulsion to making love to Asiak violated one of the Eskimo's mores, as can be inferred from Asiak's weeping and Ernenek's violent reaction (normative dimension of culture).

Folkways, mores, laws, values, beliefs, and material objects, then, do not exist as separate entities but are complexly interrelated. Material objects, such as Asiak's comb, simply have no meaning apart from the cognitive and normative aspects of the culture that define their construction, utility, and importance. Once you have understood this basic premise of the structural perspective—that social phenomena cannot be reduced to, and explained in, terms of their separate components—then it becomes clear that the components comprising culture take on meaning only within the context of their interrelationships within a particular social structure.

CULTURAL DIVERSITY

Cultural diversity among societies

Members of a society at any given point in time must fulfill needs felt to be important within that society. For the most part, human behavior represents a legacy resulting from numerous problem-solving activities of preceding generations within that society. Of course, the perception of societal members of important "needs" varies from place to place and from time to time. Consider the movement for air- and water-pollution control, which has gained significant public and governmental attention in the United States in recent years. Air and water pollution are problems perceived primarily among members of highly industrialized countries. Environmental pollution is not a major problem in economically underdeveloped societies, which have few automobiles, factories, or power plants. And, although the United States has been highly industrialized for some time, it is only recently that environmental protection forces have had anything resembling an effective voice. Thus the perceived needs of some societies are irrelevant for other

Pro Pix, Monkmeyer

societies, and the perception of problems to be solved varies from one historical moment to another within societies. As a result, one factor that promotes cultural diversity is the societal perception of problems to be solved, and because societies have different problems, they evolve unique solutions that are expressed in cultural variations.

Yet cultural diversity among societies has sources beyond the perception of their problems. Solutions to problems are not arbitrarily chosen—they are rooted in existing culture and natural environment. Thus not only what is defined as a need but the ways in which the need is attended to are heavily conditioned by the cultural legacy of a particular society and the natural environment within which it has to work. Of these, existing culture is the most influential. However, the interaction between culture and natural environment (as underscored in Chapter 2) is important for both the definition of needs and the means devised for meeting them; this interaction should not be overlooked.

A series of qualifying statements is in order with respect to culture and problem-solving. First, not all aspects of culture are the result of attempts to meet perceived needs. Economically underdeveloped societies are more closely tied to problems of survival. A crop failure in such a society may mean massive starvation. Under these conditions there tends to be a more intimate connection between the needs of the society and culture. But as societies become more economically advanced and complex, cultural patterns come into existence that are difficult to relate to social needs. Such societies can afford luxuries like waging war for further economic gain or carrying out imperialistic policies aimed at world domination, as well as more humanitarian efforts (for example, missionary work and the Peace Corps). Further, within all societies, there is a tendency for man to elaborate and diversify beyond the needs of problem-solving; that is, spiritual and aesthetic inclinations cause man to paint, compose music, write poetry, dance, or sing—and these activities are not undertaken solely as a response to societal problems.

Second, cultural developments intended to solve perceived problems may also have negative repercussions. Negative repercussions may become immediately operative or they may occur at a later time. The large quantity of waste emitted by a mammoth jet airplane is immediately recognizable as a negative consequence accompanying improvements in air transportation. Yet it took decades before the potentially negative impact of the earlier social pressure for having large families was expressed in the current concern with overpopulation.

Third, part of culture consists of vestiges of the past that are no longer relevant to the present, vestiges that exercise neither a positive nor a negative effect. Does it really matter whether the man walks on the outside when a couple is strolling down the street? Should wives defer to their husbands merely because of the authority of tradition? For most Americans the first question is easier to answer than the second. For women's liberationists, on the other hand, the answers are equally obvious. This illustration provides a transition to cultural diversity within societies.

Cultural diversity within societies

The day of the Renaissance Man is behind us. Where in modern society are the Thomas Jeffersons and Leonardo da Vincis? Where are those persons in the contemporary age who have mastered nearly all of our current knowledge? If it is difficult for physical and social scientists today effectively to share in each others' bodies of knowledge, it is nearly impossible to bridge the knowledge gap that exists between scientists and humanists. So it is with the sharing of culture. As a society becomes more complex, the portion of the total culture that is shared by all members decreases. Even within very simple societies cultural sharing is not complete, for even the least complex cultures are too variegated for complete comprehension and participation on the part of any individual. But within complex societies the cultural fragmentation reaches astounding proportions. In this section attention is focused on some concepts useful in understanding the extent to which cultural *knowledge* is diffused within a society and the degree to which cultural *participation* is shared by members of a society. Note the distinction just drawn between cultural knowledge and cultural participation. Cultural participation is not possible without some degree of cultural knowledge; yet it is often the case that cultural knowledge may be shared by those who nevertheless do not participate in an event or action. For instance, a woman may know in minute detail the process of giving birth to a baby but may never choose actually to participate in childbirth either as a mother or as part of an obstetrics team. Knowledge without participation applies to entire *social categories* (a number of persons who share a social characteristic such as age, sex, religion, or geographic residence). Men, for example, may also be familiar with the process of childbirth but do not have the option of personally conceiving, carrying, and giving birth to a baby. Women, whether or not they choose to exercise their capability for childbearing, and men, who have no such option, are illustrations of cultural specialties.

• CULTURAL SPECIALTIES. *Cultural specialties* are cognitive, material, and normative aspects of culture that are practiced only by certain socially recognized segments of a society.[1] While most or all members of a given society possess some degree of general knowledge about cultural specialties and have definite ideas regarding their functions, detailed knowledge and the actual practice of these specialties is reserved for designated categories within the larger society; that is, certain tasks that the larger society wants performed are assigned to certain segments of the society.

Since most cultural specialties relate to the division of labor, they are largely comprised of manual skills and technical knowledge. Aside from the division of labor along sexual lines, one of the clearest instances of cultural specialty is the division of labor expressed in occupational specialization. While each of you could make a reasonable judgment about whether a heart surgeon has performed a successful operation, whether a professor has delivered a stimulating lecture, or whether a chef has prepared a *haute cuisine* dinner, few of you could spontaneously presume to perform an operation, deliver a formal lecture, or prepare a gourmet meal. Obviously, cultural specialties proliferate as the division of labor in modern societies gains in complexity; this proliferation, in turn, leads to ever greater cultural diversity within societies.

• CULTURAL ALTERNATIVES. Cultures provide some range of choice for meeting any given situation. Let us use the means of transportation selected for a vacation as a case in point. Some Americans will travel in sedans or station wagons. Wealthier ones will go in small campers or in the luxury of their Winnebagos. Still others will jet to their destination. Young people are more likely to travel in groups; some will ride motorcycles; and some will hitchhike. These are *cultural alternatives*—cognitive, material, and normative patterns that may be adopted only by certain persons.

All cultural alternatives represent different ways of meeting an identical situation. Each of the alternatives would presumably achieve the same end or meet the situation equally well. Cultural alternatives are not shared by all members of a society. And, unlike cultural specialties, cultural alternatives are not assigned to socially recognized categories as part of the societal division of labor. Persons carrying out the patterns attached to widely diverse cultural specialties may share the same cultural alternatives. Businessmen may become weekend hippies, sharing cultural alternatives that include bell-bottoms, beads, group sex, and pot parties. At the same time, their straight counterparts may wear more conventional clothes, sleep with their own wives, and work on alcohol highs. Or, to cite another illustration, some nontraditional marital arrangements are appearing in the United States. Homosexual marriages and cohabitation without legal sanction are alternatives shared by persons without regard to their locations in the societal division of labor.

The complexity of the matter of cultural alternatives has not yet been revealed. First, the extent of cultural alternatives varies according to the complexity of the society. Appropriate behavior for a given situation in simple societies tends to be judged within a narrow range of alternatives. Because cultural alternatives in simple societies are well known by their members and are few in number, cultural freedom of choice is severely limited. As societies become more complex, the cultural repertoire from which their members may draw becomes larger. However, even in a society as complex as contemporary America there are limits to the acceptability of cultural alternatives. Despite what is thought to be considerable sexual flexibility exhibited in the United States, very few persons choose the alternative of offering their mate to a house guest for the latter's sexual gratification. And, while our culture provides for wide religious latitude, human sacrifice is not permissible.

Second, while individuals may choose cultural alternatives, the fact that cultural alternatives also tend to be *shared* by members of identifiable social structures and social categories is more important from a sociological viewpoint. In addition to underscoring the sharing of culture, this phenomenon partially accounts for the structure of culture.

• CULTURAL ALTERNATIVES IN SUBCULTURES AND CONTRACULTURES. Sociologists find the concepts subculture and contraculture extremely useful in the study of the distribution (degree of sharing) of cultural alternatives. A *subculture* refers to patterns for thinking, feeling, and behaving that are in some important respects different from the larger culture and that have been developed by either identifiable societal subunits or social categories.

Residents of southern Appalachia may be considered an example of a subculture. These people subscribe to ways of thinking, feeling, and behaving that are said to be quite different from those of what might be called "middle-class America." According to Jack Weller, middle-class Americans believe in such things as freedom to determine one's destiny, progress, planning ahead, status-seeking, education, and social participation.[2] In contrast, southern Appalachians are fatalistic, present-oriented, non-status-seeking, and nonparticipative.

The designs for living of the southern Appalachians are different from middle-class American patterns, but they cannot be considered to be in opposition to the larger culture. Their ways of living were neither created in reaction to, nor are they sustained by, opposition to American cultural patterns. Rather, the existence of the southern Appalachian subculture represents an adaptation to the reality of living a deprived and frustrating existence.

In contrast to a subculture, a *contraculture*, whether by deliberate design or slow unconscious development, stands in direct opposition to certain important aspects of the larger culture. Edward Suchman presents evidence regarding the existence of the "hang-loose" ethic among a particular segment of the contemporary college and university communities.[3] The "hang-loose" ethic is fundamentally irreverent and takes as its point of attack such previously unquestioned tenets of conventional culture as "my country right or wrong," the sanctity of marriage and premarital chastity, the accumulation of wealth, and the right of parental, educational, and governmental authorities to impose decisions on those in their charge. In brief, the Establishment is their target of repudiation.

Thus far, a subculture has been portrayed as merely being different from the larger culture, while a contraculture has been described as conflicting with its host culture. Although this distinction is basically sound, to a certain extent it creates a false dichotomy. Shades of meaning are precluded. In the real world, subcultures have conflicting designs for living and contracultures exhibit similarities with the larger culture. The pattern of permanent welfare support exhibited among many southern Appalachians conflicts as much with the middle-class work ethic as does the "hippie" rejection of work. And, while a certain type of college student defiantly smokes pot, rejects the concept of virginity, and rails against the accumulation of wealth and the exercise of hard work, the fact remains that he is also participating in the Establishment's educational institution in order to secure a job in the Establishment's economic system.

The concepts of subculture and contraculture are also used in reference to social categories like religion, sex, and geographic region. In the case of social categories, the usage is necessarily looser than it is when applied to definite social structures, because social categories cut across identifiable social structures. Social structures contain members of several different social categories—members who are of varying religions, of both sexes, and of varying ages. This creates confusion and conflict within social structures. There are women who belong to ethnic subcultures that strongly define the home as the only proper place for women, but who, as members of the social category "woman," may subscribe to one or more alternative roles for their sex.

Such is the complexity of cultural alternatives. That cultural diversity exists among societies and interlaces any one society has been illustrated in this section. Intersocietal and intrasocietal cultural diversity are not without their consequences, one of which is ethnocentrism.

ETHNOCENTRISM AND CULTURAL RELATIVISM

Ethnocentrism—the judgment on the part of members of one social structure that their particular patterns for thinking, feeling, and behaving are superior to those of members of other structures—is a consequence of cultural diversity that has both advantages and disadvantages.

Ethnocentrism

To be ethnocentric is to use the cultural patterns of one's own social structure as yardsticks to measure the real and ideal behavior patterns of other structures. If members of an outside structure think, feel, and behave in ways that seem strange because they are not the same as ours, we may downgrade that structure. An ethnocentric mind views cultural and behavioral differences as manifestations of inferiority.

Examples of ethnocentrism between and within societies are plentiful. Although Hitler's Germany went overboard both in theory and practice, members of all societies tend to offer themselves as exemplary models of what the gods really had in mind for human beings. The Olympic Games are much more than an arena for young men and women to engage in healthy and exuberant competition. In addition to this stated purpose of the games, they are also an expression of ethnocentrism. Influential political and nationalistic undercurrents run through the Olympics. A country's final ranking in this athletic competition for gold, silver, and bronze medals is frequently taken as a reflection of its worth and status on the world stage.

Consider some intrasocietal instances of ethnocentrism. Boston is said by some (mostly Bostonians) to be the hub of the universe. Some inhabitants of the Northeastern Seaboard have been known to express the belief that only a wasteland separates them from the Pacific Ocean; some more enlightened Easterners are willing to concede the addition of California to the East Coast in describing all that is good in the United States. Of course, this long-standing ethnocentric viewpoint has been subject to attack by those in Middle America who have always felt that virtue actually resides with them. Finally, the members of country clubs, churches, and schools all over America feel that their particular ways of living are eminently suitable for social and cultural duplicating.

To this point, ethnocentrism has been portrayed as either villainous or ridiculous. It may be both. But it is inevitable. And its inevitability is partly rooted in the advantages it offers to social life. Imagine the expense and effort required to create from scratch the integration, high morale, loyalty, and stability within a structure that ethnocentrism—based on natural cultural learning—provides. Few things draw people closer together than the shared conviction of their superiority vis-à-vis others. Such a certainty makes people feel good about themselves and their fellow members. The fires of nationalism and patriotism, prominent forms of social loyalty, cannot be kindled by propaganda proclaiming national inferiority. Indeed, because of ethnocentrism, life itself is the loyal patriot's freely offered gift for the common cause. Finally, social stability is promoted because the need for change is seldom entertained by those armed with the conviction that truth and beauty are already theirs.

Not only does ethnocentrism encourage group integration, loyalty, morale, and stability, it also provides a justification for the script by which structure members can make their way in their social orbits. Released from the need for attending to routine matters, members have more time and energy for creativity in handling either novel situations or more pressing and enduring problems. That excessive ethnocentrism can transform this asset into a liability is an observation that will be elaborated on shortly.

People are not ethnocentric simply because they consciously realize the advantages of ethnocentricity for social life. No. Ethnocentrism would be pervasive even if it did not offer these advantages. Ethnocentrism is inevitable largely because of successful socialization. We are taught the rightness of our culture from a variety of sources (home, church, peers, schools, mass media), and thus it is only natural that this "rightness" becomes the yardstick for evaluating the ways of thinking, feeling, and behaving of social structures other than our own. Judgments of all kinds are nearly always alloyed with socially derived convictions regarding right and wrong. Ethnocentrism, then, is a predictable by-product of the transmission and learning of culture.

That ethnocentrism carries certain advantages has just been noted. However, a price may have to be paid for the integration, morale, loyalty, stability, and cultural justification it supplies. Extreme ethnocentrism has ill effects within societies as well as between them. On the intrasocietal side, extreme ethnocentrism may create such a high degree of integration and stability that innovation is hampered. Societies whose members are too firmly convinced of their righteousness may experience a choking-off of internal exploration for new solutions to persistent problems. Further, they may reject, without examination, solutions that might be gleaned from the experience of other societies. If heightened ethnocentrism impedes both the internal creation and the external borrowing of ideas for solving old problems, it may create an even greater disadvantage in meeting the challenge of new problems and unfamiliar circumstances.

While extreme ethnocentrism may contribute to rigid integration within a society, it may also promote injurious intrasocietal fragmentation. A society fragmented by ethnocentrically induced barriers separating subcultures or social categories also suffers from the damper placed on innovation. Thus, within societies, extreme ethnocentrism, whether it fosters societal integration or fragmentation, works counter to the general societal welfare.

On the intersocietal front, conflict is nearly always the result of extreme ethnocentrism. Global peace and welfare become secondary goals in a world in which ethnocentrism intensifies intersocietal conflicts based on power struggles for economic superiority and/or military supremacy.

Cultural relativism is a perspective that can be helpful in combating the intrasocietal and intersocietal disadvantages of excessive ethnocentrism.

Cultural relativism

Offering one's mate for sexual dalliance with an overnight guest is not approved within most social structures. There are, however, some societies in which trading spouses is not only acceptable but expected behavior. As noted, in traditional Eskimo society it was a serious personal affront to the husband if a guest refused to "laugh" with his wife. *Cultural relativism*— the idea that any given aspect of a particular culture must be evaluated in terms of its place within the larger cultural context of which it is a part, rather than according to some alleged universal standard that applies across all cultures—gives us a unique window from which to observe these variations.

Let us begin with another excerpt from *Top of the World*. In the passage below, some time has elapsed since Ernenek's rage caused him accidentally to kill the guest who had insulted his family. Ernenek and Asiak are talking with a potential ally in the matter, a white man whose life Ernenek had saved.

"You have saved my life, Ernenek," the white man said, "and I wish to straighten things out so that you need no longer fear my companions. But you will have to stand before a judge. I will help you explain things."

"You are very kind," said Ernenek, happy.

"You said the fellow you killed provoked you?"

"So it was."

"He insulted Asiak?"

"Terribly."

"Presumably he was killed as you tried to defend her from his advances?"

Ernenek and Asiak looked at each other and burst out laughing.

"It wasn't so at all," Asiak said at last.

"Here's how it was," said Ernenek. "He kept snubbing all our offers although he was our guest. He scorned even the oldest meat we had."

"You see, Ernenek, many of us white men are not fond of old meat."

"But the worms were fresh!" said Asiak.

"It happens, Asiak, that we are used to foods of a quite different kind."

"So we noticed," Ernenek went on, "and that's why, hoping to offer him at last a thing he might relish, somebody proposed him Asiak to laugh with."

"Let a woman explain," Asiak broke in. "A woman washed her hair to make it smooth, rubbed tallow into it, greased her face with blubber and scraped herself clean with the knife, to be polite."

"Yes," cried Ernenek, rising. "She had purposely groomed herself! And what did the white man do? He turned his back to her! That was too much! Should a man let his wife be so insulted? So somebody grabbed the scoundrel by his miserable little shoulders and beat him a few times against the wall—not in order to kill him, just wanting to crack his head a little. It was unfortunate it cracked a lot."

"Ernenek has done the same to other men," Asiak put in helpfully, "but it was always the wall that went to pieces first."

The white man winced. "Our judges would show no understanding for such an explanation. Offering your wife to other men!"

"Why not? The men like it and Asiak says it's good for her. It makes her eyes sparkle and her cheeks glow."

"Don't you people borrow other men's wives?" Asiak inquired.

"Never mind that! It isn't fitting, that's all."

"Refusing isn't fitting for a man!" Ernenek said indignantly. "Anybody would much rather lend out his wife than something else. Lend out your sled and you'll get it back cracked, lend out your saw and some teeth will be missing, lend out your dogs and they'll come home crawling, tired—but no matter how often you lend out your wife she'll always stay like new."[4]

It is clear from this conversation that cultural blindness and ethnocentrism are making communication between the Eskimos and their white friend quite difficult. It was automatically assumed by the white man that Ernenek's rage was for an attempted sexual assault on Asiak. This interpretation by the white man provides amusement for the Eskimos, who go on to explain that not only did the dead man refuse to "laugh" with Asiak, but he rejected the delicacy of old meat containing the freshest worms. Ernenek plays a game of cultural one-upmanship by responding to the white man's explanation to Asiak that his own people are accustomed to a different kind of food with a sly "so we noticed." Upon comprehending the final provocation for the murder, their white friend immediately tells them of the hopelessness of their case in a white man's court. In fact, ethnocentrism, if not mild culture shock, overtakes their white friend who attempts to shut the case with a dogmatic "It isn't fitting, that's all." But to Ernenek and Asiak it is by no means unfitting to lend wives. With resentment fired by ethnocentrism, Ernenek forcefully explains that of all the possessions a man owns, only a wife stays like new with use. And if you ask Asiak, use brought on by "laughing" adds to her value (not to mention her pleasure).

Ernenek's heated justification for wife-lending is an excellent illustration of the cultural-relativistic perspective—the Eskimos' possessions were handmade, difficult to replace, subjected to hard use, and easily destroyed. Within this context, the lending of wives served a positive function and made good sense. As a perspective, cultural relativism directs that any judgment regarding the goodness or badness of one or more of the ways of think-ing, feeling, and behaving of a particular society be based on how well they fit with other aspects of its culture. In this perspective, the test of goodness is whether an aspect of culture is sufficiently consistent with other aspects of culture to be considered acceptable within a given social structure.

Since under cultural relativism any particular aspects of a culture are to be evaluated in relation to other parts of that same culture, it follows that one culture cannot be judged to be either better or worse than another. Yet if aspects of a culture as expressed in social behavior are to be evaluated only within their larger cultural context, does this mean that nothing is immoral? Have sociologists and anthropologists ruled out moral judgments by their appeal to cultural relativism? It is true that there are no absolute moral standards on which members of all societies could agree. However, this does not mean that moral judgments are never to be made. Cultural relativism is not a license permitting members of a social structure to be-have in any way they choose. Within social structures, behavior is morally evaluated in terms of those prevailing aspects of culture that are relevant. Wife-lending meshed easily with traditional Eskimo culture but could not be easily integrated into the larger American culture at any historical mo-ment to date. Thus, the sexual use of another's wife or husband generally draws strong social disapproval in America.

Cultural relativism and value-neutrality

For sociologists, cultural relativism means never having to say "you're wrong." This philosophy of withholding moral judgments in the study of social structure has come under fire lately. Some sociologists now believe that for a scientist to try to rule out standards of good and evil while doing his work is itself immoral. Cultural relativism, they contend, is unacceptable because it says that aspects of social life are neither good nor bad, they just are. Instead of remaining neutral and standing on the sidelines, these sociologists urge the active involvement of social scientists in the creation of a more humane, just, and equitable society.

Should the social scientist also be the social fixer? More specifically, do sociologists as scientists have a moral responsibility to speak out against and attempt to change aspects of social life they believe to be wrong? From the time of its appearance on the American academic scene in the late 1800s, sociology has steadily attempted to move from its origins as a social problem-solving discipline to a nonsocially involved science. During the intervening years, disagreement has periodically surfaced on the compatibility of these two role prescriptions. A central argument against the involvement of social scientists in the eradication of social ills is that science is *value-neutral*—that is, the conduct of scientific research is supposed to be directed at discovering what *actually* exists, with no room for personal judgments as to what *ought* to exist. This idea of value-neutrality—that scientists are not supposed to permit their own value judgments (ideas of what is good and bad) to influence their scientific work—has dominated sociological thought for a long time. And although science as a value-neutral enterprise remains the prevailing stance among sociologists, those favoring the interjection of standards of good and bad into scientific activity seem to be on the increase. If the debate regarding the moral responsibility of the social sciences to improve society is not a new one, it is an issue that has once again gained considerable prominence.

Whatever the attitudes of sociologists toward cultural relativism, ethnocentrism, because of its inevitability, will always operate within and across social structures. And because of its contributions to social life, ethnocentrism probably should not be completely eradicated.

Although people will probably always evaluate and thus judge other persons and social structures against the standards that they have learned, ethnocentrism does need to be kept within bounds. The perspective known as cultural relativism is helpful to this end by serving as a constant reminder that such judgments are not grounded in absolute values that hold for all times and all places. Of immediate importance to you is that viewing social life from the standpoint of cultural relativism is crucial for developing the sociological imagination. Only by removing to some extent the cultural and social blinders created by ethnocentrism can your mind be free enough to detect the interplay between self and society, to pursue the debunking theme, and to achieve a measure of intellectual liberation.

In spite of the existence of ethnocentrism within and between societies that is based on cultural diversity, some important threads of cultural similarity are also present.

CULTURAL SIMILARITY

Some degree of integration must exist within any society if it is not to fly apart in several directions and cease to exist. In simple societies the degree of integration is considerable and is quite apparent to the perceptive observer. Integration is much less visible in more complex societies—torn as they are with a multiplicity of subcultures and contracultures—but some ties that bind exist within them nevertheless. To cultural specialties and cultural alternatives Ralph Linton added a third category by which the content of culture can be classified—cultural universals.[5] Contrary to one's first reaction to the term "universals," Linton was not referring to cultural sharing among various societies. A cultural universal in one society may be a cultural alternative in another or it may be totally absent. *Cultural universals* are those aspects of culture within a particular society that are shared by nearly all adult members of sound mind. Language, housing, and customs of dress are illustrations of cultural universals.

Similarity in cultural forms

Are there shared cultural attributes that can be discerned both within and across societies? All of the discussion about cultural diversity, ethnocentrism, and cultural relativism would suggest a negative answer to this question. Yet a strong case for cultural similarity within and across societies can be made. The analysis of culture that has occupied the last two chapters applies to all cultures. Each culture is man-made, learned, abstract, and differentially shared. All cultures have cognitive, material, and normative dimensions and every culture is structured. Cultures have similarities that are somewhat less abstract than the analytical categories just noted.[6] To cite only a few, all known cultures have language, incest taboos, funeral rites, penalties for lawbreakers, music, art, personal names, and basic institutions (religion, family, education, polity, and economy).

Similarity in cultural forms across societies can be established. What about specific content for shared cultural forms? What about specific patterns for thinking, feeling, and behaving that are shared among societies? Similarity in specific cultural patterns across societies cannot be pushed to great lengths with any validity, for even cultural patterns that have equivalent labels are often expressed quite differently in various societies. Take the value of freedom. Freedom in the Soviet Union is defined within the framework of its brand of communism. Freedom in the Soviet Union does not extend very far when it comes to dissident intellectuals, artists, and Jews. In America, considerable latitude is given to intellectual, artistic, and religious expression. Yet the conception and practice of freedom in America reside within a capitalistic setting. A socialist has never been elected to the presidency in the United States, and there are still institutions of higher learning that would deny a public platform to an avowed or even a suspected communist.

Societies, then, share in a significant number of cultural forms. Cultural diversity across societies exists because the specific patterns attached to these shared forms vary from society to society. The presence of diversity in cultural patterns among societies should not be used to belittle the degree of similarity in form that has been identified among societies. It is also important to know why similarity in form exists among societies.

Factors promoting similarity in cultural forms

Because members of every society must grapple with many of the same problems, a certain amount of cultural similarity among societies is inevitable. Two basic problem areas that every society faces are the necessity of handling certain biological characteristics, shared by all humans, and the need for sustaining social life.

Consider first the biologically determined problems that all societies must solve. To select a few important ones, each society must find ways of providing food and shelter, of gratifying adult sexual needs, and of extending to human infants the close care they require.

In addition to sharing in these common biological problems, members of all societies face certain problems that must be solved if their social life is to continue. It would be difficult for any society to survive for very long without such things as a system of communication, techniques for coordinating the activities of members toward the achievement of societal goals, ways for passing on knowledge to new members, provisions for government, and means for selecting persons to lead in various spheres of social activity.

Common societal problems—whether biologically or socially based—are met with a limited number of common forms on which members of all societies tend to rely. It should not be forgotten that the specific patterns involved in solving socially and biologically generated problems result in considerable cultural diversity among societies. Cultural diversity also exists because not all aspects of culture can be thought of as solutions to problems. Finally, as noted in the beginning of the section on cultural diversity, the perception of societal problems is not the same from society to society and may differ from one time period to another within any society. But because all societies face some of the same problems at the same time with a limited number of available cultural forms from which to choose, similarities across societies can be detected.

OVERVIEW AND PREVIEW

The discussion of culture, one of the most important sociological concepts, has required two full chapters. In Chapter 3 the central characteristics of culture were presented and the content of culture was divided into cognitive, material, and normative dimensions. The diversity and structure of culture took center stage in the present chapter.

One way to see the structure of culture is to examine the cultural diversity and similarity that exists both within any given society and among different societies. Cultural diversity among various societies is related to two factors: (1) Societies have different problems, and solutions to these different problems are reflected in cultural diversity; and (2) solutions to societal problems are based on existing culture and natural environment. Some qualifications to the idea that cultural diversity among societies is related to societal problem-solving followed these two major points. Cultural diversity within each society comes from the differential sharing of culture by societal subunits and social categories. Cultural specialties, cultural alternatives, subculture, and contraculture were central to this topic.

Ethnocentrism—the conviction that one's social structure and its patterns for thinking, feeling, and behaving are superior to others—may be viewed as a consequence of cultural diversity within and among societies. An antidote to enthnocentrism is cultural relativism—the idea that any given aspect of a particular culture must be evaluated in terms of its place within the larger cultural context of which it is a part, rather than according to some alleged universal standard that applies across all cultures. Some advantages and disadvantages of ethnocentrism were cited.

The vast extent of cultural diversity should not act as a blinder to the considerable degree of intrasocietal and intersocietal cultural similarity. Within societies, cultural similarity appears partly because of the presence of cultural universals or those aspects of any culture that are shared by nearly all sane adults. While the specific patterns for thinking, feeling, and behaving will not be the same in various societies, similarity in cultural forms across societies can be documented. Cultural similarity can be detected across societies because all societies must find solutions, from a limited number of cultural forms, to many of the same problems. These common societal problems stem either from the fairly constant biological nature of man or from some common requirements for the continuation of social life.

The diversity and structure of culture have been considered in this chapter. Chapter 5 pursues the structure of culture as it is reflected in human behavior that sociologists call social structure. After distinguishing between culture and social structure, the relationships among the major concepts that link culture and social structure will be presented. These major concepts—role prescription, social position, role behavior, social interaction, role expectation, and social relationship—are then discussed in some detail.

REFERENCES

1. Cultural specialties, cultural alternatives, and cultural universals are the original thoughts of Ralph Linton, a noted anthropologist. If you wish to pursue

these concepts further, see Ralph Linton, *The Study of Man* (New York: Appleton, 1936), pp. 271–287.

2. See Jack E. Weller, *Yesterday's People* (Lexington: University Press of Kentucky, 1965) for an analysis of the southern Appalachian subculture.
3. Edward A. Suchman, "The 'Hang-Loose' Ethic and the Spirit of Drug Use," *Journal of Health and Social Behavior*, 9 (June 1968), 146–155.
4. Hans Ruesch, *Top of the World* (New York: Pocket Books; 1959), pp. 86–88.
5. Linton, op. cit.
6. Much of the remainder of this section is based on A. L. Kroeber and Clyde Kluckhohn, *Culture: A Critical Review of Concepts and Definitions* (New York: Random House, 1971), pp. 344–354.

ADDITIONAL SOURCES AND READINGS

Benedict, Ruth. *Patterns of Culture* (New York: Mentor, 1946).

Hoebel, E. Adamson. "The Nature of Culture," in Harry L. Shapiro, ed., *Man, Culture, and Society* (New York: Oxford University Press, 1960), pp. 168–181.

Kluckhohn, Clyde. "Universal Categories of Culture," in A. L. Kroeber ed., *Anthropology Today* (Chicago: University of Chicago Press, 1953), pp. 507–523.

Kluckhohn, Clyde. *Mirror for Man* (Greenwich, Conn.: Fawcett, 1957).

Kluckhohn, Clyde, and William H. Kelley. "The Concept of Culture," in Ralph Linton, ed., *The Science of Man in the World Crisis* (New York: Columbia University Press, 1945), pp. 78–105.

Murdock, George P. "The Common Denominator of Cultures," in Ralph Linton, ed., *The Science of Man in the World Crisis* (New York: Columbia University Press, 1945), pp. 123–143.

Sumner, William Graham. *Folkways* (Boston: Ginn, 1906).

White, Leslie. *The Science of Culture* (New York: Grove, 1949).

Yinger, Milton J. "Contraculture and Subculture," *American Sociological Review*, 25 (October 1960), 625–635.

5

Social Structure

From 1960 through 1967 we have closely followed the social relationships formed by individual members of a captive pack of timber wolves . . . at the Brookfield Zoo in Chicago.

. . . The social organization of the pack is maintained by the behavior of the individuals within the group—that is, one member permits the typical social behavior of another, but restricts its antisocial behavior.

. . . The separate roles within the pack consist of the dominant, or alpha male, the alpha female, the subordinate males and females, the peripheral males and females, and the juveniles. At some time or other, the alpha male is deferred to by all the other members of the pack. He is the focal point of the "solicitous affection" of the pack; that is, the other members often run up to the alpha male, wag their tails, and paw and lick at him. Frequently, they all gather around him and do this at the same time. This is generally accompanied by howling and is called a "greeting ceremony." He is also the principal guard of the territory and patrols around the periphery of the pack, perhaps looking for intruders. The alpha female is dominant over all the other females and most of the males. She controls the relationships of the rest of the females to the pack. The subordinate males and females, together with the alpha male and female, form the effective nucleus of the pack. The peripheral males and females are kept out of the nucleus as a result of their manifest submissiveness and low rank in the social hierarchy. They are forced to remain at some distance from the nucleus most of the time, although they attempt to participate in pack activities as much as possible. The juveniles spend most of their first year in or around the den and, during their second year, gradually become part of the pack nucleus.

From "The Social Organization of Wolves" by Jerome H. Woolpy, reprinted with permission from **Natural History Magazine**, May 1968. Copyright © The American Museum of Natural History, 1968.

The behavior of these wolves in the Brookfield Zoo pack (chimpanzees, bees, ants, or any other animals or insects exhibiting a patterned social life could serve our purpose equally well) is an excellent backdrop for differentiating culturally based behavior from biologically based behavior. This topic is treated in the first major section of this chapter and is followed by an elaboration of the concepts connecting culture and social structure.

Chapters 3 and 4 dealt directly with culture. In the present chapter, social structure receives primary attention. Since culture is an abstraction that can only be inferred from human behavior and because social structure among humans cannot endure without culture, keep in mind that this analytic separation of culture and social structure is for the sake of identifying and describing the unique features of each.

CULTURE AND SOCIAL STRUCTURE

Considering the Brookfield Zoo wolves as representative of other nonhuman animals, it is clear that nonhuman animals display patterns of behavior among themselves. Some species may have more definite patterns than others, and patterns observed among animals in captivity may be stronger in degree than those observed among animals in their natural habitats. Nonetheless, most of the patterns of behavior exhibited among nonhuman animals are the product of their biological inheritance. According to Woolpy, to take only one case, the social organization* observed among these wolves had a genetic origin. It had developed among a group of cubs who had been separated from adult wolves before any social transmission or learning could possibly have taken place. Without the capability for transmitting the past or the future through the creation of *arbitrary symbols* (symbols that have no intrinsic relationship with the thing for which they stand), the social learning of nonhuman animals is tied to the present. Each generation of nonhuman animals must learn by personal experience and observation; they cannot be taught apart from a concrete situation. Because the transmission and accumulation of ideas and behavioral patterns among nonhuman animals is not possible on any large scale, culture does not exist among them.[1] The significance here is that without culture there can be no social structure. Nonhuman animals can and do exhibit patterns of behavior, but because of their inability to create and transmit culture, these patterns cannot be characterized in terms of social structure.

That human beings are the only culture-creating, culture-bearing animals is generally conceded among social scientists. Therefore, the presence

---

*Many sociologists use the concepts social organization and social structure interchangeably. In this context they do not mean the same thing. As Woolpy uses the term social organization, it refers to patterned behavior that is not based on culture.

Joe Van Wormer, National Audubon Society

of culture and social structure among humans makes them unique in the animal kingdom. Social structure and culture are concepts that allow us to put a handle on a basic difference between human and nonhuman social life. It is *social structure* (an interrelated set of social relationships based on man-made patterns for thinking, feeling, and behaving) that especially captures the attention of sociologists.

Culture and social structure exercise reciprocal influence. The argument that one supersedes the other carries with it all of the impact of the chicken and the egg controversy. Culture is defined as abstract patterns for thinking, feeling, and behaving. These patterns must be acted out and transmitted through human behavior. When the acting out and transmitting of abstract patterns occurs, social structure may be said to exist. At the same time, culture must also be created and changed, and since the creation and alteration of culture is achieved *through* human behavior, culture at any point in time is affected by existing social structure. Of course, this continuous interaction between culture and social structure is conditioned by natural environment and biological heritage.

CONCEPTS BASIC TO SOCIAL STRUCTURE

Now for a brief treatment of the concepts that sociologists have developed for linking culture and social structure. Chapter 2 contained the concepts and their definitions that are basic to culture and social structure. Those cited as central to social structure were role prescription, social position, role behavior, social interaction, role expectation, and social relationship. Before turning to detailed elaborations of each, a graphic presentation of the interrelationships among these concepts, accompanied by a concise summary statement, should be helpful to you. A firm grasp of the next few paragraphs and of Figure 5.1, which graphically illustrates the ideas they contain, will make the rest of this chapter seem considerably more comprehensible.

In Figure 5.1 you can see the manner in which culture and social structure are linked. The interaction between culture and social structure is denoted by the two-headed arrow. Starting on the left side of this figure, the first major bond between culture and social structure is found in the concept *role prescriptions*—culturally defined rights and duties expected of all persons occupying a particular social position.[2] A location within a system of social relationships is a *social position*, the second link in this conceptual chain. Role prescriptions are attached to each position within a system of social relationships. It is through role prescriptions that culture enters the picture. Yet, for various reasons to be stated later, there is nearly always some slippage between the role prescriptions that receive their specific content from culture and the actual behavior displayed by persons acting out the rights and duties expected of them in a particular social position. The manner in which role prescriptions are actually executed by any holder of a social position is termed *role behavior*. Role behavior is the third link.

CULTURE

via

role prescriptions

attached
to

social positions

guides

role behavior

through

social interaction

which may be
observable as

social relationships

which
constitute

SOCIAL STRUCTURE

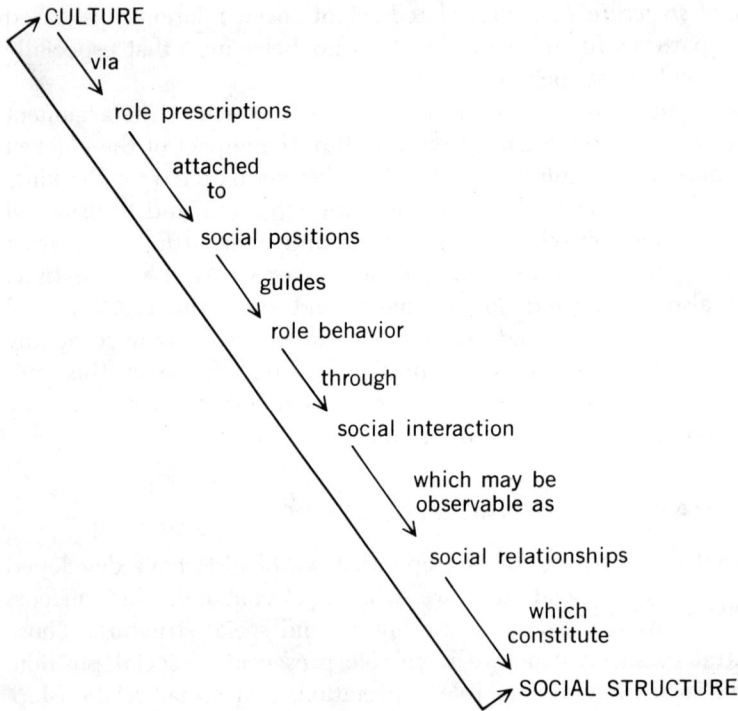

Figure 5.1 Conceptual framework linking culture and social structure

It is through the process known as social interaction that role behavior occurs. *Social interaction* is the exchange of social influence in which the actions of one person affect the behavior of another person, whose reactions in turn affect the first person, and so on. A particular type of social interaction of greatest interest to sociologists occurs when persons occupying interrelated social positions exhibit role behavior that is based on their mutual understanding of their reciprocal rights and duties. Such mutual understanding is possible because occupants of social positions have expectations for their own behavior as well as expectations for the behavior of others in the situation. *Role expectations*, then, are the repertoire of behavior expected for oneself and anticipated from others within the context of interrelated positions. Role expectations exist as a result of experience and learning, a basic concern that will be pursued in a later chapter on socialization. Because role expectations exist, much human social interaction is orderly, predictable, continuous, and recurrent.

Social interaction, based on role expectations and role behavior, is observable as social relationships, as shown in Figure 5.1. Social relationships may be of two general types: An *episodic social relationship* is a pattern of social interaction that is over quickly (clerk-customer) or engaged in only periodically (nurse-patient); a *continuous social relationship* is a pattern of social interaction that is participated in on a constant basis (husband-wife). The link between role behavior, social interaction, and social relationships is the fourth bond.

It is the social structure that emerges as a result of this sort of social interaction—along with the change and conflict that accompany it—that is sociology's starting point. That is, social interaction observable as social relationships brings us to the end of the conceptual chain between culture and social structure. *Social structure*—an interrelated set of social relationships based on man-made patterns for thinking, feeling, and behaving (culture)—can be identified as a result of all the conceptual links that have preceded it, as shown in Figure 5.1. And in turn, existing social structure affects creation and change in culture.

Is a conceptual game being played here? Yes, it is. But it is a process of conceptualization as legitimate and important for sociology as it is for nuclear physicists who have never directly observed an electron or seen an atom split. For both sociologists and nuclear physicists deal with abstractions, with unobservable things whose presence and operation must be inferred from observable things. Like culture, social structure is an abstraction, something inferred from human behavior. When sociologists infer the presence and operation of social structure, they have done so by observing culturally based social interaction that is displayed as an interrelated set of social relationships. Sociologists, then, are interested in social interaction that has coalesced into social structures. At the same time, sociologists are also engaged in the study of social interaction that reflects conflict and change in social structure.

Thus, much of human behavior is neither random nor the action of isolated individuals. Human behavior may change, conflict may exist. Nevertheless, considerable order, stability, and predictability persist because persons engage in social interaction as holders of social positions (nurse, patient, doctor) with learned role expectations that receive their content from culture (role prescriptions). That is, occupants of positions bring to a given social situation some mental map of the behavior expected of themselves as well as the behavior anticipated from others in that situation.

This concise statement of the concepts basic to social structure will have made clear to you both the integration and complexity of these concepts. The remainder of the chapter will be devoted to an elaboration of each in turn. There is a tendency to lose sight of the overall connection among the concepts basic to social structure when each is discussed in detail. Any such tendency should be firmly resisted.

Social position

A *social position* is a location within a system of social relationships. The assumption of social positions begins at birth; the newly born infant instantly becomes a child and a son or daughter. Depending on the number of children already in the home and the number of living relatives, a still-screaming baby girl may have thrust on her a number of positions including sister, granddaughter, great granddaughter, cousin, and niece. And from birth on, the number and variety of positions that a person has occupied are countless. Even the number of positions held at one particular point in time is staggering. As a college student you may have, in addition to positions related to the family, such diverse positions as bank depositor, football player, sorority member, freshman, consumer, and band member. This touches only the tip of the iceberg. Naturally, the more complex the social structure, the greater the number and diversity of positions occupied by any one person over a lifetime or at a specific stage in life. That persons occupy multiple positions is unmistakable.

Not only do persons hold a number of positions at the same time, the positions they occupy do not exist in isolation. Positions are interrelated in a very specific sense. From a sociological viewpoint it is not so important that the positions held by any one person at a point in time tend to be interrelated. Sociologists are not interested so much in how a given prostitute may balance her own positions of prostitute, mother of illegitimate children, daughter, and drug addict. What is more important sociologically is the reciprocal nature of positions held by one person with positions held by one or more other persons. A sociologist investigating prostitution either as a deviant social activity or simply as an occupational type would focus on the position of prostitute as it is connected with other positions such as policeman, judge, customer, pimp, and pusher. Emphasis on a network of positions permits the focus of interest to be shifted from the individual and his personal characteristics. Positions can be viewed as slots that must be filled in order for social structure to exist. When individuals are considered as occupants of positions, they are no longer individuals. They become position holders who think, feel, and act within a web of positions. The importance of the interrelationship of positions can readily be grasped—any single position has meaning only in relation to one or more other positions held by other persons. How can the position of mother exist without a child? Where is the meaning of a college football referee without athletes? Furthermore, positions are not related only on a one-to-one basis. Any particular position is tied into a complex of interrelated positions that are occupied by others. A sociological label for this web of positions is *social position-set*.[3]

• SOCIAL POSITION-SET. Figure 5.2 depicts an abbreviated position-set for a university athletic director. An athletic director is part of a position-set that includes the positions of golf coach, football coach, basketball coach, alumni president, university president, and member of the university board of trustees. That is, the position of athletic director is related in some manner to all of these various other positions.

Note also in this figure that any given occupant of the athletic director position will occupy additional positions outside of this position-set. These may either be indirectly related or totally unrelated to the athletic director position. These multiple positions held by different occupants of the position of athletic director will vary. One occupant of this position may be a husband, father, Little League baseball coach, and church deacon, while another may be single, an author, and a jazz musician. Each of these positions Mr. Jock has besides that of athletic director is part of another position-set. Assume, for example, that in addition to holding the position of athletic director, Mr. Jock is a part-time jazz musician (second part of Figure 5.2). This position-set then includes such positions as night-club owner, dancer, fellow musician, and a representative of the musician's union.

Moreover, the integration of positions does not stop here. Each of the other positions in the athletic director position-set is part of yet another position-set. For example, the position of basketball coach (as illustrated by Mr. Goalby in Figure 5.2) is related to such positions as assistant coach, high school coach, referee, and basketball player. Of course, the web of positions and position-sets could be traced on and on. It is enough for now to say that positions and position-sets are the building blocks of social structure.

How do persons become occupants of social positions? Sociologists answer this question with the broad classifications of ascribed and achieved positions.

• ASCRIBED AND ACHIEVED SOCIAL POSITIONS. *Ascribed social positions* are those that are assigned to persons automatically and thus are beyond their power to choose or reject. Sex, age, and race are prominent ascribed positions in all cultures. You are familiar enough with male and female as social positions. In general terms, age itself is a social position and carries with it certain other social positions. Broadly speaking, a person may be a child, an adult, or one of the aged. Each of these positions, of course, either forces people to assume, or prevents them from filling, other social positions. A child is not a father, and an adult male normally either is an employee, is self-employed, or is unemployed.

In many social structures race, social class position at birth, religion, and ethnic background operate as ascribed social positions that either prevent or require the occupation of other social positions. Within the Indian caste system Brahmins were seldom laborers and "untouchables" could not become dentists. In other types of social structures, a man who goes broke as the owner of a haberdashery may rise to the presidency, as did Harry S Truman; or a slum child can achieve renown as an outstanding professional athlete. In both cases the new social position that is occupied is an achieved one. *Achieved social positions* are those over which people have some degree of control. Achieved social positions are theoretically open for competition. By luck, cheating, politicking, or effort and ability, persons can assume a social position that was not theirs at birth, not foreordained upon their reaching a certain age, or not assigned to them because of their skin color, religion, father's occupation, or ethnic heritage.

Either ascription or achievement may be emphasized within a social structure. Ascription of social positions is more characteristic of a small and simple social structure. As social structures become more complex, they have more social positions to fill, and the rights and duties associated with social positions become more complex. As knowledge and specialization increase, it becomes more difficult to ignore the utility of leaving social positions open to the most able. Incompetency is rampant enough without compounding it through the arbitrary assignment of people to social positions. This is not to say that complex social structures cannot rest on a system of ascribed social positions, but such a pattern is more difficult and creates many problems.

Achieved social positions are supposedly filled on a competitive basis. Yet the reality of the situation—even in a relatively open system like that in America—is a mixed bag. You do not find many Blacks in high corporate positions, and there are proportionately few women executives, lawyers, doctors, or professors. In short, even with a social structure that bases the assignment of social positions on standards of achievement, the actual attainment and maintenance of social positions often involve a mixture of effort, good fortune, and ascription.

If the attainment of social positions is often a mixture of achievement and ascription—even within social structures emphasizing competition—two related questions come to mind: Who gets into which social positions? How do they come to occupy them? As just noted, within ascriptive social structures the questions of who gets what and why are fairly well answered at

MR. JOCK'S SOCIAL POSITION AS UNIVERSITY ATHLETIC DIRECTOR

Each person Mr. Jock deals with has additional social position-sets as exemplified in the case of Mr. Goalby, the university basketball coach, and one of his basketball players.

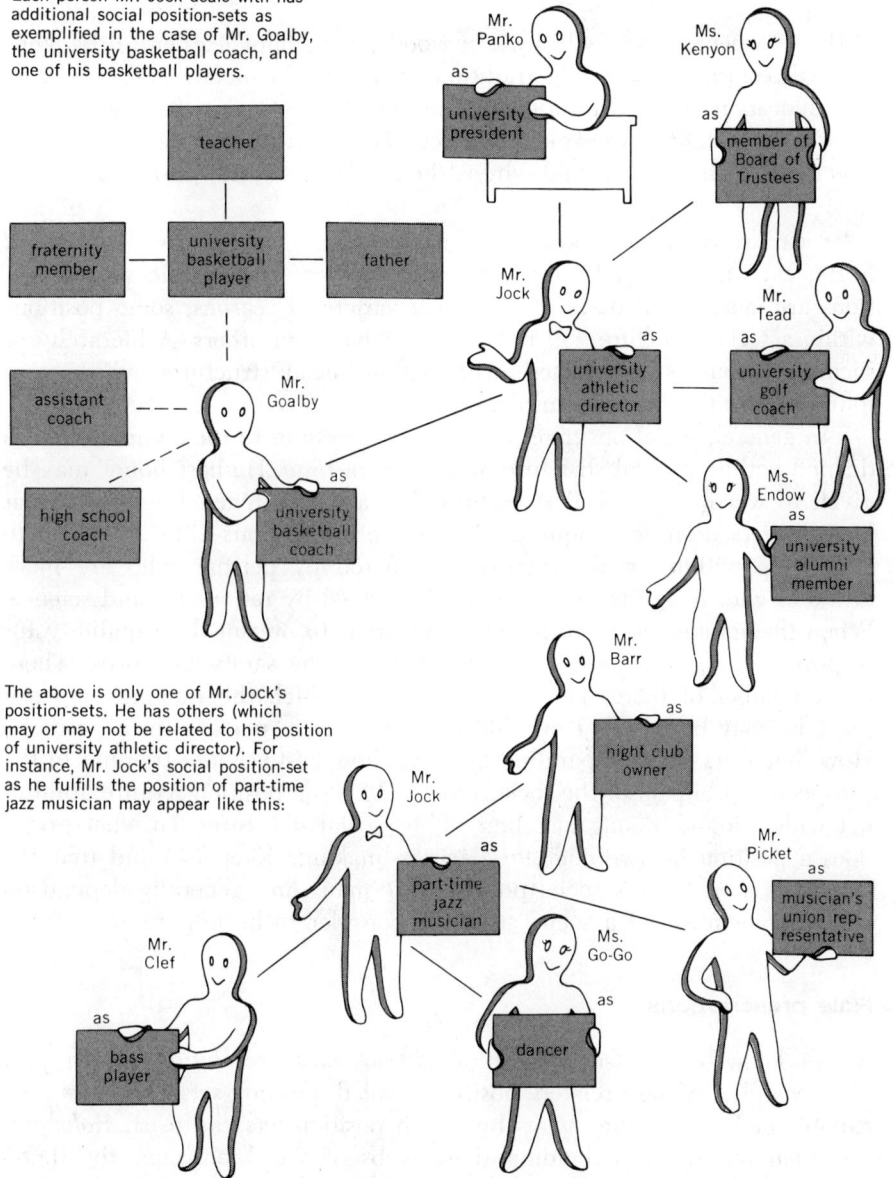

teacher

fraternity member — university basketball player — father

Mr. Panko as university president

Ms. Kenyon as member of Board of Trustees

assistant coach

high school coach

Mr. Goalby as university basketball coach

Mr. Jock university athletic director as

Mr. Tead as university golf coach

Ms. Endow as university alumni member

The above is only one of Mr. Jock's position-sets. He has others (which may or may not be related to his position of university athletic director). For instance, Mr. Jock's social position-set as he fulfills the position of part-time jazz musician may appear like this:

Mr. Barr as night club owner

Mr. Jock as part-time jazz musician

Mr. Clef as bass player

Ms. Go-Go as dancer

Mr. Picket as musician's union representative

Figure 5.2 Simplified diagram of the interrelatedness of social position-sets

birth—a carpenter's son will work in wood (or perhaps leather); a banker's son will continue the family tradition of dealing in money and influence. The allocation of social positions within social structures based on achievement is more difficult to explain. One crucial aspect of the questions of who gets into which positions and why is the ranking of social positions.

• THE RANKING OF SOCIAL POSITIONS. As in George Orwell's *Animal Farm*, even in supposedly equalitarian social structures, some social positions are more equal than others. For a variety of reasons, some positions within a social structure will be ranked higher than others. A hierarchy of social positions is established even within social structures whose very foundation is the elimination of ranking.

In general, social positions are ranked according to their importance as defined within a social structure at a point in time. Highest honor may be given to warriors in social structures that are threatened by war or that have leaders desiring conquest. Members of a religious elite are likely to be on top within social structures populated by persons who are more afraid of ghostly spirits than they are impressed by rationality and science. When the amount of waste material threatens to outrun the capability for disposing of it, more honor may be given to the sanitation corps. There are a number of more specific standards on which the ranking of social positions may be based: How difficult is it to train persons for a position? How long does such preparation take and how costly is the training to the prospective occupant of the social position? Does a position require abilities not widely found among members of the social structure? To what extent does a position involve complex decision making? Keep in mind that the standards used to rank social positions are many and generally depend on what the members of a social structure consider to be important.

Role prescriptions

As you know by now, social positions do not exist in isolation but are part of a complex of interrelated positions called position-sets. We are now capable of knowing the means by which position-sets can exist. *Role prescriptions* are the glue holding these webs of social positions together— they are culturally defined by norms that specify the appropriate ways of thinking, feeling, and behaving expected of social position occupants.

Long before sociology got its start, William Shakespeare penned these famous lines:

All the world's a stage,
And all the men and women merely players:
They have their exits and their entrances;
And one man in his time plays many parts. . . .

In *As You Like It* Shakespeare expressed an insight into the nature of social structure that mirrors one of the cornerstones of modern sociology. Social positions may be conceived as the parts held by the "actors" of real-life social situations, and, as we have seen, one man in his time does indeed hold many parts. However, as locations within a system of social relationships, social positions have no content—the actual nature of the part has not been specified. While a playwright or screenwriter specifies the content of an actor's part, the rights and duties expected of persons occupying a particular social position in the real world are "authored" by culture. Culture intersects with social structure through role prescriptions.

• ROLE PRESCRIPTIONS AND SOCIAL POSITIONS. Any single position carries with it a variety of role prescriptions. Within a position-set there is a matching of role prescriptions of one position with role prescriptions of other positions. For example, a university athletic director is expected to act in certain culturally defined ways toward his university's president, and these differ from expectations related to the university golf coach. While an athletic director may be expected to defer to the university president, the role prescriptions relating his position to that of the university golf coach places the director in control. At the same time that matching role prescriptions link the positions of athletic director and university president, there are role prescriptions relating the golf coach position to those of athletic director and university president. And so it goes with each position within the position-set.

Figure 5.3 graphically portrays the linking of social positions through role prescriptions. Although highly simplified, this figure shows that role prescriptions vary in number. Note, for example, that the span between the double lines linking the university president with the university athletic director is wider than the space between the double lines connecting the university president with the university golf coach. This means that the position of president shares more rights and duties with that of university athletic director than it does with the position of university golf coach. Similarly, you can conclude from Figure 5.3 that the positions of university athletic director and university golf coach share more rights and duties than do the positions of university president and university golf coach.

Role prescriptions attached to any position are of two kinds: rights and obligations. This fact further clarifies the way in which role prescriptions link positions into a position-set. *Rights* are what the occupant can expect from another person in the position-set. *Obligations* are those things that a

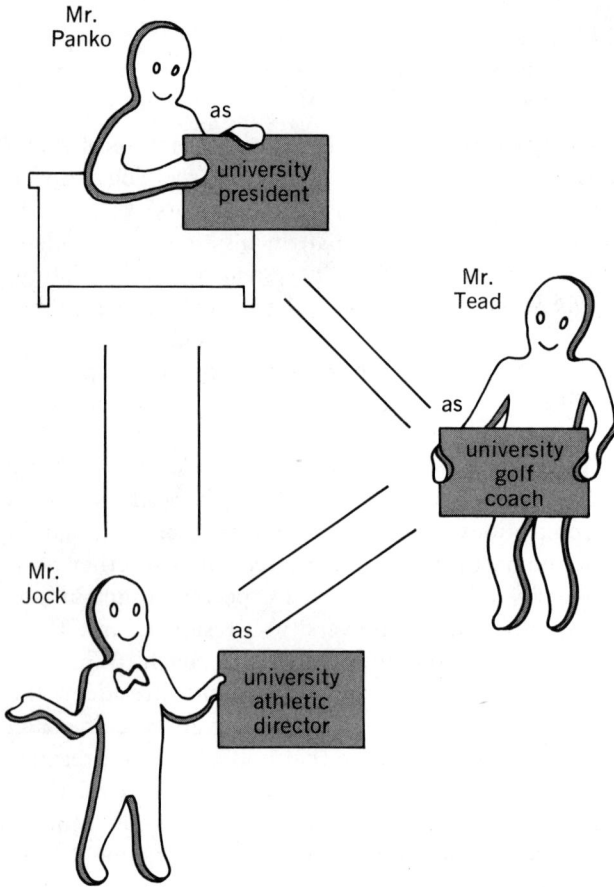

Figure 5.3   Linking of a social position-set via role prescriptions

position holder is expected to do in relation to another person within the position-set. The rights attached to one position correspond to the obligations of another position within the position-set. A baseball pitcher is expected to throw to the catcher. This obligation of the pitcher is a right of the catcher—the catcher has the right to expect this behavior from a pitcher. Similarly, the pitcher has the right to expect the catcher to throw the ball back to him after each pitch. Returning the ball to the pitcher at the appropriate time is part of the catcher's obligation to the pitcher. It is through rights and obligations that social positions become sufficiently interrelated to be labeled a position-set.

• DISTINGUISHING BETWEEN SOCIAL POSITION AND ROLE PRESCRIPTION. It is useful to keep in mind the distinction between the concepts of social position and role prescription for two reasons. In the first place, a social position in one culture may have role prescriptions different from those of the same social position in another cultural setting. The social positions may be identical among various societies but the rights and duties may not be. A religious leader in one society may be expected to appeal to a deity for relief of the sick, while in another society a religious leader may be expected to bring about a cure by his own direct action guided by a deity. Role prescriptions may also vary within societies. Within subcultures and con- tracultures, social positions similar to those in the larger culture may have entirely different role prescriptions. A father in a hippie commune has rights and obligations different from those of a father in any American suburban community.

There is a second reason for distinguishing between social position and role prescription. Any social position has a number of rights and duties or role prescriptions. A social position can be used as a single location within a system, with role prescriptions expressing the plurality of rights and obligations attached to it. Of course, position-set is also a way of introducing the idea of plurality into the social position concept. It should be clear that social positions and role prescriptions are the building blocks of social structure. They are a fundamental link between culture and socially structured human behavior.

Role behavior

Once role prescriptions are learned by occupants of social positions, then role behavior is possible. *Role behavior* is the way in which role prescrip- tions are actually carried out by a social position occupant. Let us return to the analogy between the stage and social life. If social positions are the parts and role prescriptions the lines, then role behavior is the actual performance of the play.

The danger of taking analogies at face value is that the two situations being compared are seldom exactly the same. Shakespeare's analogy be- tween social life and the stage is no exception. This does not mean that the stage analogy is not useful to you in understanding these concepts. Just the opposite is true. But in addition, further insights can be gained by look- ing at the nonparallels between real social life and the theater.

In the first place, "delivery of the lines" in real life (role behavior based on role prescriptions) is not the conscious process that actors go through in learning their script. Most role behavior occurs without forethought— persons in social positions behave in ways that just seem natural and cor- rect. In fact, these "natural" and "correct" ways have been unconsciously adopted through observation, imitation, and the efforts of others to pass them along.

There is a second and more important breakdown in the stage analogy. Considerably more variation occurs between the ideal (role prescriptions) and the real (role behavior) in social life than occurs on the stage. Actors may substitute improvised lines for momentarily forgotten ones, deliberately change lines to suit themselves, and introduce a little "business" here and there, but they either remain basically true to the written word or secure approval for marked variations. Differences between role prescriptions and role behavior are neither as easy to detect nor as easy to control as is a straying from the script on the stage. Yet—and this is a crucial point—because sufficient conformity to role prescriptions is exhibited in role behavior, orderliness, continuity, and predictability in social life can be observed.

Social interaction

Social interaction may be said to exist when persons mutually influence each other's behavior. This process is of major importance to sociology for at least two reasons. First, it is by the process of social interaction that role behavior occurs.* Second, social interaction is concrete behavior from which all of the abstract concepts in sociology can be inferred. While culture, for example, cannot be laid on the table for examination, its existence can be inferred from the direct observation of persons interacting. Sociologists are especially concerned with social interaction that is grounded in role prescriptions. To pick up Shakespeare's stage analogy once again, role prescriptions are the script for role behavior. When role prescriptions have been learned by social position occupants, they become *role expectations*—the repertoire of behavior expected for oneself and anticipated from others within a social position-set. With appropriate role expectations in mind, the behavior of one position holder becomes a cue for certain behavior from another within a social position-set. A response to this initial cue by the second position holder is a cue for further behavior on the part of the first position occupant.

This description of social interaction has been simplified. On the stage

---

*Although role behavior may involve behavior on the part of a person in isolation —a professor preparing a lecture, a student cramming for an exam—it is role behavior observable as social interaction that is most pertinent from a sociological standpoint.

there is a one-to-one relationship among cues—one performer's lines are the cue for quite specific lines from another performer. Not so for social interaction based on role expectations. In this case there is a range of cues and appropriate responses. Consider a man who, having committed armed robbery to the tune of $100,000, is about to be arrested by FBI agents. Let us consider two actions from the many that he might choose, each of which will draw quite different but equally appropriate responses from the FBI agents. Should the thief surrender, he would be handcuffed, escorted to a waiting car, and taken to jail. If on the other hand he chooses to take the money and run, he would very likely provide an opportunity for the agents to make effective use of their hours of target practice.

So it is with most instances of social interaction based on role expectations. You have a range of possible behaviors that you can direct toward the professors in your college or university. For each of those possible behaviors on your part, you can make a fairly accurate general prediction of the reaction of most professors. There may be certain professors who will not act in the anticipated manner, and each professor may carry out the anticipated action in a slightly different way. But, for professors as a whole, their action in relation to a particular cue is predictable within certain limits of variation.

This process of reciprocal cue-giving and cue-responding is called social interaction. When based on role expectations, this type of social interaction is known to the sociologist as role behavior.

Social relationships

Sociologists show the greatest interest in social interaction that occurs with enough regularity to be observed as stable patterns of behavior. Stable and enduring patterns of social interaction can be observed because occupants of social positions within a social position-set have role expectations based on culturally defined role prescriptions. Since role expectations refer to behavior expected of oneself as well as the behavior anticipated from occupants of related social positions, persons can affect each other's behavior in predictable ways. When this is the case, patterns of social interaction exist, labeled *social relationships*.

You are part of countless patterns of social interaction. Some of these patterns do not last long at any one time. It does not take very long to interact with personnel at the library circulation desk when checking out a book. Certain patterns of social interaction may be conducted over a reasonably long period of time but will not be engaged in on a continuous basis. As a hospital patient with mononucleosis, you may interact daily with nurses, orderlies, and doctors for a month or more. Once you are discharged, it is unlikely that the need for hospitalization will arise again soon. Patterns of social interaction of either short duration or infrequent occurrence are called *episodic social relationships*.

You engage in still other patterns of social interaction on a relatively constant basis. Your mother remains your mother forever, and barring death or familial problems, the two of you continue to interact regularly. Communication between you and your mother may now be more often by letter or phone than in person. The topic of conversation may have shifted from the unfairness of a parentally imposed curfew to the political and economic future of Europe. Nevertheless, social interaction between mother and daughter or mother and son tends to continue on an enduring basis; such enduring patterns of social interaction are labeled *continuous social relationships.*

Both episodic and continuous social relationships are stabilized and recurrent. These social relationships are stable and recurrent because the role expectations held by the social position occupants are culturally well defined. In contrast, there are social relationships that occur on the basis of little or no cultural definition. Persons thrown together during a disaster, for example, may be forced to interact without any clear idea of culturally acceptable behavior. Or, an English tourist who does not speak Japanese may have to endure an incredibly disconcerting social exchange with a non-English-speaking waiter in Tokyo if she is not to break her habit of afternoon tea. Between these two extremes are social relationships with varying degrees of cultural definition. Whatever the type of social relationships, they are abstractions, inferred from social interaction. That is, when patterns of social interaction are observed, the existence of social relationships may be assumed to exist. And when an interrelated set of social relationships exists, we can infer the presence of social structure.

Social structure and social structuring

The difference between social structure and social structuring, while implied throughout this chapter, has not been specifically mentioned. To this point social structure has been portrayed as something stable and fixed. In an important sense this is quite accurate—social structure is an interrelated set of culturally based social relationships. This definition, with its emphasis on culture, depicts *social structure* as a relatively stable product of social interaction. Yet, as you see from the conceptual chain developed in this chapter, the creation of social structure is a dynamic process, based on social interaction. This dynamic process by which patterns of social interaction become stabilized, recurrent, and predictable is labeled *social structuring.*

The concept of social structuring reveals the dynamic interplay between human behavior and culture noted in Figure 5.1. As you know, culture is a human creation. It is through the process of social structuring that new aspects of culture may emerge. At the same time, it is certain that existing aspects of culture help to shape social structure. Thus, social structure is a culturally based set of social relationships; social structuring is the process by which social structures are created.

In a real sense, then, social structures are constantly in a state of becoming; social structures are constantly undergoing modification. But because of their relative stability, recurrence, and predictability, social structures can be the subject of sociological study either at one point in time or over a period of time. Social structures can be viewed from either of the two perspectives central to this text—the structural or the social-psychological viewpoints.

Structural and social-psychological perspectives

It is through the social interaction of social position occupants attempting to carry out the role prescriptions attached to their social positions that culture and human behavior are fused into social structure. From the social-psychological perspective, which underlies the conceptual framework being developed in this chapter, the focus is on the network of social relationships that emerges from role behavior through the process of social interaction. That is, it is this process of interaction that is under scrutiny from the social-psychological viewpoint.

However, according to the structural perspective, an aspect of social structure can be understood only through the study of other aspects of social structure. The existence of social interaction and all it implies for the creation and maintenance of social structure is taken for granted. This is done in order to focus on the impact of social structure on persons and the interplay among social structures. Because of its emphasis on social structure itself rather than on the process of social interaction among persons that generates social structure, this perspective is a structural one. As you must know by now, neither of these perspectives considers the individual as an appropriate unit of study for sociologists.

Perspective—whether modified by "structural," "social-psychological," or "political"—means a way of looking at something. The same thing can be described in various ways, depending on the perspective from which it is being viewed. From the vantage point of the community, inmates of a jail are lawbreakers, yet it is not uncommon to find "lawbreakers" in jail who protest their innocence and who, from their own perspective, believe they have been the victim of a bum rap.

To further illustrate the difference between the structural and social-psychological perspectives, suppose for the moment that social structures are directly observable and concrete objects, and that you are cruising at 20,000 feet at the controls of *Sociologist One*. On a clear day at this altitude you would be able to observe definite patterns and contours (social structure) just as you can observe the lay of the land from an airplane. At 20,000 feet you will see no movement in the form of social interaction. Suppose you wish to get a closer look and start descending. As you reach 10,000 feet, the movements of persons engaging in role behavior will appear as tiny insects. The closer you get to ground level, the more constricted your view will be. Finally you will be forced to put aside the overall view of social structure—the structural perspective—and will be able to observe only the social interaction among social position occupants—the social-psychological perspective.

While the individual per se is not important from the social-psychological perspective, social interaction among persons is. And the more that social interaction among persons is considered, the easier it is to observe unintentional slippage between role prescriptions and role behavior, and to detect deliberate nonconformity to role prescriptions. Social-psychological aspects of social interaction and role behavior are developed further in Part IV.

OVERVIEW AND PREVIEW

Social structure—the main concern of sociology—is an interrelated set of social relationships based on man-made patterns for thinking, feeling, and behaving. These man-made patterns for thinking, feeling, and behaving are called culture. Since social structure is a network of human behavior based on culture, it follows that social structure cannot exist without culture. Nonhuman animals are without social structure because they cannot create culture. Because the social behavior observed among wolves, bees, ants, and so forth is biologically determined, their behavior is organized but not socially structured. It is not created and changed but comes to them as their unalterable birthright.

All of this, however, does not mean that all human behavior has a cultural foundation. On the contrary, considerable human behavior can be observed for which there is a lack of cultural definition (for example, panic behavior) or which is determined by the situation as it exists at a point in time (for example, a soldier going into battle for the first time). While sociologists are interested in such nonculturally defined behavior, their primary thrust has been on social structure and its alteration. In reality, sociologists tend to investigate human behavior that is "more or less" culturally flavored. Social structure is not an all-or-none matter but rather one of degree.

Culture and social structure are linked via a series of interrelated concepts, each of which was briefly introduced and subsequently covered in greater detail. Sociologists have developed a conceptual framework for linking culture and human behavior into what has been labeled social structure: Culture—in the form of role prescriptions—defines the behavior expected of social position occupants. A social position does not exist in isolation but is part of a social position-set, a complex of interrelated social positions. Occupants of social positions may have gotten there either by their own efforts (achievement) or by arbitrary assignment (ascription). Role prescriptions attached to social positions also tend to come in sets and are the force that holds social position-sets together. Role behavior—the actual performance of role prescriptions—is accomplished through the process of social interaction. The social intraction—the process of mutual influence among persons—of most interest to sociologists occurs as the result of learned role prescriptions or role expectations. From social interaction guided by role expectations emerge episodic and continuous social relationships. Social structure is any interrelated set of such social relationships.

If social structure is a culturally based set of social relationships, social structuring is the process by which social structures are created. At the social-psychological level, social structuring occurs through the process of social interaction between persons. At the structural level, social interaction remains important but it is either interaction among social structures (rather than among persons) or interaction between persons and social structures that is of significance. Both the social-psychological and structural viewpoints assume that social structure cannot be reduced to the level of individuals—as a totality, a social structure is a synthesis that is more than the mere addition of its separate parts (separate parts being individuals).

Some define sociology as the study of society. But society is only one type of social structure. Within any society there are several types of social structure that are the object of sociological scrutiny. The most central ones are group structure, formal organizational structure, social stratification structure, community structure, and institutional structure.

One reason that some sociologists bill sociology as the science of society is that all of these social structures exist within any particular society. Society, then, exclusive of a world or interplanetary social system, is the broadest and most abstract social structure. Aside from the characteristics it shares with other social structures, a *society* may be defined as a comprehensive political and territorial unit that contains an adequate number of social structures for its operation and survival. Societies are not always totally independent for they may require economic ties with other societies. But they can be identified by political and territorial boundaries, and contain at least those social structures required for their own perpetuation.

It is the study of the major social structures existing within societies that occupies the next two major sections of this text. Social stratification and community structure will be viewed from a structural perspective while socialization and group structure will be explored from the social-psychological perspective. Formal organizational structure will be examined from each perspective in turn.

Societies—even those founded on the principle of equality—appear to contain a rank order of social positions, persons, and social categories. It is clear that all persons and social categories are not treated as equals in any society. Whether inequality must always exist is a topic of vital interest in sociology, one that will be returned to in the next two chapters on social stratification structure.

REFERENCES

1. For an extended discussion of human versus nonhuman society as conceived here, see Kingsley Davis, *Human Society* (New York: Macmillan, 1949), pp. 36–50.
2. The concepts of role prescription and role behavior are the contribution of Theodore M. Newcomb and appear in Theodore M. Newcomb, Ralph H. Turner, and Philip E. Converse, *Social Psychology* (New York: Holt, Rinehart and Winston, 1965), pp. 327–333.
3. The concepts of social position-set and role-set were the original contribution of Robert K. Merton in "The Role-Set: Problems in Sociological Theory," *British Journal of Sociology*, 8 (June 1957), 106–120. The ways in which these concepts are used here, however, differ from Merton's original formulations.

ADDITIONAL SOURCES AND READINGS

Biddle, Bruce J., and Edwin J. Thomas, eds. *Role Theory* (New York: Wiley, 1966).

Davis, Kingsley. *Human Society* (New York: Macmillan, 1949).

Greer, Scott A. *Social Organization* (New York: Random House, 1955).

Nadel, S. F. *The Theory of Social Structure* (London: Billing, 1957).

Nisbet, Robert A. *The Social Bond: An Introduction to the Study of Society* (New York: Knopf, 1970).

Olsen, Marvin. *The Process of Social Organization* (New York: Holt, Rinehart and Winston, 1968).

part III

SOCIAL STRUCTURE: STRUCTURAL ASPECTS

6

Social Stratification Structure

As he sank low in the water, a strange hollow voice sounded within him. There's no way around it. I am a seagull. I am limited by my nature. If I were meant to learn so much about flying, I'd have charts for brains. If I were meant to fly at speed, I'd have a falcon's short wings, and live on mice instead of fish. My father was right. I must forget this foolishness. I must fly home to the Flock and be content as I am, as a poor limited seagull.

.   .   .

It happened that morning, then, just after sunrise, that Jonathan Livingston Seagull fired directly through the center of Breakfast Flock, ticking off two hundred twelve miles per hour, eyes closed, in a great roaring shriek of wind and feathers. The Gull of Fortune smiled upon him this once, and no one was killed.

.   .   .

His thought was triumph. Terminal velocity! A seagull at two hundred fourteen miles per hour! It was a breakthrough, the greatest single moment in the history of the Flock. . . .

When they hear of it, he thought, of the Breakthrough, they'll be wild with joy. How much more there is now to living! Instead of our drab slogging forth and back to the fishing boats, there's a reason to life! We can lift ourselves out of ignorance, we can find ourselves as creatures of excellence and intelligence and skill. We can be free! We can learn to fly!

Sometime later—

"Jonathan Livingston Seagull! Stand to Center!" The Elder's words sounded in a voice of highest ceremony. Stand to Center meant only great shame or great honor.

.   .   .

"Jonathan Livingston Seagull," said the Elder, "Stand to Center for Shame in the sight of your fellow gulls!"

It felt like being hit with a board. His knees went weak, his feathers sagged, there was roaring in his ears. Centered for shame? Impossible! The Breakthrough! They can't understand! They're wrong, they're wrong!

". . . for his reckless irresponsibility," the solemn voice intoned, "violating the dignity and tradition of the Gull Family. . . ."

To be centered for shame meant that he would be cast out of gull society, banished to a solitary life on the Far Cliffs.

". . . one day, Jonathan Livingston Seagull, you shall learn that irresponsibility does not pay. Life is the unknown and the unknowable, except that we are put into this world to eat, to stay alive as long as we possibly can."

"Why is it," Jonathan puzzled, "that the hardest thing in the world is to convince a bird that he is free, and that he can prove it for himself if he'd just spend a little time practicing? Why should that be so hard?"

An interpretive reading of the preceding passages indicates that its author, Richard Bach, has managed the ideologically impossible—a literary mixture of Horatio Alger with the New Left, achievement with autonomy, excellence with freedom. Jon Seagull wants to be as good as he can be, and his quest requires freedom from flock restrictions.

This seagull was unknowingly trying to start something. He was introducing the idea of achievement through effort. The flock elders, however, weren't buying it. Had Jonathan been successful in his campaign, these seagulls would have had the beginnings of a new social stratification structure on which their numbers could be *ranked* according to the level of their aerodynamic performance rather than their seniority. In this case, Jon's incomparable 214 miles per hour airspeed would have placed him at the pinnacle of this new seagull hierarchy. And he would have received the anticipated *rewards* of praise and prestige rather than the condemnation that wilted his momentarily proud feathers. Jonathan had the *resources* to be a great seagull—he could soar like an eagle. Yet these resources did not fit into the socially accepted stratification structure.

Flock elders were sufficiently powerful to enforce their decision for *retention* of the traditional seagull stratification structure founded on seniority. *Repercussions* generated by any social stratification structure are many. In this case, flock elders placed a high price on Jon's flight of fancy for he was banished for daring to exceed the commonly accepted definition of maximum seagull airspeed. Isolation from old acquaintances is only one type of repercussion. More important are the unique behavioral and cultural patterns associated with social class level.

Humans and seagulls are even—in real life people can't fly, and these birds are without a complex social stratification structure. But humans do indeed have highly developed social stratification structures complete with rankings, resources, rewards, retention, and repercussions—the "five R's" of stratification. Before launching into detail on each of these, some preliminaries are necessary.

THE NATURE OF SOCIAL STRATIFICATION STRUCTURE

Social differentiation, social ranking, and social stratification structure

Social stratification structures develop from the processes of social differentiation and social ranking. Therefore, distinguishing between social differentiation and social ranking within human social structures is of first order importance and can begin with a parallel and a contrast from the nonhuman world.

If bees are to survive as an insect species, they must continue to reproduce the intricate division of labor by which their cycle of work and life is accomplished. While there is only one queen bee in each hive, there must be countless workers, each of which has a particular task—that is, to fertilize eggs, to protect the hive against enemies, to care for the queen's eggs and babies, or to keep the hive clean. Each type of bee has specialized jobs to perform that are not done by other types within the hive.

Like nonhuman animals, humans within a social unit also develop a division of labor by which tasks are divided and ultimately performed by individuals. Unlike nonhuman species, man's division of labor rests primarily on a cultural base. Specialized tasks are not actually assigned to individuals but are attached to social positions. This allocation of specialized duties to specific social positions is called the process of *social differentiation*.

There is another crucial difference between social differentiation in human societies and the division of labor among animals, that of ranking of positions. On the basis of cultural values man everywhere tends to evaluate or rank certain social positions as higher than others. If the performance of brain surgery were a part of the social position of barber (assuming that brain surgery had considerable cultural value), then barbers would have a high rank. Yet the social position of barber is considerably

Beckwith Studios

below that of surgeon, precisely because cutting hair is less culturally valued than cutting brains.

This process of evaluation occurs in even the most primitive social structures. In such structures, persons are ranked primarily in terms of a few broad social positions like age or sex, or in terms of such physical attributes as strength and speed. In modern societies, differential evaluation is placed on an infinitely greater number of social positions, most of which are culturally rather than biologically defined. When social differentiation is accompanied by evaluation, the process of social ranking becomes operative. Thus the allocation of particular tasks to specific social positions is social differentiation. The process of hierarchically arranging social positions on the basis of cultural values is *social ranking*.

An inevitable outgrowth of the process of social ranking is the emergence of particular kinds of social relationships that are geared to the social position hierarchy. The rights and obligations of these social relationships attached to social position hierarchies vary from culture to culture, partly because social rankings of positions vary from culture to culture. For example, in medieval times, the social relationships between barber-surgeons and their patients were quite different from those of today's surgeons and their patients. In those days, barbers were not automatically accorded respect or high reward for the "surgery" they performed. In fact, being a surgeon then was not without its threats to personal health and safety. With the low level of medical knowledge and equipment, patient injury or death was a frequent occurrence, and barber-surgeons were often held accountable, either by law or by irate relatives, for such failures. A *social stratification structure*, then, is composed of a hierarchy of social positions and the accompanying network of social relationships. Both of these components are produced through the process of social ranking. In sociology, one can examine the social stratification structure in several ways—by looking at the actual hierarchy of social positions, by examining the network of social relationships, or by viewing the two in combination.

Must social differentiation become social stratification?

Radicals and revolutionaries in all ages have sought the dream of a classless society, a society in which all people are considered equal in terms of material rewards, power, and prestige. So far, each attempt to realize this vision has been marred by the emergence of some sort of social stratification structure. The animals in George Orwell's *Animal Farm* were no more successful than have been the Russians and the Israelis. Just as the pigs in Orwell's classic redefined the rules from "all animals are equal" to read "all animals are equal—but some are more equal than others," evidence indicates the existence and persistence of social classes in the Soviet Union and the kibbutzim system of Israel.[1] Why does the dream of a classless society seem so elusive? Why does social differentiation always seem to involve social stratification? Two theories of stratification—functional and conflict—answer this question quite differently.

• FUNCTIONAL THEORY OF STRATIFICATION. The functional* explanation of the universal presence of social stratification, developed by Kingsley Davis and Wilbert Moore, contends that social inequality exists because societies require it.[2] That is, they argue, all societies must locate their members in social positions in order to get the necessary tasks accomplished. Not only must members be located in social positions, they must also be motivated to perform the duties associated with their respective social positions; therefore, motivation is necessary on two fronts—getting persons into positions and securing performance at an acceptable level. Some social positions are more agreeable to occupy than others, some require more talent and training, and some are more crucial for survival. Consequently, getting those persons with the appropriate abilities and skills into the requisite social positions cannot be left to chance. And neither can the extraction of good performance from position holders be merely assumed. It is at this point that rewards become important—a society must offer some rewards and have a means for differentially distributing them. Distribution of the rewards is a central factor in the creation of a social stratification structure.

The principle by which rewards are distributed in the functionalist theory is this: Social positions with the highest rank receive the greatest compensation. Moreover, positions with highest rank—and therefore the greatest rewards—are those that are judged to be the most important for the larger social structure and that require the most talent or training. As importance, talent, and training decrease, so does the rank of the position. Davis and Moore's contention that social systems need a social stratification structure to ensure the accomplishment of tasks (which they assume is not guaranteed by the mere presence of social differentiation) seems sound enough. However, as indicated earlier, their ideas regarding the reasons

---

*The functional school views aspects of a social structure in the light of their positive or negative impacts on the structure as an integrated whole. In the present case, the functionalist reasoning is that since social stratification structures exist universally, they must be making a necessary contribution to all social structures. This is not to say, on the other hand, that negative ramifications of social stratification structure do not also occur.

certain social positions receive the greatest rewards have not gone unchallenged.[3]

• CONFLICT THEORY OF STRATIFICATION. Those convinced that stratification structures are the product of power-based conflict approach from an entirely different angle the question of whether social differentiation must become social stratification. Scarce and highly desirable rewards are said to be distributed according to the outcome of conflicts. In this conception, those who can exercise the most power in the struggle obtain more of the scarce desirables and, at the same time, prevent those who have less power, prestige, and economic benefits from securing greater amounts of them. Thus, persons and families have more or fewer rewards as a direct result of the amount of power they are able to exercise in conflict with others. According to the conflict perspective, social differentiation becomes social stratification because those with the most power, and consequently the most desirables, want it that way. It follows, the conflict adherents believe, that social stratification need not exist. If the power is taken from the elite and equally distributed among all members of the social structure, social differentiation need not become social stratification.

Further discussion of the functional and conflict theories of stratification is reserved for the following chapter. Whatever the underlying reason, the ranking of social positions tends to be associated with social differentiation. It may not inevitably be so, but as far as we know it has been the common human experience.

Social class

The existence of a hierarchy of social positions means that some positions have a higher rank than others. Except in a very small social structure, however, it would be impossible to study a social stratification structure if an attempt were made to consider each social position in the hierarchy. For one thing, it is difficult to conclude that some social positions are higher in rank than others. Many social positions may be at roughly the same level in the hierarchy. Moreover, there is the question of how much higher certain positions are than others. Physicians have higher rank than professors, but is the difference large enough to warrant a separate classification for each of them within the context of the total stratification structure? Sociologists generally answer this question by classifying together social positions that, within some range, share a similar location in the hierarchy of social positions. Surgeons and professors, for example, although they are not at the same rank in the hierarchy of social positions, would be categorized together. Social positions having a sufficiently similar rank are termed a *social class.** This strategy of grouping social positions explains why the

*Social status and social stratum are sometimes used synonymously with social class.

sociological literature is filled with such designations as upper-upper class, lower-middle class, lower-lower class, and working class.

Social classes can be identified because, once created, they tend to take on relative permanence. A social stratification structure and its rank order divisions called social classes display considerable stability and persistence for at least two reasons. In the first place, social positions are ranked according to culturally derived criteria. Since cultures do not ordinarily change dramatically and rapidly, the criteria for ranking tend to remain intact, and thus there is continuity in the ranking of social positions. A second factor promoting the maintenance of a social stratification structure is the fact that social class levels tend to be either directly inherited or the result of resources (power, wealth, or the lack of same) of one's family. Relative permanence of a social stratification structure stems in large part from the passing of social class level from one generation to the next.

• ELITES, IDEOLOGY, AND THE PERMANENCE OF STRATIFICATION STRUCTURE. Certainly those at the top of a stratification structure, the *elites*, and sometimes those at the bottom, have their own *ideology*, their own set of ideas that serves to justify their values. In the hands of the powerful, ideology is a justification for keeping things the way they are. If the powerless develop an ideology, it is directed toward altering the status quo. Elites and non-elites will use ideology in this way, according to Karl Marx, because each formulates a set of ideas justifying their values in order to serve or protect their economic interests. While not all sociologists would agree with the argument that ideologies are based squarely on economic interests, most would agree that many ideologies involve economic interests to varying degrees.

Whatever the basis of the ideology, an important reason for the relative permanence of stratification structures, for the passing of social class from one generation to the next, appears to be the presence of an ideology among those at the higher levels that attempts to justify why they and their kind should be there. That is, elites, whether they are conscious of it or not, have a vested interest in forging and keeping alive an ideology justifying their social class level. In America, for example, a part of the stratification-related ideology traditionally has been that those at the top are there because of their efforts and talent. One important effect has been to cause nonelites either to accept their lower social class level or to try to be upwardly mobile. Since the ideology places the blame for lower social class on individuals, it makes no sense to challenge the nature of the stratification structure. That the stratification-related ideology has been changing over the years in America in no way undermines the contribution of ideology to the maintenance of social stratification structures.

Families and persons as basic units of stratification structure

In some instances the family is taken as the smallest unit of analysis in the study of social stratification structure. This is possible because all resident members of a family belong to the same social class. Social class level is assigned to the entire family on the basis of the rank of the head of the household.* The degree of prestige, power, and wealth attached to the head of the household is unavoidably shared by family members so long as they reside with the family. Members of the same family also share in similar ways of life as a result of the rewards connected with their social class level.

• SOCIAL MOBILITY. It is true that one's initial social class is determined by his family of birth. Nevertheless, it should be quickly added that the inheritance of social class across generations is a relative matter. *Social mobility*—movement of individuals or families within a stratification structure—is something that we know occurs. Movement up and down the social stratification structure varies according to the strength of the boundaries separating social classes. Social class boundary strength ranges from the impassable—as in the traditional Indian caste structure—to the relatively permeable boundaries in American society. In achievement- and mobility-oriented societies, persons can establish themselves at levels on the stratification structure that are higher or lower than that of their parents. *Intergenerational* mobility is measured by comparing a father's occupational level with that of a son. Comparing the same person's occupational level at different intervals in his career is a measure of *intragenerational* mobility. When the research focus is on either intergenerational or intragenerational occupational mobility, persons rather than families are the smallest unit of sociological analysis.

Location on a social stratification structure can be heavily influenced by four very general social positions—age, sex, ethnicity, and race. These may best be viewed as master social positions.

---

*The head of the household in most societies is a male. Gerhard Lenski contends, however, that in advanced industrial societies it is no longer valid to assign wives a social class level on the basis of their husband's rank. With large numbers of women in such societies engaged in gainful employment, their traditional dependence on the male is disintegrating. See Gerhard Lenski, *Power and Privilege: A Theory of Stratification* (New York: McGraw-Hill, 1966), pp. 402–403.

MASTER SOCIAL POSITIONS
AND STRATIFICATION STRUCTURE

Like more delimited social positions, age, sex, ethnicity, and race are locations in a system of social relationships that have expected patterns of
behavior attached to them. Yet expectations associated with these broad
social positions are not explicitly defined and are carried out in very subtle
ways. In fact, certain of these expectations within a culture may be denied.
In America, for example, women and Blacks are, like all people, said to be
created equal. Yet when men feel superior to women and Whites believe
they have a mental edge on Blacks, these feelings are covertly translated
into behavioral expectations, which at the same time may be denied by
their possessors.

The importance of age, sex, ethnicity, and race as social positions is
not diminished by their covert and subtle nature. Actually, they are best
thought of as *master* positions—ascribed positions that significantly affect
the likelihood of achieving other social positions within a stratification
structure.[4] Age categories, the sexes, and various racial and ethnic minorities do not normally constitute social classes because all social classes contain males, females, the young, the old, and persons of various racial and
ethnic backgrounds. But they are especially influential in social class placement because they affect other social positions that a person may occupy.
When will the United States have a female president? How many women
doctors, lawyers, and executives are there in America? Would you let a 19-
or 90-year-old handle your case in court or remove your appendix? What
about the absurdity of a black Ku Klux Klan Grand Dragon, Cyclop, or
Kleagle? Or, less frivolously, why have so many Blacks in America turned
to sports and show business to make it?

Age as a changing master position

"You're not old enough to stay out all night." "Why, he's old enough to
be her father." "Act your age!" What is considered appropriate behavior is
very much tied to age in all social structures.

The universal practice of relating age to the performance of role prescriptions attached to social positions is deeply embedded in culture and
may have little connection to mental and physical realities. During the
Middle Ages the son of a nobleman was considered ready for the rigors of

squirehood at the age of 14. Fourteen-year-old boys in America are judged to be ready for very little aside from a growing interest in girls, cars, sports, and smoking "weeds" of all varieties.

Nonetheless, although ideas on age vary from culture to culture, the assignment of social positions is very much geared to the number of years persons have been around. Why not trust your legal or medical fate to a 19- or 90-year-old? Why is it assumed that a better job will be done by those in the middle years? In part, the exclusion of the very young and the very old from certain social positions is based on biological reality. It takes a certain number of years to acquire sufficient knowledge and experience to occupy some social positions, and "childhood," with all its mental and physical incapacities, can occur at both ends of the age distribution.

However, it has also been argued that the more things stay the same in a society, the more valuable the cumulative knowledge and experience of its older members. Yet, we are losing the long-standing conviction that competence and wisdom must be a by-product of age mixed with training and experience. Within the context of a "future shock" society, it makes more sense to place trust in younger persons because they are often more flexible and adaptable than the old. A more important force increasing the number of the young in higher level positions is the relationship between education and employment. Because of the recent explosion in opportunity for college education in highly industrialized societies, the younger generation is more educated than the older. While this difference lasts (it cannot last forever because today's well-educated younger generation will become tomorrow's well-educated older generation), the young have a distinct advantage because hiring is heavily based on educational background.

Before we agree to consign everyone over 30 to nursing homes or quiet deaths, some realities must be faced. While members of the younger generation are increasingly considered acceptable for important governmental, commercial, and professional positions, they are not likely ever to outnumber representatives of the older generation in these areas. This is partly because tomorrow's younger generation will not have the educational edge enjoyed by today's. The older generation will prevail for two additional reasons. First, members of the younger generation are barred from adulthood for a longer period of time precisely because of the expanded opportunity for higher education. Second, industrialized societies, even highly advanced ones, are dominated by bureaucratic structures that perpetuate leadership in the hands of the older generation via the practice of advancement according to years of service.

An analysis of age and stratification structure could be easily extended. However, the examples just given amply illustrate that age is a master social position, an ascribed position affecting the probability of occupying other social positions.

Sex as a changing master position

In all societies the differences between men and women have been translated into social differentiation. Sex is used everywhere as a basis for the assignment of social positions. Social differentiation by sex normally has implications for stratification structure. Although some societies have displayed a reasonable equality between the sexes, the most common historical experience is the dominance of males over females.

Why is social differentiation and social stratification along sex lines a constant feature of social life? There are two conflicting explanations. Some offer a cultural argument. These people, cheered on by women's liberationists, attribute all but the most obviously physical differences between the sexes to learning. If Russian women, the argument goes, can load boxcars and become doctors, why are these considered odd occupations for women in other cultures? In this view, the most important difference between men and women is their cultural heritage. Opposing these environmentalists are those who contend that the basic sexual division of labor (women working at home, men employed outside the home) finds its origin in unavoidable biological facts. So far, this debate has created more heat than light.

While it is not possible at this time to settle the cultural-biological disagreement, it is safe to say that the real answer lies between the two extremes. Whichever set of factors turns out to be the most influential, it is clear that culture reinforces the universal differentiation and stratification by sex. In America any female interest in traditionally male social positions must fight incredible odds if it is to survive the cultural assault launched by parents, peers, and lovers during childhood, adolescence, and adulthood. Starting in infancy with pretend tea parties and mother's purses, girls are bombarded with a sufficient cultural barrage to make their preference for traditional female activities seem "natural," whether it is partially rooted in nature or not.

It is difficult for females to translate their learned interests in things like dolls, fashion, and homemaking into the capacities required to succeed in business, government, or the professions. It is infinitely easier for males to make the transition into the world of work because so many of their play activities—cowboys, spacemen, and sports—prepare them for a "man's world." Consequently, many women never question their traditional social positions, some consciously choose marriage instead of employment, and others find the barriers to occupational achievement in traditionally male positions too high and the social-psychological costs too great to merit a prolonged struggle.

Yet, an increasing proportion of women in advanced industrialized countries are working outside the home. For this reason, the discrimination against women in the labor market assumes more importance. It is true that women have made significant legal gains in this century. In the United States women can vote, hold political office, obtain an education, and cannot be legally barred from any job for reason of sex. These same trends exist in other industrializing societies.

If female "slavery" is a thing of the past in highly industrialized economies, its prior existence still affects the occupational life of the contemporary woman. Whether you look at the occupational, economic, or political spheres of modern life, a very small percentage of women reach the upper levels. There are several reasons for this inequality between the sexes. In the first place, as just stated, women may choose marriage and family because their cultural background tells them it is the right course to take, or they may go this route because of the difficulties they must face when competing with men. Second, despite the strong current of liberation for women, it is still they who must bear the children. Moreover, they are still expected to handle their primary responsibility—the home—before pursuing a career. Attempting to balance both puts women at a disadvantage.

Third, because women may stop working either for marriage or other family responsibilities, employers are discouraged from placing them in responsible positions and from investing money and training time in them. Finally, it is primarily men who hire, fire, and reward women. Doubtlessly, culturally derived biases often cause men to evaluate and reward women on grounds unrelated to qualifications and performance. However, it must be kept in mind that these are *current* rules of the game; the future may show that "anatomy is not destiny."

As Table 6.1 unmistakably shows, American women earn less than

TABLE 6.1 Comparison of average earnings for men and women in the same occupational categories

Occupational Categories	Men	Total for Women	WOMEN WITH WORK EXPERIENCE Percentage of Adult Life Worked for Women			
			100%	75%–99%	50%–74%	Less than 50%
Total	$7,529	$4,362	$5,618	$4,727	$4,155	$3,655
Professional, technical, and kindred	$9,868	$6,236	$6,705	$6,013	$6,155	$5,540
Clerical workers	$7,006	$4,743	$5,570	$4,846	$4,531	$4,172
Operatives	$6,452	$3,988	$3,666	$4,556	$4,082	$3,744
Service workers	$5,778	$2,749	$3,272	$3,034	$2,614	$2,688

SOURCE: Adapted by permission from Larry E. Suter and Herman P. Miller, "Income Differences Between Men and Career Women," **American Journal of Sociology,** 78 (January 1973), 966. Copyright © 1973 by the University of Chicago.

males even when both are in identical occupational categories. This is so despite recent federal legislation requiring equal pay for equal work regardless of sex. It should be noted that the income gap between men and women definitely narrows as women spend a larger percentage of their adult lives in the labor force. Even conceding the long-run favorable impact of the Equal Pay Act of 1963 on earnings of females relative to males, a significant problem remains—this legislation fails to cover higher status occupations such as managers and professionals because they are exempted from the wage and hour law. Not only, then, must women hurdle the obstacles to entrance into higher status occupations, but even when they arrive, they are without legislation calling for equal pay for equal work. And as shown in Table 6.1, women in higher status occupations are just as subject to discriminatory pay practices as their sisters at lower rungs of the occupational ladder.

Functionalists contend, you will recall, that higher rewards go to the occupants of the most important social positions and that the best-qualified persons—by training, talent, or both—are recruited to fill the most important positions. The fact that women receive lower economic rewards than do men at the same occupational level places a strain on the functional theory of stratification structure. Strain of a similar nature comes from evidence on the relationship of race and ethnicity to stratification structure.

Race and ethnicity as changing master positions

Age and sex affect the chances for holding certain social positions. However, the impact of age is more critical among the young and the old; in the wide expanse of the middle years, age is less important. If age is a temporary matter, the same may be said for sex in at least one significant sense. That is, women have the widely accepted option of deriving their place on a stratification structure from their husbands. This remains true in spite of the recent push for female economic and social independence and the increasing proportion of working women. In contrast to age and sex, the influence of race and ethnicity as master social positions appears to be more widespread and permanent.

Although a race may be an ethnic subculture and vice versa, this is not uniformly the case. Therefore, these two concepts should be distinguished. An *ethnic subculture* is a minority whose subculture often includes a distinct language and religion. An ethnic subculture differs from other subcultures in that its members generally, although not always, trace their recent origins to other societies and have not yet become diffused throughout their new society to any great extent. Prominent ethnic subcultures in America have been formed by the Chinese, Jews, Puerto Ricans, Italians, as well as by others. The American Indian subculture is testimony to the existence of ethnic subcultures with native origins. And, of course, all "Americans" must find their ancestors' origins on other soils.

While ethnic subcultures are identified by way of unique cultural characteristics, *races* are categories of persons who share certain physical features. Distinguishing physical features include skin and eye color, body size, and contours of the nose, head, ears, eyes, and lips. The sharing of physical characteristics is a matter of degree. Races do not always display physical features that are unique to them alone; more than one race may share an anatomical similarity. The traditional classification of the major races—caucasoid, mongoloid, australoid, and negroid—are based on the fact that a greater number of each of these peoples share certain physical characteristics than do other peoples. It should be noted that these classifications are social definitions stemming from the social needs and culture of the peoples who use them, and they have little scholarly dependability.

Social classes are not formed on the basis of age and sex. Similarly, races and ethnic subcultures normally cannot be neatly categorized as social classes, because members of races and ethnic subcultures may be distributed from top to bottom on the economic, prestige, and power hierarchies within a society. Yet, at a particular point in time members of a racial category or ethnic subculture may find themselves sharing a common location on a stratification structure. Some sociologists, for example, offer the view that Blacks in America were at one time a *caste*—they inherited a location on the stratification structure that was, for practical purposes, unchangeable. This location determined such matters as which jobs were open to them, where they could live, whom they could associate with, and the amount of education they could obtain.

If race and ethnicity are generally not sufficient for the creation of social classes, their influence is heavy in the sense of creating master social positions that affect initial placement and subsequent movement of their members on a stratification structure. Educational, economic, and occupational inequality in America reflects this phenomenon. For simplicity's sake, the positions of Blacks compared to those of Whites will be emphasized.

Blacks were in the spotlight in the 1960s partly because they represent a sizable proportion of the United States population (now roughly 11 percent). Another reason for the attention given Blacks is their standing relative to other American minorities. For example, while Spanish Americans* lag considerably behind "Anglos" occupationally, educationally, and eco-

*Persons in the United States who are of Latin American—Mexican, Puerto Rican, or Cuban—or Spanish origin.

nomically, with the exception of Puerto Ricans they are better off than Blacks in the same geographic area.[5]

The difference between Blacks and other ethnic and racial minorities in America is even more pronounced when the referent is those non-Blacks who came to this country in the late nineteenth and early twentieth centuries. These immigrants, who started at the bottom, gradually became part of the American culture, and they and their descendents moved up the stratification structure. This was particularly true for those immigrants who shared a religious or linguistic bond with American culture.

Evidence of the presence, proportion, and recalcitrance of the Black stratification problem in America is quite clear. Since sudden equality between Blacks and Whites is no more likely than the discovery of Camelot, we can only look at the current trends in education, income, and occupational status. Some indication of a closing of the gap would be the only realistic expectation. According to Blau and Duncan's study based on 1962 national data, gains in the advancement of Blacks compared to Whites have occurred only with respect to the acquisition of minimum education and to decreased discrimination on entrance into the labor market.[6] But, when it comes to higher education—the ticket to movement up the stratification structure—the distance between Blacks and Whites has continued to widen. As Blau and Duncan state, it is hardly startling to find Blacks at an occupational disadvantage to Whites.

An interesting dimension is added, however, in their finding that the discrepancy between black-white occupational status and income level widens as education increases. This means that more-educated Blacks are further behind comparably educated Whites than are less-educated Blacks. Table 6.2 contains the average occupational prestige scores of Whites and Blacks in 1962 as well as the difference between them according to educational level. The trends are consistent—look at columns 1 and 2 of Table 6.2 and you will see that the average occupational prestige scores rise for both Blacks and Whites at each higher educational level. Column 3, however, reveals that the difference between the races increases to the advantage of Whites at each successively higher level of schooling. It is important to note that the rate of increase in differences in average occupational prestige scores appears to level off among Blacks and Whites with at least some college. Yet, the average occupational prestige scores of high-school-educated Whites are only three points below that of non-Whites with one or more years of college (38 versus 41).

TABLE 6.2 Education, race, and occupational status

AVERAGE OCCUPATIONAL PRESTIGE SCORES*
(1962)

Education	White (1)	Nonwhite (2)	Difference Between Average White and Nonwhite Occupational Prestige Scores (3)
0 to 8 years	24	17	7
High School 1 to 3 years	30	19	11
High School 4 years	38	23	15
College, 1 or more years	57	41	16

*Occupations are ranked on a scale of 0 to 96. Occupational prestige increases as score number increases.
SOURCE: Adapted by permission from Peter M. Blau and Otis Dudley Duncan, **The American Occupational Structure** (New York: Wiley, 1967), p. 208.

In short, Blacks need a college education in order to reduce the rate of increase in occupational inequality, and college-educated Blacks have only a slight occupational edge over white high school graduates. In fact, Whites with eight years of education or less are occupationally superior to non-Whites who have either had some high school or who hold a high school diploma.

There is reason to believe that the picture painted by these 1962 statistics is overly pessimistic. After all, the federal legislation forbidding employment discrimination for reason of race, color, sex, age, religion, or national origin was not passed until 1964, two years after the survey used by Blau and Duncan. More recent information was presented in the 1970 *Manpower Report of the President*, information that evokes only muted optimism.[7] While the statistics indicated that Blacks made some educational, occupational, and economic advances in the 1960s, the spread between Blacks and Whites continues to be substantial. Actually, the gap in average income between the two races has lengthened for those at the top and bottom of the national income scale from 1959 to 1968. Whereas the dollar difference in average income between the two races in the lowest fifth of the national income hierarchy was $1350 in 1959, the difference had increased to $1500 by 1968. Looking at the highest fifth in family income, the black and white average dollar difference was $6300 in 1968, a considerable increase over the $4500 disparity in 1959.

However, Ben Wattenberg and Richard Scammon, using the latest U.S. Census data, present a picture of far greater economic, educational, and occupational improvement for Blacks during the 1960s.[8] While recognizing the huge social and economic gap that still remains between Blacks and Whites in America, Wattenberg and Scammon document a significant narrowing of the disparity between the two races. Their most startling assertion is that Blacks have made such tremendous progress over the last 12 years that a majority of them—slender though the majority may be—can now be classified as middle class. Using the annual family income figure of $8,000 outside the South and $6,000 in the South as the income cutting point for the lower-middle class, Wattenberg and Scammon report that slightly more than half (approximately 52 percent) of black families in the United States are presently economically in the middle class. Also the annual family income for white families in America rose 69 percent between 1960 and 1970, while the increase for black families was nearly 100 percent. Moreover, they state, changes in the ratio of black annual family income to white annual family income have been dramatic over the last decade. In 1961, annual black family income was 53 percent of the white family income. From 1961 to 1971, the percentage reached 63 percent, a 10 percent increase. Given that black families are still at a serious disadvantage—they have an annual income 37 percent below white families—Wattenberg and Scammon point out that the ratio of black to white income remained the same during the 1950s. The gap between black and white annual family income is even less when region, age, and family type are taken into account. The disparity is lower outside the South, among the young, and among those families with husbands present; thus, among black husband-wife families, in the North and West, with the head of the family under 35 years old, the average annual family income was 96 percent of similar white families (the figure was 78 percent in 1959).

Wattenberg and Scammon also cite progress for Blacks in employment and education during the 1960s. Table 6.3 contains the statistics on these areas used by these two researchers to support their assertion that Blacks are making good strides toward becoming middle-class Americans. Briefly, these figures indicate that the difference between black and white unemployment rates is decreasing, that the percentage of Blacks in white-collar, craft, and operative occupations is on the rise, and that Blacks are becoming better educated.

Attempting to place the social and economic situation in perspective, Wattenberg and Scammon are saying that Blacks have made tremendous social and economic progress since 1959. They are *not* taking the position that equality between Blacks and Whites exists in America or that the problems of poor Blacks have been solved so that all efforts in their behalf can now be stopped. They note, in fact, that during this period when the percentage of black families in poverty has decreased, the percentage of those receiving welfare has increased, and the proportion of female-headed black families has risen. There are some other facts that should not go un-

TABLE 6.3 Indicators of progress among American Blacks

EMPLOYMENT

Unemployment Rate and Black-to-White Ratio for Married Men,
20 Years and Over, With Spouse Present, 1962 to 1972

	Negro & Other Races	White	Ratio
1962	7.9%	3.1%	2.5 to 1
1963	6.8	3.0	2.3 to 1
1971	4.9	3.0	1.6 to 1
1972	4.4	2.6	1.7 to 1

Numbers of White-Collar Workers, Craftsmen, and Operatives,
in Millions

	Negro	White
1960	2.9%	46.1%
1970	5.1	57.0
Percentage increase	76.0	24.0

EDUCATION

Median School Years Completed, Negroes, Aged 25–29

1940	7.0 years
1950	8.6 years
1960	10.8 years
1970	12.2 years

Percent of Persons, Aged 18–24, Enrolled in College 1965–1971

	1965	1971
Negro	10%	18%
White	26	27
"Gap"	16	9

SOURCE: Ben J. Wattenberg and Richard Scammon, "Black Progress and Liberal Rhetoric," **Commentary**, 55 (April 1973), 37–38. Copyright 1973 by B. Wattenberg and R. Scammon, reprinted by permission of Harold Matson Co., Inc.

noticed. For one thing, those black families that are the most similar to white families economically—those headed by a black male under 35 years of age, living outside the South—constitute less than 20 percent of all black husband-wife families in the United States and represent only 10 percent of all black families. Also, the high-school dropout rate among black males is 50 percent higher than among white males, the rate of college graduation is four times higher among white males under 35 than among their black counterparts, and unemployment among black teenagers is over 35 percent.

Wattenberg and Scammon have been accused of painting an excessively rosy picture of the socioeconomic situation of black Americans, of providing ammunition for those who would stop all efforts to achieve equality between Whites, Blacks, and other minorities. But, rather than advocating complacency in the face of the social and economic progress made by Blacks in the 1960s, Wattenberg and Scammon point to the long distance to travel before parity between black and white Americans is reached. According to their reasoning, the significant progress of the 1960s should stimulate rather than discourage further efforts. Why? Because this progress demonstrates that efforts can produce the desired results. Those who believe the socioeconomic condition of American Blacks either to be no different from what it was a decade ago or to have worsened are simply not facing the facts, say Wattenberg and Scammon.

While inequality between Blacks and Whites presently seems to be persistent, it is too early to offer a definite long-term judgment. According to the latest data, there is some evidence that Blacks will eventually move up the stratification structure and, like ethnic minorities before them, they will enter the appropriate mobility channels. If so, then those who consider the situation of Blacks to be the same as that faced and conquered by other American minorities will be right. And those who fear the lasting accuracy of the couplet "If you're White, you're right; if you're Black, stay back" will be wrong. It remains to be seen if color is going to stand as an enduring obstacle to social mobility in a way that ethnic differences have not. There seems to be reason for optimism, assuming that the trends reported by Wattenberg and Scammon continue.

With these ascriptive master social positions as background, we can now turn to a concise look at the five R's of social stratification structure.

THE FIVE R's OF SOCIAL STRATIFICATION STRUCTURE

Each of the five R's was mentioned in connection with *Jonathan Livingston Seagull*. Some further indication of the nature of three of them—ranking, retention, and rewards—has been implicit in the preceding discussion. At this point, a concise view of each should be helpful.

Ranking

The first R of social stratification structure—*ranking*—is the process of vertically arranging social positions on the basis of criteria rooted in cultural values. Ranking pertains to the stratification structure per se.

In any but the simplest societies, there is an incredibly large number of social positions to be filled. An attempt to take into account this unwieldy array of social positions in the determination of social class placement would be as foolish as it is impossible. Fortunately—particularly from the viewpoint of sociological research—some social positions are clearly more crucial than others for social class placement.

In industrial societies, occupation generally is the single social position utilized in the ranking process. The higher the prestige of the occupation, the higher it is ranked on the social stratification structure. Since income and education tend to increase with occupational prestige in industrial societies, they are used in conjunction with occupation to produce a measure of *socioeconomic* status—so labeled because of its social components (occupational prestige and education) and its economic dimension (income).

Retention

The *retention* dimension of social stratification structure signifies that the hierarchy of positions and associated social relationships tend to endure. Although upward and downward social mobility may occur within a given stratification structure, the amount of social mobility that does occur—even within relatively open stratification structures—does not create enough turnover to change social class membership substantially from one generation to another. That is, members of social classes and their descendents tend to remain in the same social class over long periods of time.

Rewards

The rewards dimension centers on the "good things" associated with social class placement. *Rewards* are the differential benefits derived from social class placement. Socially desirable rewards such as respect, wealth, and influence increase as social class level increases. Rewards may serve as a motivating device for encouraging persons to train for occupational positions and to perform the associated duties on at least an adequate level.

Resources

Whereas rewards relate to the compensation forthcoming from placement at a particular social class level, the study of resources focuses on how class level is determined. *Resources* are the means by which persons and groups attain social class placement on a stratification structure. They are the assets that are negotiable in the process of achieving, maintaining, or passing on to others a social class level. Prominent resources in some societies may be family of birth or physical prowess. In other societies the best assets for social class placement may be money, power, or education.

Repercussions

Did you ever wonder why it's always the blue-collared "Joe" who is popularly depicted as the cigar-smoking, beer-drinking television addict or baseball nut? Why, at the other extreme, is the advertising model for Seagram's Extra Dry Gin a suave, handsome young man with a compliant-looking female companion draped around his well-dressed shoulders? It is certainly true that many workingmen like gin, scotch, or bourbon as much as your average upper-class gentleman. And beer often flows over well-cultivated palates. Nevertheless, the stereotypes should not be completely dismissed, for they do reflect an important aspect of social stratification structure— social class level carries with it a host of distinctive behavioral and cultural patterns ranging from such trivial matters as dress, speech, manners, and alcohol preferences to such vital things as death, fertility, and divorce rates. Distinctive behavioral and cultural patterns that can be associated with certain social classes are those *repercussions* of social stratification structure of the most interest to sociologists. In fact, it is common in sociology for social classes to be referred to as subcultures.

OVERVIEW AND PREVIEW

Two processes—social differentiation and social ranking—lead to the creation of stratification structures. Social differentiation is the process of assigning specialized duties to specific social positions; differentiation is the division of labor. When the positions within a social structure have been evaluated and located in a hierarchy from high to low, social ranking has occurred. Because networks of social relationships are associated with the hierarchy of positions, we may speak of it as a social stratification structure.

If social differentiation occurred without the accompanying evaluative ranking of positions, then classless societies would emerge. Why are non-stratified social structures so difficult to find? Functionalists see social inequality as a necessity for the survival of social structures; hence social classes emerge. Proponents of conflict theory believe that stratification structures are the product of power-based conflict.

Social classes are comprised of a number of social positions with a similar location on a stratification structure. Because certain positions can be categorized with others, sociologists depict stratification structures as class structures rather than as elaborate hierarchies of specific social positions. Although the members of social classes and their descendents tend to remain in the same social classes over long periods of time, social mobility or movement up and down the stratification structure does occur.

In investigating stratification structures, it is generally the family or persons who are taken as basic units of analysis. That is, in order to determine the nature and composition of a stratification structure, either persons are ranked or a family representative—usually the male head—is used to assign a rank to all household members.

Age, sex, race, and ethnicity are social positions in a broad sense. Within stratification structures they are best thought of as master positions, as ascribed positions that either open or close avenues to other social positions. Research reveals that these ascribed social positions are associated with inequality.

In the last major section of this chapter, the five R's of stratification were concisely introduced. Since ranking, rewards, resources, retention, and repercussions constitute the heart of the sociological study of stratification structure, they are given more detailed attention in Chapter 7.

REFERENCES

1. For the case of Russia, see Alex Inkeles, "Social Stratification and Mobility in the Soviet Union," in Reinhard Bendix and Seymour Martin Lipset, eds., *Class, Status, and Power: Social Stratification in Comparative Perspective*, 2nd ed. (New York: Free Press, 1966), pp. 516–526. Substantiation for statements about Israeli kibbutzim may be found in Eva Rosenfeld, "Social Stratification in a 'Classless' Society," *American Sociological Review*, 16 (December 1951), 766–774.
2. Kingsley Davis and Wilbert E. Moore, "Some Principles of Stratification," *American Sociological Review*, 10 (April 1945), 242–249.
3. Melvin Tumin, "Some Principles of Stratification: A Critical Analysis," *American Sociological Review*, 18 (August 1953), 387–394.
4. The idea of master position comes from Everett C. Hughes, "Dilemmas and Contradictions of Status," *American Journal of Sociology*, 50 (March 1945), 353–359.
5. *Manpower Report of the President* (Washington, D.C.: U.S. Government Printing Office, 1970), pp. 100–103.
6. Peter M. Blau and Otis Dudley Duncan, *The American Occupational Structure* (New York: Wiley, 1967), pp. 208–227, 238–241.
7. *Manpower Report of the President*, op. cit., pp. 90–95.
8. Ben J. Wattenberg and Richard M. Scammon, "Black Progress and Liberal Rhetoric," *Commentary*, 55 (April 1973), 35–44.

ADDITIONAL SOURCES AND READINGS

Barber, Bernard. *Social Stratification* (New York: Harcourt Brace Jovanovich, 1957).

Bendix, Reinhard, and Seymour Martin Lipset, eds. *Class, Status, and Power: Social Stratification in Comparative Perspective*, 2nd ed. (New York: Free Press, 1966).

Chambliss, William J., ed. *Sociological Readings in the Conflict Perspective* (Reading, Mass.: Addison-Wesley, 1972).

Dahrendorf, Ralf. *Class and Class Conflict in Industrial Society* (Stanford, Calif.: Stanford University Press, 1959).

Heller, Celia S., ed. *Structured Social Inequality: A Reader in Comparative Social Stratification* (New York: Macmillan, 1969).

Keller, Suzanne. *Beyond the Ruling Class: Strategic Elites in Modern Society* (New York: Random House, 1963).

Mayer, Kurt. *Class and Society* (New York: Random House, 1955).

Mills, C. Wright. *The Power Elite* (New York: Oxford University Press, 1959).

Tumin, Melvin M. *Social Stratification* (Englewood Cliffs, N.J.: Prentice-Hall, 1967).

Wrong, Dennis H. "The Functional Theory of Stratification: Some Neglected Considerations," *American Sociological Review*, 24 (December 1959), 772–782.

7

The Five R's of Stratification Structure

MULTIDIMENSIONALITY OF SOCIAL STRATIFICATION STRUCTURE • Economic dimension • Prestige dimension • Power dimension • Interrelatedness of the economic, prestige, and power dimensions
RANKING • Standards for social class placement • Diversity of social stratification structures • Approaches to the study of social stratification structure • Occupational prestige as an indicator
REWARDS AND RESOURCES Types of rewards • The distribution of rewards • Rewards as resources
RETENTION • Varieties of social mobility • Open and closed stratification structures • Social mobility • Some influences on upward social mobility
REPERCUSSIONS • Life chances • Life style • Personality correlates of stratification structure • Psychological costs of social mobility • Status inconsistency

"Money, position, honor, respect—you can keep it!"

Reprinted from **Bums vs. Billionaires** by Al Ross. Copyright © 1972 by Al Ross. Used with permission of Dell Publishing Co., Inc.

Al Ross' happy "King of the Road" in the cartoon opening this chapter has put his finger on the factors central to the five R's of stratification structure. Add "power" to money, position, honor, and respect and you have isolated the economic, prestige, and power dimensions so important to the socio-logical study of ranking, rewards, resources, and retention. The amount of power, prestige, and economic assets that persons or families possess also has definite repercussions. Ross' lighthearted vagabond may not want money and prestige but he has to pay a price—he is not the distinguished-looking success story reading a newspaper in the comfort of the Union League Club. On the other hand, he seems to be spared the pressures accompanying high achievement on a stratification structure.

MULTIDIMENSIONALITY OF SOCIAL STRATIFICATION STRUCTURE

Although intellectual concern over stratification structure did not get its start with Karl Marx, his analysis of social classes in industrial society remains one of the most influential. The most important aspect of Marx's theory in the present context is the criterion on which he was convinced social class was determined. For Marx, only one factor separated social classes—ownership of the means of production. Although recognizing the existence of several social classes in nineteenth-century industrial society—laborers, servants, factory workers, craftsmen, proprietors of small businesses, mon-eyed capitalists—Marx predicted that society would ultimately be reduced to two social classes. Those who owned capital would be the rulers, the *bourgeoisie*; those without ownership of the means of production would be the ruled, the *proletariat*.

According to Marx, then, social classes may be identified if one piece of information is known—does a person or family own capital or not? Writing in the first part of the twentieth century, Max Weber criticized Marx's one-dimensional approach, contending that other criteria were involved in social stratification structures. By introducing three orders of stratification—economic, prestige, and power—in place of the one used by Marx, Weber gave sociologists the lead that stratification structure is a multidimensional matter.[*]

---

[*]Weber's actual terms were "class" (economic), "status" (prestige), and "party" (power). Although Weber's definitions have generally been retained here, his labels have been changed to make them consistent with the other concepts used in this chapter. For Weber's original work, "Class, Status, and Party," see Hans Gerth and C. Wright Mills, eds., *From Max Weber: Essays in Sociology* (New York: Oxford University Press, 1958), pp. 180–195.

Economic dimension

According to Weber, one basis on which social classes are determined is a person's or family's economic situation. This basis for social stratification structure is akin to the Marxian one of ownership of the means of production, although Weber saw a number of social classes rather than merely two. Moreover, Weber elected to underscore "life chances" rather than ownership of the means of production. *Life chances*—the likelihood of securing the "good things of life" such as housing, education, health, food, and various other desirable goods and services—are clearly dependent on the economic condition of a person or family. Obviously, the probability of possessing these desirables is directly related to such economic resources as real estate, wages, inheritance, and profits from various investments.

Prestige dimension

It has already been made clear that in Weber's mind social class placement does not occur solely because of economic resources. A second dimension of social stratification is *prestige*, or favorable evaluation of some persons by other persons.

The basis for prestige is varied, ranging from wealth and power to acts of heroism or the demonstration of personal character. The most stable source of prestige, however, is associated with social position, particularly with occupation.

Prestige is always a cultural and social matter. In the first place, favorable social evaluation is based on the norms and values professed and practiced within a social structure. Honor, admiration, respect, and deference are extended to "family" dons within the Mafia, but despite America's fascination with the underworld, they do not have high prestige outside their tightly controlled social structure.

Second, honor, deference, and the like must be given to one person by another person. To paraphrase comedian Rodney Dangerfield, Robinson Crusoe "never got no respect" until his man Friday came along.

The sociocultural nature of prestige is evident in yet a third way. Those persons or families who are accorded a similar rank in the prestige hierarchy form social classes that share identifiable life styles. As you will discover when another important R of stratification—repercussions—is examined, social classes tend to share everything from food tastes to levels of education.

Finally, prestige is social and cultural because, while the assignment of rank in the prestige hierarchy to a person or family does not come from unanimous agreement among all members of a social structure, there is sufficient consensus among social structure members to make the evaluation endure.

Power dimension

Power is the capability of a person to exert his will on other persons, whether or not they wish to cooperate. This aspect of social stratification structure is much more elusive than are the economic and prestige dimensions. Reasonably satisfactory methods have been devised for measuring rank in the economic and prestige hierarchies. Not so with power. Sociologists have displayed considerable interest in the distribution of power on the community and societal levels. Yet disagreement exists regarding the way in which power is distributed within a stratification structure. Consequently, power is frequently not included by sociologists who devise indexes of social stratification structure, on the assumption that wealth and prestige are normally used to gain power and thus no great damage is done to accuracy by relying exclusively on them.

Interrelatedness of the economic, prestige, and power dimensions

It is generally true in industrial societies that high rank in one of these dimensions is used to gain high rank in the others. Power—particularly political power—is a decided economic advantage to its holders. For example, the wealthy will pay for political favors either directly (as with money) or indirectly (as through inside information on lucrative business deals). And the Kennedys are by no means the only Americans who have used their wealth to achieve high political rank.

Prestige and wealth are also closely intertwined. High prestige is heavily dependent on economic resources. One cannot maintain the life style expected of persons with high prestige without the economic clout to purchase such necessities as the "nice" home in the "proper" neighborhood or to send one's children to the "right" schools. But those with high prestige normally have no cause for concern, for with prestige comes special economic rewards and unique business opportunities for generating wealth. Most of the wealth amassed by Arnold Palmer and Jack Nicklaus does not come directly from prize money in professional golf tournaments. Because of their prestige, people want to buy Arnold Palmer sweaters and Jack Nicklaus golf clubs as much as corporations want their endorsement of products. And as their wealth increases, so does their prestige.

Prestige and power mix quite well. Prestige is attached to social positions requiring important decision making. And prestige may be converted into power. Consider Ronald Reagan, the actor who became California's governor, or Jack Kemp, the professional quarterback who became a congressman in Washington.

Despite the tendency for the economic, prestige, and power dimensions to coalesce, it is useful to think of each as a separate factor. While a person's rank in each dimension will be roughly the same in stable societies, in rapidly changing societies inconsistencies in rank in the three dimensions are likely to occur. In dynamic societies, for example, you will find a greater incidence of the newly rich who are capable of purchasing homes, cars, education, and health care but who suffer from a lack of the appropriate life style. CBS made a fortune by portraying this phenomenon in the popular television series, "The Beverly Hillbillies." And at the same time that changing societies create the Jed Clampetts, the opposite condition is created among the old-rich who attempt to maintain their prestigeful life style in the absence of the economic resources they once enjoyed.

Without a recognition of the multidimensionality of social stratification structure it would be difficult to analyze such discrepancies as occur among the old- and new-rich. Also obscured would be the consequences that may flow from being high in some dimensions and low in others. This phenomenon—called *status inconsistency*—is discussed at the end of this chapter as one of the repercussions of stratification structure.

The economic, prestige, and power dimensions underlie each R of social stratification structure. They are useful for ascertaining the *rank* of persons and families. Wealth, prestige, and power can be used singly or in combination as *resources* for the maintenance of present rank or for attainment of a higher rank. Each is also a desirable, a *reward* attached to social positions. When used for maintaining and passing on a social class level to a future generation, wealth, prestige, and power are forces of *retention*. Finally, the possession of varying amounts of the desirables that these three dimensions represent has *repercussions* for life chances, life style, and personality.

RANKING

Standards for social class placement

Of course, sociologists do not simply manufacture from their fertile imaginations the appropriate indicators of stratification structure location. Rather, through observation they discover the characteristics that seem to confer placement within a stratification structure. These characteristics may not be uniform from one stratification structure to another, but they always reflect a cultural context.

Mark Twain was acutely aware of social stratification structure and the weapon that high social class placement can be in the hands of the pretentious. He also knew that the standards for placement on the stratification structure were not the same in all places. Twain unleashed both of these insights when, in *What Paul Bourget Thinks of Us*, he wrote: "In Boston they ask, How much does he know? In New York, How much is he worth? In Philadelphia, Who are his parents?" Within some stratification structures

Tim Egan, Woodfin Camp & Associates

the most accurate barometer of rank may be an economic one. In others, education or the family tree may tower over all other considerations. Actually, placement on a stratification structure is the result of rankings on a number of criteria that may include religion, ethnicity, neighborhood, family, wealth, formal organization memberships, and occupations.

• DIVERSITY OF SOCIAL STRATIFICATION STRUCTURES. Social stratification structure qualifies as a type of social structure because of the social relationships that result from the formation of social classes through the process of social ranking. In addition to viewing it as a social structure in its own right, sociologists also study stratification structures as one aspect of other social structures. Stratification occurs in all social structures—in societies, communities, formal organizations, and social groups* of all types (for example, work groups, delinquent gangs, and bridge clubs). And a person's rank may vary from one social structure to the next. A man, for example, may have low rank in the factory where he is employed but possess high rank among his on-the-job friends and in his church or lodge. This is because the standards for location in one stratification structure may be irrelevant in another—in industrial societies education is crucial for high rank in formal organizational structures but it is unimportant for assuming the presidency of a local Moose club. It also happens that a person or family may rest at the top of their own community stratification structure but not be recognized in the stratification structure of other communities.

Because of the diversity of stratification structures—both across and within communities—it is essential that the stratification referent be specified before the location of persons or groups can be meaningfully pursued. Such specification can be at the societal, community, organizational, or group level.

However, sociologists have devoted most of their efforts in the study of stratification structure at the community and societal levels. This is easily explained. While stratification occurs in all types of social structures, it is not conventional in sociology to speak of the presence of social classes within formal organizational structures or social groups. Unquestionably, differences in rank exist within these two types of social structures, but sociologists reserve the delineation of social classes for communities and societies. A brief examination of the approaches used in the exploration of stratification structure at the community and societal levels will be helpful in understanding why certain standards are more useful than others for the social class location of individuals.

• APPROACHES TO THE STUDY OF SOCIAL STRATIFICATION STRUCTURE. Three basic approaches have been advanced in the study of stratification structure

---

*A *social group* is the type of social structure created through the patterned interaction of a relatively few persons who share a common identity, goals, rules for thinking, feeling, and behaving, and direct or indirect lines of communication. Chapter 12 is devoted to group structure.

at the community and societal levels—reputational, self-location, and objective. Although each of these approaches may be used in combination, they represent distinct strategies for determining the nature and shape of a given stratification structure.

One way of handling social class placement is to ask members of a stratification structure to rank others in the social class hierarchy—the *reputational* approach. When persons are asked to rank themselves, a *self-location* tact is being taken. In the *objective* approach, members of a stratification structure are not consulted. Instead, researchers establish standards that reflect the beliefs of stratification structure members. More on this shortly.

As indicated, societal and community stratification structures are of the greatest interest to sociologists. Which of these three approaches to the study of stratification—reputational, self-locational, or objective—is the most appropriate for each type of stratification structure? Although the reputational and self-location strategies have been applied at the national level, their use presents some definite problems. In local communities where people and their life styles are known to each other, the reputational and self-location approaches are dependable for determining the number of social classes and for locating persons in these classes. But where "communities" are the size of large metropolitan areas like Los Angeles, Chicago, and New York, the reputational approach is capable of identifying only those at the very top of the stratification structure because only the most visible are sufficiently known to be classified by others. And in these mammoth communities the self-location technique is adequate only within residential segments that are small and cohesive enough for community members to rank themselves in relation to a variety of other members.

In social structures where people do not know each other, then, subjective approaches (self-location and reputational) are inappropriate. Such social structures call for objective criteria. Those most commonly used are income, education, and occupation. Not only are these socioeconomic indicators easier to use and more accurate in such cases, they also are predictive of class differences in birth, death, and divorce rates, in mental health states, and similar data.

A final point should be made on the study of stratification structures in societies and communities. Because particular communities are likely to have their own unique variations of the national stratification structure, distortion usually accompanies attempts to infer or describe the stratification structure of one from the other. A coal-mining town in America, for example, will exhibit a stratification structure with only a few social classes, the most prominent ones being the mineowner and his managers versus the mine workers and their families. The stratification structure in this type of community cannot easily be compared to that of a community containing a variety of white-collar industries. And neither of these types of communities accurately depicts the national stratification structure. It is possible, of course, to categorize communities into general types (for example, one-industry, blue-collar, and white-collar) and to generalize across those within the same category.

As indicated, the determination of social class placement is a multidimensional affair. Measurement of social class is difficult enough in a small community where objective criteria can be supplemented with the perceptions of its residents. You can appreciate, then, the seemingly insurmountable difficulties sociologists face in outlining social stratification structure at the national level. Forfeiting to some extent the conviction that stratification structure involves several dimensions, many sociologists have settled on occupational prestige as the best available indicator of social class.

• OCCUPATIONAL PRESTIGE AS AN INDICATOR. Some rather strong arguments can be offered for the use of occupational prestige in studying social stratification structure.[1] In the first place, the use of occupation as an indicator of social class is consistent with the idea that a hierarchy of social positions is basic to any stratification structure. Occupations are not only the most important positions held by persons in highly industrialized societies, they are the most easily identified. Thus a second advantage of occupational prestige as an indicator of social class is that occupations are relatively easy to ascertain because they are an objective characteristic. Of course, the advantage of objectivity would be worthless if the information gathered on occupations did not reflect some important dimensions of stratification structure. A third and necessary advantage is that occupation serves to reflect several crucial dimensions of ranking—prestige, income, and education; close correspondence between occupation, income, and education has been a consistent research observation. Furthermore, income and education in turn reflect life style and life chances, other central dimensions of social class that are dealt with later in this chapter. Because occupation is linked with a number of social and economic characteristics, it can be billed as a measure of socioeconomic status.

A fourth advantage of using occupation as a measure of social class is its applicability to a variety of settings. Research has shown a general correspondence in the rank-order of occupations among both industrialized and nonindustrialized nations, indicating that occupational prestige comparisons can be made across societies as well as within communities and societies.[2]

Further, the stability of occupational prestige rankings can be tested within a society or community. For example, the occupational prestige rankings in the United States assessed in 1963 corresponded, with some minor variations, to those obtained in 1947 (see Table 7.1).

TABLE 7.1 Occupational prestige in America

Occupation	Rank in 1947	Rank in 1963
U.S. Supreme Court justice	1	1
Physician	2.5	2
Nuclear physicist	18	3.5
Scientist	8	3.5
Government scientist	10.5	5.5
State governor	2.5	5.5
Cabinet member in the federal government	4.5	8
College professor	8	8
U.S. representative in Congress	8	8
Chemist	18	11
Lawyer	18	11
Diplomat in the U.S. foreign service	4.5	11
Dentist	18	14
Architect	18	14
County judge	13	14
Psychologist	22	17.5
Minister	13	17.5
Member of the board of directors of a large corporation	18	17.5
Mayor of a large city	6	17.5
Priest	18	21.5
Head of a department in a state government	13	21.5
Civil engineer	23	21.5
Airline pilot	24.5	21.5
Banker	10.5	24.5
Biologist	29	24.5
Sociologist	26.5	26
Instructor in public schools	34	27.5
Captain in the regular army	31.5	27.5
Accountant for a large business	29	29.5
Public-school teacher	36	29.5
Owner of a factory that employs about 100 people	26.5	31.5
Building contractor	34	31.5
Artist who paints pictures that are exhibited in galleries	24.5	34.5
Musician in a symphony orchestra	29	34.5
Author of novels	31.5	34.5
Economist	34	34.5
Official of an international labor union	40.5	37
Railroad engineer	37.5	39
Electrician	45	39
County agricultural agent	37.5	39
Owner-operator of a printing shop	42.5	41.5
Trained machinist	45	41.5
Farm owner & operator	39	44
Undertaker	47	44
Welfare worker for a city government	45	44
Newspaper columnist	42.5	46
Policeman	55	47

Table 7.1 (Continued)

Occupation	Rank in 1947	Rank in 1963
Reporter on a daily newspaper	48	48
Radio announcer	40.5	49.5
Bookkeeper	51.5	49.5
Tenant farmer	51.5	51.5
Insurance agent	51.5	51.5
Carpenter	58	53
Manager of a small store in a city	49	54.5
Official of a labor union local	62	54.5
Mail carrier	57	57
Railroad conductor	55	57
Traveling salesman for a wholesale concern	51.5	57
Plumber	59.5	59
Automobile repairman	59.5	60
Playground director	55	62.5
Barber	66	62.5
Machine operator in a factory	64.5	62.5
Owner-operator of a lunch stand	62	62.5
Corporal in the regular army	64.5	65.5
Garage mechanic	62	65.5
Truck driver	71	67
Fisherman who owns his own boat	68	68
Clerk in a store	68	70
Milk route man	71	70
Streetcar motor man	68	70
Lumberjack	73	72.5
Restaurant cook	71	72.5
Singer in a nightclub	74.5	74
Filling station attendant	74.5	75
Dockworker	81.5	77.5
Railroad section hand	79.5	77.5
Night watchman	81.5	77.5
Coal miner	77.5	77.5
Restaurant waiter	79.5	80.5
Taxi driver	77.5	80.5
Farmhand	76	83
Janitor	85.5	83
Bartender	85.5	83
Clothes presser in a laundry	83	85
Soda fountain clerk	84	86
Sharecropper	87	87
Garbage collector	88	88
Street sweeper	89	89
Shoe shiner	90	90

SOURCE: Adapted by permission from Robert W. Hodge, Paul M. Siegel, and Peter H. Rossi, "Occupational Prestige in the United States, 1925–1963," **American Journal of Sociology**, 70 (November 1964), 290–292. Copyright © 1964 by the University of Chicago.

The occupational prestige ranks in Table 7.1 are derived from the application of the North-Hatt technique to national samples of the U.S. population in 1947 and 1963. Each occupation was rated according to each respondent's own opinion of its *general standing* in American society. Possible ratings included *excellent, good, average, somewhat below average,* and *poor.* From these individual ratings a single prestige score was assigned to each of the 90 occupations in 1947 and 1963. Note that the rank in 1963 is much the same as it was in 1947.

A close examination will reveal that white-collar occupations are generally accorded higher prestige than are blue-collar ones. Also, higher prestige is associated with those occupations requiring skill and training and those offering the rewards of authority and wealth.

Despite the association between occupational prestige and the economic and power dimensions of social stratification, there is no one-to-one correspondence between occupational prestige ranking and stratification structure. The slippage is sufficient to require that occupational prestige rank be viewed as an *indicator* of social class rather than as a synonym for it.

For one thing, where are the dividing points between, say, upper, middle, and lower social classes? An approximation is not so difficult for the middle and lower classes. The traditional demarcation is made between blue-collar and white-collar occupations. Yet this division is not clear-cut because of the blurring that exists at the dividing line: Are clerical and sales workers any more middle class than craftsmen? No definite answer can be offered, for some highly paid craftsmen may be middle class while some bottom level white-collar employees are lower class. Moreover, what about the upper class? Some difficulty arises in determining from occupational prestige rankings who belongs in the upper class, because many of the occupations of these persons have the same labels as those of middle-class persons. Are local politicians and national political leaders in the same social class?

This brings up a second reason why occupational prestige ranking can be considered as only an approximation of social class: There may be considerable variation in the prestige, power, and economic situations of persons with identical occupational rankings. It is one thing to be a manager, proprietor, or professor and quite another to be the chief executive of IBM, a major stockholder in the Ford Motor Company, or the dean of the Harvard Law School.

Revealing the inadequacies of occupational prestige ranking as an indicator of social class should be taken as a signal for caution in interpretation; it should not be construed as sufficient reason for doubting its utility or rejecting its application. Despite its shortcomings, occupational prestige is the best index of social stratification structure presently available. Fortunately, its credibility is enhanced by its workability—as already stated, occupational prestige is highly correlated with such indicators of social class as prestige, income, education, life style, and life chances.

REWARDS AND RESOURCES

Social stratification structures exist within all communities and societies and their composition can be at least approximated. Having established their presence, some further questions arise. What are the rewards that are differentially distributed according to rank on the stratification structure? Why are some social positions more highly rewarded than others? Are these rewards also resources that are useful either for the maintenance of present social class level or for the attainment of even higher rank for oneself and family?

Types of rewards

Rewards involved in stratification structures are, by definition, in scarce supply. If they were plentiful, if every person or family shared equally in these rewards, then the process of ranking social positions could not occur, since many of the criteria used for locating persons or families on a stratification structure are also rewards. Income and occupational prestige, for example, serve this dual purpose. Although there are many specific rewards, some of which are emphasized in certain stratification structures more than in others, three broad types of rewards may be identified—economic, power, and prestige. Again, we are reminded of the multidimensionality of stratification structure and the interrelationships among its various dimensions. There are cases on the societal stratification structure in which similar amounts of these three types of rewards are not all attached to the same social position. It is possible to be eminently powerful and rich and yet be without societal prestige. Mafiosi like Vito Genovese and Carlo Gambino are prime illustrations. "Professor" is an often-cited example of a nationally prestigeful social position that lacks equivalent amounts of power or wealth.

Of course, statements like these are entirely dependent on the stratification structure in question. On a local level, underworld kingpins may do everything but set up an office in city hall, and their local prestige may be as great as is their power in local politics and business. And professors may wield considerable power within a university or college and may be quite well-off economically compared to the rest of the community. The unit of analysis has to be kept in mind. Whatever the unit of analysis, there is a tendency for these three types of rewards to coalesce for persons and families.

The distribution of rewards

An enduring question explored by sociologists interested in social stratification structure is, Who gets what and why? Answers to this question constitute attempted explanations of the principles of reward distribution in society.

The most widely accepted sociological explanations for the unequal distribution of power, prestige, and economic rewards have come from two sources—functionalists and conflict or power theorists.

As indicated in Chapter 6 the functionalists believe that social inequality exists because of the contribution it makes to the operation and survival of a social structure. The mechanism for distributing rewards in the functionalist explanation lies in the increasing of rewards in line with increases in positional rank. This occurs, they argue, first because social positions with the highest rank are the most crucial for society and require the greatest talent or training. Second, rewards are used to motivate persons to undergo the preparation necessary to qualify for the most important positions and to perform successfully the duties of those positions.

In the conflict perspective, rewards are distributed not to serve society but to serve those with the most power. Scarce rewards are said to be captured by those who, in conflict with others, are able to work their will.

There has been an important attempt to combine the functional and conflict explanations of reward distribution. Gerhard Lenski places the pursuit of self-interest near the center of man's nature.[3] Consistent with this view of human nature, Lenski formulates two "laws of distribution"—one that applies to societies insufficiently developed to create a surplus of goods and services, the other that operates in societies with a surplus. The first law of distribution, drawing from the functional theory of stratification, says that men will share the fruits of their labors with others when it contributes to their own survival. According to the second law of distribution, power determines the distribution of almost all the surplus goods and services produced by a society. This second law of distribution is consistent with conflict theory.

Exceptions to both the functionalist and conflict interpretations are easily observed in social life. It is difficult for conflict theorists to explain why powerful characters like leaders of organized crime find it almost impossible to gain widespread public prestige and why those without power—the Albert Einsteins and Jonas Salks of the world—are accorded extremely high prestige. It is equally hard for functionalists to explain the fact that Blacks and women occupying positions identical (both in terms of functional importance and occupational title) to those held by Whites and males are not as highly rewarded. Also, why are teachers, who are conceded high functional importance, not highly rewarded economically?

Such exceptions suggest that neither of these theories can, by itself, adequately explain social stratification structure; both appear to reflect different realities of stratification structure. It has been demonstrated that power is generally associated with economic rewards and prestige. At the same time, observation has revealed an association between stratification structure rewards and the social definition of the functional importance of social positions. Both functional importance and the exercise of power are undoubtedly at work in most stratification structures.

Whether because of functional importance or the exercise of power, rewards increase with social class level. These rewards, in turn, become resources for the preservation or enhancement of social class level or, as in the more homely adage, "the rich get richer."

Rewards as resources

Rewards attached to stratification structures do not always go to the good and the swift. Certain of the inept and the lame may pick up the marbles if their families hold a sufficient concentration of prestige, power, or economic resources. Although, at least in nonsubsistence societies, power and economic resources are the primary sources of prestige, any one of the three major types of rewards may be used as a resource for gaining greater amounts of the other two. Public affection for actors like Shirley Temple Black, Ronald Reagan, Frank Sinatra, and Sammy Davis, Jr., to name a few, can lead to wealth and political influence. Joe Kennedy's wealth was translated into prestige and power through Jack, Bobby, and Teddy. Although these are selected examples, they reflect a basic reality in stratification structures.

There is not enough evidence to show conclusively the causal connections among the three types of stratification-related rewards; power may lead to prestige and wealth, or prestige may lead to power and wealth. Whichever way the causal relationship may run initially—whether a person or family uses wealth to obtain power or vice versa—eventually there is a tendency for the types of rewards to coalesce at approximately equal levels, with changes in one affecting the other two.

The fact that one or more of the three types of rewards is generally used as a resource in the maintenance or attainment of social class level is reflected in the extent of social mobility—the amount and kinds of movements persons and families make on a stratification structure. Rags to riches within one generation, à la Horatio Alger, has always been more of a comfort to the poor and to those desiring upward mobility than a portrait of reality. Even when upward social mobility does occur, it tends to be only a short step from the socioeconomic status of one's family. In broad terms, parental social class is the best predictor of future social class level of offspring.

This last statement has to be qualified. The more that achievement rather than ascription is honored within a stratification structure, the less do family power, prestige, and economic resources affect the future social class level of children. Still, even in stratification structures based on social class placement through achievement, stratification-related rewards are resources used by offspring either to maintain or to improve on their parents' social class level. Because power, prestige, and economic rewards are resources that are translated into social class level, the location of persons and families on stratification structures is marked by stability and continuity. The perpetuation of stratification structure, its quality of retention, is pursued in greater detail in the next section.

RETENTION

Social mobility—movement of individuals or groups within a stratification structure—evokes the feeling of motion, of flux and change. Yet social mobility is being presented within the context of continuity, perpetuation, retention. This seems contradictory partly because the concept of social mobility is defined in terms of movement and partly because American society places so much emphasis on upward mobility. Without question, changes in social class composition occur in all except the most rigid stratification structures, but the extent of change clearly is not so dramatic as the "American dream" would have it. Even within a relatively open stratification structure like that of the United States, the social class movements that do occur tend to be small ones. Moreover, there is a type of social mobility that is neither upward nor downward.

Varieties of social mobility

Movement within a stratification structure may be horizontal or vertical. A movement from one social position to another that involves no increase or decrease in social class level is called *horizontal* social mobility. A carpenter may become a bulldozer operator, a retired military officer may become a manager in private industry. This kind of social mobility has been neglected in favor of the study of vertical social mobility.

If a move from one social position to another carries with it a change in social class level, then *vertical* social mobility has occurred. Vertical social mobility may be either upward or downward, involving either greater or lesser prestige, power, or economic rewards. Upward or downward social mobility for persons can be measured in two ways. *Intragenerational* social mobility occurs within an individual's lifetime. This variety of social mobility is measured by comparing a person's social class level at one point in time with his social class level at a later time. Social mobility that occurs from one generation to another is *intergenerational*. Measurement of intergenerational social mobility takes the form of comparing a father's (or grandfather's) social class level with that of a son.

Open and closed stratification structures

The retention dimension of stratification has two aspects. In the first place, the hierarchy of social positions (especially occupational positions) tends to remain the same over the years. Second, persons generally inherit through their family the location on the hierarchy they eventually assume as adults; that is, those persons within a particular social class have generally come from families at the same social class level. To the extent that this hereditary transmission of social class occurs from generation to generation, there is a lack of social mobility within the stratification structure. Retention is greatest within those stratification structures that restrict the interchange of persons between social classes.

In *closed-class* stratification structures, inheritance of social class is the rule. At the time of birth, the education, occupation, prestige, power, neighborhood, and a host of other stratification-related characteristics of persons and families are known. Closed-class stratification structures are not only closed in the sense of severely limiting social mobility; they may be characterized as closed because "superiors" keep "inferiors" at a social (and sometimes physical) distance. By reason of religious, biological, magical, or legal justification, those in one class marry only their own kind and limit social relationships of all types with those below them in the stratification structure. The caste system, as in ancient and modern India, is the most closed stratification structure. Even within that type of stratification structure, however, some small degree of movement across caste lines has always occurred.

Whereas in closed-class stratification structures a variety of justifications are erected to prohibit social mobility, the culture within *open-class* systems defines social class movement as a desirable event. Without social origin as a brake on mobility, members in an open-class stratification structure are able to translate achievement efforts into social class improvement.

Just as social mobility exists in closed stratification structures, there may be castelike pockets within an open-class system. A prominent illustration in American society—which has a relatively open-class system—is the traditional black-white dichotomy. Because some degree of social mobility is present in closed-class systems and because social class rigidity can be observed within open-class hierarchies, these two types of stratification structures must be viewed as ideal types. That is, actual stratification structures will either approximate each extreme or lie somewhere between them. Figure 7.1 graphically depicts the retention of social class composition (measured by the de-

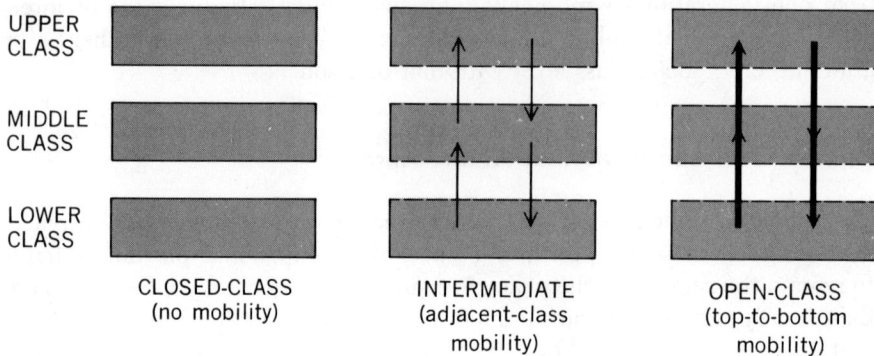

Figure 7.1 Retention of social class level within types of stratification structure

gree of movement across lines) as it varies by the degree of openness of a stratification structure.

Most industrialized countries, America included, cannot accurately be considered as either purely closed-class or open-class stratification structures. While the trend over the last few hundred years has been away from the closed-class model, industrialized societies still have stratification structures that fall between the two extremes of achievement and ascription. This means, as shown in Figure 7.1, that within "intermediate" stratification structures, upward or downward social mobility is primarily to the nearest social class.[4] This does not suggest that movement from the bottom to the top and vice versa does not occur in industrialized and urbanized societies; it does mean that the predominant pattern is adjacent-class social mobility.

Social mobility

The study of social mobility has, for the most part, focused on upward and downward occupational movement. A hierarchy of occupational groups has been established for this purpose. Table 7.2 contains the rank ordering of major occupational categories applied by sociologists in social mobility research. Often intergenerational and intragenerational social mobility is measured along a manual- versus a nonmanual-occupations dividing line. For simplicity, this manual versus nonmanual movement will serve as an illustration of social mobility in the following discussion. It should be kept in mind, however, that movement on other levels does occur.

TABLE 7.2 Prestige ranking of major occupational categories

	OCCUPATIONAL CATEGORY	Average Prestige Score
Nonmanual Occupations	Governmental officials*	90.8
	Professional and semiprofessional workers	80.6
	Proprietors, managers, and officials	74.9
	Clerical, sales, and kindred workers	68.2
Manual Occupations	Craftsmen, foremen, and kindred workers	68.0
	Farmers and farm managers	61.3
	Protective service workers	58.0
	Operatives and kindred workers	52.8
	Farm laborers	50.0
	Service workers (except domestic and protective)	46.7
	Laborers (except farm)	45.8

*Includes Supreme Court justice, state governor, Cabinet member, mayor of a large city, United States representative, diplomat, county judge, head of a department in a state government.
SOURCE: Reprinted with permission of Macmillan Publishing Co., Inc. from "Jobs and Occupations: A Popular Evaluation" by Paul K. Hatt and C. C. North in **Class, Status, and Power** by R. Bendix and S. M. Lipset, editors. Copyright © 1953 by The Free Press.

With the predominant pattern of adjacent-class social mobility, movement across the manual-nonmanual line will usually mean that upwardly mobile sons of electricians, truck drivers, assembly-line workers, and so forth will in all probability become part of the lower middle class as clerical workers or salesmen. Clerical and sales occupations, in turn, are the most hospitable launching pads for movement into business and professional jobs. In the United States about one-third of the sons of manual workers move from blue- to white-collar occupations, and about the same proportion of the sons of nonmanual workers assume manual jobs. In both instances, then, two-thirds of the sons of American workers remain in the same broad occupational category as their fathers. Whether or not sons assume exactly the same occupation as their father, the inheritance of social class level as measured by occupation is considerable in American society.

If intergenerational mobility is experienced by a minority of Americans, the same is true for intragenerational mobility. Of those American workers whose first job was nonmanual, over two-thirds were still in white-collar jobs at a later period in their careers. Similarly, almost exactly two-thirds of those who began full-time employment performing manual work were in the same occupational category later. This supports a frequent finding in social mobility research—a person's first job is an excellent indicator of the occupational category in which he will ultimately settle.

Although there is controversy on the matter, some evidence indicates a similarity in the amount of total social mobility (upward and downward mobility *combined*) within such industrialized countries as the United States, Australia, Great Britain, Sweden, West Germany, Japan, France, Switzerland, Denmark, and Italy. If the rates of total social mobility in these societies are not identical, they do seem to bear a reasonable resemblance to each other when movement across the manual-nonmanual line is the meas-

uring point, as shown in Table 7.3.* If valid, this finding damages the enduring belief that America's stratification structure is much more open-class
than those of other industrialized countries. It may also be taken as indirect
support for the functionalist theory of stratification structure, at least with
reference to economically developed societies—industrialized and urbanized
societies tend to be more open-class because of the pressure to place the best
qualified persons in the most functionally important positions.

Still, a plurality of persons in industrialized countries inherit their location on the stratification structure. While from a historical perspective the
current trend in these societies is toward the open-class type of stratification
structure, they presently display an intermediate degree of openness. Retention of social class level from generation to generation as well as from the
outset of persons' careers to their conclusion remains descriptive even of
those stratification structures conceded to offer the greatest opportunities
for social mobility.

**TABLE 7.3 Percentages of total occupational mobility
across the manual-nonmanual line in nine
industrialized countries**

COUNTRY	TOTAL OCCUPATIONAL MOBILITY
United States	34%
Sweden	32
Great Britain	31
Denmark	30
Norway	30
France	29
West Germany	25
Japan	25
Italy	22

SOURCE: Reprinted by permission from Gerhard Lenski, **Power
and Privilege. A Theory of Social Stratification** (New York:
McGraw-Hill, 1966), p. 411.

*Some researchers have challenged the existence of similarity in total social mo-
bility among industrialized societies, questioning the quality of the data on which this
proposition is based and presenting evidence that the statement holds only if farm
occupations are excluded. Of course, the findings contained in Table 7.3 are based only
on movement between manual and nonmanual occupations. See Leonard Broom and
F. Lancaster Jones, "Father-to-Son Mobility: Australia in Comparative Perspective,"
American Journal of Sociology, 74 (January 1969), 333–342; and F. Lancaster Jones,
"Social Mobility and Industrial Society: A Thesis Re-Examined," *Sociological Quarterly*, 10 (Summer 1969), 292–305.

Some influences on upward social mobility

Industrialized societies, as you have seen, have relatively open-class stratification structures. One important reason for the higher social mobility occurring within these societies is that, as industrialization proceeds, greater
dependence on machines causes the elimination of lower-level jobs. At the
same time, modern technology creates more jobs at higher levels. The shrinking of job opportunities at the bottom means that some of the sons of lower-
level manual workers simply cannot follow in their fathers' occupational
footsteps. Some of them will move up to meet the demand at higher occupational levels. This type of social mobility, which occurs because of changes
in the distribution of occupational opportunities, is called *structural*
mobility.

A second major influence on stratification structures in industrialized
societies is their characteristic emphasis on education as the avenue to social
mobility. Chances for upward mobility are enhanced as the level of education increases. This is particularly true for lower-class persons. Generally
those sons of manual workers who achieve marked occupational mobility
are backed by a college diploma.

Social mobility is also affected by the extent to which equal access to
education for all societal members is actually practiced. Equal opportunity
for education increases with industrialization, partly because of the need for
capable and trained people to perform more complex and specialized work.

Retention of social class across and within generations in industrial societies is heavily influenced by two facts: first, education is generally the
ticket to middle- and upper-level occupations; and second, chances for a
high level of education diminish markedly as family social class level declines. Table 7.4 reveals that as education level increases, so do occupational
prestige and average annual income. Although these income figures are low
by contemporary standards (they are based on 1962 incomes), the link between education, occupational prestige, and income is clear. And since the
educational level of a family increases with its social class level, Table 7.5
can be used to demonstrate in an indirect way that social class affects the
chances of children to become educated. Table 7.5 shows that the educational level of the father very much influences the son's likelihood of
achieving a given level of education. It is clear from Table 7.5 that the
percentage of sons who reach a progressively higher level of education increases as their fathers' educational attainment increases. Look at the bottom
row of figures and you will see that the percentage of sons who achieved at
least some college education steadily increases from 23 percent among
fathers who did not graduate from high school to 88 percent among fathers
who are college graduates.

Family prestige, power, and economic resources affect sons' occupational
attainment primarily through this differential access to higher education;
such differential access occurs in part because higher education is expensive

TABLE 7.4 Seventeen occupational categories by income and education

OCCUPATIONAL CATEGORIES*	MEDIAN INCOME	MEDIAN YEARS OF SCHOOLING
Professionals		
Self-employed	$12,048 ⎫	
Salaried	6,842 ⎭	16.4
Managers	7,238	12.8
Salesmen, other	6,008	13.0
Proprietors	5,548	12.1
Clerical	5,173	12.5
Salesmen, retail	3,044	12.3
Craftsmen		
Manufacturing ⎫		
Other ⎭	5,482†	11.2
Construction	5,265	10.2
Operatives		
Manufacturing	4,636	10.0
Other	4,206	10.4
Service	3,233	10.3
Laborers		
Manufacturing ⎫		
Other ⎭	2,189	8.9
Farmers	1,992	8.8
Farm laborers	488	8.3

*For males 14 and over employed in 1962.

†Excludes foremen, who are concentrated in manufacturing and whose median income is $7,073.

SOURCE: Adapted from Peter M. Blau and Otis Dudley Duncan, **The American Occupational Structure** (New York: Wiley, 1967), p. 27.

and in part because sons from middle- or upper-class families acquire at home and school some crucial tools for coping in the educational arena. Through parental encouragement and school experiences, middle- and upper-class offspring are more likely to possess educational and occupational motivation, verbal capacity, appropriate manners, ability to defer gratification, and capability for independence and responsibility than are their lower-class peers. As Jewish folk wisdom would have it, "the rich have heirs, not children."

In addition to acquiring a higher education, persons within an open-class stratification structure can improve their chances for upward social mobility by being an only child or coming from a small family, having a dominating mother and weak father, living in an urban area, delaying marriage, and producing small families.

Such a blueprint or pattern for successful upward mobility leads us to the last R of social stratification structure—repercussions.

TABLE 7.5 Fathers' and sons' educational attainment

	FATHERS' EDUCATIONAL ATTAINMENT			
Sons' Educational Attainment*	Less Than High School Education	High School Education Only	Some College	Completed College
Less than high school education	43%	10%	6%	4%
High school education only	34	36	24	8
At least some college	23	54	70	88
	100%	100%	100%	100%

*Aged 20–24 as of October 1962.
SOURCE: Adapted from U.S. Bureau of the Census; **Current Population Reports, Population Characteristics,** Series P-20, No. 110 (July 24, 1961), table A, p. 1.

REPERCUSSIONS

Despite its absurdity, *Mad* magazine's portrayal of the contrasting life styles of liberals, conservatives, leftists, and reactionaries presented in Table 7.6 makes an essential point. It may not be true that conservative couples sleep in twin beds, that reactionaries are suspicious of FM radio, that liberals always try to see the other guy's point of view while being mugged, or that leftists rooted for the Mets until they started winning. But sociological research has demonstrated the association of distinct ways of thinking, feeling, and behaving with social class level. This association between social class and life style has led some to think of social classes as subcultures.

You have seen the inequality among social classes. In fact, social classes are defined and measured in terms of the unequal distribution of desirables such as power, prestige, and wealth. Once obtained, these desirables become resources usable for the retention or perpetuation of social class level across generations. Such attempts are generally successful, for parental social class is highly related to subsequent social class. An important consequence is the relative stability and permanence of stratification structures. Even a modest degree of social class continuity permits the training of children in ways of thinking, feeling, and behaving that are somewhat distinctive of their social class. It is not wealth, power, or prestige that directly cause class-related cultural and behavioral differences. Rather, differences in life style, norms, and values are the result of learning experiences within a social class. Parents, peers, teachers, churchmen, and others all get into the act.

Caution is required in stating that social class level *causes* distinctive patterns of thinking, feeling, and behaving. There are other forces at work besides location in a stratification structure. Stratification structures always exist within a larger social structure. And the cultural aspects of these larger social structures impinge on the relationship between social class and life style. If, for instance, a society is in the midst of a war or a depression, either condition could affect, for example, the differences in suicide rates among

TABLE 7.6 Mad magazine's portrait of liberals, conservatives, leftists, and reactionaries

LIBERALS . . .				CONSERVATIVES . . .			
Feed their pets organic foods.	Watch Dick Cavett.	Try to see the other guy's point of view while being mugged.	Bicycle.	Wet their finger before turning the page of a book.	Sleep in twin beds.	Take pride in their penmanship.	Waltz.
Say "peace!"	Take up yoga.	Support nonprofit TV.	Have tried pot.	Own Irish setters.	Are reliable pallbearers.	Work out at a gym regularly.	Mail in warranties.
Secretly wish William F. Buckley were a liberal.	Secretly wish David Susskind weren't.	Walk around nude in front of the children.	Know the name of their congressman.	Are life members of the National Geographic Society.	Refer to Muhammad Ali as Cassius Clay.	Drive cars with low license plate numbers.	Overdecorate their homes at Christmas time.
Sign petitions.	Are cremated.	Get psychoanalyzed.	Distrust Nixon.	Undertip.	Take pride in their "regularity."	Are on a first-name basis with their bank officer.	Distrust Nixon.
Subscribe to **Consumer Reports**	Grind their own coffee.	Make it a habit to call Negroes "Blacks."	Hate being called "leftists."	Are disgusted with Jim Bouton.	Read historical markers.	Wear vests.	Hate being called "reactionaries."

Table 7.6 (Continued)

LEFTISTS . . .

Phone all-night radio talk shows in order to argue with the Emcee.	Drive VW minibuses.	Organize amateur film festivals.	Scratch.
Save newspaper articles.	Eat thick soups.	Take in stray cats.	Work in secondhand bookshops.
Enjoy folk dancing.	Wear caps and mittens.	Rooted for the Mets until they started winning.	Omit zip codes.
Do not eat breakfast.	Make bookshelves out of old bricks.	Sit in cafeterias alone, reading underground newspapers.	Distrust Nixon.
Carry their money in snap-clasp pocket purses.	Have missing shirt buttons.	Do not shave their legs.	Hate being called "new left extremists."

REACTIONARIES . . .

Pay cash.	Are suspicious of FM radio.	Wear suspenders.	Do not mix flavors in ice-cream cones.
Erect high fences around their backyards.	Enjoy Philadelphia.	Never heard of John Lennon.	Own canaries.
Are convinced "Sesame Street" is subversive.	Have middle-aged secretaries.	Hate Astroturf.	Cross picket lines.
Take baths.	Do not sleep past 7:00 A.M.	Are pleased with Mt. Rushmore except for Jefferson.	Distrust Nixon.
Carry their money in snap-clasp pocket purses.	Wear jackets and ties to football games.	Like meat well done.	Hate being called "right-wing militants."

SOURCE: Reprinted by permission of Mad magazine, September 1972, pp. 28–29. © 1972 by E. C. Publications, Inc.

social classes. Because of the difficulty in specifying all of the factors causing class-related differences, it is more correct to think of these differences as being *associated* with social class level. This does not in any way downgrade the impact of social class on human behavior. It does mean that while social class is a highly significant causal factor, it is only one of several factors contributing to the variations observed in social life.

Given the principles of class-related repercussions on social life, some of the specific consequences substantiated by sociological research can be examined. Three umbrellalike dimensions of class-related social repercussions are life chances, life style, and personality.

Life chances

The term *life chances* refers to the likelihood of possessing the "good things in life," including health, happiness, wealth, legal protection, and, of course, life itself. The probability of acquiring and maintaining the material and nonmaterial rewards in life is significantly affected by social class level. As indicated, power, prestige, and economic rewards increase with social class level. And education—the single most important gateway to these rewards—also increases with higher placement on a stratification structure. But there are additional life chances, much more subtle ones, that vary among social classes. These less-obvious life chances are in good part the product of inequality in the distribution of education, power, prestige, and economic rewards.

The probability of possessing life itself—the most precious life chance—declines with social class level. Whether measured by the death rate or by life expectancy, the likelihood of a longer life is enhanced as persons move up a stratification structure. This disparity in the most fundamental life chance is due to differences in the value placed on medical attention, the concern with proper nutrition, the attention to personal hygiene, and the ability to afford what these things cost. A reduction in the life expectancy difference among social classes is occurring in advanced industrial societies. The narrowing of this gap is the expected result of rising incomes in all social classes, widespread diffusion of health-related information through mass media, presence of high-level medical care, insurance policies, and government aid such as Medicare and Medicaid.

In light of life expectancy differences, it is not surprising that physical health among the living is affected by social class level. Those lower on a stratification structure are more likely to be sick or disabled and to receive poorer medical treatment once they are ill. It is no different for mental health. Persons at lower-class levels have a greater probability of becoming mentally disturbed and are less likely to receive therapeutic help, adequate or otherwise.

There are innumerable other life chance inequities, only a few of which can be mentioned. The poor often pay more for the same goods or services. They are more likely to get caught for committing a crime, and they stand a greater chance of being convicted and serving prison time for their alleged crime. They are less likely to have connections to help them beat the system, as in obtaining tickets to a football game or getting a favor from a political figure. And the public services they receive, like garbage collection, police protection, and street repair, are inferior.

Life style

Max Weber linked life chances to the economics of social class—he thought of them as a result of the ability to generate money and to purchase goods and services. Since life chances can be improved with access to wealth, they are a relatively open matter. Life style, in contrast, is a more closed affair.

Moving from a lower-class area to an expensive home in an upper-class neighborhood carries with it instantaneous improvement in city services. And money can buy a good lawyer, a life-lengthening doctor, a competent psychiatrist, or a college education. But why is it that a family with newly acquired financial resources does not seem to "fit" into the new social environment surrounding their $150,000 house? It is a matter of social class differences in life style, in ways of thinking, feeling, and behaving that class members have been exposed to from birth. Partly because of ethnocentrism, members of higher social classes view the life styles of the upwardly mobile as not only strange, but inferior. The "snobbery" associated with the upper class reveals the closed quality of class-related life styles. Of course, an attitude of superiority is not only characteristic of the upper class. Members of the middle class display their own kind of rejection of lower-class norms, values, and behavior.

You simply cannot purchase a new cultural outlook. It is also quite difficult to adopt a new class-related life style, even when the desire is great. For one thing, one's culture is like the air he breathes; it is not easy to change to a new medium, for it seems unnatural. In the second place, exposure to a new life style must precede its acceptance and execution, and the closed quality of class-related life styles only increases the barriers. That is to say, persons who already share a similar life style tend to associate with each other, thus excluding culturally dissimilar persons. Since the acquisition of a new class-related life style or subcultural world view takes time, and since the lack of the appropriate life style can lead to social exclusion, acceptance in a higher social class may be a slow process. Thus, if life style is a repercussion of stratification structure, it also contributes to the retention of social class membership because of the exclusivity of social interaction that it generates.

As research has shown, the rich and the poor really are separated by much more than money. Social class dissimilarities have been observed in a variety of areas of American life including education, marital and family relations, child-rearing, political attitudes and behavior, religious affiliation, and participation in social activities. Only a few of the many and varied class differences need to be specifically mentioned.[5]

Those in higher social classes marry later, display greater family stability (for example, lower divorce rates), and have better marital adjustment. Although working- and middle-class parents are more alike in child-rearing practices than in the past, some differences remain. Compared to the middle class, lower-class parents tend to be less permissive, less attentive to their children's social and emotional needs, more inclined to use physical punishment rather than logic and reasoning in disciplining their children, and more authoritarian in parent-child relationships.

Regarding political behavior, the incidence of voting and involvement in politics, either through formal organizational structures or in informal social relationships, increases with social class level. Varying political attitudes are also associated with location on a stratification structure—those in the lower class tend to be more liberal than middle- and upper-class Americans on economic issues but more conservative on social issues. Thus, lower-class persons are more in favor of labor unions, government control of business, and social welfare programs, but tend to exhibit less tolerance and sympathy than do higher social classes for social issues involving civil rights and international affairs.

In regard to religion, the rate of church membership and attendance is the lowest at the extremes of the stratification structure. Among those of all social classes who do attend church, there seems to be a discernible pattern of affiliation by social class. Episcopalian, Congregational, and Presbyterian churches are significantly less populated by members of the lower class. Lower-class Americans lean more toward Baptist, Catholic, and fundamentalist churches. Middle-class Americans are disproportionately drawn to Methodist and Lutheran churches.

Finally, social participation is not the same in all social classes. Membership and participation in voluntary formal organizations is more characteristic of the middle and upper classes. Even considering only those members of each social class who do participate in voluntary organizations, it is found that they belong to identifiably different types of organizations. You have just seen this with respect to church membership. To cite some other grossly representative examples, you are more likely to find the upper class in country clubs, the middle class in the Rotary club, and the upper-lower class in the American Legion.

Personality correlates of stratification structure

Just as life chances and life styles may be thought of as correlates of stratification structure, there is reason to believe that social class is associated with different personality patterns. *Personality* is comprised of the patterns of thinking, feeling, and behaving that are characteristic of a person. You will recall from Chapter 3 that culture is learned through social interaction and is, in turn, inferred from the behavior of persons. Although most sociologists recognize the impact of biological traits on the human personality, they tend to leave that aspect of the matter to psychologists. For practical purposes, then, personality to the sociologist is the subjective and personalized side of culture.

Whether the reference is to personality characteristics or to psychological consequences, the discussion of the social psychology of stratification structure that follows focuses on the *internal* states of persons. The structural perspective, you will remember, focuses on the external dimensions of social life such as the rank order of social positions and social mobility. However, that the social-psychological perspective was also represented is evident in the sections on life chances (in the discussion of incidence of mental illness) and life styles (in the differentiation of political attitudes). This illustrates that most sociological problems can be approached from both perspectives, but that each should be recognized for what it is. At this point, the relative emphasis on the repercussions of stratification structure switches from the structural to the social-psychological.

If many personality characteristics are the subjective expression of culture and if social classes possess distinctive cultural patterns, then unique personality traits should appear among members of each social class. This is not to say that *all* members of a social class share a given personality trait. It does mean that, as a whole, members of one social class exhibit a given characteristic more than do persons in another class. Although research on the social psychology of stratification has not been as extensive as on other aspects, it is possible to sketch some class-related personality characteristics, including some of the psychological costs of social mobility and some of the psychological consequences of status inconsistency.

For one thing, achievement motivation drops off markedly from the higher to the lower social classes. The lower class exhibits a greater tendency to accept what they presently have than to take risks for possible self-gain. It has also been observed that lower-class children have less anxiety than do middle-class children. The ability to defer gratification seems to be less prevalent among lower-class children. This is manifested in a variety of ways. Compared to the middle class, lower-class children are more likely to satisfy their immediate desires through physical violence, sexual intercourse, spending money, and dropping out of school. Finally, a greater proportion of authoritarian personalities appear in the lower class than in either the middle or upper class.

• PSYCHOLOGICAL COSTS OF SOCIAL MOBILITY. Because some degree of social mobility occurs among members of all classes in an open-class stratification structure, whatever the class level, those who move up or down have a psychological price to pay. Most people find personal responsibility for failure an extremely unpleasant burden. All but the neurotic avoid continuous self-blame. This places persons in an open-class stratification structure in a vulnerable situation. In the first place, because there is a high ceiling on upward movement, persons feel a responsibility to keep trying to improve their status. And since failure to achieve ever higher status cannot be blamed on a system that permits upward mobility, the fault must lie with each individual, with his innate inferiority or lack of effort. Thus, there are few places to hide.

Anxiety generated by an open-class stratification structure is at its height among those in the middle class because they have the greatest opportunities to rise and a good distance to fall. Those in the upper class have only to maintain their present privileged status and, as you have seen, they have the resources to do so. While the upper class has neither to struggle for status nor fight hard to retain it, the middle class is not so fortunate. More members of the middle class want to go higher on the stratification structure, and many have just arrived at their present level. Those who have just arrived in the middle class are generally more insecure than members of long standing, and those with the goal of ever higher status seldom feel serene in their current class "launching pads."

Whether wanting higher status for themselves or their children, or fearing downward mobility, many in the middle class suffer stratification-related insecurities. Among those who have only recently moved from the lower to the middle class, these insecurities may be consciously and directly felt. Those who have been in the middle class for several generations express their insecurities in more indirect and subtle ways. For example, they show concern that their children finish their education; they may fear that their children will marry someone of a lower social class; and they attempt to build some financial security through savings, investments, or insurance.

The lower class has insecurities of a different kind. Their worries run to matters of survival like unemployment, sickness, and the lack of food and money; anxieties about mobility are much less a factor. Members of the lower class seem more likely to evidence resignation; they do not anticipate upward mobility and do not instill in their children the desire to achieve. It is obvious, then, that the degree of stratification-related anxiety is conditioned by the security persons feel in their class location and the intensity of their desire for upward mobility.

As just shown (and contrary to popular opinion) the quest for upward mobility does have some negative psychological repercussions, of which insecurity and anxiety are most prominent. There are reasons for this anxiety and insecurity aside from the fear of failure. In the first place, persons who move across class lines find themselves in unfamiliar cultural territory. Because social classes are subcultures, the upwardly mobile must absorb some new ways of thinking, feeling, and behaving if they are to be accepted. You simply do not say "amen" during a sermon in a Methodist or Lutheran church, and T-shirts are not part of the standard dress for dinner at an exclusive country club. It takes time and effort to feel comfortable with the trade of familiar cultural patterns for strange ones. But until this cultural transition has been made successfully, upwardly mobile persons are a type of marginal man—each foot is grounded in a different cultural world, and full acceptance is denied in both. Their marginality often is intensified because they themselves cannot decide which cultural map to follow. Persons who lack adequate cultural ties or who fail to achieve integration into a culture or subculture feel the anxiety and insecurity that such isolation breeds.

Upwardly mobile persons experience emotional as well as cultural isolation. Not only must they attempt to think, feel, and act in new ways, they must do so with a new set of friends and acquaintances. Some long-standing personal relationships often have to be forfeited because a move to a different neighborhood or city is usually associated with an upward shift in social class. If geographical moves are frequent—as they often are with the upwardly mobile—the formation of strong and stable emotional ties is nearly impossible. Even if the status shift is slight and geographical change does not occur, personal relationships are frequently disturbed. Executives in many companies, for example, are not supposed to associate regularly with those below them. Golfing matches, drinks, and lunches with old friends often become casualties of assuming a vice-presidency. The psychological costs of upward social mobility are reflected in the association between mental illness and movement up a stratification structure.

Of course, upward mobility has its positive psychological pay-off. "Success" can be used to build self-esteem. Since self-regard does increase with social class level, it follows that the downwardly mobile are likely to suffer a loss of self-esteem. When others equate success with ability and self-worth, it is the exceptional "failure" who can avoid a harsh self-judgment. As already stated, self-dislike is one of the most painful attitudes known to man.

It is, therefore, no surprise that people will go to great lengths to avoid its psychological repercussions. The ultimate avoidance technique is suicide, an alternative that is disproportionately chosen by the downwardly mobile.

Rather than take this ultimate stand against oneself, those skidding down a stratification structure may shift the blame to forces outside themselves. A convenient scapegoat is ethnic and racial minorities. Blacks and Jews, for example, may be blamed by either the downwardly mobile or those who seem to be blocked in their efforts for upward movement. By choosing an external target, they can attempt to excuse themselves and at the same time vent their hostility and frustration on others. This may be quite effective because it plays on prejudices against minorities that already exist; not only can people rationalize away personal accountability for perceived failure, they can do so with considerable support from those around them. Research has revealed a relationship between social mobility and prejudice.

However, not all of the unsuccessful place the burden of personal "failure" on outside forces, and those who do so are not completely able to avoid self-blame. This is reflected in the high incidence of emotional disturbances—anxiety, depression, schizophrenia—among both the downwardly mobile and those persons blocked in their thrust for higher status.

• STATUS INCONSISTENCY. There is a tendency for those at one level on a particular ranking dimension to be at a similar level on other dimensions of rank. Amounts of power, prestige, and wealth held by members of a social class generally vary together. A close correspondence on the various dimensions of rank is especially characteristic of closed-class stratification structures. Such a correspondence is less characteristic of open-class stratification structures, in good part because relatively frequent social mobility increases the chances of inconsistencies on the dimensions of rank. In open-class structures, money may precede prestige by some time, or power may trail prestige by some distance because one may be achieved before the other. This is obviously not possible in stratification structures in which location on the various dimensions of rank are ascribed at the same level. Thus, *status inconsistency*—marked variation in location on one or more dimensions of rank—is a much more frequent occurrence in rapidly changing industrial societies than in stable agricultural ones. Mobility is not the only source of status inconsistency in open-class stratification structures. It has been seen that a certain amount of status inconsistency is built in. In America, for example, some occupations offer high prestige that is not matched by economic rewards (teachers, ministers), while others have monetary rewards that outstrip their prestige (skilled construction workers, truck drivers).

More important than the sources of status inconsistency in the present context are the social-psychological repercussions. Why, in the first place, would status inconsistency be expected to have any impact at all? According to Gerhard Lenski, it is a matter of "one-upmanship."[6] That is, people attempt to place themselves in a good light, even if it means putting others down. Thus, if a person is higher on one dimension than he is on the others, he will define himself in those terms and expect others to do the same. Yet, in order to enhance their own self-esteem, others will not only fail to comply, they will relate to him on the basis of his *lowest* rank. A young white minister may approach a banker believing that he will receive a sizable loan because the banker will respect and trust him. To the banker, however, prestige is not collateral. Ignoring social standing, the banker will probably make a decision grounded on the minister's financial situation. Or, a black doctor may be responded to on the basis of his skin color rather than his occupational rank or income.

Predictable consequences of this discrepancy between self-image and the actions of others include frustration and anger, as well as other psychological stresses. Such repercussions seem to be associated more with instances of conflict between ascribed rank and achieved rank than when the conflict pertains to achieved ranks only. Black physicians whose ascribed racial features supersede their achievements would be expected to suffer more than white ministers whose status inconsistency involves achieved ranks only (income and prestige).

OVERVIEW AND PREVIEW

Some of the major aspects of stratification structure have been summarized in the five R's—ranking, rewards, resources, retention, and repercussions. Opening the chapter was the idea of the multidimensionality of stratification structures. Whereas Karl Marx based his analysis of social classes on the economic dimension alone, Max Weber influenced sociology by underlining two additional dimensions, power and prestige. This insight opens for consideration the extent to which persons or families hold a dissimilar rank in each of the three hierarchies, that is, whether or not status inconsistency exists. While the ranks on each dimension tend to settle at the same level, it is particularly in rapidly changing societies that inconsistencies emerge.

A multidimensional approach to stratification structure is useful because the economic, power, and prestige dimensions are intimately involved in each of the five R's. However, the practice of using occupational prestige as a single indicator of social class level can be defended by its relationship to the other dimensions of stratification structure.

The economic, power, and prestige dimensions are also broad types of stratification structure rewards, which become resources for either the maintenance or improvement of social class level. There is a difference of opinion regarding the mechanism of reward distribution. While the functionalists link reward inequities to societal welfare, conflict theorists attribute inequities to differences in power, that is, rewards go to the powerful. The correct answer seems to lie in a synthesis of these two angles of vision.

Because stratification-related rewards are resources for either the consolidation or enhancement of social class level, they contribute to the retention of class membership. This is true even in open-class stratification structures. In western industrialized societies—all of which have relatively open-class stratification structures—both intergenerational and intragenerational mobility is experienced by only a minority of persons. And those who do move up or down make only short gains or losses. The extent of social mobility in industrial societies is affected by alterations in the distribution of occupational opportunities—modern technology tends to eliminate lower-level occupations and to create more higher-level ones.

Power, prestige, and economic inequalities also have repercussions, some of which are social-psychological. Access to the finer things of life—life chances—is conditioned by social class level. Social classes are so intimately related to life style that they may be viewed as subcultures. Different personality characteristics are associated with social class level, including mental illness, willingness to take risks, and the ability to defer gratification. Although often overlooked, there are psychological costs attached to upward social mobility. Finally, inconsistency among the dimensions of rank is associated with psychological stress, particularly when a clash exists between achieved and ascribed ranks.

The next chapter pursues community structure in terms of its social characteristics. Urban growth is often identified with unique social characteristics that are said to differentiate it from a rural way of life. This allegedly distinctive urban social structure is referred to as urbanism. As you will learn, urban community structure is more complex and varied than the freely used phrase "urban way of life" implies.

REFERENCES

1. Parts of this section draw heavily from Leonard Reissman, *Class in American Society* (New York: Free Press, 1959), pp. 144–164.
2. For a review of these findings, see Robert W. Hodge, Donald J. Treiman, and

Peter H. Rossi, in Reinhard Bendix and Seymour Martin Lipset, eds., *Class, Status, and Power: Social Stratification in Comparative Perspective*, 2nd ed. (New York: Free Press, 1966), pp. 309–321.

3. Gerhard Lenski, *Power and Privilege. A Theory of Social Stratification* (New York: McGraw-Hill, 1966).

4. The description of social mobility presented here is a distillation of several sources: Elton F. Jackson and Harry J. Crockett, Jr., "Occupational Mobility in the United States: A Point Estimate and Trend Comparison," *American Sociological Review*, 29 (February 1964), 5–15; Seymour Martin Lipset and Reinhard Bendix, *Social Mobility in Industrial Society* (Berkeley: University of California Press, 1964); Otis Dudley Duncan, "Occupational Mobility in the United States," *American Sociological Review*, 30 (August 1965), 491–498; Peter M. Blau, "The Flow of Occupational Supply and Recruitment," *American Sociological Review*, 30 (August 1965), 475–490; Peter M. Blau and Otis Dudley Duncan, *The American Occupational Structure* (New York: Wiley, 1967); Leonard Broom and F. Lancaster Jones, "Career Mobility in Three Societies: Australia, Italy, and the United States," *American Sociological Review*, 34 (October 1969), 650–658.

5. Many of the following findings are cited in Bernard Berelson and Gary A. Steiner, *Human Behavior: An Inventory of Scientific Findings* (Harcourt Brace Jovanovich, 1964), pp. 476–490.

6. Lenski, op. cit., pp. 86–88.

ADDITIONAL SOURCES AND READINGS

Barber, Bernard. *Social Stratification* (New York: Harcourt Brace Jovanovich, 1957).

Feuer, Lewis S., ed. *Marx and Engels: Basic Writings on Politics and Philosophy* (Garden City, N.Y.: Doubleday, 1959).

Fox, Thomas G., and S. M. Miller. "Economic, Political and Social Determinants of Mobility: An International Cross-Sectional Analysis," *Acta Sociologica*, 18 (1965), 76–93.

Heller, Celia S., ed. *Structured Social Inequality: A Reader in Comparative Social Stratification* (New York: Macmillan, 1969).

Hodges, Harold. *Social Stratification: Class in America* (Cambridge, Mass.: Schenkman, 1964).

Jencks, Christopher. *Inequality: A Reassessment of the Effect of Family and Schooling in America* (New York: Basic Books, 1972).

Kahl, Joseph A. *The American Class Structure* (New York: Holt, Rinehart and Winston, 1957).

Kohn, Melvin L. "Social Class and Parent-Child Relationships: An Interpretation," *American Journal of Sociology*, 68 (January 1963), 471–480.

Mayer, Kurt. *Class and Society* (New York: Random House, 1955).

Tumin, Melvin M. *Social Stratification* (Englewood Cliffs, N.J.: Prentice-Hall, 1967).

8

Community Structure: Urbanism

NOW I LAY ME DOWN TO SLEEP
Now I lay me down to sleep
I pray the double lock will keep;
May no brick through the window break,
And no one rob me till I wake.

FEE, FI, FO, FUM
Fee, fi, fo, fum,
I smell the blood of violence to come;
I smell the smoke that hangs in the air
Of buildings burning everywhere;
Even the rats abandon the city:
The situation is being studied
by a crisis committee.

THERE WAS A MAN
There was a man of our town
And he was wondrous wise—
He moved away.

Eve Merriam, **The Inner City Mother Goose** (New York: Simon & Schuster, 1969), pp. 21, 92–93, 95. Reprinted by permission of Eve Merriam. Copyright © 1969 by Eve Merriam.

It is fashionable to depict life in the city in the grim terms of Eve Merriam's poems from *The Inner City Mother Goose*. While it is true that many a "wise" man who can afford it is moving to the suburbs and that parts of the core of large cities require emergency treatment, it is incorrect to portray all of the central city as socially disorganized. The popular view of urban life is based on an antiurban bias, a bias that yearns for the good old days when life was pastoral and peaceful. This slanted perspective on rural versus urban life ignores the backbreaking tasks associated with self-sufficiency, the crimes that occur in allegedly pastoral and peaceful settings, and the grinding poverty found in rural areas of the world. Of course, inner-city slums exist, replete with roaches, rats, crime, pollution, drug addiction, prostitution, and poverty. Nevertheless, exclusive preoccupation with the negative side of urbanism ignores the diversity of urban community structure.

Urbanization involves the concentration of large numbers of people within a relatively small geographic area. More specifically, *urbanization* is the process by which an increasingly larger proportion of a society's population resides in urban areas. Chapter 14 is devoted to this topic. Associated with urbanization are some distinctive patterns of culture and social structure that contrast sharply with the rural way of life. The "urban way of life" called *urbanism* is examined in this chapter. The chapter opens with an introduction to the concept of community structure. Other topics include the antiurban bias, the social convergence of rural and urban areas, urbanism as a way of life, and the urban crisis associated with the concentration of the poor—mostly the black poor—in the inner cities of America.

WHAT IS COMMUNITY STRUCTURE?

Of all sociological concepts, that of community has been one of the most difficult on which to achieve a consensus. Some sociologists emphasize the community as a psychological entity; self-conscious identification, sharing of goals and interests, and a sense of belonging distinguish this view of community. Others see the spatial aspect of community as the most important; community is defined by its territorial boundaries. Still others contend that the existence of social relationships is the most prominent dimension of community. The definition that will be used in this text is a combination of the latter two perspectives. *Community structure* is an interrelated set of social relationships that fulfill on a daily basis the major social and economic needs of the population living within a delimited geographic area.

Missing from this definition is the psychological dimension. This omission reflects the continuing transformation of our planet from a rural to a highly urban world. It is not logical to define any concept in terms of a characteristic that is not constant, that is not the same for all phenomena to which the concept refers. For example, until something like the Wankel engine or the electric car makes an impact, the defining characteristics of an automobile would have to include such things as four-wheeled, piston-driven, and gasoline-powered. To define the automobile in terms of color or style—both of which are extremely variable—would be as bewildering as it would be ludicrous.

Thus, whereas the psychological conception of the community was descriptive in a rural society, it is out of joint in an urban one. Identification, a feeling of unity, and loyalty may characterize the residents of rural and relatively small urban communities but may or may not exist among the inhabitants of a metropolitan community. If a majority of San Franciscans have left their hearts in that city, they exhibit an atypical response to metropolitan living. Why have so few ever left their hearts in Detroit or Newark? In metropolitan communities, people seem to be searching for, and clinging to, particular limited aspects of their community with which they can identify and to which they can give their allegiance. Inhabitants of metropolitan communities may be able to "identify" their community— as in "I'm from Chicago," or Los Angeles or St. Louis—but they generally do not have deep psychological roots in their communities as a whole. Sheer size plus frequent and extensive geographic mobility tend to create a community of strangers. The extent of psychological attachment to a community, then, decreases as community size increases. Therefore, just as the Wankel engine may usher in a new definition of the automobile, urbanization has made obsolete the psychological definition of community.

The concept of community followed in this chapter is heavily influenced by the emergence of the urban community as the dominant form in industrial society. While urbanization has undermined the generalizability of a psychological definition of community, this process has left the geographic and social structure dimensions reasonably well intact. You will recall that social stratification structure encompassed two elements—the ranking of social positions and the social relationships based on this ranking. Community structure is analogous to this; its two major elements are geographic area and the social relationships that exist within given territorial limits.

From this discussion what kinds of places would qualify as communities? Rural towns and villages and cities of all sizes would fit the definition of community structure. But what about popular applications of this concept as in "scientific community," "religious community," "prison community," or "world community"?

References like the scientific or religious community would clearly be inappropriate because the alleged members of such "communities" do not share a sharply delimited geographic area. Scientists are located all over this country, and Baptists are not confined to the South.

Sociologists generally refer to places like prisons, mental hospitals, and concentration camps as "total institutions" rather than as communities. It is true that total institutions have very precise geographic boundaries and fulfill those needs necessary for the survival of their inhabitants. The term total institution itself reflects the self-containment of such places. However, the social relationships within total institutions are sufficiently different from those in communities in the "outside world" that the two should not be conceptually lumped together. More importantly, the goals of total institutions are few and can be clearly specified, while the goals of communities are many, diffuse, and ill-defined. For this reason, total institutions are considered to be formal organizational structures rather than community structures.

To think sociologically of the "world community" or the "communist community" is to stretch the concept of community structure beyond usefulness. Among other difficulties, such referents are too broad and heterogeneous to be meaningfully analyzed as social structures.

There is one final point on the definition of community structure. It may have occurred to you that large metropolitan communities seem to contain within their boundaries social units that might also be termed community structures. Do not New York City's Bedford-Stuyvesant, Philadelphia's Germantown, and Los Angeles' Watts constitute communities without reference to their larger metropolitan areas? Do they not illustrate the existence of communities *within* communities?

Although disagreement exists among sociologists, two arguments can be used against viewing such social units as communities in themselves. In the first place, it is difficult to establish geographic boundaries separating each from its larger community. Where does Germantown end and the rest of Philadelphia begin? Second, these smaller social units rarely fulfill all or even most of the social and economic needs of their residents on a daily basis. The phenomenon of residents having to find work outside of the area in which they live is a notable illustration of the dependence of these subunits on the larger community structure. Public transportation and utilities are still other examples. While it is less than ideal, it is probably best to think of these smaller social units as subcommunity structures.[1] This stance leaves open for empirical study the extent to which any particular subcommunity is geographically separable from the larger community and the degree to which it can operate on a self-contained basis.

Urban community structure has rapidly emerged as the dominant form in industrialized societies. Highly industrialized societies have made the dramatic transition from farms and villages to densely populated cities. Developing nations are on the road to this transformation. As reflected in

Bob Combs

the poems opening this chapter, this transition has not been without its critics.

THE CITY AS THE SOURCE OF ALL EVIL

Reflected in Thoreau's love of nature was a strong bias against urban life. His view of civilization was biased because he tended to emphasize the negative side of city existence and to praise the positive aspects of living in communion with the elements. Thoreau had plenty of intellectual company in his bias against the city, for he was neither the first nor the last to see urban life as the fountainhead of all that is worth deploring. The description of the destruction of Sodom and Gomorrah in Genesis is an example of wholesale condemnation of the decadence of urbanites. Thomas Jefferson feared the passing of democracy if cities ever became the seat of influence. Mark Twain, always more subtle, went beyond the city to blast civilization in general when he wrote, "Soap and education are not as sudden as a massacre, but they are more deadly in the long run." A more contemporary antiurban statement was offered in the 1960s by those American youths who preferred organic foods to the Student Union, chose to till the land rather than make money, or considered poetry reading more important than soap and formal education.

Studies of ethnocentrism have showed that people tend to like things familiar to them, things that they think of as "natural." Although civilization has been advanced by cities, the fact is that rural living has been the experience of most people for most of history. American society, despite its relative youth, is not excluded from this generalization. It was scarcely over one hundred years ago that buffalo on the American western frontier saw wagon trains, buffalo hunters for the railroad, and the westward retreat of Indians. Wherever urbanism has emerged as a new mode of living, it has been viewed as "unnatural" and therefore an easy target for those who believe in the correspondence between rurality and righteousness.

The city has not been without friends. Many have praised the city as the center of all that is good. Where else, they have asked, can you find the intellectual, artistic, and technological enlightenment characteristic of city life? From this perspective, the poverty, crime, pollution, and congestion accompanying urban living are human costs well worth paying. Moreover, they can argue, urban misery and degradation are often equaled in areas of rural poverty.

Such contradictory judgments of urban life mean that cities offer both the good and the bad. The reference point of the observer determines whether the judgment will be positive or negative. Clearly, most past and contemporary observers have been critics. But curiously enough, these critics often take the "cafeteria approach"—they choose to take advantage of what they find desirable in the city, while downgrading less favored aspects. Hippies transport "free love"—a decidedly urban practice—to their rural communes, and rural residents shake their heads at the decadence of city dwellers as portrayed on their cable TV.[2] Apparently, a blanket rejection of urban life without some facts is as premature as it is erroneous.

Although we have been discussing, and contrasting, rural and urban viewpoints, the question must be asked: How rural is rural?

RURAL-URBAN CONVERGENCE

Prior to the middle of the twentieth century, sociologists found the distinction between rural and urban ways of life meaningful. Much was written on "folk" or peasant society versus urban society. But it became apparent that it was primarily in underdeveloped societies, in places where cultural contacts between rural and urban people were either nonexistent or severely limited, that such contrasts retained their accuracy. Social and cultural distinctions between urban and rural areas have been nearly obliterated in industrialized societies. Not only has a steadily increasing proportion of the population in economically advanced countries become urban dwellers, but those living in clearly rural areas physically beyond metropolitan communities are no longer immune to the influence of urbanism. A casualty of this influence has been the disappearance of distinctive social structures identified with the rural way of life.

Consider American society. One factor promoting the diffusion of urbanism throughout the continental United States is the heavy dependence of nearly all communities on federal government funds. This dependence was dramatically illustrated in the early part of President Nixon's second administration with the advent of revenue-sharing. Nixon's program of revenue-sharing was partially designed to diminish the centralization of power in Washington by strengthening the autonomy of local communities: Urban renewal projects, for example, were to be decided on, and financed at, the local community level. The outcries from mayors and U.S. senators and congressmen clearly reflected the dependence of communities (and states) on the federal money machine. Of interest here is that the sharing of a common and important reference point like Washington promotes social and economic convergence between urban communities and the shrinking proportion of our population still living in rural communities.

Another source of rural-urban integration is the loss of social and economic independence among rural communities. On the economic side, it is well known that residents of New York City do not grow corn and that Butler, Oklahoma, is not an industrial center. Consequently, there is a trade-off of raw food supplies for manufactured goods between rural and urban areas.

Economic ties breed cultural sharing. In the present case most of the influence is in one direction. Rural and urban residents purchase the same television sets, radios, and national magazines, view similar motion pictures, and read newspapers. The cultural impact is one-way because the people who determine the content of television and radio programs, movies, and national magazines live in our major cities. And much of the content of local newspapers comes from national wire services. Thus the culture of the largest cities is diffused throughout the country. Modern transportation, along with communication, serves to spread the urban life style. Automobiles, buses, and planes make visits to the city a commonplace occurrence.

There is another aspect of rural-urban interdependence that has caused sociologists to view both small and large communities within the context of the larger society rather than as autonomous social structures. This aspect of interdependence is the existence of an unnumbered variety of national formal organizations, each of which has suborganizational units representing them in local communities. This goes beyond businesses such as Kroger or Sears stores to include organizations related to social activities. A Boy Scout troop in the Iowa corn belt is much like one in Chicago or Miami; churches teach the same basic philosophy from place to place; local United Automobile Workers unions have the same bargaining goals whether they are in Detroit, Michigan, or in Lorain, Ohio. Since the tentacles of so many special-interest national organizations are wrapped around both rural and urban communities, it is little wonder that members of each type of community display some similarities in attitudes and behavior.

Of course, there is no one-to-one correspondence between the social structures of mammoth cities and smaller communities. But if rural and urban areas are not exactly the same, they are infinitely more alike in modern societies than in traditional ones. And even if differences persist in the short run, the future belongs to urbanism. This is particularly the case for Western societies and will probably hold true for the rest of the world as well. What, then, is urbanism?

URBANISM AS A WAY OF LIFE?

Early urban ecologists at the University of Chicago were interested in the social aspects of urban life; they examined such phenomena as slums, the poor, the Jewish ghetto, and "high society." The member who best formulated the Chicago School's keen interest in the social structure of the city was Louis Wirth, who in 1938 wrote an influential essay entitled "Urbanism as a Way of Life."[3] As a representative of his colleagues, Wirth was attempting to answer this question: How can the distinctive social structure of urban areas be explained?

Wirth's view of urbanism

Wirth's starting point was that the city was more than a physical entity and therefore deserved a distinctly sociological definition. In Wirth's mind, the city exhibited a unique type of social structure that could be traced to three central physical characteristics: population size, population density, and heterogeneity of city dwellers. In the first place, these three characteristics of the city are interrelated. As larger numbers of people settle in a limited geographic area, the density of the population increases. The larger the number of people living in a given area, the greater the cultural, social, and economic diversity or heterogeneity among them. And the closer that people are physically (that is, the higher the population density), the more their differences will surface and affect each other.

Second, Wirth contended, these three interrelated features of the city exert a homogenizing effect on the social relationships of its inhabitants. Even though urban dwellers are dissimilar occupationally, culturally, racially, and ethnically, they share in a common way of life. In fact, according to Wirth, the heterogeneity of city people, brought about through the concentration of large numbers of persons in a relatively small land space, was a major contributor to their participation in a common social structure.

City people interact more on the basis of rigidly defined role expectations than do rural residents. A patient of a country doctor may bring him some meat or vegetables from the farm and ask about the health of his wife and children. In turn, the doctor may accept farm products rather than money in payment for his services simply because he knows the patient is experiencing hard times. Contrast this with the city surgeon who operates with a complicated accounting procedure that demands the same charge for a particular operation, whatever the personal economic situation of the patient. Heavy reliance on role expectations occurs in the city partly because there are so many people that it is impossible to know them all personally. Urbanites may actually know more people than do rural residents, but they know fewer people well enough to interact with them on a personalized basis.

The extremely high degree of occupational specialization found in cities also promotes impersonal, segmental, superficial, and transitory social relationships. Instead of relying on a family doctor for nearly all medical treatment, for example, urbanites must visit a variety of medical specialists. This example is easily multiplied because urban residents perform almost no services for themselves, depending as they do on a staggering number of persons and organizations to fulfill their needs.

This fundamental shift in the nature of social relationships from the personal and permanent to the impersonal and fleeting is accompanied by other features unique to urban social structure. Urbanites may exhibit an air of reserve, indifference, and bored cynicism in their social relationships. Cultural relativism is more characteristic of city dwellers who believe they have seen everything at least twice. Consequently, they are quite tolerant of the new and bizarre. People living, working, and playing together without emotional and personal bonds relate to each other in competitive, selfish, and exploitive ways. Friction and hostility abound. Formal social controls, including traffic lights and policemen, must replace the informal social controls operating among people who know each other personally and care what others think of them.

Even memberships in formal organizations do not compensate much for the impersonality and other characteristics of urban social relationships because such organizations, too, are segmental rather than encompassing. Whereas a rural church may satisfy a variety of needs, the members of an urban church generally have only their religious needs serviced. Thus, each of the organizations to which urbanites belong engages only a limited segment of their personalities. Furthermore, because urbanites are physically mobile—they are typically renters rather than homeowners—the memberships of special-interest organizations have a rapid turnover, making personal relationships even less likely.

According to Wirth, city dwellers suffer depersonalization from still another source. People in the city relate to each other primarily in terms of the goods and services they supply for each other. This market mentality means that persons see most others not as individuals but as one of a social category—a customer, a client, a collector of garbage. And regardless of personal differences that may exist among them, customers are customers and nothing more.

Wirth saw some basic consequences flowing from this urban way of life, most of which were negative. To be sure, city life frees people from the tight social and emotional control exercised in small, intimate groups and increases their sophistication and cultural relativism. But the price of liberation includes low morale, a loss of the sense of participating in, and belonging to, a total community, the absence of a basis for social solidarity, the decline of importance of the family and neighborhood, depersonalization, and loneliness. That the price of emancipation is not cheap is said to be reflected in the high urban rates of mental illness, suicide, delinquency, crime, and corruption.

There are two parting comments to be made on Wirth's theory of urbanism. In the first place, Wirth portrayed urbanism as a continuum. As population size, density, and heterogeneity increased, the characteristics of urbanism would be pushed toward their extremes. Second, he emphasized maintenance of the distinction between urbanism on the one hand and industrialism and modern capitalism on the other. That is, while industrialism and capitalism promoted urbanization (heavy concentration of people within a small geographic area), he believed that preindustrial cities also shared in the social structure of urbanism.

The diversity of urbanism

Wirth's view of urbanism, not unrepresentative of the Chicago School, was decidedly negative. Urbanism was unfavorably compared with rural life, a stance that dominated sociological thought in this area until the 1950s. At that point, criticism of the Chicago School flowered into a new image of the city. The Chicago School was accused of inappropriately generalizing from the inner city to urban life in general. Some critics even began to doubt the validity of Wirth's theory for the inner city. Herbert Gans has developed a most penetrating countertheory, grounded in more recent research conducted by himself and others.[4]

Gans reexamined Wirth's theory of urbanism because the latter failed to distinguish ways of life in the inner city from other urban districts. Most importantly, Gans' theory deals (as Wirth's did not) with the massive move of people and industry from the central city to the suburbs—a population exodus that gained its greatest momentum after the 1930s. Central to Gans' analysis were the distinctions he made among the inner city, the outer city, and the suburbs. The *inner city* encompasses the transient residential areas surrounding the central business district. Both the rich and the poor occupy these areas. In the *outer city* are those stable residential areas holding working-class and middle-class people. The main differences between the outer city and the suburbs is that the *suburbs* are further from the inner city and have a lower population density.

• INNER CITY. If Wirth's theory was descriptive of any urban area, Gans believed it depicted the inner city. And even there he argued that the diversity was greater than Wirth pictured it, for within the inner city were relatively homogeneous types of residents, some of whom had unique social structures insulating them from the alleged adverse repercussions of population size, density, and heterogeneity. Gans isolated five homogeneous types of inner city residents: cosmopolites; unmarried and childless; ethnic villagers; deprived; and trapped and downwardly mobile.

Cosmopolites—including students, artists, writers, musicians, entertainers, intellectuals, professionals—live in the inner city by choice. They wish to be near the "cultural" advantages the central city offers. Single persons and childless couples also live in the central city by choice, to be near their jobs and/or entertainment facilities. For many, this is a temporary arrangement until marriage and children send them home-hunting in the suburbs.

Ethnic villagers—members of urban enclaves who live much as they did in Europe, Puerto Rico, or Mexico—remain in the inner city partly by choice (continued participation in their native culture) and partly by necessity (poverty and lack of job opportunities). Aside from their jobs, each ethnic minority isolates itself from city social structures outside their own.

While some of the so-called ethnic villagers may have the unacted-upon option of leaving, the last two types of inner city residents remain of necessity. Where can the deprived—the poor, the psychologically and physically handicapped, and the non-Whites—go? For many of them, the inner city is a dead end. The trapped and the downwardly mobile are also anchored to the inner city, primarily because neither can afford to move to better areas. Downwardly mobile persons differ from the trapped in that the former were higher on the stratification structure earlier in their lives. Many of the downwardly mobile are older people living on small fixed pensions.

According to Gans, it is only the deprived, trapped, and downwardly mobile inner-city residents who experience the negative impacts of population size, density, and heterogeneity. Sociocultural barriers isolate and protect the other three types of inner-city dwellers. Cosmopolites are involved in their own subculture, leaving them detached from the rest of the surrounding neighborhood social structures. Detachment from the neighborhood also characterizes the unmarried and childless, who are without familial responsibilities in the present and have an eye to moving out of the inner city in the future. Although many ethnic villagers may have to remain in the city, they are members of a distinct imported subculture. Contrary to Wirth's theory of urbanism, these ethnic minorities emphasize kinship ties and personal relationships. By being suspicious of anything outside their neighborhoods, they avoid anonymity and impersonal social contacts. Whereas cosmopolites, the unmarried, and the childless are protected by their detachment from neighborhood life, ethnic villagers are sheltered by their total involvement in their separate neighborhoods.

• OUTER CITY AND SUBURBS. If some of the homogeneous resident types in the inner city are shielded from the alleged devastation of population size, density, and heterogeneity, says Gans, even more protection is offered to those in the outer city and suburbs. In these areas people live in homogeneous neighborhoods formed around similarities centered on such characteristics as occupation, location of work, income, racial and ethnic background, education, tradition, and preference. Another important characteristic is that most of these people are in the process of rearing children. While neighborhoods in the outer city and suburbs are not necessarily socially and culturally self-contained, Gans described the social relationships within the neighborhoods in both areas as "quasi-primary"—not fully open and personal but yet not closed and impersonal. This is partly due to the separation of residence and workplace. Social contacts, even those involving local merchants, do not reflect a market mentality. Instead, social interaction is guided by the desire for sociability and friendship. In fact, Gans notes, a hallmark of life in these areas is a lack of anonymity, impersonality, and privacy. In many ways, he says, such neighborhoods are like small towns, particularly when compared to the way small towns actually are rather than to the way romanticists have portrayed them.

Not only does Gans see many ways of life associated with the city, he has an explanation for them that is different from the one offered by Wirth. Since Wirth was an ecologist, he explained social structure via the ecological concepts of population size, density, and heterogeneity. This is fine, Gans counters, when the subjects being studied (plants, animals, or human beings) have no *choice* regarding where they will live. As you have seen, the lack of choice is most characteristic of those inner city residents without the resources to move. People who can make choices regarding housing and neighborhood can also make demands as to their nature. Most significantly, argues Gans, choices and demands are not determined by ecological factors but result from the characteristics of people. In his view, social class and stage in the life cycle are the two most useful characteristics for explaining the types of housing and neighborhoods people will occupy and the ways of life they will attempt to construct within them.

In the inner city, the unmarried and childless can be detached from their social surroundings because they have not yet entered the life cycle stage associated with familial responsibilities. For instance, they do not have to worry about the physical safety of their children or the quality of inner city schooling. Cosmopolites can be detached because of their stage in the life cycle and their class-based subculture. Ethnic villagers can choose to remain within their distinctive subcultures. However, low financial resources lock in the deprived, trapped, and downwardly mobile. Those in the outer city and suburbs have the resources to exercise some choice in residential areas and build a life style around the rearing of children.

Where does the clash of Gans' and Wirth's theories of urbanism leave us? There has not been enough research to say whether Wirth's ecological factors (population size, density, and heterogeneity) or Gans' social factors (stage in the life cycle and social class) have the greatest validity in explaining urban social structure. Probably both sets of factors are at work. Available research, however, does indicate that family, kinship, and personal social relationships exist to a much greater extent in the city than Wirth's description would suggest. Others have concluded that preindustrial cities and cities in currently developing areas do not conform to Wirth's picture of urbanism. As noted earlier, Wirth viewed urbanism as a continuum—urbanism reaches its heights where population size, density, and heterogeneity are the greatest. It appears that Wirth can be faulted for dealing with only one extreme of the continuum—the inner city, where population size, density, and heterogeneity are at their peak—and for attempting to generalize his theory to cover both industrialized and non-industrialized cities of the world. This left ample room for Gans and others to fill in additional gradations on the continuum of urbanism, particularly the outer city and the suburbs, and to challenge the accuracy of Wirth's theory of urbanism for all times and places. And even in the inner city, it is charged, Wirth overemphasized the decline of family, kinship, and personal ties.

Still, the fact remains that impersonal, temporary, and segmental social relationships do occupy a greater proportion of urban dwellers' time. While those living in the outer city engage in "quasi-primary" social relationships within their neighborhoods, the majority of their waking hours are spent either at work in the city or commuting. And even Gans' "ethnic villagers" can isolate themselves only during nonwork hours. Finally, Gans could go no further than "quasi-primary" in characterizing urban social relationships, relationships that some would label "pseudo-primary."

AN URBAN CRISIS

The contemporary urban crisis in America has so many faces that it is misleading to speak of *the* urban crisis. Modern urban society provides a variety of crises; its assorted ills include air pollution, noise pollution, water pollution, transportation paralysis, crime, high cost of living, and physical deterioration. A crisis of considerable interest to sociologists is the one associated with the massive concentration of the poor—particularly Blacks—in inner-city slums.

Suburbanization and urban slums

Color the inner city black. Metropolitan growth has been a major trend in recent American history; three-fourths of all Americans now live in cities with a population in excess of 50,000. This growth has been made possible through suburbanization, a process that permits people to be near their place of work and yet allows them to escape the inner city for the fresh air, grass, and private homes available in outlying areas. But, of course, all people cannot afford to vacate the central city for suburban life. When suburbanization began to be noticeable in the 1930s, only the upper and middle classes could bear the cost. It was not until the 1950s that they were joined by the working class. While suburbanites may belong to different social classes, they share the same skin color—white. Only about 5 percent of those persons living outside the central city are nonwhite.

Although nearly all of the white metropolitan population growth since

1950 has taken place in suburbs, black urban population growth has been confined overwhelmingly to central cities. The percentage of non-Whites in central cities has more than doubled since 1950, while the increase among Whites has been below 5 percent. At present there is no sign of a slackening in this differential growth rate of the inner-city population. In fact, in every metropolitan area outside the South the number of black men and women between 15 and 24 years of age doubled between 1960 and 1970.

The concentration of any race or ethnic minority in a given area does not necessarily mean that slums will develop. Slums have appeared in black ghettos partly because the residents are poor and lack the educational and employment opportunities to change their conditions. In addition, even those Blacks who can afford suburban living face housing discrimination that persists in spite of recent federal legislation prohibiting it. Because of inferior education and discrimination in housing and employment, the movement of Blacks out of inner-city slums has been infinitely slower than it was for white minorities. Names can be changed and nationalities can be denied, but skin color is indelible. Even with a reduction in employment and housing discrimination, the foreseeable future of urban Blacks includes living in the central city and within ghettos.

Consequences of suburbanization

The creation and persistence of inner-city slums are only partly due to the socioeconomic characteristics of their residents. Actually, their socioeconomic characteristics are intertwined in a much larger picture, of which residential, educational, and employment discrimination are only a part. As the poor, unskilled, and uneducated migrate into the city, they are figuratively passed in the outbound lanes by members of the middle class and by manufacturers and retailers who are headed for the suburbs. It is there that commerce and industry find lower tax rates, less expensive land, less congestion, and many of their customers who have already left the central city. Accompanying the exodus of the middle-class residents, manufacturers, and retailers is the shrinking of the central city tax base. Their tax allegiance shifts to the more affluent suburban areas.

Yet services must continue for those remaining in the central city. Further, heavy migration into the central city has increased the demand for services; yet many of those requiring municipal services such as education, sanitation, police and fire protection, and public transportation are in no financial position to support their costs. Without adequate funding, these services continue to deteriorate along with the physical facilities in the central city. If city government attempts to rally by raising taxes, it runs the risk of driving even more of its tax base to the suburbs. If nothing is done about the decay of physical facilities and services, those who can afford it will escape the mess, taking their tax and consumer dollars with them. And, all the while, those who have already left the city for suburban living continue to commute to work, using public transportation, streets, and sidewalks without compensating tax support.

This, then, is the dilemma of the central city—diminishing public revenues are not sufficient to cope with the influx of the poor, unskilled, and uneducated who have difficulty in supporting themselves, let alone contributing to the financial health of the inner city. Poor inner-city residents—mostly black—face consequences of this urban dilemma in addition to the deterioration of physical surroundings and public services.

Consequences of the central-city dilemma

Poor rural Blacks come to the city primarily to improve their economic situation. In fact, they probably are better off in this respect in the city. But relatively few of them or their children experience integration into the social and economic "good life" of middle-class American society. Poor inner-city black children are handicapped by inferior education (facilities and teachers) and the dropout rate among them is considerably higher than among Whites. Like that of their parents, their unemployment rate is going to be at least twice as high as it is for urban Whites during prosperous times and will skyrocket when the economy falters. Those who are employed generally must take dead-end, low-paying jobs because more desirable jobs go to the better educated. As pointed out in Chapter 6, not only are Blacks in general at an occupational and income disadvantage compared to Whites, the income and occupational status disparity increases with educational level. If anything, this situation is worse when inner-city Blacks are compared with Whites.

A catalogue of social ills flows from this socioeconomic condition in the inner city. Blacks in big-city slums exist in a social structure involving poverty, congestion, prostitution, drug addiction, broken homes, and brutality.

Until the riots of the 1960s, Whites in America were either unaware of or unconcerned about the plight of inner-city Blacks. The civil disorder and violence directed by Blacks against symbols of the white Establishment raised public awareness of ghetto life. Many Whites whose consciences were not touched did become concerned for economic or safety reasons. The Kerner Commission, established to study the civil disorders of the 1960s, expressed fear that America was becoming two societies—the largely black poor in the central cities and the affluent Whites in the outer cities and suburbs.[5] The potential for either renewed violence or deadening apathy in such a polarized society is all too easily imagined.

OVERVIEW AND PREVIEW

Community structure is an interrelated set of social relationships that fulfill on a daily basis the major social and economic needs of the population living within a delimited geographic area. Obviously, community structure has a social dimension—social relationships—and some physical dimensions—population and delimited geographic area. This chapter focused on the social dimension of community structure, featuring the concept of urbanism.

Despite a long-standing antiurban bias, the process of urbanization has proceeded so far in highly industrialized societies that the distinction between a rural and an urban way of life has lost most of its validity. While the social structures associated with major cities are not identical to those found in smaller communities, the sociocultural impact of the urban sector on rural areas is tremendous.

The Chicago School, through its representative, Louis Wirth, depicted a distinctively urban way of life called urbanism. Using three central physical characteristics—population size, density, and heterogeneity—Wirth's theory proposed a basic difference in social relationships between rural and urban areas. In urban areas social relationships among all people were said to become impersonal and temporary. The 1950s saw a challenge to the Chicago School's negative view of urban social structure. Differentiating among the inner city, outer city, and suburbs, Herbert Gans argued that considerable social structural diversity exists in urban areas. Gans also attributed different ways of city life to social factors (stage in the life cycle and social class) rather than to the ecological forces of population size, density, and heterogeneity.

An important "urban crisis" is the concentration of the poor in the inner city. Because those who can afford it have fled to the suburbs, and because those who can afford it are predominantly white, the inner city is heavily populated by poor non-Whites. The inner-city poor cannot afford to move to the suburbs; moreover, they cannot adequately support city services and facilities. Consequently, such services and facilities deteriorate because economically able persons and organizations have shifted their tax and consumer dollars to suburban areas. These facts create a central-city dilemma—public monies are not sufficient to handle the poor, unskilled, and uneducated who come to the city for its alleged economic benefits. Without adequate schools or job-training programs, the urban poor face unemployment at worst and dead-end, low-paying jobs at best. A host of social problems flows from the socioeconomic condition of the inner city.

The long-range position of the federal government on urban problems remains to be seen. In the short run, governmental money and effort promise to be less than they were during the 1960s.

A more clearly definable type of social structure—formal organization—is explored in the next two chapters. The next chapter opens with the idea that industrialized societies cannot survive without formal organizational structures. Most of the chapter is devoted to the main characteristics of formal organizational structures, known as bureaucracies.

REFERENCES

1. This suggestion, as well as some other ideas contained in this introductory section, may be found in Leo F. Schnore, "Community," in Neil J. Smelser, ed., *Sociology* (New York: Wiley, 1967), pp. 84–96.
2. For an interesting study of small-town ambivalence toward the city, see Arthur J. Vidich and Joseph Bensman, *Small Town in Mass Society* (Garden City, N.Y.: Doubleday, 1960).
3. Louis Wirth, "Urbanism as a Way of Life," *American Journal of Sociology*, 44 (July 1938), 1–24.
4. Herbert J. Gans, "Urbanism and Suburbanism as Ways of Life: A Re-evaluation of Definitions," in Arnold M. Rose, ed., *Human Behavior and Social Processes* (Boston: Houghton Mifflin, 1962), pp. 625–648.
5. *Report of the National Advisory Commission on Civil Disorders* (New York: Bantam, 1968), pp. 21–22.

ADDITIONAL SOURCES AND READINGS

Banfield, Edward C. *The Unheavenly City: The Nature and Future of Our Urban Crisis* (Boston: Little, Brown, 1968).

Bernard, Jesse. *The Sociology of Community* (Glenview, Ill.: Scott, Foresman, 1973).

Breese, Gerald, ed. *Urbanization in Newly Developing Countries* (Englewood Cliffs, N.J.: Prentice-Hall, 1966).

Feagin, Joe R., ed. *The Urban Scene: Myths and Realities* (New York: Random House, 1973).

Gist, Noel P., and Sylvia F. Fava. *Urban Society*, 5th ed. (New York: T. Y. Crowell, 1964).

Liebow, Elliot. *Tally's Corner: A Study of Negro Streetcorner Men* (Boston: Little, Brown, 1967).

Sennett, Richard, ed. *Essay on the Culture of Cities* (New York: Appleton, 1969).

Stein, Maurice R. *The Eclipse of Community* (Princeton, N.J.: Princeton University Press, 1960).

Suttles, Gerald D. *The Social Order of the Slum* (Chicago: University of Chicago Press, 1968).

Thomlinson, Ralph. *Urban Structure: The Social and Spatial Character of Cities* (New York: Random House, 1968).

Tönnies, Ferdinand. *Community and Society (Gemeinschaft and Gesellschaft),* Charles P. Loomis, ed. and trans. (East Lansing: Michigan State University Press, 1957).

Walton, John, and Donald E. Carns, eds. *Cities in Change: Studies on the Urban Condition* (Boston: Allyn & Bacon, 1973).

Warren, Roland L. *The Community in America*, 2nd ed. (Skokie, Ill.: Rand McNally, 1972).

[9]

Formal Organizational Structure

The Circumlocution Office was (as every body knows without being told) the most important Department under government. No public business of any kind could possibly be done at any time, without the acquiescence of the Circumlocution Office. Its finger was in the largest public pie, and in the smallest public tart. It was equally impossible to do the plainest right and to undo the plainest wrong, without the express authority of the Circumlocution Office. If another Gunpowder Plot had been discovered half an hour before the lighting of the match, nobody would have been justified in saving the Parliament until there had been half a score of boards, half a bushel of minutes, several sacks of official memoranda, and a family-vaultful of ungrammatical correspondence, on the part of the Circumlocution Office.

Charles Dickens, **Little Dorrit** (New York: Dutton, 1963), p. 103.

Substitute "The Registrar's Office" for "The Circumlocution Office" and Charles Dickens' scathing indictment of governmental bureaucracy will become quite personalized. Dickens' sharp pen, directed at bureaucratic organizations as early as 1857, shows that recognition of the ill effects of this type of formal organization is not an insight reserved for contemporary social critics. Even Max Weber, the German sociologist responsible for the early formulation of the bureaucratic model as an ideal type, expressed fear that bureaucracy would breed excessive conservatism among persons within such organizations. Neither Dickens nor Weber needs to file a retraction from the Beyond. And yet the bureaucratic form of organization—the predominant model in industrial and postindustrial societies—should not be dismissed because of its well-known disadvantages or criticized without knowledge of its not-so-well-known merits. It is toward an increased understanding of formal organization that this chapter is directed.

THE ORGANIZATIONAL DILEMMA OF MODERN SOCIETY

"Organizational revolution" and "organizational society" are pat phrases offered by radicals and conservatives alike to describe modern society. Radicals rail against the bureaucracy or the Establishment, claiming it to be the locus of decision making that dictates the fate of an essentially powerless and apathetic public. Conservatives deplore the encroachment of the governmental bureaucracy on the free enterprise system. Although certainly at odds about what "ails" our society, the thinking of both conservatives and radicals converges on this point: Organizations in modern society are too numerous and too large. In fact, the term organizational revolution refers to the quantum jump from small to vast organizational structures; organizational society describes a social system that, as presently constituted, depends on a pervasive organizational network for its maintenance and survival at an acceptable level of economic and social development. For example, in the absence of careful economic and social planning, a dismantling of the automobile manufacturing complex would have a number of interacting reverberations. The thousands of automobile workers would become unemployed, which alone would significantly raise the national unemployment rate. An unbelievable number of small auto-allied companies, which feed the automobile manufacturing monolith with everything from brake drums to Pitman arms, would go out of business, increasing still further the unemployment rate. General chaos would occur in the larger sectors of the economy that are geared to automobiles and trucks as forms of transportation. Chaos would also ensue in such businesses as motels and hotels, service stations, and vacation facilities. While a big industry like automobile manufacturing contributes to the *economic* well-being of our capitalistic society, it also inadvertently promotes the general *social* well-being through the provision of employment and the creation of tax dollars for a myriad of governmental welfare programs. At the same time, this industrial behemoth leaves in its wake such deleterious side effects as air and water pollution—as well as injuries and deaths caused by vehicles that are inadequately designed for safe operation at the high speeds for which they are deliberately geared.

Therein lies the organizational dilemma: Although essential for the achievement and maintenance of an affluent society, large organizational complexes also create undesirable side effects. Since it is quite unlikely that the positive benefits of the organizational revolution are going to be forfeited, the most that can be done is to combat the negative consequences. And, paradoxically enough, such a fight requires the creation of yet other organizations.

Given the impact and pervasiveness of organizational society, it is necessary to gain some understanding of formal organizations. This chapter has two objectives: first, to differentiate formal organization from other types of social structure; and, second, to examine the key principles of bureaucracy, the currently predominant type of formal organization in modern society.

FORMAL ORGANIZATION AS A
TYPE OF SOCIAL STRUCTURE

When asked to name the organizations to which one belongs, formal organization like Students for a Democratic Society, the National Association for the Advancement of Colored People, the Society for the Preservation and Encouragement of Barber Shop Quartet Singing in America, or the Ku Klux Klan are apt to come to mind. It would hardly seem appropriate to include other social structures like the family, the economic system, or the Sunday afternoon touch-football game. Yet each of these is a socially structured activity. What is distinctive about formal organizations as compared to other social structures?

As you know, sociology is the scientific study of social structure. Sociologists devote much of their research efforts to explaining, understanding, and predicting patterns of social relationships characteristic of humans. Relative stability in patterns of social relationships is possible because human social life is predicated on systems of social positions, norms, and values that provide for regularity and predictability in social interaction. Social structure develops when people interact continuously and regularly in the pursuit of common goals.

Early man evolved a family structure partly because of the need to place exclusive claim on a mate and to establish a home base to which he could expect to return after the day's hunt. Early humans did not call a meeting to discuss and plan designs for family structure. Rather, such structures emerged unconsciously and spontaneously over a long period of time. In contrast, there are social structures that are not the product of spontaneous development but have been deliberately and consciously formed for the achievement of clearly specified goals; it is for this type of social structure that the concept *formal organizational structure* is reserved.

An example will help to clarify the distinction between formal organization and other social structures. In the pre-1960 South, by law Blacks were to occupy only back-of-the-bus seats. This, of course, was just one part of the broader "Jim Crow" pattern of social structure that perpetuated racial segregation. On December 1, 1955, Rosa Parks, a black woman, exhaustedly took a front seat in a Montgomery, Alabama, bus, a seat reserved for Whites only. More importantly, she failed to "know her place" by refusing to relinquish her seat to a white woman who later boarded the bus. The ensuing uproar, during which Rosa Parks was arrested, reveals that not only was a law broken, but an expected social pattern was violated. A part of the social structure of segregation had, at that time and on that bus, momentarily collapsed. An informal committee that existed at the time, composed of black Montgomery ministers, would not let the issue die. This ad hoc committee created an organization—the Montgomery Improvement Association —to push for integration, with the relatively unknown Reverend Martin Luther King, Jr., as its leader. Through bus boycotts and protest marches, the newly formed organization achieved its goal; slightly over one year after the bus incident, the first desegregated buses traveled the streets of Montgomery. Out of the Montgomery Improvement Association grew the Southern Christian Leadership Conference under the direction of Dr. King. Their goal of eradicating segregation was subsequently extended to regional and national arenas.

As the Montgomery events illustrate, when persons have a goal requiring collective effort, they set up a formal organization that has characteristics and processes designed to promote the achievement of that goal. In sum, the differentiation of formal organization from other types of social structure is based on this characteristic of conscious establishment for the achievement of certain specified goals.

BUREAUCRACY AND FORMAL ORGANIZATION

Bureaucracy as a dominant model of formal organization

Gore Vidal rather delicately captured the popular stereotype of bureaucracy and bureaucrats when he wrote "there is something about a bureaucrat that does not like a poem." It has been popular for some time to write off bureaucracies as "people-eating" machines. Because of the negative judgment by the public, some sociologists avoid use of the term bureaucracy altogether. The creation and use of more neutral concepts in social science is laudable. Yet bureaucracy remains a viable organizational form, and while it is a heavily value-laden concept, it nevertheless is the organizational form that is predominant in our society. For that reason, the popular tendency to emotionally reject bureaucracy (often on the basis of inadequate information) should be replaced by an attempt to understand its nature.

The nature of bureaucratic organization

Bureaucratic organization is the type of social structure traditionally applied when persons desire to achieve specific goals in the most rational manner. The ideal characteristics of bureaucracy were first analyzed by Max Weber through an elaboration of its four basic organizing and operating principles.[1] A *bureaucracy* may be defined as a formal organization based on the following principles: (1) hierarchy of authority; (2) division of labor; (3) system of rules and procedures; and (4) universalism.

• HIERARCHY OF AUTHORITY. Application of bureaucratic principles increases effectiveness and efficiency through the coordination of people and their activities that is accomplished via a *hierarchy of authority*. Before pursuing this characteristic of bureaucratic organization, it will be necessary to define two concepts—power and authority.

Power is the capability of a person or group to exert its will on other persons or groups, whether or not they wish to cooperate. The exercise of power can be accomplished in one of several ways. Madison Avenue has perfected the power-wielding technique of *manipulation*. Whatever the biological pleasures attendant on cigarette smoking, they are alloyed with overtones of masculinity, feminine independence, love, and sexual prowess. We know enough about the Mafia to recognize the degree to which it has developed techniques of *coercion*. One's knowledge or *expertise* is often a basis for controlling the behavior of others. Bureaucratic organizations have a mechanism for exercising power within the organization that structures social relationships in an infinitely more stable and predictable fashion than could be accomplished by relying primarily on manipulation, coercion, or expertise. Although suffused with actual relationships based on manipulation, coercion, or expertise, as will be apparent in a subsequent discussion of informal organization, power relations in bureaucratic organizations are primarily grounded in legitimate power or authority. *Authority* is power attached to a social position that is considered legitimate by persons subjected to it. The statement "authority always rests with those to whom it applies" means that persons in a social system comply with directives from above because they feel it is the proper and just way to behave.

The concept of authority can be illustrated by the following example. Does a ship's captain maintain his authority when a mutiny occurs on his ship while at sea? If authority actually is granted to superiors by subordinates, then, by definition, a ship's captain is stripped of his authority when his crew ceases to recognize as legitimate his right to control their behavior. However, this is true only so long as the ship remains at sea under the control of the mutineers. Once the ship reenters the larger society where the captain's right to issue orders is still honored, the crew is subject to whatever punishment that society deems just. It is important, then, to realize that authority exists by virtue of group consent. However, in order to determine if authority actually exists in a social unit, it is necessary to specify the boundaries of the social unit. In the case of the ship's captain, the larger society, through law, grants him the right to control his crew. Of course, should crew members be able to convince a court-martial of the captain's incompetency, their act of denying authority would be vindicated. Normally, the initiation of such proceedings is like spitting against a cold, hard wind, precisely because authority already has been granted by the larger society as evidenced by its encasement in law.

The definition of authority as power resting on social recognition of its legitimacy has just been discussed. Authority as power attached to a social position also requires comment in order to understand how control is exercised in bureaucratic organizations. There is in fact not one pure type of authority but three: legal authority, traditional authority, and charismatic authority.[2]

In bureaucratic organizations, *legal authority* is attached to the position regardless of the particular person occupying it at any given time. Presidential authority, for example, does not vary from incumbent to incumbent, except as it is altered by law or public consent.

Particularly in nonbureaucratic organizations, and at times in bureaucratic ones, obedience is granted to superordinates by subordinates on traditional or charismatic grounds. In the case of *traditional authority*, compliance is based on personal loyalty to a superordinate. To illustrate, in Japan, employment with a company is considered to be a lifelong commitment. In this paternalistic system, a Japanese employee is supposed to feel a deep personal allegiance to his employer. Charismatic authority is similarly exemplified by commitment to a person rather than to a position but in a more intense way. Traditional authority is based on acquiescence to the person occupying the traditionally approved position of authority. In the case of *charismatic authority*, no legal or traditional position exists, but rather obedience is given to another person as a result of his magnetic personal characteristics or the trust he elicits. Hitler and Jesus are excellent illustrations of authority granted on a charismatic basis.

There are at least two qualifications to this analysis of legal, traditional, and charismatic authority. First, any concrete instance is likely to exhibit a mixture of these types of authority, although one of the three will normally be the dominant source of compliance. Second, in each of the three types of authority there are boundaries on the obedience given. Even a charismatic leader cannot control all aspects of his followers' lives. And in bureaucratic organizations compliance is expected only for those areas of behavior related to one's formal position.

Figure 9.1 is an abbreviated bureaucratic organization chart, representing a hypothetical oil refinery. Bureaucratic organizations tend to assume a pyramidal shape because of the nature of authority distribution. Authority is distributed in decreasing amounts from the top down. Decisions are made by a relatively few persons at higher organizational levels and passed down to the much larger number of employees who perform the functions required to translate a decision from abstraction to reality.

That the organizational hierarchy is composed of many strata of authority is apparent in Figure 9.1. Except for the members of the board of directors at the summit and the production workers at the bottom, each position holder is subject to control from above and at the same time exercises control over the occupants of some positions below him.

This hierarchy of authority constitutes one of the basic organizing principles of bureaucracy. A second principle is that of the division of labor.

• DIVISION OF LABOR. A basic process derived from the Industrial Revolution, the *division of labor* can be defined as a breaking up of total production or service operations into their component parts. Specialization is the key principle in the division of labor. Component parts of a total operation are delegated to various organizational divisions. These component parts are further divided and assigned as specialized work tasks to individuals or groups. From this process emerges a functionally integrated system of occupational positions.

The fundamental division of labor underlying the organizational structure is that of the authority hierarchy (composed of those positions connected by solid lines in Figure 9.1) and is known as the *line organization*. While the line organization is the most obvious product of the division of labor, it is not the only one. In addition to the line organization, which is based on authority, there is the *functional organization*, which is based on the type of work performed.

Functional organization and line organization are closely intertwined, the main difference being that the line organization is seen from a vertical view while the functional organization is best understood from a horizontal perspective. When examining the organizational structure from a line viewpoint the question is: Who has the right to control whom? The salient question for determining the functional aspect of organizational structure is: Who does what?

It is important to view an organization from both line and functional perspectives. When a difference of opinion (for example, a disagreement as to which of several departments deserves priority with respect to its requests) cannot be settled in terms of authority levels (line perspective),

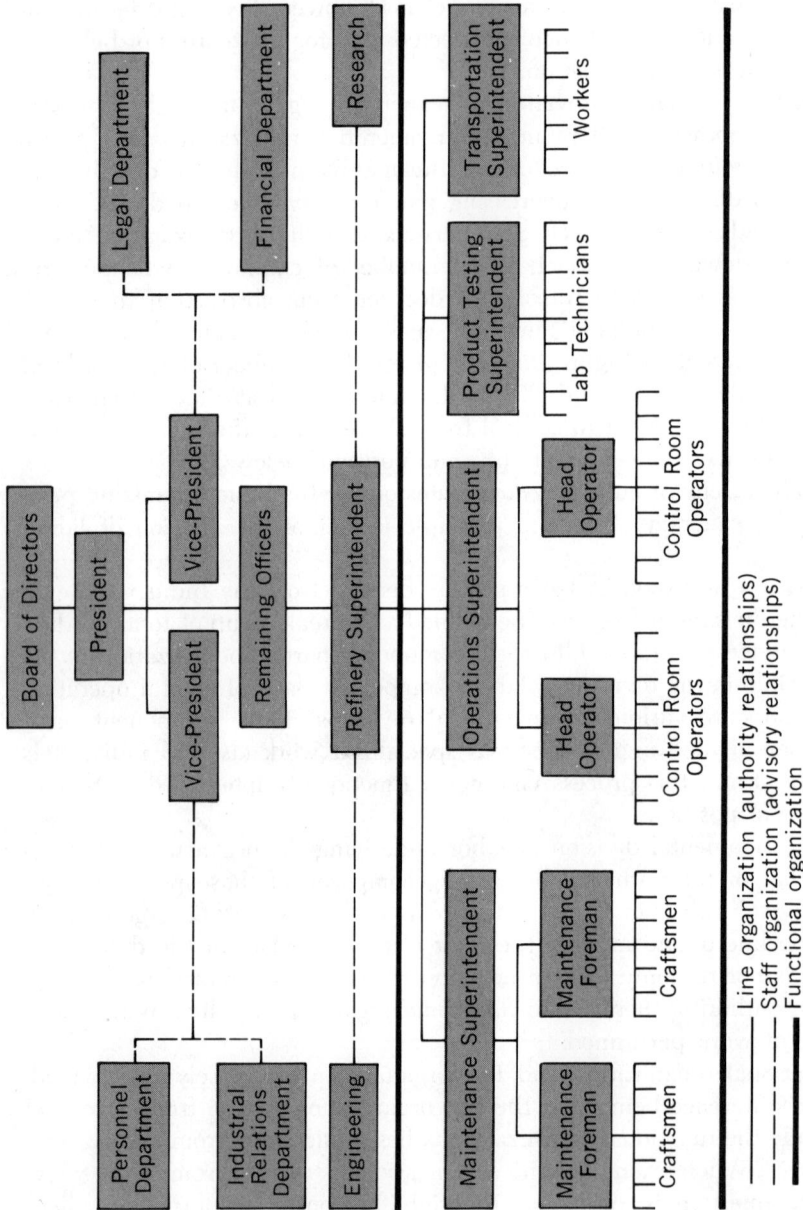

Figure 9.1 Line, staff, and functional organization of a hypothetical oil refinery (abbreviated form)

conflict is likely to arise within an organization. To illustrate, in Figure 9.1 the functional organization is represented by the four departments within the two heavy black lines—Maintenance, Operations, Product Testing, and Transportation. These are functional departments performing quite different tasks. Yet the fact that they are at the same level in the organization's authority structure can lead to difficulties. There is considerable danger of fire or explosion in an oil refining plant. Such an incident can be very costly in both human and financial terms. While one of the functions of the Maintenance Department is to arrest a fire, it is the Operations Department that can prevent such a fire by being alert to warning signals in the control rooms. Further, since the Operations Department stands in the closest relationship to the processing of crude oil and its derivatives, there is a tendency for management to favor it; operators, who are considered semiskilled workers, may be paid at a slightly higher hourly rate than the skilled maintenance craftsmen. If the Operations Department in this hypothetical refinery were at a higher position in the line organization, the inequity would be more justifiable and more easily accepted by the Maintenance Department. Because the two departments are at the same line organizational level, this pay inequality would be extremely difficult to explain to company maintenance employees, and as a result, interpersonal hostility could arise between maintenance craftsmen and control room operators.

The final aspect of bureaucratic structure created by the division of labor is the *staff organization*, which is based on expertise gained through specialized and technical training.[3] Staff personnel are of two broad types, those directly involved in production and those without a direct input in production. For example, when an automobile manufacturing firm decides to produce a new-model car to compete in a developing market, its executives must consult with designers and engineers regarding the feasibility and cost of alternative models. In other words, such members of the staff organization are directly involved in production. Staff with no direct relationship to production are illustrated by personnel in financial, actuarial research, and legal departments, who are consulted by insurance executives when considering, for example, a reduction in premium rates for nondrinking drivers. Theoretically, neither of these types of staff personnel have a place of authority within the line organization. They are supposed to function in a purely advisory capacity. In practice, they may occupy a formal position with limited authority in the line organization, or they may exercise authority informally because of their special personal qualities or technical competencies.

• SYSTEM OF RULES AND PROCEDURES. The division of labor involves the assignment of specific work tasks to organizational divisions and persons, with the hierarchy of authority drawing the lines of control. The third facet of bureaucracy is a *system of rules and procedures* that prescribes and proscribes the manner in which organizational members perform the various facets of their jobs. Rules and procedures cover a good deal more than, for

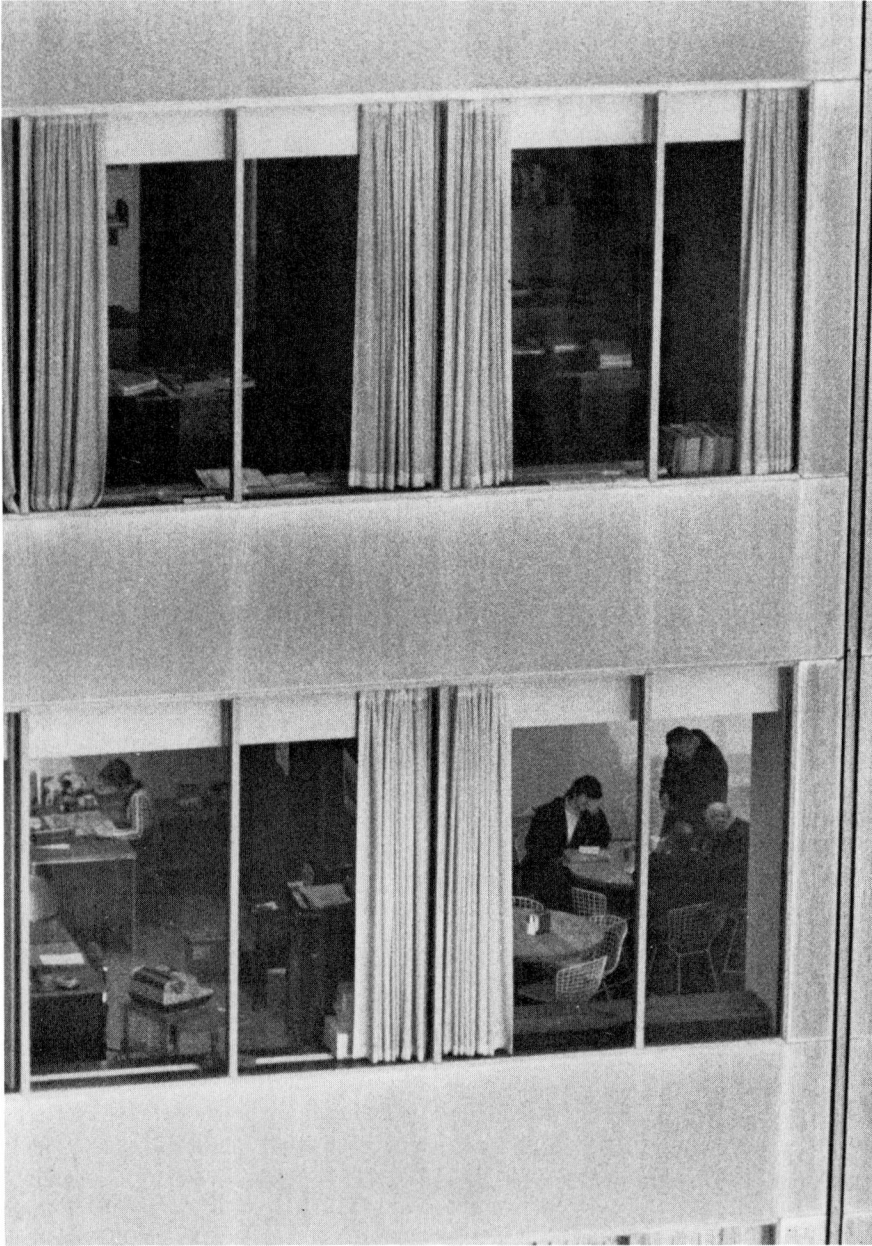

Beckwith Studios

example, the responsibility of a group of operators for the boiler room functions of an oil refinery, the duty of a clerk in an insurance company to process the premium payments of customers whose last names start with the letters A through H, or the duty of a department manager to report to the general manager. In addition, if a bureaucratic organization is to be effectively coordinated, activity must be disciplined. A decision, although rational from one person's vantage point, in reality may be quite the contrary from an overall organizational viewpoint. For example, a supervisor may decide that her clerical staff has higher morale when permitted to work at their own pace. The difficulty arises if these employees, because of their slower work pace, fail to process the amount of data regularly required by the computer. As a result, the office work groups to which the computer output is delivered the next morning do not have sufficient data to perform their duties. It is easy to imagine the ensuing chaos if many such out-of-phase decisions were made.

• UNIVERSALISM. Universalism, the final basic characteristic of bureaucracy, pervades all aspects of the organization. *Universalism* refers to an impersonal attitude toward, and treatment of, another person. Internal and external organizational transactions are supposed to be conducted without regard to any special relationship that exists between interacting persons. Nepotism—favoritism toward one's relatives because they are relatives—is one example of particularism, the opposite of universalism. There is always the danger in a bureaucracy that a person in a decision-making position will promote or hire a relative or friend without regard to the latter's qualifications or without realizing the superiority of other candidates for the position. This natural tendency toward organizational actions based on personal relationships is taken as sufficient reason for the removal of such temptations. Impersonal or universalistic treatment is supposed to apply to internal organizational relationships such as promotion and qualification for a position, as well as to relationships with clients or customers. The intended advantage of the norm of universalism is equitable treatment for all concerned.

Bureaucracy as an ideal type

Although Weber was well aware of variation, inconsistency, and irrationality within bureaucratic organizations, he used the ideal type method of analysis in order to formulate a generalized description of bureaucracy. The *ideal type method* involves constructing a model by abstracting the most characteristic elements of a social structure under observation. While determination of these typical elements is based on the observation of concrete cases, the ideal typical model itself is not meant to match any particular instance.

In the *ideal* sense, then, formal organizations of a bureaucratic type are based on the four principles just outlined: hierarchy of authority; division of labor; system of rules and procedures; and universalism. This does not mean that a specific bureaucratic organization will put any or all of these principles into effect to a maximum degree. The actual nature of any particular bureaucratic organization is conditioned by complicating factors. That is, some bureaucracies personify these operating principles; for others, the existence of certain pressures may attentuate them. For example, universities, because they employ a large number of professionals who demand autonomy and independence, are considerably less bureaucratic than are factories or offices.

For practical purposes, most formal organizations in economically advanced societies can be placed on a continuum ranging from highly bureaucratic to scarcely bureaucratic. Most formal organizations do not operate strictly according to the principles just outlined. The more closely that their actual operations are geared to these principles, the more bureaucratic they are considered to be.

Negative consequences of bureaucracy

These bureaucratic principles were found attractive at the outset of the Industrial Revolution because they represented a rational solution to problems of organization. Organizational behavior guided by logic and consistency was considered more effective than other organizational methods that were rampant with nepotism, subjugation, cruelty, arbitrariness, and purely personal judgments. Actually, while the attempt to be rational through bureaucratization generally has been a good thing, it has often been carried to a fault. An organizational member may lose the ability to alter his attitudes and behavior when conditions change; this lack of flexibility may affect his capacity effectively to carry out the role prescriptions attached to his formal organizational position. The narrowness of vision and inability to change with the times that is based on training and experience is known as *trained incapacity.*[4]

Let me offer an illustration based on personal experience. At one point during my graduate training in sociology, the federal government was giving me financial support. With a child on the way, it seemed necessary to earn some additional money. The chairman of the sociology department consented to let me teach one course, providing the university administration agreed that the rules would permit receiving money from the federal government and the university at the same time. Upon posing this question to the appropriate university official, I watched a perplexed bureaucrat fumble through the code of regulations for a pat answer, which simply would not present itself. After minutes of obvious discomfort—stemming from his inability to find a rule to support the refusal he seemed bent on issuing—he found what he was looking for. With the relief of a winner at Russian roulette, this man said excitedly, "Here it is!" While the regulation actually could have been interpreted as permitting the earning of additional income by a recipient of a federal research grant, this administrator chose the interpretation that bolstered his original inclination to deny permission. I later learned that former policy had prohibited persons receiving federal money from obtaining additional financial support from the university. This bureaucrat had become so accustomed to this old way of doing things that he could not interpret the new ruling in any way other than as supporting the viewpoint that had become so indelibly his own. By past training and experience he had developed an incapacity to meet the new organizational realities.

Another illustration of the application of bureaucratic principles gone awry is that of *goal displacement*, which exists when organizational means are elevated to ends in themselves.[5] For example, members of a social welfare organization sometimes become more concerned with eligibility requirements than with service to their clients; the original organizational goal of service to those with low income may be displaced by concern with rules, which were actually intended to be merely a *means* to such service.

OVERVIEW AND PREVIEW

Formal organizations have an important characteristic that distinguishes them from other social structures. Whereas other social structures emerge spontaneously over a period of time, formal organizational structures are the product of a conscious set of decisions designed to coordinate efforts toward the achievement of stated goals. It is in this sense that they are formal social structures.

While it is not the only possible organizational model, modern formal organizational structures tend to be cast in a bureaucratic mold. As such, these social structures take their character from four basic organizing principles: hierarchy of authority; division of labor; system of rules and procedures; and universalism. Since organizing principles represent an ideal type, actual formal organizations based on them may be placed on a continuum from personification to extreme dilution.

It is easy to gain the impression today—particularly on college campuses and health food farms—that bureaucracy is a concept so repugnant as to disqualify it from all Password and Scrabble games. While some may make bureaucracy an Orwellian nonword, they cannot make the reality disappear. Because formal organizational structures seem necessary for the achievement and continuity of life at a high level of economic and social well-being, the current detractors of bureaucracy are not about to make it completely disappear in the near future. With its persistence, an organizational dilemma is maintained—formal organizations, which contribute to the good life for some and make possible any life at all for others, simultaneously create undesirable side effects. Because of these negative consequences, it must be concluded that the critics of bureaucracy are not without justification. Trained incapacity and goal displacement are but two of the negative repercussions of this type of formal organizational structure. Some additional ones are pursued in the next chapter.

Trained incapacity and goal displacement—two observable negative side effects of formal organizational structures predicated on the bureaucratic model—are clearly on a more person-to-person level than are the other aspects of formal organization covered in this chapter. In fact, they provide a transition from the structural to the social-psychological perspective. The next chapter, "Social Psychology of Formal Organizational Structure," is a continuation of concern with formal organizational structure but from the social-psychological perspective. The emphasis in Chapter 10 is on the conflict between man and bureaucracy.

Chapter 10 opens with an examination of the changing images of the nature of man as related to organizational life. An extremely important reason why bureaucracies do not operate according to their blueprint is the presence of informal organizational structures within the formal structure, a force that has implications both for groups and for the formal structure itself. The potential clash between human personality needs and the needs of the formal organizational structure is also pursued, along with some possible solutions to the conflict. The chapter ends with an examination of alternatives to the bureaucratic model of formal organizational structure, for there are those who believe that the bureaucratic pattern is on the way out.

REFERENCES

1. H. H. Gerth and C. Wright Mills, eds. and trans., *From Max Weber* (New York: Oxford University Press, 1958), pp. 196–204. Although Weber described more than four characteristics of bureaucracy, these four capture its essential nature.
2. These three types of authority were also elaborated by Weber. See A. M. Henderson and Talcott Parsons, eds. and trans., *The Theory of Social and Economic Organization* (New York: Free Press, 1957), pp. 328ff.

3. The distinction between functional organization and staff organization is made in Delbert C. Miller and William H. Form, *Industrial Sociology*, 2nd ed. (New York: Harper & Row, 1964), pp. 125–129.
4. This term was derived from Thorstein Veblen, *The Engineers and the Price System* (New York: Viking, 1933).
5. David L. Sills, *The Volunteers* (New York: Free Press, 1957), pp. 62–77.

ADDITIONAL SOURCES AND READINGS

Blau, Peter M., and W. Richard Scott. *Formal Organizations: A Comparative Approach* (San Francisco: Chandler, 1962).

Caplow, Theodore. *Principles of Organization* (New York: Harcourt Brace Jovanovich, 1964).

Downs, Anthony. *Inside Bureaucracy* (Boston: Little, Brown, 1967).

Etzioni, Amitai. *A Comparative Analysis of Complex Organizations* (New York: Free Press, 1961).

Etzioni, Amitai, ed. *A Sociological Reader in Complex Organizations*, 2nd ed. (New York: Holt, Rinehart and Winston, 1969).

Grusky, Oscar, and George A. Miller, eds. *The Sociology Of Organizations: Basic Studies* (New York: Free Press, 1970).

Hall, Richard H. *Organizations: Structure and Process* (Englewood Cliffs, N.J.: Prentice-Hall, 1972).

March, James G., and Herbert A. Simon. *Organizations* (New York: Wiley, 1958).

March, James G., ed. *Handbook of Organizations* (Skokie, Ill.: Rand McNally, 1965).

Perrow, Charles. *Complex Organizations: A Critical Essay* (Glenview, Ill.: Scott, Foresman, 1972).

Peter, Lawrence F., and Raymond Hull. *The Peter Principle* (New York: Morrow, 1969).

part IV

SOCIAL STRUCTURE: SOCIAL-PSYCHOLOGICAL ASPECTS

{10}

Social Psychology of Formal Organizational Structure

The drill sergeant came into the barracks at six in the morning and shouted, "Wakey, wakey, everyone! It's a glorious morning and you're all invited out on the veranda to join me for exercises."

"Say Sarge," one of the privates said, "I'm tired. Do you mind if I sleep this morning?"

"Why not, Wozinski? It's your Army. Could you meet us at the rifle range when you're in the mood?"

"I'll try," the private said, "but I'm not making any promises."

"That's a good boy, Wozinski. Now, everybody out on the veranda."

Only half the platoon was dressed. The other half had stayed in their sacks.

The sergeant seemed pleased. "Well, we have more than enough to start with. I have a surprise for you men. We're going to march over to the mess hall together and I'm going to count cadence."

The platoon started catcalling and booing.

"Now, come on, fellows. That's not nice. After all, I'm your drill sergeant. Why don't we try it? If you don't like it, we won't do it again."

The men shrugged their shoulders and started marching toward the mess hall.

"Smith and O'Malley," the sergeant said, "you're out of step."

"Out of step with what?" O'Malley wanted to know.

"The rest of the platoon."

"That's no way to talk to a recruit," Smith said. "We're doing the best we can."

"We've only got two feet," O'Malley shouted.

"I'm sorry," the sergeant said. "Forget I brought it up."

"Okay, but don't forget we're human too," Smith muttered.

Later in the morning the drill sergeant held inspection in the barracks.

"Barstow," he said, "why didn't you make up your bed this morning?"

"I forgot."

"Suppose everyone in the Army forgot, Barstow? Then we'd all be living like pigs."

"Look," said Barstow, "a guy's got a right to make a mistake once in a while. I made it up yesterday morning, didn't I?"

"I suppose you're right, Barstow. Do you want me to make the bed
for you today?"

"Suit yourself, since it bothers you and it doesn't bother me."

Art Buchwald's humor always runs from the sublime to the ridiculous. "The
New Army" depicts democratization—participation by subordinates within
a formal organization—as a waking nightmare of impracticality and in-
efficiency. Is Buchwald right? Is debureaucratization strictly for the funny
papers? There are those who think not. This chapter examines some conditions under which modifications of the ideal type model of bureaucracy
may not only be workable, but necessary.

There are contemporary critics of bureaucracy who contend that the
bureaucratic organizational form was quite well suited to the social and
economic conditions under which it was adopted and developed. However,
they argue, these social and economic conditions have changed, and organizational models and managerial practices adapted to contemporary
realities are necessary. Such criticism regarding the appropriateness of the
bureaucratic model has been heard among scholars from many disciplines.
Elaborating on the often stated observation that bureaucratic organization
breeds conservatism and parochialism, some point out that bureaucratic
organizations stifle the generation and implementation of new ideas. Structural principles like centralized control from the top, use of extrinsic reward (money, power, and prestige) to assure compliance, and emphasis
on accountability on all organizational levels create a psychological and
social climate inappropriate for individual and thus organizational creativity. Other alleged negative consequences of bureaucracy include lack of an
appeal mechanism to mitigate authority, wastage of human resources, and
prevention of personal growth.

One implication of all this is the presence of a conflict between formal
organizational structures and the needs of persons within them. This chapter
is organized around this general theme, a theme that requires a switch from
the structural to the social-psychological perspective.

ORGANIZATIONAL AND PERSONALITY NEEDS

Organziations do not have "needs" in the same way persons do. Yet hierarchy of authority, division of labor, a system of rules and procedures, and universalism may be considered principles that have traditionally been judged as necessary for the achievement of organizational goals in economically developed or developing societies. In a sense, this is tantamount to saying that for effective and efficient goal attainment, organizations *need* to be based on these bureaucratic principles to some degree.

Social scientists contend that certain personality needs clash with these organizational needs. This point of view, while currently in vogue, has not been dominant in the past. Whether or not individual needs and bureaucratic principles are at odds depends on one's view of the nature of man.

Since the turn of the century, beliefs regarding the nature of man have varied. In pursuing the conflict of needs between organizations and individuals, it will be helpful to briefly discuss the several views of human nature that have been influential in the past.

Changing images of man

During the nineteenth century and until the 1910s, the market ideology prevailed.[1] Social Darwinist theory explained that success was not a product of accident but a result of the survival of the fittest. In the *market ideology*, then, life was viewed as a pit of competitiveness, with the superior people rising to the top. In organizational terms, persons at the bottom of the hierarchy of authority were merely fulfilling their destinies; they had gone as far as their abilities would permit. It obviously followed that those on top of the hierarchy were social superiors. And it was only natural and right for social superiors to exercise complete authority over the lower members of the species.

Financial incentive gained early acceptance as the most important motivator of higher productivity. Man, it was assumed, would work harder if such additional labor were rewarded by a greater amount of money. *Scientific management*, which gained influence in the second decade of this century, personified the economic-man assumption. According to this view, man is by nature selfish and competitive. It seemed only logical that money was the single most important motivator of man.

A slight break in the economic-man interpretation occurred during the 1920s. The managerial philosophy now known as *benevolent paternalism* conceded to man some noneconomic dimensions. Organizations began to offer workers a voice, instituting such democratic mechanisms as suggestion boxes. Other activities—for example, company newspapers and athletic teams—also became prominent. However, the economic view of man was largely unquestioned until the mid-1920s, when studies were undertaken at the Hawthorne plant of the Western Electric Company in Chicago.[2]

• "DISCOVERY" OF INFORMAL ORGANIZATIONAL STRUCTURE. The Hawthorne research findings contradicted the idea that man was motivated solely by money and working conditions, and that he existed as an isolated entity within the organization. Prior to these studies, industrial psychologists and industrial engineers had dominated the organizational research scene. They had assumed that variations in worker productivity and job satisfaction were produced by changes in such factors as lighting, temperature, fatigue, and wages. However, early experiments with production workers at the Hawthorne plant failed to find the expected positive relationships between output and, for example, illumination, rest pauses, and wages. Failure to find these expected relationships led the researchers to suspect the existence of some unknown factor that affected productivity.

A clue to the identity of this factor came from an experiment with female workers in the Relay Assembly Test Room. These women, who at the outset exhibited shyness, uneasiness, silence, and suspiciousness, later displayed openness, frankness, and self-assurance. The explanation for this transformation lies in what is now known as the *Hawthorne effect*; that is, because these employees were permitted to participate in decision making pertinent to the experiment, they came to feel important and worthwhile. More importantly in the present context, these women had developed a social structure, that is, an informal organization within the formal organizational structure.

Although sociologists had been aware of informal group relations, it was not until this research that the existence of informal organization was "discovered" and accepted as exerting an influence within the formal organization. This new focus on the nature of social groups and the consequences for formal organization was further pursued in a study of 14 male operators in the Bank Wiring Observation Room. It was discovered from observing these workers that a web of social relationships existed among them. These social relationships were based on cultural norms and were enforced by social sanctions. Norms included prohibitions on excessive production ("rate-busting"), underproduction ("chiseling"), and passing to supervisors information harmful to another worker ("squealing"). Sanctions encouraging conformity to these norms included ridicule, sarcasm, criticism, expressions of hostility, and the delivery of sharp blows to the arm ("binging").

There was also a status structure within the group. Inspectors were at the top of the group status hierarchy while soldermen were on the bottom. Social relationships were influenced by the status structure. For example, it was inappropriate for a solderman to ask a wireman to switch jobs temporarily; job switching was customarily initiated by wiremen.

The Bank Wiring Observation Room study illustrates the development of informal organization within the formal organization. Later studies have clearly indicated this to be a common circumstance. That is, within any formal organization there also exists *informal organization*—patterned personal relationships that have developed spontaneously as a result of social interaction. These personal relationships and the spontaneous manner in which they emerge stand in sharp contrast to the nature of social relationships as defined by the formal organizational blueprint. Given this contrast, how does it happen that these personal and spontaneous social relationships so frequently arise in the impersonal and meticulously programmed environment specified by bureaucratic organizing principles?

• FUNCTIONS OF INFORMAL ORGANIZATION FOR GROUP MEMBERS. Informal organization emerges for two basic reasons. First, it permits personal relationships that are not provided for by the formal organizational blueprint. By the principle of universalism, bureaucratic organizations are deliberately designed to be impersonal. Individual likes, dislikes, animosities, and bonds of affection are considered extraneous to the fulfillment of organizational duties.

Second, informal organization serves as a control or power mechanism for its participants. On the internal side, informal organization curtails deviant behavior among group members. The emergence of norms and rituals has the effect of structuring behavior, and the development of sanctions encourages conformity through the application of punishments and rewards. On the external side, informal organization gives power to group members because they are afforded a measure of protection from outside control, that is, controls stemming from other segments of the formal organization.

The appearance of informal organization in the midst of (and often having goals in opposition to) the formal organizational structure substantiates the existence of conflict between the needs of man and the needs of formal organization. The Hawthorne findings, which refuted the idea that man was motivated solely by money or working conditions, sparked a more optimistic view of man.

• A NEW IMAGE OF MAN. In this more current view, which can be identified in the human relations and human resources philosophies, various personality needs are recognized and given such labels as ego and self-fulfillment needs, ego motive, and need for self-actualization. According to these theories, mature adults desire self-determination, self-initiative, independence, responsibility, and self-integrity. Yet these personality needs, it is argued, are frequently thwarted at work because they clash with the structure of the formal organization; formal organizational structure, based

Thomas Hopker, Woodfin Camp & Associates

on extreme job specialization, strict hierarchy of authority, and close super-vision, is felt to be an environment inimical to the needs of the mature human personality. Work in a bureaucratic organization, the argument goes, permits little individual control over job activities, provides minimal outlet for use of creative abilities, and gives rise to expectations that employees should be passive, dependent, and submissive. What, in turn, is the impact on formal organizational structure?

Implications for formal organizational structure

Because the needs of people are unmet, it is contended, the organization itself suffers; its efficiency is impaired by high turnover rates, excessive ab-senteeism, production restriction, and malingering—the hallmarks of an increasingly apathetic work force. Further, what effect does the existence of informal organization have on the functioning of formal organization? In the case of the Bank Wiring Observation Room, informal organization had negative repercussions for the larger organization, partly because the production rate was systematically suppressed. Studies immediately follow-ing this experiment generally concluded that behavior detrimental to formal organizational goals tends to occur within cohesive work groups.[3] Problems, concerns, and goals of the members of the informal work group were often found to be substituted for the larger organizational goals. But is it gen-erally true that the emergence of informal organization spells trouble for the achievement of organizational goals? Later studies have shown the relationship between work group cohesion and productivity to be more complicated than was earlier supposed.

Some studies concluded that informal organization was not only benefi-cial to but was *necessary* for organizational success.[4] Contributions of in-formal organization to the formal organization include communication channels that are needed to avoid blockages in the formal communication lines, heightened morale, and means for solving difficulties unanticipated by those in control. Yet while cohesiveness contributes to employee morale, it does not necessarily promote increased productivity. The most accurate statement is that high group cohesiveness in informal organization may or may not improve organizational performance.

Harnessing informal organization for formal organizational benefit may depend in part on the group members' perception of their superordinates. One study indicates that if management wants to ensure positive benefits from informal organization, it should create an atmosphere of supportive-ness in regard to employees.[5]

It seems obvious, then, that organizational needs and the current op-timistic view of man as having distinct personality needs are in conflict, with results detrimental to both the organization and the worker. This new view of man has given rise to the human relations and human resources schools of thought, which have attempted to resolve the conflict between man and organization by simultaneously fulfilling mature personality needs and achieving organizational goals. The following discussion centers around these philosophies and the solutions advocated by their proponents.

Solutions to the conflict between man and organization

After the Hawthorne studies it was widely believed that increased worker morale translated into higher productivity. However, numerous later studies have yielded mixed results on this score. While positive relationships between morale and productivity have been found, so have instances of low morale with high productivity and high morale with low productivity. There is, however, strong evidence that the style of leadership plays a crucial role in work-related attitudes and behavior.

• STYLES OF LEADERSHIP. Authoritarian leadership and democratic leadership are the two basic styles of supervision exercised in organizations. Under an *authoritarian style of leadership*, those in charge determine and/or enforce group goals, activities, and rules. The absence of a challenge to the authority structure means that subordinates accept decisions from above—decisions that have been made without consideration of the subordinate group's ideas or opinions. The authoritarian style of leadership is obviously quite consistent with the bureaucratic principle of hierarchy of authority.

In contrast, a *democratic mode of leadership* permits persons affected by a decision to contribute their viewpoints on various aspects of the matter. Discussion, consultation, and group decision making are characteristic of democratic leadership. Prior to the Hawthorne studies, little or no credence was given to the use of democratic leadership in bureaucratic organizations. After all, a democratic style of leadership contradicted the basic bureaucratic principle of hierarchy of authority. But various research has documented the emergence of positive group attitudes and behavior as a result of supervisory consultation with subordinates. Consequently, the democratic pattern has become a reasonable, although by no means the predominant, alternative in the choice of a leadership style.

Employee participation in work-related decisions is seen by the human relations school as one solution to the conflict between organizational objectives and personality needs. Yet, from its inception, accusations were made that the human relations philosophy is used by management to manipulate employees for organizational benefit—that the human relations emphasis on employee participation in decision making is used merely to enhance morale and satisfaction only so that resistance to authority will be lowered. In short, it is said that employee participation is callously used as a means to better performance on the part of the individual worker.

Growing out of the controversy of organizational versus individual needs, a new viewpoint has emerged—that of human resources. Human resources is a theory of democratic management that considers subordinate contributions as valuable in themselves; such contributions are seen as a direct input to *improved* decision making.[6]

Thus, these two schools see the benefits of a democratic style of leadership in different lights. The *human relations* approach considers participation in decision making as a means to improved attitudes on the part of subordinates. Increased morale and job satisfaction, in turn, are said to lead to better employee performance. The *human resources* philosophy contends that inasmuch as mature personality needs are fulfilled by direct participation in decision making, the organization itself benefits from the creative resources of subordinates that are released by a democratic environment. Higher morale and job satisfaction, according to the human resources model, are the result of improved job performance (see Figure 10.1).

Whatever the differences in evaluating the benefits of democratic leadership, the two schools are in agreement that participative or democratic management is a means of simultaneously fulfilling mature personality needs and achieving organizational goals. Thus, participative management is seen as one viable modification of the ideal type bureaucratic model. Another modification deals with the nature of job design.

• JOB DESIGN. Historically the predominant job design philosophy held that job specialization was the best form of work arrangement because it promoted the greatest efficiency and economy. *Job specialization* can be defined as the minute subdivision of work tasks so that any given worker performs only one operation, or a few small operations, in the production process. Advantages of extreme job specialization include the hiring of

HUMAN RELATIONS

Employee participation ⟶ Higher morale ⟶ Improved job
in decision making   and job satisfaction   performance

HUMAN RESOURCES

Employee participation ⟶ Improved job ⟶ Higher morale
in decision making   performance   and job satisfaction

Figure 10.1   Human relations and human resources models of participative management
SOURCE: Adapted from Raymond Miles, "Human Relations or Human Resources? **Harvard Business Review**, 43 (July–August 1965), 152.

cheap labor with minimal qualifications, holding training costs to a minimum, reducing the possibility of errors that result in rejected output, and producing a greater quantity within a shorter time-span.

Minute job specialization, however, is not without its disadvantages. Much of the pertinent research done to date shows that extreme job specialization is associated with negative work attitudes. Studies of work attitudes in mass production settings indicate that lower levels of job satisfaction and higher levels of alienation characterize workers performing small and repetitive tasks.

Several solutions, including increased leisure time, money, and more meaningful work, have been offered to buffer these negative social-psychological consequences. Some authorities contend that proper use of the increased leisure time made possible by advanced technology will achieve the psychological restoration of workers. Aside from the fact that increased leisure time may well prove to be a fiction, it may also be that meaning is derived from either work or leisure separately only when *both* activities are self-fulfilling in their own right. Engagement in alienating work may reduce leisure to the status of a first-aid station for psychological repair. Moreover, when leisure is utilized as an escape from meaningless work, it may be stripped of its regenerative faculty and become as empty as work. Additional income will probably be ineffective since it is not innately satisfying and is used primarily as an instrument in the futile pursuit of a leisure-time solution to the problem of unfulfilling work. Some alteration in work patterns may represent the most meaningful solution to the problem.

Automation is heralded as a form of technology that will return to the worker the meaning in work that mass production seems to preclude. It has recently been argued that automation represents a dramatic change in production technology, since it is characterized by a *less* specialized division of labor and by more responsibility, authority, job control, freedom, and meaning for the worker. Research done in both semiautomated (transfer technology or "Detroit" automation[7]) and automated (continuous-process) work settings reveals improved attitudes toward work among production personnel.[8] This research suggests that alienation and other negative work attitudes are lower among workers in automated settings than among those laboring in traditional mass production systems. Such changes in man's relationship to technology may resuscitate work as an integral part of life for many industrial employees. Although it is a hopeful sign, it may not be enough; the fact remains that the bulk of the labor force is likely to remain in industries that are not affected by automation. Since automated technology may or may not prove to be the worker's ally, other steps must be taken if his work is to become meaningful. One such step is the deliberate alteration of jobs within mechanized production systems. Job enrichment is the form of job alteration that is currently gaining in acceptability.

Job enrichment is a recently coined umbrella-concept embracing both participative management theory and the job design philosophy of job enlargement. *Job enlargement* is the theory of job design based on the idea that employees can be given more meaningful jobs either by assigning them more of the same kinds of tasks or by giving them a larger number of completely different operations out of a total production process. Proponents of job enrichment see job enlargement as inadequate, as failing to fulfill mature personality needs while simultaneously contributing to the achievement of formal organizational goals. According to one of its primary developers, Frederick Herzberg, the principles of job enrichment include removing some controls over employees while increasing their personal accountability; assigning each employee a complete, natural unit of work; increasing job freedom; giving work-related feedback to each employee; periodically introducing employees to new and more complex tasks; and allowing employees to become experts in a designated area. These major principles of job enrichment, along with the alleged contribution of each principle to the mature human personality, are presented in Table 10.1.

Some concrete instances of job enrichment may be helpful. General Motors has experimented with a team approach to the assembly of one of its new expensive motor homes. By tradition, this motor home would be put together on an assembly line, with each worker performing only one or two functions. In this experiment, by contrast, teams of three to six workers are building some coaches from the ground up. Ford and Chrysler are also

TABLE 10.1 Principles of job enrichment and their contribution to the mature human personality

PRINCIPLE	CONTRIBUTION TO PERSONALITY
1. Removing some controls while retaining accountability	Responsibility and personal achievement
2. Increasing the accountability of individuals for own work	Responsibility and recognition
3. Giving a person a complete, natural unit of work (module, division, area, and so on)	Responsibility, achievement, and recognition
4. Granting additional authority to an employee in his activity; job freedom	Responsibility, achievement, and recognition
5. Making periodic reports directly available to the worker himself rather than to the supervisor	Internal recognition
6. Introducing new and more difficult tasks not previously handled	Growth and learning
7. Assigning individuals specific tasks, enabling them to become experts	Responsibility, growth, and advancement

SOURCE: Adapted by permission from Frederick Herzberg, "One More Time: How Do You Motivate Employees?" **Harvard Business Review**, 46 (January–February 1968).

experimenting, although all American automobile plants are, in this respect, lagging behind several European factories, which have already introduced job enrichment programs into their regular manufacturing processes. As another illustration, Indiana Bell Telephone now has one employee assembling an entire directory—a job that used to be done in 21 steps by as many employees. While this latter example may seem trivial, Indiana Bell Telephone cites a reduction in employee turnover as high as 50 percent in some locations as one consequence of their job enrichment program.

In summary, according to the current image of man, there is a conflict between his needs and the structure of formal organization. Participative management and changes in job design are two possible solutions to the conflict that are presently being explored in both theory and practice. Such solutions, of course, modify the ideal type bureaucratic structure. Research findings support the efficacy of these changes. But are these modifications sufficient? Or will the future see more drastic changes?

THE FUTURE OF BUREAUCRACY

Those who see modification or qualification of the bureaucratic model as insufficient predict the complete demise of this type of formal organizational structure.

According to Warren Bennis, for example, two factors will lead to the ultimate destruction of the bureaucratic model.[9] In the first place, there is an increasing demand for a balance between individual goals and organizational objectives. This is essentially a reference to the growing recognition and acceptance of the human relations and human resources philosophies. But this problem of "reciprocity" between individuals and organization, according to Bennis, is not the factor that will succeed in destroying bureaucracy. Rather, Bennis contends, it is the necessity of adaptation in a rapidly changing society that will deliver the *coup de grâce* to bureaucratic organization. In this view, bureaucracy is ideal in a society that is competitive and stable, and for work tasks that are routine and predictable. Organizational flexibility, on the other hand, is required if an organization is to survive under conditions of rapid and continuous change. According to some analysts, the trend toward debureaucratization or flexibility in organization is beyond the control of those in organizational power positions. They locate the source of this trend in the contemporary and future nature of our social and economic institutions.

What are some of the specific conditions, then, that may erode the viability of the bureaucratic model? Among the most prominent are the increasingly high level of education of the population in general, the changing nature of work tasks within organizations, and the tremendous influx of professionals into the ranks of the bureaucratically employed. Professionals, of course, perform relatively nonprogrammed and unpredictable work tasks, precisely the types of work tasks that clash with bureaucratic rigidity. A movement toward a less bureaucratic formal organizational structure may occur as the proportion of professionals in the organization increases.

It is projected that the creation of a highly educated work force will alter the orientation toward work. Education and a predisposition for responsibility and autonomy tend to go hand in hand. As the educational level rises, therefore, the work orientation may encompass a desire and capability for autonomy, responsibility, and participation. A second major condition threatening bureaucracy is the change toward more complex, technical, and nonroutine work. Of course, these two factors are intertwined. As work tasks become more complex and unprogrammed, increasing numbers of highly educated people are needed. At the same time, the existence of a pool of highly educated employees permits organizations to pioneer in sophisticated areas of production and service that would otherwise remain unexplored.

Consensus regarding the future of bureaucracy does not exist. The current majority opinion projects the persistence of the bureaucratic model into the distant future; however, there is a definite parting of the ways on the question of the *degree* of organizational change that will occur as a result of the factors discussed above. Nonetheless, a part of the majority stance clearly emphasizes the necessity of modifying and qualifying the bureaucratic model. And these modifications and qualifications are in an important sense consistent with the ideas of those predicting the demise of bureaucracy. These more conservative analysts agree with Bennis that certain kinds of organizations operate best along nonbureaucratic lines. Research and development firms and advertising agencies are prime examples.

Those envisioning radical organizational change project the emergence of an entirely nonbureaucratic organizational format. Others contend that only segments of bureaucratic organizations will be based on nonbureaucratic principles. According to this view, segments within a bureaucratic organization that perform routine tasks will continue to adhere to the principles of hierarchy of authority, rules and regulations, universalism, and minute division of labor. Within this same organization, units handling nonprogrammable and unpredictable work tasks will minimize bureaucratic principles.

Undoubtedly, complete democracy in the armed forces, as Buchwald humorously depicts, would lead to unimagined absurdities. Subordinate participation in decision-making does have to be tailored to such limiting factors as organizational goals, subordinate capabilities, existing technology, and economic conditions. In short, it can be argued, a variety of organizational models may be necessary, each based on, among other things, the nature of the task to be accomplished. These models are likely to range along a continuum from something closely resembling the ideal type model of bureaucracy to entirely nonbureaucratic organizations. At this early stage of the debate, and lacking the assistance of a crystal ball, no concrete predictions can be made about the ultimate future of bureaucracy.

OVERVIEW AND PREVIEW

There is more to the study of formal organization than its structural side. This chapter focused on some important social-psychological dimensions of the bureaucratic model of formal organization. It is currently believed that bureaucratic organizing and operating principles are in conflict with the nature of man. Although it has not always been so, an optimistic view of the inherent capabilities of man is currently in vogue—it is contended that persons generally prefer, for example, self-determination, self-initiative, independence, and responsibility. Since bureaucracies tend to promote a working atmosphere prohibiting fulfillment of these desires, they carry in their wake negative consequences for both persons and formal organizations. Employee participation in decision making and changes in job design are two possible solutions to this conflict between man and formal organizational structure.

Informal organization—patterned personal relationships that have developed spontaneously from social interaction—emerges within formal organizations for two basic reasons. First, persons desire personal relationships and no provision for them is made in the organizational blueprint. Second, informal organization controls behavior of group members and offers protection from other segments of the formal organization.

The existence of informal organization is not without its consequences for the formal organization. If an atmosphere of subordinate supportiveness is created within the formal organization, the effects of personal relationships may contribute to the achievement of formal organizational goals. In its absence, detrimental side effects may flow from informal organization.

There is disagreement regarding the future of bureaucracy as the dominant formal organizational model in modern society. One camp believes that social and economic change is occurring at a pace too fast to be handled by the bureaucratic form. Bureaucracy with its basic conservatism, they contend, was well suited to earlier times when relative social and economic stability reigned, but in rapidly changing society, bureaucracy is no longer viable. Some specific changes that challenge the bureaucratic model are the rising educational level of work forces in advanced industrial societies, the changing nature of work tasks, and the employment of professionals within formal organizational structures. Another camp stresses the continued existence of the bureaucratic model but with basic modifications. They envision formal organizational structures that have bureaucratic as well as nonbureaucratic segments. Which organizational units will be nonbureaucratic, according to this viewpoint, is contingent on the nature of the work to be done, the abilities of those who do the work, and the technology involved.

The four preceding chapters have dealt with some primary social structures of interest to sociologists—stratification structure, community structure, and formal organizational structure. The present chapter on the social psychology of formal organizational structure has been a transitional one. In the following chapter you will move into the heart of the social-psychological perspective. Its central concepts and theories are socialization, social interaction, and symbolic interactionism. A counterpoint to sociology's traditional accent on the social origins of human nature appears in the form of a discussion of heredity and human nature. Closing the chapter on socialization is a brief treatment of deviance and conformity.

REFERENCES

1. A fuller discussion of managerial philosophies is presented in Richard A. Lester, *Economics of Labor* (New York: Macmillan, 1964), pp. 137–143.
2. In the present context, the Hawthorne studies are intended only to be illustrative of some basic points. Anyone interested in details should see an original report of the research, which appears in F. J. Roethlisberger and William J. Dickson, *Management and the Worker* (Cambridge, Mass.: Harvard University Press, 1939). A much briefer summary may be found in Delbert Miller and William H. Form, *Industrial Sociology*, 2nd ed. (New York: Harper & Row, 1964), pp. 660–667.
3. For example, see Donald Roy, "Efficiency and the 'Fix': Informal Intergroup Relations in a Piecework Machine Shop," *American Journal of Sociology*, 3 (November 1954), 255–266.
4. An illustration may be found in Raymond H. Van Zelst, "Sociometrically Selected Work Teams Increase Production," *Personnel Psychology*, 5 (Autumn 1952), 175–185.
5. Stanley E. Seashore, *Group Cohesiveness in the Industrial Work Group* (Ann Arbor: Survey Research Center, University of Michigan, 1954), especially pp. 97–102.
6. Raymond Miles, "Human Relations or Human Resources?" *Harvard Business Review*, 43 (July–August 1965), 148–157; R. Likert and D. G. Bowers, "Organizational Theory and Human Resource Accounting," *American Psychologist*, 24 (1969), 585–592.
7. William A. Faunce, "Automation and the Automobile Industry: Some Con-

sequences for In-Plant Structure," *American Sociological Review,* 23 (August 1958), 401–407; Floyd C. Mann and L. Richard Hoffman, *Automation and the Worker* (New York: Holt, Rinehart and Winston, 1960); Charles R. Walker, *Toward the Automatic Factory* (New Haven, Conn.: Yale University Press, 1957).

8. Robert Blauner, *Alienation and Freedom* (Chicago: University of Chicago Press, 1964); Jon M. Shepard, *Automation and Alienation: A Study of Office and Factory Workers* (Cambridge, Mass.: MIT Press, 1971).

9. Warren G. Bennis and Philip E. Slater, *The Temporary Society* (New York: Harper & Row, 1968), especially pp. 53–76.

ADDITIONAL SOURCES AND READINGS

Argyris, Chris. *Personality and Organization* (New York: Harper & Row, 1957).

Blau, Peter M. *The Dynamics of Bureaucracy,* rev. ed. (Chicago: University of Chicago Press, 1963).

Ford, Robert N. *Motivation Through the Work Itself* (New York: American Management Association, Inc., 1969).

Haas, J. Eugene, and Thomas E. Drabek. *Complex Organizations: A Sociological Perspective* (New York: Macmillan, 1973).

Herzberg, Frederick. *Work and the Nature of Man* (Cleveland: World Publishing, 1966).

Katz, Daniel, and Robert L. Kahn. *The Social Psychology of Organizations* (New York: Wiley, 1966).

Likert, Rensis. *The Human Organization* (New York: McGraw-Hill, 1967).

McGregor, Douglas. *The Human Side of Enterprise* (New York: McGraw-Hill, 1960).

Sheppard, Harold L., and Neal Q. Herrick. *Where Have All the Robots Gone? Worker Dissatisfaction in the 70s* (New York: Free Press, 1972).

Tannenbaum, Arnold S. *Social Psychology of the Work Organization* (Belmont, Calif.: Wadsworth, 1966).

Work In America: Report of a Special Task Force to the Secretary of Health, Education, and Welfare (Cambridge, Mass.: MIT Press, 1973).

Socialization

Nurses who worked with Mr. A noticed that he seemed to sense the disability by the time a new patient walked from the reception room into his office. Thus challenged, he admitted that he psychically grasps much of the problem, and he completes the diagnosis by listening to the heart, without aid of stethoscope. They asked for an explanation, and he said: "There are thirty-six different frequencies. Each individual operates on three waves at different frequencies, making numerous combinations of magnetic field control. The moment that I see a person, I know on which three life rays he operates. With that knowledge, the rest is easy. I then listen to his heart to get the physical picture. The pattern of the heartbeat tells me precisely where the trouble is located, and then I go to work."

"What in the world are life rays?" I asked.

As patiently as a teacher would try to explain the principle of television to a backward child, he said: "The solar rays give us life, but the position of the planets at the time of birth makes us the individuals that we are. Characteristics and personality occur at conception; individuality occurs at birth. Your individuality is governed by your fixed sign. This establishes your magnetic field, which consists of three different frequencies derived from the Power of Powers. You are thereafter influenced by the vibrations of all the planets of this universe. We are no stronger than our magnetic field. Shortness of breath, irritability, and illness are among the signs that insufficient energy is being distributed. When the depletion of the magnetic field continues, the nerves are partially starved for their fuel or energy, creating spasms or nerve tension through the body. This depletion, unless corrected, can develop into serious ailments. Now do you understand?"

What could I say? We accept without argument the influence of the moon on tides, because scientists tell us it is true. We do not dispute the revolving planets and changing seasons in relation to the sun. We have no reason to doubt that a magnetic electrical field governs planetary action; why then is it too strange that a magnetic electrical field might govern human action as well? After all, the atom with its electrons has the same pattern as the sun and planets in a solar system. Remember the old adage, "As above, so below"? Yet we are inclined to view as "superstition" the idea that the position of the planets and the sun can influence our own personality or affairs.

Reprinted by permission of William Morrow & Company, Inc., from **A Search for the Truth** by Ruth Montgomery. Copyright © 1966, 1967 by Ruth Montgomery.

Throughout history there have been those who have attempted to explain social life in biological terms, believing that one's genes determine one's destiny. If Aristotle and Lombroso were biological determinists, Ruth Montgomery's Mr. A goes them one better by patiently revealing the source of biological programming. He is satisfied that the source of biological, and therefore personality, differences rests with the position of the planets at the time of birth.

While sociologists do not deal with astrology as an explanation for personal or social life, there is currently a revival of interest in the impact of biology on "human nature." Traditionally dominating sociological thought on the nature of man has been the conviction that biological factors may *limit* human options, but they do not *determine* the course of human events. In this view, infants possess the raw material to become human beings, but their promise is fulfilled only through years of physical care and social nurturance. The renewed interest in the place of biological factors in social life is not a new form of genetic determinism; it is more a reaction to mainstream sociology for its nearly total reliance on a social explanation of personality and social structure.

The first part of this chapter will place the concept of socialization within the context of social structure. The second section provides coverage of mainstream sociology's ideas on socialization and human nature, together with a discussion of the biological revival. Closing the chapter is a section on social deviance and conformity.

SOCIAL STRUCTURE, SOCIAL INTERACTION, AND SOCIALIZATION

In Chapter 5 a distinction was made between social structure and social structuring. Social structure is a culturally based set of social relationships whereas social structuring is the dynamic process by which social structures are created. Central to social structuring is social interaction, which occurs when persons mutually influence each other's behavior. Social interaction based on perceptions of role prescriptions is of the most interest to sociologists. The question arises: How do members of a social structure develop perceptions of the ways they are expected to behave toward others within the context of the many social position-sets in which they are participants? Since the content and structure of culture are not part of the biological package, human beings must learn about culture and their parts in social structures through some social process; sociologists call this basic process *socialization*. It is through socialization that persons learn enough to become integrated into various social structures.

If human infants enter the world without a knowledge of culture and social structure, they are also born without an awareness of themselves as distinct beings. Thus, socialization has a second outstanding feature—it is the process through which humans develop a self-concept. This happens in two ways. In the first place, children develop a conception of themselves as persons by interpreting the ways in which they are treated and responded to by others. Although it is never quite this simple, if they are treated as likable by others whose opinion they value, they will feel that they are likable persons. Second, as they grow up, children forge a more fully developed social self by acting out, in play and in games, various social positions. For boys in American society it is not merely idle play when they ride the range all day and want to sleep with their boots on. This is serious business, for it is through playing at masculine social positions that the initial foundation for later, real social performance is laid.

While socialization is particularly crucial for making a human being out of the raw material that is an infant, this process continues throughout life. Just as an eight-year-old Little League third baseman has to learn the rules of a baseball game, the new vice-president, college freshman, and army recruit must learn how to make his way socially. Appropriate values, norms, attitudes, and behaviors must be absorbed whenever a person enters a new social structure; thus the process recurs from the time he plays his first childhood game to the time he enters a home for the elderly or begins living with his children.

Crucial to the process of socialization is social interaction. This is particularly the case in the beginning of life. Interaction between an infant and one or more others must be intensive and prolonged. It must go beyond physical care to include emotional support and mental stimulation. Said another way, man is a social animal. The next section examines the outcome when the social nature of human beings is ignored.

THE SOCIAL NATURE OF MAN

Inadequate socialization

The socialization of man is a mixture of the biological and the sociocultural. Most sociologists take as given the biological nature of human beings and emphasize the importance of social experience in the development of personality and social integration. How can we have confidence in this assumption? How do we know that the planets or some other form of biological programming is not sufficient for human development? The best proof would be an experiment with a control group of normally socialized infants and an experimental group of socially isolated infants. Assuming that these two groups of children were biologically the same, any differences between them at the end of the experimental period could be attributed to sociocultural factors. For obvious reasons, no such evidence exists. There are, however, documented cases of children who have been kept alive physically but deprived socially, emotionally, and mentally. Fortunately, documentation includes changes in these children when placed in an environment designed to socialize them. Case histories of two unrelated girls, fictitiously named Anna and Isabelle, were reported by Kingsley Davis.[1]

• ANNA. Anna was the second illegitimate child born to her mother. Because they lived with Anna's grandfather, who was incensed by the latest evidence that his daughter did not measure up to his strict moral code, the mother and child were forced to move out of the house. After several months of being moved from one place to another, repeated failures at adoption, and with no further alternative, at the age of five and a half months Anna was returned to the grandfather's house. Anna's mother so feared that the sight of the child would anger the grandfather that Anna was confined to an attic-like room on the second floor of the farmhouse. While there, Anna was given little physical attention beyond the exclusive diet of milk that sustained her until she was discovered at the age of five. Barely alive, she was extremely emaciated and undernourished, with skeletonlike legs and a bloated abdomen. Apparently Anna had seldom been moved from one position to another, and her clothes and bed were filthy. Positive emotional attention was unfamiliar to her. When found at age five, Anna could exhibit no signs of intelligence, nor could she walk or talk.

During the first year and a half after being found, Anna made some developmental progress in a county home for children—among other things she learned to walk, understand simple commands, eat by herself, tend to personal neatness somewhat, and recall people she had seen. Her speech was that of a one-year-old. Anna was then transferred to a school for retarded children where she made some further progress, even though at age seven her mental age was only 19 months and her social maturity level was that of a two-year-old. A year later she could bounce and catch a ball, participate as a follower in group activities, eat normally (although with a spoon only), attend to her toilet needs, and dress herself aside from handling buttons and snaps. Significantly, she had acquired the speech level of a two-year-old.

By the time of her death at age ten, Anna had made some additional progress. She could carry out instructions, identify a few colors, build with blocks, wash her hands, brush her teeth, and try to help other children. Her developing capacity for emotional attachment was evidenced in the love she had learned to have for a doll.

Was Anna's lack of personal and social development perhaps due to her original biological inadequacies rather than to the effects of her early and prolonged social isolation? There is reason to believe that Anna could have been mentally deficient from the start. Her mother, for example, tested out with a very subnormal I.Q. of 50. Whether or not Anna was mentally deficient at birth, the physical, personal, and social skills she developed in the few years between the time she was found and the time of her death are testimony to the indispensability of social interaction for the development of basic characteristics generally thought to be just "naturally human." The case of Isabelle is even more dramatically supportive of this conclusion.

• ISABELLE. Found nine months after Anna, Isabelle too was an illegitimate child kept in isolation for fear of social disapproval. Isabelle's mother, a deaf-mute since the age of two, stayed with the child in a dark room secluded from the rest of her family. When found at the age of six and a half, Isabelle was physically ill as a result of inadequate diet and lack of sunshine. Her legs were so bowed that when she stood, the soles of her shoes rested against each other, and her walk was a skittering movement. Unable to talk except for a strange croaking sound, Isabelle communicated with her mother by means of gestures. Upon seeing strangers, especially men, she acted like a wild animal because of fear and hostility. Some of her actions were those of a six-month-old infant.

In spite of the interpretation that Isabelle was feeble-minded—her first I.Q. score was near the zero point and her social maturity was at the level of two and a half years—those then responsible for her started an intensive program of rehabilitation. After a slow start, Isabelle progressed through the usual stages of learning and development much like any normal child progressing from ages one to six. Although the pace was faster than normal, the stages of development were in their proper order. It took her only two years to acquire skills mastered by a normal six-year-old. By the time she was eight and a half, Isabelle was on an educational par with other children her age. By outward appearances, she was an intelligent, happy, energetic child. At age 14, she passed the sixth grade and, according to her teachers, participated in all school activities as normally as other children in her grade.

The implication of these two cases is unmistakable—the personal and social development associated with being human is acquired through intensive and prolonged social contact with others. Cases of extreme social isolation are not the only evidence supportive of this generalization. Children may be negatively affected when the degree of social interaction is simply limited. René Spitz compared the infants in an orphanage with those in a women's prison nursery.[2] Both groups were similar in terms of hygiene and diet. Yet after two years some of the children in the orphanage were re-tarded and all were psychologically and socially underdeveloped for their age. By the age of four, one-third of them had died. No such problems were observed among the prison nursery infants. Not one of them died during this period, even though the physical environment was not as clean as that of the orphanage. Spitz traced the difference between the two groups of in-fants to the relative emotional, physical, and mental stimulation offered in each setting. In the prison nursery the infants' mothers were with them for the first year of their lives. Of course, the mothers were not present in the foundling home and the infant-nurse ratio there was seven or eight to one. Also in contrast to the prison nursery, the infants in the orphanage lacked the stimulation normally provided by toys and were isolated from the other children. As has been shown, such isolation is detrimental to social and per-sonality development.

SELF, SOCIALIZATION, AND SYMBOLIC INTERACTIONISM

Socialization is the process by which persons learn about culture and social structure so that they can participate in social life. For infants it is the very process of becoming human. At the core of socialization is the development of the *self*, the conception a person has of himself. Since a newborn child has no conception of himself as a distinct object, he must develop a self-concept. This is accomplished through social interaction, by making judg-ments of himself from personal interpretations of the attitudes and behavior of others toward him. Although it does not pertain to infants, a favorite story of many social psychologists (liberally embellished here) illustrates the importance of social interaction for the formation and maintenance of the self.

It seems that several students in a sociology course wanted to test first-hand the principle that a person's concept of himself is derived from the way he imagines he appears to others. As their unknowing subject for study they selected a female who, by the standards of the times, did not attract the attention of many males. Her personal dress code—uncombed hair, no makeup, sloppy clothing—made her a perfect target for the students who wanted to see if their pretended attraction would change her attitude to-ward herself. They bombarded her with requests for dates, praised her beauty, and openly competed for her favor. She responded as predicted.

Slowly she began to change both her attitude and appearance until she did meet the standards of femininity of that time. Then this Eliza Doolittle turned the tables on her multiple Professor Higginses. In the end, she rejected all their advances because they simply failed to meet her new-found standards of male attractiveness.

Among other things, social psychologists are interested in how persons become human, develop the capacity for participation in various social structures, and in the part played by agents of socialization—family, teachers, peers, ministers, and so forth—in the development and maintenance of a self-concept. One explanation of this process, the theory of symbolic interactionism, has been especially influential in sociological circles. *Symbolic interactionism* emphasizes the emergence of the mind, the self, and social structure through social interaction based on mutually understood symbols, especially the symbolic system known as language.

Looking-glass self

One of the first proponents of what is now known as symbolic interactionism was Charles Horton Cooley, a man who formulated some ideas about the acquisition and maintenance of a self from carefully watching his own children at play.[3] Cooley noted the pleasure children derive from exercising influence over others. By observing the reactions of others to their behavior, children learn that they can attract attention to themselves in certain ways. A child may cry as if mortally wounded—even though scarcely touched by a brother or sister—in the belief that his tears will elicit compassion and tenderness from mother. Or a child in the presence of adult company may create so much noise and confusion that it is impossible for the mother to continue her "neglect." With this insight highly polished with persistent use, it is a short step to reading one's worth from the imagined reactions of others. A main difference between children and adults in this regard is that, as they mature, people learn to make their efforts to elicit social approval less obvious.

Others, then, become mirrors whose reflections we use in the process of creating, maintaining, and changing our self-concept. According to Cooley, the looking-glass process occurs in three stages—an image of how one appears to another person, a personal judgment of the other's reaction to that imagined appearance, and some kind of self-evaluation, such as pride or shame. In practice, this process operates instantaneously without persons being aware of it.

• IS THE LOOKING GLASS ACCURATE? There is no claim that the figurative looking glass is free of distortion. Quite the contrary seems to be true. A study by Quarantelli and Cooper showed that the self-conceptions of a sample of dental students were nearer to the evaluations they *thought* the dental faculty would give them than it was to the *actual* evaluations the faculty made.[4] Serious misreadings, however, occur primarily among persons with some type of emotional problem. At the very least, there is evidence of a relationship between one's self-concept and the evaluation of oneself imagined to be made by others.

• SIGNIFICANT OTHERS. Of course the looking glass does not tell us what we should think of ourselves. We tell ourselves. This point has tremendous significance for symbolic interactionism, which, as you will see later, views people as active participants in their social life rather than mere passive reactors to social stimuli. A more limited observation is intended here. Since we communicate to ourselves imagined judgments others are making of us, room is made for assigning more or less importance to any given imagined judgment. Those persons whose evaluation of us we consider the most important are *significant others*. They have the greatest impact on our self-concept and on our learning about culture and social structure. Children look to parents, teachers, and friends, while teen-agers are more strongly peer-oriented. Adults are not immune, for they have significant others, ranging from their family members to the boss, whose good opinion they believe to be important for job advancement.

Learning to participate in social structures and developing a self-concept is not exclusively tied to other individuals, whether significant others or not. *Reference groups* are social structures or social categories used by persons to evaluate themselves and to acquire attitudes, values, norms, and beliefs. Membership in a social structure or social category is not necessary, but identification with it is. A teen-ager need not be a musician or a groupie in order to pattern himself after his perception of the life style associated with the current rage in popular music. As stated above, a reference group may be a fairly well-defined social structure or a social category. A high school girl, for example, may identify with college students in general or she may use as a reference group a particular sorority in a university attended by a friend.

Mind, self, and social interaction

Challenging the biological interpretation of human nature dominant at the time, Cooley was influential in proposing the idea that human nature is the product of processes distinctly social. But it was George Herbert Mead who, pursuing the links between the mind, self, and social structure, is credited with the fullest original elaboration of symbolic interactionism.[5]

• THE IMPORTANCE OF LANGUAGE. The label "symbolic interactionism" implies the pivotal place of language in Mead's theory of socialization. He was literally focusing on social interaction based on arbitrary or *significant symbols*, symbols that have no intrinsic relationship with the thing they represent but that mean the same things to two or more people because of mutual understanding. The gesture of "whistling" may stand for approval in one social structure and intense disapproval in another. And the act we know as whistling has other labels in other societies. Thus, the meaning of the physical act of whistling as well as its label are not dictated by the event itself. Its meaning and label within a given social structure are reached by usage and consensus. It follows, then, that significant symbols must be learned.

It is only through the acquisition of language that significant symbols become part of the human repertoire. Once learned, physical and verbal significant symbols used in social interaction have the same meanings for all participants. This fact is crucial for most of the social interaction engaged in by socialized humans. As defined in Chapter 2, social interaction is the exchange of social influence in which the actions of one person affect the behavior of another person, whose reactions in turn affect the first person, and so on. Clearly, in order to be predictable, social interaction must be based on the mutual understanding of symbols. Otherwise, inappropriate responses would disturb, prevent, or terminate social relationships.

As language is learned, two other vital things are being developed—the mind and the self. Social interaction based on "natural" signs such as voice inflection and facial expressions prepares the child for learning a language. Before learning a language, a child's knowledge of the meaning of physical things and behaviors far outstrips his ability to label them verbally. A young child also learns to control his responses to certain events and objects before he can label them. Feeling heat waves, an experienced child will avoid them. When a child can manipulate and understand the words hot, burn, and hurt, he can think about avoiding intense heat without feeling its presence. The ability to think symbolically reflects the development of a mind. And as the mind is used to think abstractly about oneself, one's behavior, and the behavior of others toward oneself, the existence of a self is apparent.

• ROLE TAKING, SELF, AND SOCIAL STRUCTURE. With only a small repertoire of significant symbols gained through the initial stages of learning a language, a child is able to carry on internal conversations. He tells himself something and responds internally to it. With this capacity it is possible to anticipate the responses of another. He can imagine what his own thoughts, feelings, and behavior would be in a similar situation. Because this can be done prior to any behavior on his part, the child or adult can guide his actions in light of the behavior likely to come from another person.

Imagine that your sociology professor has just returned an examination on which you have done so poorly that you fear it threatens the good grade you want in the course. You may decide to try to get your examination score raised. This can be a delicate matter, probably affecting the final grade in the course. So, you might ask yourself the important question: How can I get this teacher to change the examination grade? From that point the internal conversation might go something like this: I will tell him that he has made an error. But, you think, that might be taken as a questioning of his competency. The same is true if I say that the test was not a very good one. Perhaps my chances are better if I explain that my dog died and I simply couldn't concentrate. The last approach is laughable. Why? Because you have just imagined what your response would be to such a story if you were the professor on the receiving end. The search for a strategy either goes on in your mind or you abandon any effort to improve the grade on this examination.

This process of assuming the viewpoint of another person by thinking of yourself as that person and then mentally responding to yourself as you think the other person would, Mead called *role taking*. When applied to the self-concept, Mead's role taking is similar to Cooley's looking-glass process. But Mead went beyond Cooley to offer an explanation of how the capacity for role taking and the self are developed.

According to Mead, the self and the role-taking facility emerge from a two-stage process. The first of these, the *play* stage, follows the first few years of life, when children merely imitate the behavior of others. Near the age of three or four, you can observe children assuming a position and acting out some of the roles associated with it. Within a very short time, a child may have been a mother, father, truck driver, or cowboy. In each instance the child's "play" involves the serious business of learning to put himself in the position of another and behaving as he thinks that person would. This sort of play often involves taking the role of two persons. A boy may be a sheriff making an arrest one moment and in a flash be the outlaw shooting the sheriff. A perfect illustration of taking the attitudes of others toward oneself is the little girl who spanks her doll, puts her to bed without dinner, and calls her a "bad girl." During the play stage, role taking is confined to specific other persons. A child may be a sheriff and an outlaw within the same 10-second period but he can only think about one of them at a time.

Within a few years after the play stage is begun, a second phase is entered during which the capacity for the simultaneous consideration of several social positions and their interrelationships emerges—the *game* stage. A solitary child can play at one or more social positions alone, but games involve several participants. Moreover, behavior in games is guided by rules to cover the expected behavior of each participant. In order to play a game it is necessary to know what you are supposed to do. But you must also know the roles of every other person in the game and the relationship of these roles to your own position. Five people can play a genuine basketball game only if each can mentally anticipate the appropriate behavior of the guards, forwards, and center. Otherwise, there is no way to know how to behave toward each of the other players when occupying any one of these positions. It is no longer sufficient in this stage to take the role of one person at a time. It is necessary to be able to take the role of a number of persons simultaneously and to know the interrelationships among them.

A game is a good analogy for understanding the way in which persons learn to participate in social structures. What are games if not several interrelated social positions, or a social position-set? Participation in a social position-set is possible only if one has the capability of responding to a number of others at the same time. Prior to the game stage, children are capable only of thinking of the attitudes and behavior of specific people. Standards of "goodness" and "badness" are associated with what significant others say and do. Beginning during the game stage, a child's conception of appropriate ways of thinking, feeling, and behaving gradually become less tied to specific others and take on a more generalized character. Being honest, for example, is not important just because one's parents say so; it just does not seem right to behave dishonestly. As this occurs a *generalized other* is forming—an integrated picture of the norms, values, beliefs, expectations, and attitudes of the social structure in which socialization has taken place. Unity of self and consistency in behavior are made possible because the generalized other is a relatively stable reference point from which to view oneself and with which to make one's way in a variety of social situations.

Having developed a generalized other, persons can enter new social position-sets and form a generalized conception of the mutually shared role expectations operating in each of them. And they can respond to others without reference to the particular individuals occupying the social positions. Without the learned capacity for role taking—with reference to both specific others and the generalized other—it would be impossible to have a self or to become integrated into social structures.

• A SOCIAL STAMP? Is the process of socialization and the social interaction that it makes possible so easy, so programmed, so complete as some of the above may make it seem? Is social interaction merely the result of past learning? Are all of us the undeviating products of a social stamp? Symbolic interactionists do not think so. In addition to the obviously active processes of role taking, thinking, and self-evaluation, Mead introduced some other ideas further emphasizing the active part human beings play in social interaction.

In the first place, symbolic interactionists follow Mead in the belief that the self is more than the incorporation of the generalized other and the attitudes of specific others. To them the self operates on two abstractly separable dimensions. One dimension, which Mead called the *me*, represents the internalized social attitudes derived from socialization in a social structure. From this dimension of the self comes predictability and conformity in social behavior. But why is it that people are not always able to predict how they might react in a given situation? Even though the generalized other clearly prohibits it, a rejected lover may spontaneously and unaccountably kill the one he loves. Afterward, his dazed reaction may be, "I don't know what came over me. How could I do that to the person I cared the most about?" To account for this spontaneous, unpredictable, often creative side of the self, Mead postulated another dimension to the self that he labeled the *I*.

The "I" operates not just in extreme situations of rage or excitement. It constantly interacts with the "me" as persons conduct themselves in social situations. According to Mead, the first reaction of the self comes from the "I," but before one acts, the initial impulse is directed in socially acceptable channels by the "me." Thus, the "I" normally takes the "me" into account before acting. However, the uniqueness and unpredictability of much human behavior demonstrates that the "me" does not as a rule totally dominate the innovative dimension of the self.

Another denial of the social stamping of persons is Mead's conception of human behavior as the outcome of active individual construction rather than as mere automatic responses to social stimuli. Social acts are consciously and deliberately constructed by persons taking into account, among other things, the behavior of other persons. Aside from reflexes and ingrained habits, human behavior is guided by an internal decision-making process involving all of the aspects of symbolic interactionism presented in this chapter. Actually, the example of the student conversing with himself about attempting to have his sociology examination grade changed indicates the active, reflective, constructional nature of human conduct.

Thus, symbolic interactionists accept the assumption that the mind, self, and social structure are the products of distinct social processes but reject the idea of human beings as passively stamped social products. They envision a certain amount of freedom from the socialization process. However, there are others who think that the degree of freedom has been seriously underestimated. They do not believe that the biological factors in human development have received recognition equal to their impact.

BIOLOGY AND SOCIALIZATION

Freud and the biological basis of personality

Although writing at the same time as Mead, Sigmund Freud developed a different view of socialization and human nature. As noted, Mead emphasized the social side of human nature. Freud, while recognizing the tremendous imprint of the first years of life, gave a central position to the instinctual, biological facets of man. In Freud's theory the human personality can be analytically separated into three parts—the id, ego, and superego.[6] The *id* consists of the impulses and desires—especially the sexual and aggressive tendencies—that are part of any human being's biological equipment. Since one of the functions of socialization is to control such "antisocial" impulses and desires, the id has to be harnessed to some degree. During the first few years of life the norms, values, and beliefs of a social structure become part of the personality. This part of the personality, akin to Mead's "me" and to what is popularly thought of as a conscience, Freud labeled the *superego*. Once internalized, the superego and the id wage a continual battle, a conflict mediated by the ego. The *ego* is the conscious and rational part of the personality that attempts to keep the id within the boundaries set by the superego. A rage to murder someone may be overcome by rational consideration of the consequences. If so, in Freud's model, the ego would have done its job.

It is not Freud's theories that are of primary interest here. In fact, many of his ideas have been under critical attack for some time. It is his biological emphasis that concerns us, since it fits in with the current revival of the place of genetics in human nature.

Sociology's "oversocialized" view of man

Predating the contemporary revival of genetic influence by several years, Dennis Wrong argued that sociology had accepted the superego concept but used it without reference to the existence of the biologically based impulses that Freud called the id.[7] For Freud, the superego operated to hold these selfish, antisocial impulses in check. Attempts to repress urges and desires is said to generate considerable internal conflict. Without a picture of man that includes biological impulses and desires, Wrong says, sociologists are free to conclude that the forces of socialization meet with little resistance. According to Wrong, sociologists find the answer to conformity in the incorporation of norms into the personality and in the desire of people to maintain a favorable self-image, which is more likely to come when the expectations of others are met.

Wrong is saying that sociologists have an "oversocialized" view of the human animal. By leaving out the biological nature of man, sociologists are ignoring the fact that socialization is never completely victorious. While socialization makes man human, it does not succeed completely in molding him. The biological equipment of human beings carries a natural resistance to absolute conformity. In Wrong's view, sociological theories that overemphasize socialization are not as incorrect as they are limited. While far from being a biological determinist, he does see an important niche for biological factors in sociological theories. By refusing to consider psychological and biological forces, Wrong contends, sociologists leave the impression that man's nature is completely formed by his cultural heritage.

In the present context the specific ideas of Freud and Wrong are not as important for their accuracy as for their emphasis. While both have been challenged on many fronts, their position on the pivotal place of biology in human nature may be on the verge of a renaissance.

A new challenge to the social stamp

There is renewed interest in the heredity-environment debate among social scientists, particularly among psychologists. Psychologists of the stimulus-response school (behaviorism) are being challenged by cognitive psychologists. While behaviorists see human behavior as the result of learned reflexes to stimuli, cognitive psychologists underscore the centrality of the human mind in the construction of behavior. This point would come as no surprise to symbolic interactionists. But cognitive psychologists as well as some linguists and anthropologists are going further. They are theorizing that a greater proportion of individual and group behavior may be due to genetic inheritance than has been supposed in contemporary social science.

A good illustration is language, which is a human capability normally thought to be completely learned. How is it that even very young children can speak so many sentences that they have never heard before? Linguist Noam Chomsky believes that this creative facility with language cannot be accounted for by stimulus-response learning theory, because it is quite clear that a great many sentences are created rather than learned.[8] He proposes the presence of innate rules of "deep grammar" that underlie all human languages. Without these biologically transmitted rules of deep grammar, Chomsky contends, it would be impossible for children to master one or more languages in the brief time that they do.

Another controversial set of ideas are currently coming from some anthropologists. Two notable advocates of the biological roots of human nature, Lionel Tiger and Robin Fox, write of inherited behavior patterns that they label "biogrammar."[9] They point to cultural similarities across societies—marriage, incest taboos, religious ideas and practices—to buttress the claim that more human behavior originates from the genes than social scientists are now willing to admit.

At this time, evidence to back the ideas of Chomsky and Tiger and Fox is scant. But some earlier research on children can be used to support the notion of inherited behavioral patterns.

Studies have been conducted comparing male and female children, including infants. Psychoanalyst Erik Erikson invited about 150 boys and girls, from 10 to 12 years old, into his office one at a time, asking each to use toy furniture, human figures, blocks, and the like to construct an exciting imaginary movie scene.[10] These children were not psychiatric patients. Among other things, Erikson found in girls a tendency to create peaceful scenes while boys preferred active and strong scenes involving Indians, animals, motor cars, and policemen. But surely, you may be thinking, these male-female differences merely reflect the success of socialization. It is true that boys in American society are expected to be more aggressive and active than girls; girls who fail to fulfill this cultural definition become "tomboys" in the eyes of adults.

Other research, however, suggests that such male-female dissimilarities may be more deeply embedded in genetic heritage. It has been found that male infants even in the first two or three months of life display, on the average, greater aggressiveness and activeness than do females of the same age. Male infants, as a whole, tend to thrust with their arms and legs, and express demands through crying, more than do females. The case for some sexual biological programming is further strengthened by similar findings among other mammalian species, especially other primates.[11]

Where does all of this leave us on the issue of cultural versus biological determinism? The currently dominant stance in sociology—biology sets limits on human behavior; it does not determine it—will very likely remain unchanged. Of course, the further one probes on the social-psychological level, the wider the latitude given to genetic influence. But even given a fuller recognition of biology's impact on human nature, sociologists need not abandon their concentration on social structure. They will simply have to pay more than lip service to their often repeated position that biology serves only to limit cultural and social development. More serious attention will have to be paid to the specific ways in which innate and learned aspects of human nature are intertwined.

DEVIANCE AND CONFORMITY

Deviance and its relativity

Since sociologists are preoccupied with social structure, with the predictability and recurrence of social life, it is inevitable that most of their efforts will be directed to the study of conformity to social norms. Yet, as Mead, Freud, Wrong, and others tell us, cultural determinism misrepresents reality. It does

Dan Budnik, Woodfin Camp & Associates

not take an announcement from the FBI to convince you that human beings, as a whole, are not completely conforming creatures. *Deviance* occurs when social norms are violated.

Two factors make deviant behavior harder to pinpoint than one might expect. First, norms are not thin lines; they are bands of varying widths. By law, the driver of an automobile is supposed to come to a complete halt at a stop sign. But coming to a near stop is generally close enough for the police. Knowing how near to a full stop one must come is a matter of knowing the territory. Some police forces are strict with everyone; others delight in reacquainting out-of-towners or lower-class residents with the letter of the law. Moreover, the limits of socially acceptable deviance are not the same for all people. An unemployed man caught stealing a car may receive a longer jail sentence than a bank president who is caught embezzling a large sum of money; teen-agers are held less accountable for their crimes than are adults; and children can do and say things that would make adults blush. While norms such as those expressed in traffic laws may have fairly wide bands, it is hard to convince a judge or jury that you are guilty of only a little murder or a half-rape. As the importance of the norm increases, the limits of permissible deviance shrink.

A second obstacle to identifying deviance is its relativity. A business-man with a flat-top haircut would appear to be just as much a deviant in a hippie commune as a flower child at an IBM stockholder's meeting. By the principle of cultural relativism—the idea that any aspect of a culture must be evaluated within the context of the larger culture—labeling an act as deviant can have no ring of absoluteness or finality. Behavior can be considered to reflect conformity or deviance only within the context of a specified social structure. This means that in a complex society with many diverse and conflicting social structures, it is virtually impossible not to be a deviant from the point of view of the members of some social structure. In fact, slavish conformity to the norms of one social structure may earn you intense disapproving social pressure from another, as any teen-ager can tell you. Or, to take a political example, were the disclosers of the Pentagon Papers, Daniel Ellsberg and Anthony Russo, serving their country or weakening the Vietnam war and peace efforts?

Not only is deviance relative to social structures, it is conditioned by time within the same social structure. Imagine convincing a collection of nineteenth-century manufacturers that children should be in school rather than putting in long days in factories beside their mothers or sisters. Imagine persuading twentieth-century middle-class American boys that hard work is worth doing for its character-building qualities alone.

Theories of deviance

Several theories of deviance have been developed, some attempting to explain specific types of deviance such as crime or delinquency, others dealing with the violation of norms on a general level. Two of these general theories of deviance will be introduced here. One, anomie theory, is formulated to account for deviance at the structural level. The other, labeling theory, deals with deviance on the social-psychological level, in the tradition of symbolic interactionism.

• ANOMIE THEORY. The anomie theory of deviance, formulated by Robert Merton, has been one of the most influential.[12] *Anomie* occurs when members of a social structure are unable to reach culturally defined goals through socially acceptable avenues. Anomie within a social structure is more likely to lead to deviant behavior among members of those subcultures or social categories whose efforts toward goal achievement meet with built-in barriers.

Merton's analysis was directed at American society, in which the accumulation of wealth as a symbol of success is a paramount goal. Most Americans subscribe to the goal of success, but certain segments of society are without the means (money, education, social class background) to make any progress toward its realization. Because of this disparity between cultural goals and socially approved means for their realization, deviant behavior is particularly prevalent within the lower class and among poor minority groups.

Also, as Merton recognized, material success is a purely relative matter. With regard to money and success, Americans tend to be insatiable. Besides, as one rises in the social stratification structure, the standards for measuring material success rise. A young stockbroker on Wall Street may be able to portray himself as the epitome of the American Dream to his friends in Beaver Falls, Pennsylvania. But he knows that to the big-money men on the stock exchange he is just another young man on the make. Such young men may believe that they, too, are blocked from material success and may turn to illegitimate means, as can be seen from the statistics on white-collar crime.

Deviant behavior, according to anomie theory, does not occur on a large scale just because segments of a social structure are denied the means to reach the goal of success. Rather, widespread deviance is likely to appear when *all* members of a society are encouraged to value success while significant portions of the society face social structural barriers to achievement through socially acceptable means.

Turning to nonsocially approved means to attain success is one major adaptation to this discrepancy between cultural goals and social structure. This type of adaptation is reflected in crime, delinquency, gambling, and prostitution. Merton called this course *innovation*—the cultural goal of success is maintained but nonsocially approved means are used in its pursuit. Table 11.1 shows this mode of adaptation as well as four others discussed by Merton.

Two of these modes of adaptation—retreatism and rebellion—also lead to deviant behavior. *Retreatism* involves the rejection of success and of the approved means to success. Moreover, no socially illegitimate means for the attainment of the goal are adopted. Retreatists include social dropouts, alcoholics, drug addicts, and bums. *Rebellion* entails the attempt to replace present cultural goals and approved means with a new or somewhat different social structure. The student movement of the 1960s is an example of this type of adaptation, as would be any radical social movement.

Of course, there are adaptations to the conflict between culture and social structure that do not lead to deviance. Probably the most common of these is *conformity* to cultural goals and social structural means. A more extreme adaptation without deviance is *ritualism*—the rejection of success with strict conformity to the means. Ritualists deflate their aspirations to the point that, in effect, their goals have already been reached. Even though they have forsaken the cultural directive to "get ahead," they continue to engage in the pursuits that would presumably pull them up the stratification structure. In fact, the devotion to the means tends to take on a compulsive cast. Ritualists are "deviants" only in the sense that they effectively remove themselves from the success game participated in by most other members of the society.

• LABELING THEORY. By its accent on social interaction, labeling theory is clearly a social-psychological perspective on deviance. In fact, part of its roots can be traced to symbolic interactionism, to the ideas of Cooley and Mead. Central to the *labeling theory* of deviance are the principles that the self emerges through social interaction, and that attitudes toward the self and actual behavior both result from the process of taking the role of the other.

The developers of labeling theory, Edwin Lemert and Howard Becker, start with the central assumption that no act is inherently deviant.[13] Behavior may be considered to be deviant in a particular place at a particular

TABLE 11.1 Types of adaptation to anomie

DEVIANT ADAPTATIONS	NONDEVIANT ADAPTATIONS	CULTURAL GOALS	SOCIALLY APPROVED MEANS
Innovation		Accept	Reject
Retreatism		Reject	Reject
Rebellion		Reject/Substitute new goals	Reject/Substitute new means
	Conformity	Accept	Accept
	Ritualism	Reject	Accept

SOURCE: Reprinted with permission of Macmillan Publishing Co., Inc. from **Social Theory and Social Structure**, rev. ed., by Robert K. Merton. © Copyright The Free Press, a Corporation, 1957.

point in time only because others have labeled it as deviant. Once persons have been socially defined or labeled as deviants, others begin to interact with them as deviants. If the process continues, the socially labeled deviant, through role taking, begins to see himself as a deviant and ultimately fulfills the expectations others have of him in this regard.

In essence, negatively labeled persons are said to assume the social position of deviant and to carry out the role prescriptions associated with it. The more prolonged the process, the more likely are labeled deviants to incorporate the social position of deviant into their self-concept and to guide their behavior in line with it and with the expectations of others.

The anomie and labeling theories are not without fault; nevertheless, both theories have stimulated considerable thought and research on deviant behavior and must be viewed as two major points of departure in the study of deviance.

The further complexity of deviance

Attempts to unravel the nature and sources of deviance reveal even greater complexity. It is a difficult enough task to explain why some persons want to, and do, conform to social norms while others desire to, and do, deviate from them. But what about persons who prefer not to violate norms but do so anyway, and those who wish to be deviant but nevertheless conform? Judith Blake and Kingsley Davis have emphasized these latter two cases.[14] Assuming the existence of some broader set of norms from which the behavior of individuals may be judged to be either conforming or deviant, they interrelate motives and actual behavior. Table 11.2 shows the types of

TABLE 11.2 Types of conformists and deviants

PERSON'S MOTIVE	PERSON'S BEHAVIOR	
	Conforming	Deviating
To Conform	Intentional Conformists	Unintentional Deviants
To Deviate	Unintentional Conformists	Intentional Deviants

SOURCE: Adapted from Judith Blake and Kingsley Davis, "Norms, Values, and Sanctions," in Robert E. L. Faris, ed., **Handbook of Modern Sociology**, © 1954 by Rand McNally and Company, Chicago, p. 468. Reprinted by permission of Rand McNally College Publishing Company.

deviants and conformists that can be isolated when individuals' motives with respect to a set of norms are cross-classified with their real behavior. Of interest here are unintentional deviants and unintentional conformists.

- UNINTENTIONAL DEVIANTS. Those who violate norms against their own desire do so because of existing conditions beyond their control. Conditions may be physical, psychological, or social. A sick employee may work only half a day, or a mentally disturbed person may commit some act that he cannot even remember later. Less obvious is the unintentional deviation promoted by social structure itself. What is a person to do when the role prescriptions of one social position are in conflict with those attached to another position? It is often a no-win situation. A major league baseball player has to be on the road, away from his family, for much of the year. These circumstances, combined with the tensions associated with big-time athletics, may very well interfere with the role prescriptions of husband or father.

If unintentional deviation is generated from conflicting social positions, it may also come from some incompatible role prescriptions related to a single position. College students who complain that the quality of their professor's teaching is low, and that he or she is never available for advising, may be correct in tracing it to the "publish or perish" ethic. Although doing research and writing articles and books do not necessarily lower the performance level of teaching-related activities, it is difficult for many professors to balance both teaching and research duties at the same time. While an emphasis on research and writing may not result in conflict with some in a social position-set (dean, department chairman), the incompatibility may surface with respect to others (students).

- UNINTENTIONAL CONFORMISTS. Several factors operate to cause persons who really want to violate norms to resist the temptation. Even though the members of a social structure have internalized its norms, there is ample room for them to want to violate these norms under some circumstances: An ex-Eagle Scout in banker's clothing may attempt to reinterpret the motto "Be Prepared" to mean that his chance to embezzle without detection should not be neglected. He may not succeed in translating this new interpretation of an old moral code into the behavior of stealing other people's money. Why? For one thing, after a mighty internal struggle he simply may not have been able to wash out, even temporarily, the norms he internalized from the Boy Scouts or other social structures. A second inhibitor on the behavioral expression of desired deviancy may be the need for approval from significant others. The imagined disapproval from his wife, children, or colleagues may not be worth the newly acquired wealth. Or he may not want to risk the formal punishment that will come should the theft be uncovered. Not only might he lose his job and jeopardize the chances of ever getting a comparable one, he might spend some time in prison. Perhaps he will decide that the gain is simply not great enough. If the amount he feels he can get away with were $1 million rather than $10,000, it would be worth the risks. Finally, the desire to be deviant may burn unrelieved because of the absence of opportunity. A new accounting system may be installed before he gets an opportunity to steal the $10,000, thus removing the loophole the banker had spotted.

OVERVIEW AND PREVIEW

It is through socialization—the process of learning about culture and social structure—that individuals become human, develop a self, and learn to participate in various social structures. That social interaction is central to socialization is dramatized by cases of socially isolated children and illustrated by cases of children with limited emotional and mental stimulation.

Symbolic interactionism is one of the most widely accepted theories of socialization. According to this theory, the mind, the self, and social structure emerge as a result of social interaction based on gestures and significant symbols. It is through learning to take the role of others, through learning to imagine another's reactions to a situation by mentally putting oneself in his place, that the self is created and persons become capable of participating in social structures. Despite their assumption that the mind, the self, and social structure are products of distinctly social processes, symbolic interactionists envision human beings as active creators rather than passive products of a social stamp.

Others want to press further the idea that man is more than a socially created being. Although there is a revival of interest in the impact of heredity on the individual and on social life, sociologists are likely to retain their long-standing position that biological factors limit rather than determine social life. Depending on the outcome of future research, however, sociology may have to take any such limits more seriously.

Even though sociology's major thrust is social structure, with all of its predictability and recurrence, it is obvious that deviance or the violation of social norms surrounds us. It is often difficult to identify deviant acts—adherence to norms is often not an all-or-nothing matter, and some persons can break the rules with more immunity than others. Adding to the problem of identifying deviance is the fact that deviation is relative to time and place. That is, an act can be said to be deviant only with reference to the norms that operate in a particular social structure at a particular point in time.

Two theories of deviance, one structural and one social-psychological, have been especially prominent. According to anomie theory, deviance occurs when the cultural goal of success is emphasized for all while certain segments of the population are denied access to socially approved means for achieving success. Turning to nonsocially approved means to attain success is a major adaptation to this discrepancy between cultural goals and social structure. Labeling theory rests on symbolic interactionism and depicts deviants as the products of social definition and interaction.

Deviance and conformity often do not occur intentionally. Both anomie and labeling theory make this point. But often ignored are those persons who are deviant in one situation because they are conforming in another. These are "unintentional deviants." If some people are deviant as a result of circumstances beyond their control, there are others who are conformists through no fault of their own.

The social-psychological perspective is continued in the next chapter. There attention will be focused on group structure, the smallest unit of sociological analysis. Although other types of groups are of interest to sociologists, primary group structure will be spotlighted.

REFERENCES

1. Kingsley Davis, "Final Note on a Case of Extreme Isolation," *American Journal of Sociology*, 52 (March 1947), 232–247.
2. René A. Spitz. "Hospitalism," in Anna Freud, et al., eds., *The Psychoanalytic Study of the Child*, vol. 1 (New York: International Universities Press, 1945), pp. 52–74; René A. Spitz, "Hospitalism: A Follow-Up Report," in Anna Freud, et al., eds., *The Psychoanalytic Study of the Child*, vol. 2 (New York: International Universities Press, 1946), pp. 113–117.
3. Charles Horton Cooley, *Human Nature and the Social Order* (New York: Scribner, 1902).
4. E. L. Quarantelli and Joseph Cooper, "Self-Conceptions and Others: A Further Test of the Meadian Hypothesis," *Sociological Quarterly*, 7 (Summer 1966), 281–297.
5. George Herbert Mead, *Mind, Self, and Society* (Chicago: University of Chicago Press, 1934).
6. Sigmund Freud, *The Ego and the Id*, trans. by Joan Riviere (London: Hogarth, 1949).
7. Dennis H. Wrong, "The Oversocialized Conception of Man in Modern Sociology," *American Sociological Review*, 26 (April 1961), 183–193.
8. Noam Chomsky, *Language and Mind* (New York: Harcourt Brace Jovanovich, 1972).
9. Lionel Tiger and Robin Fox, *The Imperial Animal* (New York: Holt, Rinehart and Winston, 1971).
10. Erik H. Erikson, *Childhood and Society*, rev. ed. (New York: Norton, 1963).
11. Judith M. Bardwick, "Infant Sex Differences," in Clarice Stasz Stoll, ed., *Sexism: Scientific Debates* (Reading, Mass.: Addison-Wesley, 1973) pp. 28–42.
12. Robert K. Merton, *Social Theory and Social Structure*, rev. ed. (New York: Free Press, 1957).

13. Edwin M. Lemert, *Social Pathology* (New York: McGraw-Hill, 1951); Howard S. Becker, *Outsiders: Studies in the Sociology of Deviance* (New York: Free Press, 1963); Howard S. Becker, *The Other Side: Perspectives on Deviance* (New York: Free Press, 1964).
14. Judith Blake and Kingsley Davis, "Norms, Values, and Sanctions," in Robert E. L. Faris, ed., *Handbook of Modern Sociology* (Skokie, Ill.: Rand McNally, 1964), pp. 466–482.

ADDITIONAL SOURCES AND READINGS

Blumer, Herbert. *Symbolic Interactionism: Perspective and Method* (Englewood Cliffs, N.J.: Prentice-Hall, 1969).

Clausen, John A., ed. *Socialization and Society* (Boston: Little, Brown, 1968).

Clinard, Marshall B., ed. *Anomie and Deviant Behavior: A Discussion and Critique* (New York: Free Press, 1964).

Clinard, Marshall B. *Sociology of Deviant Behavior* (New York: Holt, Rinehart and Winston, 1968).

Glaser, Daniel. *Social Deviance* (Chicago: Markham, 1971).

Goffman, Erving. *The Presentation of Self in Everyday Life* (Garden City, N.Y.: Doubleday, 1959).

Goslin, David A., ed. *Handbook of Socialization Theory and Research* (Skokie, Ill.: Rand McNally, 1969).

Lemert, Edwin M. *Human Deviance, Social Problems, and Social Control* (Englewood Cliffs, N.J.: Prentice-Hall, 1972).

Maccoby, Eleanor E., ed. *The Development of Sex Differences* (Stanford, Calif.: Stanford University Press, 1966).

Manis, Jerome G., and Bernard Meltzer. *Symbolic Interaction: A Reader in Social Psychology*, 2nd ed. (Boston: Allyn & Bacon, 1972).

Mazur, Allan, and Leon S. Robertson. *Biology and Social Behavior* (New York: Free Press, 1972).

Simmons, J. L. *Deviants* (Berkeley, Calif.: Glendessary Press, 1969).

Group Structure

[The following scene takes place in a mental institution.]

McMurphy looks up at the clock and he says it's time for the game. He's over by the drinking fountain with some of the other Acutes, down on his knees scouring off the baseboard. I'm sweeping out the broom closet for the tenth time that day. Scanlon and Harding, they got the buffer going up and down the hall, polishing the new wax into shining figure eights. McMurphy says again that he guesses it must be game time and he stands up, leaves the scouring rag where it lies. Nobody else stops work. McMurphy walks past the window where . . . [Big Nurse is] glaring out at him and grins at her like he knows he's got her whipped now. When he tips his head back and winks at her she gives that little sideways jerk of her head.

Everybody keeps on at what he's doing, but they all watch out of the corners of their eyes while he drags his armchair out to in front of the TV set, then switches on the set and sits down. A picture swirls onto the screen of a parrot out on the baseball field singing razor-blade songs. McMurphy gets up and turns up the sound to drown out the music coming down from the speaker in the ceiling, he drags another chair in front of him and sits down and crosses his feet on the chair and leans back and lights a cigarette. He scratches his belly and yawns.

"Hoo-wee! Man, all I need me now is a can of beer and a red-hot."

We can see the nurse's face get red and her mouth work as she stares at him. She looks around for a second and sees everybody's watching what she's going to do—even the black boys and the little nurses sneaking looks at her, and the residents beginning to drift in for the staff meeting, they're watching. Her mouth clamps shut. She looks back at McMurphy and waits till the razor-blade song is finished; then she gets up and goes to the steel door where the controls are, and she flips a switch and the TV picture swirls back into the gray. Nothing is left on the screen but a little eye of light beading right down on McMurphy sitting there.

That eye don't faze him a bit. To tell the truth, he don't even let on he knows the picture is turned off; he puts his cigarette between his teeth and pushes his cap forward in his red hair till he has to lean back to see out from under the brim.

And sits that way, with his hands crossed behind his head and his feet stuck out in a chair, a smoking cigarette sticking out from under his hatbrim—watching the TV screen.

The nurse stands this as long as she can; then she comes to the door of the Nurses' Station and calls across to him he'd better help the men with the housework. He ignores her.

"I said, Mr. McMurphy, that you are supposed to be working during these hours." Her voice has a tight whine like an electric saw ripping through pine. "Mr. McMurphy, I'm warning you!"

Everybody's stopped what he was doing. She looks around her, then takes a step out of the Nurses' Station toward McMurphy.

"You're committed, you realize. You are . . . under the jurisdiction of me . . . the staff." She's holding up a fist, all those red-orange fingernails burning into her palm. "Under jurisdiction and control."

Harding shuts off the buffer, and leaves it in the hall, and goes pulls him a chair up alongside McMurphy and sits down and lights him a cigarette too.

"Mr. Harding! You return to your scheduled duties!"

I think how her voice sounds like it hit a nail, and this strikes me so funny I almost laugh.

"Mr. Har-**ding**!"

Then Cheswick goes and gets him a chair, and then Billy Bibbit goes, and then Scanlon and then Frederickson and Sefelt, and then we all put down our mops and brooms and scouring rags and we all go pull us chairs up.

"You **men**—Stop this. **Stop**!"

And we're all sitting there lined up in front of that blanked-out TV set, watching the gray screen just like we could see the baseball game clear as day, and she's ranting and screaming behind us.

If somebody'd of come in and took a look, men watching a blank TV, a fifty-year-old woman hollering and squealing at the back of their heads about discipline and order and recriminations they'd of thought the whole bunch was crazy as loons.

From **One Flew Over the Cuckoo's Nest** by Ken Kesey. Copyright © 1962 by Ken Kesey. All rights reserved. Reprinted by permission of The Viking Press, Inc.

McMurphy later paid dearly for the leadership he displayed in the television incident. Although Big Nurse lost both her cool and her authority at the time, she got her revenge later by having McMurphy's brain disconnected. This was a last resort, for all other efforts to control him had failed. As this incident demonstrated, the other inmates were beginning to take cues from him. Without a direct spoken word from McMurphy, the other inmates joined him in his absurd behavior. Big Nurse did not have to be struck by a television set twice to realize that her ability to control the ward hinged on breaking up the social pattern so clearly taking shape. From her vantage point, Big Nurse was not wrong. A group structure was forming around the uncontrollable McMurphy, a structure that clearly threatened to give typically socially isolated mental patients some leverage for the resistance of authority.

The first major section of this chapter is an introduction to the concept of group structure, followed by a discussion of a major type of group structure—that characterized by primary relationships. In the final section of the chapter, the functions of primary group structure for individuals are examined.

WHAT IS GROUP STRUCTURE?

A definition and illustration

It is essential to note that the term "group" as used in sociology differs from the normal usage of the word. In everyday language, group is a concept sufficiently elastic to apply to human associations ranging from a motorcycle gang to an entire society. This conventionally imprecise usage of group is too all-encompassing to be scientifically meaningful. Group as a sociological concept should have a much more narrow application. Thus, in this text, the following definition is employed: A *group* is a type of social structure that is created through the patterned interaction of a relatively few persons who share a common identity, goals, rules for thinking, feeling, and behaving, and direct or indirect lines of communication.

Let us apply certain aspects of this complex definition of group structure to McMurphy and his band of renegade mental patients. There is no arbitrary number of persons required for the existence of group structure. It may involve only two persons; under 10, as in the case of McMurphy's crew; or more, as in military prison camps. The number is important only in this respect: As the number of persons in a group increases, it becomes increasingly difficult to maintain the central characteristics of a group structure.

McMurphy was able to marshal a common identity held by the mental patients—they were all essentially powerless, and they knew it. Normally this was an accepted fact of existence among them, but under McMurphy's leadership, a common and immediate goal had developed—get Big Nurse! Thus, even though the lines of communication were indirect (McMurphy said not a word), a set of social relationships were obviously being engaged in by these usually compliant men. It was precisely in order to short-circuit this growing group structure that Big Nurse had McMurphy's mind defused.

Sharing a common identity and goals is basic to the emergence and maintenance of group structure. In some instances these revolve around the desire to accomplish a specific objective, such as undermining Big Nurse's authority. On the other hand, group members may be seeking fulfillment of needs for sociability and emotional support, as was the case in the events leading up to McMurphy's inspired revolt.

Communication among group structure members may be direct or indirect. It may be as direct as talking to each other face-to-face or conversing by telephone. It may be as indirect as McMurphy's message. And group structures may be maintained when the members are not interacting or communicating at all. This state of noncommunication, of course, must be temporary, as is the case for members of professional athletic teams during the off-season or family members taking separate vacations.

Group is one of the most frequently used concepts in sociology—many professionals define sociology as the scientific study of social groups. Generally, the definition of a social group is much the same as the above definition of group structure, except that absolutely no limit on numbers would be specified. From this standpoint, as noted earlier, a social group could include every kind of social unit, ranging from two interacting persons to an entire society. In contrast, this text is based on the concept of social structure rather than on social group, in order to avoid the confusion caused when such abstract and diffuse objects of sociological investigation as stratification structure, communities, and formal organizations are called social groups.

To think of a community structure as a group, for example, stretches the meaning of a perfectly good concept too far. Thinking of community structure in terms of sharing a common identity, subscribing to the same goals, and direct or indirect lines of communication creates some theoretical and conceptual problems. For one thing, viewing communities as social groups glosses over sociocultural diversity, particularly within urban communities. A similar argument can be made for stratification and formal organizational structures. Greater clarity is promoted by reserving the characteristics of identity, goals, and communication for group structures—considerably smaller social units of which these characteristics are infinitely more descriptive.

Persons and group structure

Persons, regardless of their number, are not a social structure; however, people acting in concert do create, maintain, and change the sets of culturally based social relationships by which they live. Thus, when group members interact among themselves on the basis of interrelated social positions, they are participants in a group structure. But because a relatively small number of people are involved in a group structure, there is a tremendous temptation to see members as distinct individuals rather than as position holders interacting within a social position-set. By definition, group structures have small memberships. Consequently, it is possible to focus on the social interaction among persons. While dealing with social structure on the social-psychological level, it is all too easy to forget the essence of the structural perspective: Social structures are not reducible to individuals.

If individuals do not a group make, it is also true that persons who have one or more things in common, or who are in physical proximity, are not necessarily joined in a group structure. Taxpayers, Methodists, and Howdy Doody buffs are examples of a *social category*—a number of persons who share one or more social characteristics. A *social aggregate* is a number of persons who are physically located together. For example, persons waiting at the Port Authority bus terminal in New York City constitute a social aggregate. Some of these people may interact with each other, they may complain about the bus service or talk of an anticipated March vacation in Miami Beach. But until these same people have developed a common identity, shared goals, norms, and stable communication links, they do not constitute a group in the sociological sense of the term. They are merely an aggregate of persons who may or may not engage in sporadic interpersonal relations.

Neither social categories nor social aggregates qualify as social structures of any kind, group or otherwise. However, as just implied, members of either a social category or a social aggregate may become part of a group or other social structure. Some of the taxpayers in the $30,000-and-below bracket in Brookline, Massachusetts, for example, could mount a drive for tax relief. Such a drive might become a formal organizational structure, or it might evolve no further than a group structure composed of a few irate people who get together to remind each other how bad things are and that they are going to do something about it. A social aggregate may become transformed into a social structure as well. This would be true if, say, soccer fanatics formed vigilante groups in order to intimidate referees.

Although there are others, only one type of group structure will be covered in this chapter: groups characterized by primary social relationships.

THE NATURE OF PRIMARY GROUP STRUCTURE

All group structures have the several characteristics noted in the above definition. Special kinds of groups have additional and distinctive features. Thus the set of culturally based social relationships involved in a primary group structure are of a particular nature—the social relationships are "primary." In order to clarify the meanings of primary group structure and primary social relationships, it is necessary to return to the ideas of Charles Horton Cooley.

Primary group structure and primary social relationships

You will recall from the previous chapter on socialization that Cooley was influential in forging the idea that the self is the product of social interaction. Cooley reserved the term *primary group* for those groups that figured the most prominently in making human beings human.[1] These groups—family, play groups, small neighborhoods, and others—were designated by Cooley as being primary in several respects. In the first place, they are primary because they are the first groups known to human infants and children. Second, they are primary because they are instrumental in the formation of the human self and personality. In fact, Cooley depicted primary groups as the nursery of human nature.

Sociologists since Cooley have used the concept of primary group in a variety of contexts, contexts extending far beyond the initial years of socialization. Examples include motorcycle gangs, combat units, bridge clubs, and work groups within formal organizational structures in industry. What, then, is the similarity between primary groups like the family and those entered into as adolescents or adults? Diverse group structures may be classified as primary if persons within the group interact with each other on the basis of *primary social relationships*, which are intimate, laden with personal and emotional overtones, considered as ends in themselves, and involve many aspects of the group members' personalities. It follows, then, that *primary group structure* is a social group engaged in a set of social relationships that are intimate, personal, ends in themselves, and that encompass many aspects of each member's personality.

Secondary group structure and secondary social relationships

All of the above is not to say that every episode of social interaction among primary group members will be intimate, personal, encompassing, and satisfying in itself. Some of the interaction may be the opposite; social interaction that is impersonal, nonemotional, serves as means to other ends, and involves only a limited aspect of each participant's personality is called a *secondary social relationship*. However, a secondary social relationship is less characteristic of primary groups than it is of secondary groups such as the Ku Klux Klan, the Democratic Party, and Weight Watchers. Secondary social relationships may be observed between a coach and an athlete, a judge and a defendant, or a policeman and an accused criminal.

If secondary social relationships occur among members of a primary group, it is equally true that members of a secondary group may relate to each other on personal and intimate terms. Consider some illustrations. One fraternity member may try to sell a car or motorcycle to another. If the price is set and the sale accomplished without reference to the personal ties thought to exist among fraternity brothers, then the transaction would be a secondary relationship. The fraternity brother purchaser would be viewed as a buyer who should receive neither a break on the price nor inside information about the real mechanical condition of the car or motorcycle. On the other hand, primary relationships occur among members of secondary groups. Weight Watchers is a formal organization dedicated to the rather limited goal of separating people from their excess fat. Yet, even within the context of formal meetings, intimate, personal, and emotional relationships are carried out. A female member may relate to the others the personal details of a new social life that has followed the transition from "circus fat lady" to neighborhood sex symbol.

In brief, primary and secondary group structures are not pure types in the real world. Members of social groups relate to each other at some point along a continuum from predominantly primary to largely secondary social relationships. What follows is a more thorough excursion into the characteristics of primary social relationships. For present purposes, it will be sufficient to think of secondary social relationships as the opposite of primary ones.

Characteristics of primary social relationships

As noted, primary group structures share the basic characteristics of other social groups. In addition to these features they have other unique features that flow from the high proportion of primary relationships within them. Primary relationships are intimate and personal, involve many aspects of each member's personality, and are considered as ends in themselves rather than as a means to some other goal.[2] Table 12.1 contains these and other

TABLE 12.1 Primary and secondary social relationships

	PRIMARY	SECONDARY
Characteristics	Personal and intimate Involves total personalities Fulfilling in themselves	Impersonal Involves only specific aspects of personalities Means to other ends
Factors affecting the nature of social relationships	Face-to-face interaction Small group size Lengthly association	Physical separation Large group size Brief association
Examples of multi-membered groups	Family Village or small neighborhood Children's play group Bridge group	Court Pressure group Committee Panel of judges at a frog-jumping contest
Examples of two-person social relationships	Friend-friend Husband-wife Minister-parishioner Parent-child	Clerk-customer Policeman-criminal Coach-athlete Nurse-patient

SOURCE: Adapted with permission of Macmillan Publishing Co., Inc. from **Human Society** by Kingsley Davis. Copyright 1948 by Macmillan Publishing Co., Inc.

features of primary and secondary relationships along with some illustrations.

• PERSONAL AND INTIMATE NATURE OF PRIMARY RELATIONSHIPS. Persons who have formed primary relationships view each other as unique and irreplaceable individuals. Persons are irreplaceable and unique in the sense that the sentiments held for one person cannot simply be transferred to another. If a mate or parent dies, or if the relationship is dissolved for some other reason, there is no immediate and direct switching of the relationship to some other person. A substitute may eventually come along but only after a period of time during which a new personal relationship has been formed. And even if a substitute is found, an exact duplication does not occur, precisely because the original relationship was based on the personal idiosyncrasies of those involved.

It follows that personal relationships must rest on intimacy, on sharing oneself, on revealing oneself, on expressing deep feelings. Sentiments in primary relationships may range from hate to love. Feelings are not always positive, although a healthy dose of positive emotion is essential in sustaining a primary relationship over a period of time.

Secondary social relationships stand in vivid contrast. Buying a new automobile from one salesman cannot, in the absence of a personal relationship, be judged to be better than doing so from another. Salesmen, nurses, and electricians are easily interchanged; they are dealt with impersonally and with a lack of sentiment, except as attitudes and feelings are related to the services rendered. The fact that secondary social relationships are limited to only specific aspects of the participants' personalities provides a clue to a second characteristic of primary relationships, their encompassing quality.

• INVOLVEMENT OF TOTAL PERSONALITIES. A primary social relationship encompasses a wide variety and number of personal characteristics and current circumstances. Although any specific encounter may not actually involve the "total personalities" of those engaged in a primary relationship, an enduring relationship, with its myriad encounters, will involve many and diverse aspects of their personalities, taking momentary situations into account. In contrast, in a secondary social relationship persons are interacting on the basis of one or a few aspects of each other's personality. If strong feelings arise in an encounter with, say, an automobile mechanic, they are expected to be related to the quality of the work done. You may be pleased or incensed over the repair job, but other facets of the mechanic's personality are not considered relevant to your evaluation. Only his performance is at issue, not whether he got a good night's sleep or is in the process of being divorced. However, if the relationship is a primary one, the mechanic's performance on a given day may be judged within the context of his relative lack of skill in doing a particular thing, his present health, or a crisis in his home life.

Briefly, primary social relationships encompass total personalities, with various dimensions actually being called into play at different times. Given this sort of personal involvement, it is easy to see why primary relationships are not transferable.

• PRIMARY RELATIONSHIPS AS FULFILLING IN THEMSELVES. Using a normally secondary relationship like mechanic-customer as an example may be somewhat misleading. It is true that secondary relationships can assume a primary cast, but such a switch is hindered by the presence of a goal beyond the pleasures derived from personal involvement. The goal of getting one's car repaired may intrude, either preventing the emergence of a more completely primary relationship or causing the termination of the partial one that already exists.

To the extent that a social relationship is entered into and maintained for the intrinsic satisfaction it provides, to that extent it is a primary relationship. You are usually correct in exercising a healthy suspicion when a car dealer, upon first meeting you in the showroom, laughs at your jokes and repeatedly interjects your first name into the conversation. When there is a reason for maintaining a relationship aside from the personal fulfillment it can supply, it normally remains a strictly secondary one. On the other hand, a primary relationship may suddenly become a secondary one. This occurs, for example, when relatives or friends go into a business venture together.

While primary relationships tend to be ends in themselves, this is not always strictly so. A real friendship may be maintained partially because of the social status it provides for one of the parties. Also, in formal organizational structures there are certain tasks that may be better accomplished when primary relationships exist among members of the work group.

What makes primary relationships and groups grow?

There is no surefire set of circumstances for creating primary social relationships or groups. But there are certain conditions that increase the odds for their development. These conditions include face-to-face interaction, small group size, and existence of interaction over a relatively long period of time. These are not always necessary conditions—primary relationships may appear in their absence. Nor are they sufficient conditions, for primary relationships may not emerge in their presence. Nevertheless, as the number of

these conditions increases, the environment for the growth of primary relationships becomes more favorable. A more detailed discussion of these conditions will make clearer their potential impact on the nature of social
relationships.

• FACE-TO-FACE INTERACTION. The intimate and personal quality of primary relationships is best nurtured by close contact. Since such contact can
come from telephone conversations or lengthy letters, it is possible for primary relationships to spark or endure without face-to-face interaction. Evidence of this is provided by families who overcome vast geographic distance
via the telephone, or soldiers and sweethearts who maintain intimate ties by
letter.

Yet if it is true that absence makes the heart grow fonder, it may also be
that the fondness will be for someone else. It is difficult to maintain intimate
and personal ties from afar, partly because the subtle interchange of feelings, ideas, and attitudes of which Mead and Cooley wrote involves considerably more than words, written or spoken. Shades and depth of meaning
are interjected by gestures, physical touch, and voice inflection.

Related to this is the severe limit on the amount and type of intimate
and personal expression that can be transmitted by impersonal means such
as the telephone. A narrowing of the range of intimate and personal expression stands in the way of taking total personalities into account.

• SMALL GROUP SIZE. Face-to-face contact alone does not ensure the
growth of primary relationships. Fifty guests at a cocktail party may interact
in close physical contact without intimacy, without regard to total personalities, and with some other goals in mind—like making a business contact.

At least two factors work against the rise of primary relationships in
large groups. For one thing, engagement in primary relationships with a
large number of people within a short span of time is beyond the emotional
and physical energies of most of us. Second, the larger the group the harder
it is for the members to know each other well enough for the web of social
relationships known as a primary group to develop.

Still, there are cases of relatively large groups becoming primary ones.
Illustrations are provided by prisons, prisoner-of-war camps, and football
teams.

• PERSISTENCE OF SOCIAL INTERACTION. If face-to-face contact does not necessarily cause social relationships to become primary, the same holds for small group size. But a small number of persons engaged in face-to-face contact has a higher probability of becoming a primary group structure if their interaction persists over a long period of time. Intimacy, involvement of total personalities, and association as an end in itself are more prone to evolve as group members' knowledge of each other deepens and widens, a process normally requiring time.

Of course, primary groups exist without the benefit of long association. Two people may marry after a few days or weeks of courtship. Combat units and athletic teams may become primary group structures almost overnight. At the same time, a primary group may fail to appear even when a relationship has lasted for a long time. Prolonged military or union negotiations do not generally produce a primary group. Each side maintains its social distance, focuses almost exclusively on those social positions related to the negotiations, and keeps its formal goals at the forefront.

Now, what *does* make primary relationships grow? Even though one of these three conditions may be sufficient in some instances and all three insufficient in others, the most fertile setting exists when each condition is present simultaneously—when the interaction is face-to-face, the number small, and the association lengthy.

But if primary relationships can fail to appear even in the presence of all three factors, there must be something else involved in their growth. There is. That "something" is sociocultural rather than temporal (length of relationship) or physical (face-to-face interaction and group size). Specifically, the nature of the social structure in which persons are situated influences whether or not primary relationships will grow.

• THE IMPACT OF SOCIAL STRUCTURE. If persons are supposed to interact with each other strictly in terms of social positions that make no provisions for primary relationships, then their emergence is stifled. Union or military negotiations are illustrations—interaction is guided by the role prescriptions attached to the social positions of "lawyer," "adviser," "interpreter," or "negotiator." Theoretically no room is made for the position of "friend" or "relative" while at the negotiating table, positions calling for personal, often intimate treatment of the occupants.

Without a doubt, primary relationships appear in spite of the hurdles flowing from the nature of social structure. Negotiators may become close friends, and as you saw in the chapter on the social psychology of formal organizations, primary groups are an integral part of factories, offices, hospitals, and other formal organizational structures. So it is not that the nature of social structure prevents the emergence of primary relationships in all cases. Rather, social structure may prevent their growth even when the interaction among a small number of persons is face-to-face and of long duration.

If this were not so, the survival of the countless secondary relationships so vital to most societies would be gravely threatened. In the absence of

Bob Combs

social structural barriers to primary relationships, for example, friendship and favoritism would operate to a greater extent in government and business. Although it is often "who you know" rather than "what you know" in politics and industry, without social structural support for secondary relationships, it would be infinitely more difficult for a Ralph Nader to have any influence at all.

FUNCTIONS OF PRIMARY GROUP STRUCTURE

John Donne, the English poet, was quite right when he wrote: "No man is an island, entire of it self." Moreover, it is the rare person who wishes to be socially isolated. Although surviving on his own, De Foe's Robinson Crusoe was overjoyed with the arrival of Friday. The social-psychological costs of social isolation are high, as prisoners of war or convicts in solitary confinement will surely confirm. Primary relationships are the opposite of social isolation. And humans require and seek intimate and personal social bonds just as much as they attempt to avoid the damaging effects of prolonged isolation. This is in large part because primary relationships serve certain functions that are vital for the well-being of man. In addition to serving individuals, primary relationships generally function for the benefit of social structures ranging from a family to an entire society. These functions include making humans of infants, socializing persons for participation in social structures, providing emotional support, integrating individuals into larger social structures, and exercising social control.

· MAKING HUMANS OF INFANTS. Cooley summarized the humanization of infants when he wrote that primary groups are the nursery of human nature. As was shown in the previous chapter, without the benefit of at least some primary relationships, persons can develop their capacities for becoming what we think of as human beings only to the most limited extent. Anna and Isabelle took on human characteristics only after several years of close and intimate care.[3] Without some semblance of the intimacy offered by primary relationships, there is no well-developed self, there is no fully integrated human personality. Human infants can survive and develop with only secondary relationships, but compared with children exposed to primary ties, they tend to be at a physical and emotional disadvantage.[4]

· SOCIALIZATION OF PERSONS. New members of any social structure must either already have or come to possess knowledge of its norms and values. Whether it be the socialization of an infant or the socialization of a plebe at West Point, primary relationships are especially crucial for learning enough about the appropriate ways of thinking, feeling, and behaving to participate in social structures. Primary group structures are instrumental in the perpetuation of recurrent, stable, and predictable social relationships.

• PROVISION OF EMOTIONAL SUPPORT. That identification with a group is a powerful social force was illustrated in Chapter 1 by Emile Durkheim's study of suicide.[5] He located the social antecedents of varying suicide rates in the nature of the relationships between individuals and social structure. With respect to primary groups, Durkheim found that those types of people without intimate social bonds had unusually high suicide rates—for example, the divorced, unmarried, childless, widowed, and urban residents.

Combat units supply other concrete illustrations of the staying power that individuals derive from participation in primary group structures. In spite of being outmanned, underequipped, and in steady retreat for a period of years, the German army in World War II did not crumble. Against all odds, German fighting men rarely deserted or surrendered. Edward Shils and Morris Janowitz, the sociologists who documented this phenomenon, traced the German army's remarkable stability and combat performance to the existence of strong primary relationships within combat units.[6] Maintenance of men in primary groups—with their bonds of affection and mutually shared expectations for good military conduct—was fostered by the German military high command in the apparently correct belief that the result would be a better fighting force. Further evidence of the emotional supportiveness of the primary group in combat situations has been provided by the Vietnam war.[7]

• INTEGRATION OF INDIVIDUALS. Whether it be a stratification, community, or formal organizational structure, primary groups often serve to tie individuals into larger social structures. Integration into a social structure is usually enhanced if there is a connection through a primary group. Examples are provided by research in formal organizational structures. It was noted above that the German military command fostered the transformation of combat units into primary groups on the conviction that both performance and commitment would be heightened. This insight resulted in loyalty, integration, and a combat record that probably could not have been achieved by appealing to individuals per se. Given proper handling, primary group structures can be used consciously for the benefit of a formal organization. Of course, as the chapter on the social psychology of formal organizations showed, improper handling of primary groups may produce a lack of integration, as when groups of workers deliberately restrict the amount of work done or cooperate in order to avoid conformity to rules and regulations.

The integrative function of primary groups is not limited to formal organizational structures. Attitudes and behavior considered appropriate for particular social classes within a stratification structure are readily learned informally, as through peer groups among the young. If one's friends think, feel, and behave in certain ways, the validity of these ways is almost unchallengeable. Should these same directives come from a school principal or teacher—that is, through some secondary relationship—they would fall on an incredible number of selectively deaf ears. By the same token, peer groups can mobilize support for nonconformity to generally accepted norms, ranging from goldfish swallowing to stealing automobiles.

• EXERCISE OF SOCIAL CONTROL. As just implied, group pressure—particularly primary group pressure—is an extremely powerful force for the exercise of social control. William F. Whyte writes of a primary group—a boy's gang in an Italian slum—in which members' rank in the group influenced their athletic performance.[8] One member, Frank, had played semiprofessional baseball and was usually considered the group's best player. Yet, because recent circumstances had caused him to fall to the bottom of the group's status hierarchy, he began playing lousy ball. By his own account, he could play better when not playing with group members.

Whyte also observed a close correspondence between rank in the group and bowling scores—bowling averages tended to rise with rank in the group. This correspondence was no accident—it was maintained by group pressure. When a lower-ranked member began to bowl better than he had in the past, verbal remarks took the form of "You're bowling over your head" and "How lucky can you get?" Such verbal attacks were deliberately used to keep members in their place. The effectiveness of these efforts to influence a member's behavior illustrates the strong social control operating within primary groups.[9]

OVERVIEW AND PREVIEW

This chapter has dealt with group structure, the type of social structure that is the most social-psychological of all. Group structure is formed through the patterned interaction of a relatively few persons, persons who share a common identity, goals, rules for thinking, feeling, and behaving, and direct or indirect lines of communication. Unlike other social structures, groups tend to be small.

Although other types of group structures exist, one has been singled out particularly in this chapter. Primary groups are in many respects similar to other groups but the "primariness" of the social relationships among their members makes them unique. Primary social relationships are personal and intimate, involve total personalities, and are fulfilling in themselves. A primary group structure, then, is a social group engaged in a set of primary social relationships. Secondary social relationships and secondary groups are on the other end of the scale—they are impersonal, segmental, and viewed as a means to other ends.

Primary social relationships and primary groups are more likely to evolve under some conditions than others. The most favorable environment exists when the interaction is face-to-face, the group size small, and the association a long-term one. Primary social relationships can be formed without these preconditions and can fail to emerge in their presence. One reason for this lies in the nature of the social structure in which the relationships are conducted. That is, a few persons involved in face-to-face interaction over a long period of time may not become a primary group because, by the role prescriptions attached to their social positions, they are supposed to remain on a secondary footing.

Primary group structures serve important functions both for persons and for social structures. In the first place, it is largely through primary relationships that infants assume the features associated with being human. Second, much of culture is learned in primary groups, whether family or work groups. Because of this learning, persons are able to participate in stratification, community, and formal organizational structures. Third, primary groups provide considerable emotional support for their members. Fourth, primary groups serve to link individuals to other social structures. Finally, primary groups are a vital force in the creation of conformity through social control mechanisms.

To this point, the stability of social structures has been spotlighted to the exclusion of change in social life. In Part V the emphasis swings from stability and order to social change. Chapter 13 introduces the concept of social change, presents some theories of change, examines selected population changes, and looks at social movements as a vehicle of social structural transformation.

REFERENCES

1. Charles Horton Cooley, *Social Organization* (New York: Scribner, 1909).
2. This treatment of the characteristics of primary social relationships as well as the following section on conditions promoting primary relationships take much of their direction from Kingsley Davis, *Human Society* (New York: Macmillan, 1949), pp. 294–298.
3. Kingsley Davis, "Final Note on a Case of Extreme Isolation," *American Journal of Sociology*, 52 (March 1947), 232–247.
4. René A. Spitz, "Hospitalism," in Anna Freud et al., eds., *The Psychoanalytic Study of the Child*, vol. 1 (New York: International Universities Press, 1945),

pp. 53–74; René A. Spitz, "Hospitalism: A Follow-Up Report," in Anna Freud et al., eds., *The Psychoanalytic Study of the Child*, vol. 2 (New York: International Universities Press, 1946), pp. 113–117.

5. Emile Durkheim, *Suicide*, trans. by John A. Spaulding and George Simpson (New York: Free Press, 1951).

6. Edward A. Shils and Morris Janowitz, "Cohesion and Disintegration in the Wehrmacht in World War II," *Public Opinion Quarterly*, 12 (Summer 1948), 280–315.

7. Morris Janowitz, *Sociology and the Military Establishment* (New York: Russell Sage, 1965).

8. William F. Whyte, *Street Corner Society* (Chicago: University of Chicago Press, 1943), pp. 14–25.

9. Testimony to the effectiveness of group pressure also comes from experimental research with small groups. Fascinating experiments are reported in Solomon E. Asch, "Opinions and Social Pressure," *Scientific American*, 193 (November 1955), 31–35; and Muzafer Sherif, *Social Interaction: Process and Products* (Chicago: Aldine, 1967).

ADDITIONAL SOURCES AND READINGS

Cartwright, Dorwin, and Alvin Zander, eds. *Group Dynamics* (New York: Harper & Row, 1968).

Hare, A. Paul. "Interpersonal Relations in the Small Group," in Robert E. L. Faris, ed., *Handbook of Modern Sociology* (Skokie, Ill.: Rand McNally, 1964), pp. 217–271.

Hare, A. Paul, Robert F. Bales, and Edgar F. Borgatta, eds. *Small Groups*, rev. ed. (New York: Knopf, 1965).

Homans, George. *The Human Group* (New York: Harcourt Brace Jovanovich, 1950).

Mills, Theodore M. *The Sociology of Small Groups* (Englewood Cliffs, N.J.: Prentice-Hall, 1967).

Mills, Theodore M., ed. *Readings on the Sociology of Small Groups* (Englewood Cliffs, N.J.: Prentice-Hall, 1970).

Ofshe, Richard, ed. *Interpersonal Behavior in Small Groups* (Englewood Cliffs, N.J.: Prentice-Hall, 1973).

Olmsted, Michael S. *The Small Group* (New York: Random House, 1959).

Shepherd, Clovis R. *Small Groups: Some Sociological Perspectives* (San Francisco: Chandler, 1964).

part V

SOCIAL CHANGE

{·13·}

Social Change, Demographic Change, and Social Movements

"When Howard and George start letting their hair grow, I think we can safely assume that long hair is on its way out."

Drawing by Weber: © 1973 The New Yorker Magazine, Inc.

One thing seems obvious from the expressions on the faces of Howard and George in the cartoon opening this chapter—they believe that they are "with it." After all those years of railing about the subversive effects of long hair on American society, these two guardians of conventional morality have

253

finally bent with the times and have apparently conceded that hair reaching the shirt collar may not spell the end of manhood and decency after all. But if these two cornerstones of the Establishment think they have made the mod scene, their wives know better. By the time their rather conservative mates have made concessions to the changing society, the thrust of innovation is in some other direction; using their husbands as an indicator of the winds of change, these ladies might well expect shaved heads to captivate the New York cocktail circuit.

In fairness to the Howards and Georges of American society—and they are the majority of us—it takes no Rip Van Winkle or Alvin Toffler to tell us that we are in a period of often bewildering and devastating social change.[1] It is a cliché to say that change is one of the most unchanging features of American society. In a very short time we have traveled from the question "Does a lady kiss in public?" to questions like "Should mothers give their daughters the Pill?" or "What is the role of the university or college in the dispensation of contraceptives to single coeds?" Most people either find it difficult to grasp the interplay between public issues and their own lives or they do not have sufficient awareness even to make the attempt. If this is true as a general statement, its accuracy is translated into poignancy in what might be termed "future shock societies," societies that change so quickly that the future often becomes the here and now. In *Future Shock*, Toffler was saying that when change occurs with such velocity that tomorrow threatens to become today, people experience a kind of bewilderment, a confusion flowing from the absence of stability, recurrence, and predictability in social life.

Until this point, this text has centered on social structure with all of the recurrence, continuity, and predictability that it implies. In the next three chapters the accent shifts from order and stability to alterations in social structures. Social change can best be analyzed within the context of social structure. Without some social structure as a referent, how can the pace, extent, and type of social transformation be gauged?

Several major aspects of social change will be covered in the present chapter, which is divided into three major parts. In the first part, attention centers on the concept of social change and theories of change currently dominating sociological thinking. The second major division explores demographic change, specifically changes in population size. Change as expressed in social movements is discussed in the final third of the chapter.

SOCIAL CHANGE

What is social change?

If sociology is the scientific study of social structure, it follows that when sociologists are concerned with change, their attention would turn to changes in social structure. Because a social structure is an interrelated set of social relationships based on culture, social change encompasses transformations in both social relationships and culture. Social change, then, is really sociocultural change.

It is, of course, possible to consider cultural change without reference to social structure. This applies to both material and nonmaterial culture. Thus, the focus could be on such technological changes as the airplane and automobile, or on alterations in language and norms. But sociologists take social structure as their province and, by doing so, they tend to concentrate on changes involving the intersection of social relationships and culture. Say, for example, that the societal prohibition on the sacrifice of children were to be lifted. Rather than dwelling on the appearance and nature of a new norm calling for the sacrifice of babies to the gods, sociologists would trace the implications of this new norm for social relationships. Of course, the new norm would affect social relationships by virtue of becoming a role prescription attached to one or more social positions. Suppose that in religious ceremonies it was the duty of the father to kill his first male child on its third birthday. Additional norms would emerge to alter the social position-set that a family constitutes. Would the father, mother, and first-born son be expected to form intimate and personal ties? Or would the eventual human offering be kept in virtual isolation to prevent his participation in the primary relationships of the family? Although the ramifications of the new norm of infant sacrifice could be traced on and on, this is enough to make the point that sociology concentrates on the narrower topic of changes in social structure rather than on the broader area of cultural change. Simply stated, *social change* refers to alterations in social structures. Of particular interest are those social changes that have relatively important consequences and that tend to be comparatively long lasting.

All social structures change. The speed of change may vary from the glacial to the mercurial, but the existence of social change is a constant. Given this fact, at least two questions are relevant: What are the *theories* of social change? What are the *processes* by which social structures are modified?

Theories of social change

If considered one by one, theories about why social structures change are so numerous that they defy coverage in anything less than an entire book. But there are ways to classify these theories more economically. A widely

Bob West

used classification breaks theories of social change into four categories—evolutionary, cyclical, functional, and conflict. Although functional and conflict theory have some overlap with evolutionary theory, they will be treated separately.

• EVOLUTIONARY CHANGE. "Every day in every way, things get better and better." In simplistic terms, this idea of progress, of societies constantly moving toward improvement, was at the heart of the brand of evolutionary theory that dominated nineteenth-century social thought. In its nineteenth-century form, evolutionary theory held that societies must pass through a set series of stages, each of which resulted in a more complex and advanced social structure.

The assumption that "things get better and better" in part accounts for the fall of the social evolution theory from sociological grace some time ago. Yet, some of the more recent evolutionary theories of social change have gained a certain degree of acceptability. These newer evolutionary theories reject the unilinear cast of earlier ones. Given the sociocultural diversity around the world, they ask, how can we believe that all societies develop in a single direction? We simply cannot, they answer. Because societies assume varied paths of development—some toward greater unhappiness and deterioration—they see evolution as "multilinear."[2] Deliberately missing from these neoevolutionary theories are the ideas of definite and ordered stages of development and the absolute inevitability of change being in the direction of progress and human happiness.

• CYCLICAL CHANGE. If the neoevolutionists are willing to concede that some societies might on occasion even become less complex, the essence of cyclical change is that societies never follow a smooth, unbroken path toward improvement. Just as living things are born, mature, degenerate, and pass on, most cyclical theorists from ancient Greece to the twentieth century have depicted societies as fluctuating from low to high points and back down again.

• FUNCTIONAL THEORY OF SOCIAL CHANGE. Now we turn to the functional model, one of the two most influential theories of social change in modern sociology. The second dominant theory—conflict—will conclude this treatment of social change theories. As revealed in the discussion of social stratification structure, advocates of the functional and conflict schools are themselves in conflict over the validity of each others' theoretical positions. This debate has generated one of the most heated clashes among contemporary sociologists. Keep in mind that both the functional and conflict theories usually consider change from the societal viewpoint.

It is perhaps best to begin with a discussion of *classical* functional theory, which may be condensed into four major assumptions: (1) A society is an integrated whole; (2) all elements of a society contribute to its well-being and survival; (3) a society tends to maintain stability, to remain in equilibrium; and (4) a society rests on the censensus of its members.

The first assumption of classical functional theory is that all elements of a society are so interrelated as to form an integrated whole. All parts of a society are depicted as meshing and operating together with a minimum of conflict and maximum of consistency.

A second assumption of classical functional theory is that each element of a society contributes to its survival. That is, a society has certain functions that must be performed, and its interrelated parts have evolved to fulfill those needs. It is for this reason, the classical functionalists contended, that all complex societies have economies, family arrangements, governments, religions, and some means for formal or informal education. If pushed to extremes, classical functionalists would have insisted that the survival of a society depended on the contribution of any given element, whether it be governmental leadership, food-gathering technology, or norms of courtship. If an element no longer served a function, it would simply vanish from the scene.

While the first two assumptions retain some influence in modern functionalism, they have become much more flexible. It is now recognized that societies are not perfectly integrated, that conflicts and inconsistencies endure within them. *Modern* functionalists contend that a certain degree of integration is necessary for the survival of a society, but they are no longer bound to the idea that all societies are perfectly integrated. The extent of integration within a society runs the gamut from high to low. But because at least some degree of integration exists, functionalists favor a *systems* point of view—they believe that a change in one part of the society will very likely lead to modifications in other parts. As an illustration, functionalists could cite something like the reduction in family size that accompanies the shift from an agricultural economy to an industrial one. Specifically, the need for a relatively large pool of farm labor (fulfilled by having many children) disappears in an industrialized, urbanized society. Taking only this one instance, a change in the economy produced a change in the family. There are obviously further interrelated repercussions flowing from the rise of a capitalistic economy.

Thanks to Robert Merton, modern functionally minded sociologists have also yielded to the reality that not all elements of a society make positive contributions.[3] The repercussions of any part of a society may be positive (functional), negative (dysfunctional), or neutral (nonfunctional). Again following the lead of Merton, modern functionalists believe that it is essential to refer to specific parts of a society in ascertaining whether the effects are positive or negative. What is dysfunctional for one part of the society may be functional for another. While corrupt political machines typical of American society in an earlier era impeded democratic government, they also served human and social needs by providing jobs, education, food, and money to the poor. An aspect of a society may remain even though its function has disappeared: A norm, value, or role prescription may outlive its usefulness. Before streets were paved, it may have been considered necessary for American men to walk on the street side of female companions in order to protect them from water or mud splashed on the sidewalk by a horse, buggy, or automobile. This custom survives in the form of etiquette, despite the switch from dirt to concrete or asphalt for road surfacing.

In modern functionalism, then, elements of a society may have diverse consequences, both negative and positive, and their impact is best assessed by examining specific parts of the structure. If each element does not necessarily make an unalloyed contribution to the survival of the society, it is now assumed that the relative balance between functional and dysfunctional consequences must be on the positive side. Otherwise, the society would probably cease to exist.

This brings us to the third assumption of the functional perspective, the assumption that societies tend to remain in equilibrium, to regain the stability and integration that is interrupted by alterations in a part of the structure. Just as the human body creates chemical ammunition in order to restore its health in the face of disease, it is assumed that societies tend to maintain their prior state of integration in the face of disturbances.

While the first two assumptions of functional theory may have seemed irrelevant to social change, it is their interrelationship that functionally oriented sociologists use to explain the equilibrium tendency. This is the line of reasoning: If the parts of a society make contributions that balance out on the positive side so that the society continues to exist, and if the parts are integrated so that a change in one may affect another or others, then a change will be absorbed in such a way as to maintain the relative stability and consistency that existed prior to the disturbance of the society's equilibrium.

In this, its classical form, functionalism has been criticized for emphasizing stability and integration to the virtual exclusion of conflict and change. Modern sociologists who use the functional approach meet this criticism with the idea that societies maintain a "dynamic equilibrium." That is, over a period of time a society surely undergoes modification, but it retains the state of equilibrium by absorbing and adjusting to changes within the basic framework of the structure.

Consider the student unrest on college and university campuses in the late 1960s. One outstanding conviction of student radicals seems to have been that the structure of American society was so noxious that dismantlement was the only hope for the future. They were not successful in reaching this goal. But while American society is now rocking along in most ways just as it did before the "revolution," the waves made by students seem to have created some changes. The students may have altered the public's tendency to accept all wars as being in the national interest, and their efforts may have made universities and colleges more democratic and more responsive to student needs and goals. These apparent changes may be of long- or short-term duration. Either way, these changes, along with others, have been absorbed into American social structures—they have not revolutionized these structures.

• CONFLICT THEORY OF SOCIAL CHANGE. Grasping the conflict theory of social change is made easier by the previous introduction to functionalism. This is because, in broad terms, the assumptions of conflict theory are just the reverse of functional theory. The basic assumptions of each school of thought are presented in Table 13.1. It is obvious from the first three assumptions in Table 13.1 that conflict theory assumes the universal presence of change and conflict in direct contrast to the stability and integration portrayed by functionalists.

Discussion of the fourth assumption of functional theory has been reserved for this point because it is especially helpful in understanding conflict theory. From the functional perspective every society rests on a general agreement or consensus regarding values. That is, most members of a society are said to be of the same mind with respect to paramount goals and

TABLE 13.1 Contrasting assumptions of functional and conflict theory

FUNCTIONALISM	CONFLICT THEORY
1. A society is a relatively integrated whole.	1. A society experiences inconsistency and conflict at every moment—inconsistency and conflict are present everywhere.
2. Elements of a society contribute to its well-being and survival.	2. Elements of a society contribute to its change.
3. A society tends to remain in equilibrium.	3. A society is subjected to change at every moment—social change is present everywhere.
4. A society rests on the consensus of its members.	4. A society rests on the constraint of some of its members by others.

SOURCE: This quotation (adapted in table form) from "Toward a Theory of Social Conflict," by Ralf Dahrendorf, is reprinted from the **Journal of Conflict Resolution** Vol. II, No. 2 (June 1958), pp. 170–183, by permission of the publisher, Sage Publications, Inc.

principles. It is due to this high degree of consensus and the relative permanence of values, say the functionalists, that social integration is achieved.
In contrast, sociologists with a conflict viewpoint believe in the constraint
of some members of a society by other members. If true, this means that
persons often behave as they do because they are forced to do so by others,
rather than because of a conviction that they are following the "right"
course. To generalize conflict theory, societies feature a conflict of values,
not—as the functionalists would have it—a general agreement on goals and
principles.

This brings us to the center of the conflict-functionalist debate. People
generally do not struggle with each other when they are in fundamental
accord. Conflict tends to arise when there is disagreement on basic goals
and principles. Conflict theorists believe that different segments of a society have their unique goals and interests and that they compete (conflict)
with other segments for the realization of their own aims and interests. It
then becomes a contest, with the paramount weapon being *power*—the
ability to control the behavior of others even against their desire. Those
with the most power will, in achieving their particular ends, force others
to behave in ways that may not be of their own choosing. Social change
occurs as power shifts from segment to segment of the society, as various
interest blocs are able to gain their ends and work their will on others. As
an illustration, conflict theorists might point to the social and economic
events following the election of Franklin D. Roosevelt to the presidency.
To single out only one change, American society has moved more toward
a welfare state since the Democrats assumed national power in 1932. By
the same token, a bucking of the trend toward a welfare society ensued
after Republican Richard Nixon took office in 1968.

The foregoing summary of the conflict perspective on social change is
based on the ideas of Ralf Dahrendorf.[4] But there are some differences
between the more contemporary Dahrendorf and Karl Marx, the intellectual
father of conflict theory.[5] In the first place, Marx saw the unfolding of
history as the result of class conflict based on the ownership of property.
Those in possession of the means of producing wealth, the bourgeoisie, were
in a struggle with those who performed the work, the proletariat. Whereas
the struggle for the ownership of the means of production was the source
of conflict and change for Marx, Dahrendorf attributes alterations in society to the fight for power among various interest blocs.

A second difference between Marx and Dahrendorf lies in Marx's exclusive emphasis on the change of entire societies—capitalism would ultimately
divide society into two opposing classes. By contrast, Dahrendorf makes
room for a multitude of interest blocs that operate at all levels of society,
from local political elections to the White House, from Ralph Nader's
Raiders to ITT.

Both conflict theorists and functionalists recognize the presence of conflict and cooperation in any society. Stability and change are two sides of
the same coin. Societies change as a result of adjustments to "disturbances"

in their current state (as the functionalists contend), and they are altered by the process and outcome of power struggles (as the conflict theorists argue). It remains for sociologists to formulate a theory of social change incorporating the insights contributed by each of these schools of thought.

Processes of social change

Explanations for change in societies have just been presented. But no mention has been made of the processes by which they change. Alterations within societies are linked to two processes—invention and diffusion.

• INVENTION. *Invention* is the forging of a new element by combining two or more already existing elements and creating new rules for their use as a combination. Examples of invention on the material side of culture come to mind easily. It was not so much *what* Orville and Wilbur fashioned into an airplane—most of the parts were available to those who failed to fly— but *how* the elements were put together and the manner in which they were manipulated.

It is no different for the nonmaterial side of culture or for social structures. What is novel about group marriages? No new sexes are required. Sexual needs must be satisfied. Housework still has to be done. Income must be generated through employment or self-subsistence labor must be performed at home. Most of the elements of group marriage, then, have been around for a while. But within the context of some new norms defining who does what and who does what with whom, a new type of social structure called group marriage may be created.

The pace of social change as influenced by invention is closely tied to the complexity of the cultural and social structural base. As the base becomes more complex and varied, the number of elements as well as the number of ways in which they can be combined into inventions increase at a fantastic rate. Therefore, the more complex and varied a social structure, the more rapidly it will change. This helps to explain why several millions of years passed between the evolution of man and the invention of the automobile and the airplane, whereas men reached the moon in the century of Henry Ford and the Wright brothers. It is by this same process of social change that we can at least partially account for the existence of the bewildering array of dissimilar life styles present in contemporary America. But invention is only one process by which social structures are changed. Diffusion is another important process.

• DIFFUSION. When members of one social structure adopt elements of another structure—whether they be norms, values, role prescriptions, or a style of architecture—change has occurred through the process of *diffusion.* If the extent of invention depends on the complexity of a cultural and social structural base, the extent of diffusion rests on contact between members of different societies or subcultures. Borrowing from other social structures may involve entire societies, as in the American importation of cotton-growing from India. Or diffusion may take place between social structures within a single society. In fact, diffusion may follow invention within a single society. This is seen in the social and cultural spin-offs of the jazz subculture originating among black musicians in New Orleans, including "funkyness" in behavior, dress, and speech.

Group marriage was offered earlier as an illustration of invention. This type of marriage arrangement was invented at some time and at some place other than now in America. It has been transported into this country but, like most elements diffused from one social structure to another, it has been altered to suit the aims of its adopters. Diffusion of sociocultural elements seldom takes the form of complete duplication. If the two social structures are dissimilar and if each is integrated, then it could hardly be any other way; to gain acceptance, a borrowed element must to some degree mesh with the rest of the social structure into which it is being introduced. Thus despite the upsurge of unisex fashions in America today, wearing a Scottish kilt could get a construction worker laughed off the top of an unfinished skyscraper. Kilts still clash too violently with the American definition of manhood. And if skirts are ever to become as acceptable for American men as pants-suits are for women, either their form will have to be modified or the conception of masculinity will have to be changed.

Integrating a borrowed element into a new social setting also involves choosing not to incorporate other, associated elements. The Japanese, for example, can accept capitalism and a host of other elements while resisting the American form of government, style of conducting business, and family structure. Sociocultural borrowing, then, is a process of social change involving modification and selectivity.

Most of the elements of complex social structures and material cultures are borrowed rather than built from scratch. While the process of invention is a vital force, especially in changing complex social structures, the proportion of elements borrowed from other social structures far outstrips the proportion created by internal innovation.

DEMOGRAPHIC CHANGE

Key concepts in the study of population size

Demography is the study of changes in the size, composition, and distribution of the population within some territorial limits. Composition involves such factors as the age, sex, racial, and educational characteristics of a population. The fact that Blacks constitute slightly over one-ninth of all people in the United States is one bit of information on the nation's population composition. Some aspects of population distribution will be covered in the following chapter on urbanization. Among other things, demographers who study population distribution are interested in the proportions of a given population living in urban places of varying sizes, factors encouraging or retarding urbanization, and the rate and extent of world urbanization.

There are some key concepts used by demographers in the study of population size, the main topic to be discussed in the next several pages. They are birth rate, death rate, fertility rate, rate of reproductive change, rate of net migration, and population growth rate. When measured annually, as it normally is, the *birth rate* is calculated by dividing the number of live births in a population by the total population as it stood at the halfway point of the given year. Multiplying this figure by 1000 gives the number of live births per 1000 persons in the population, a much more understandable and usable statistic than the proportion derived from dividing births by total population size. Table 13.2 contains the formula for this and other indicators of population size change in nonsymbolic form. If, for example, 360 live babies were born within a total population of 9000 for a given year, the percentage yielded by dividing 360 by 9000 would be 0.04. Multiplied by 1000, this percentage would be converted to a birth rate of 40 live births for every 1000 persons in the total population.

The *fertility rate* is determined in precisely the same way except that it refers to the number of live births for each 1000 women of childbearing

TABLE 13.2 Rates used for measuring changes in population size

Annual birth rate =	$\dfrac{\text{number of live births}}{\text{total population at midyear}}$	× 1000
Annual fertility rate =	$\dfrac{\text{number of live births}}{\text{women of childbearing age}}$	× 1000
Annual death rate =	$\dfrac{\text{number of deaths}}{\text{total population at midyear}}$	× 1000
Annual rate of reproductive change =	$\dfrac{\text{live births minus deaths}}{\text{total population at midyear}}$	× 1000
Annual rate of net migration =	$\dfrac{\text{in-migrants minus out-migrants}}{\text{total population at midyear}}$	× 1000
Annual rate of population growth = rate of reproductive change + rate of net migration		

SOURCE: Adapted by permission from Donald J. Bogue, **Principles of Demography** (New York: Wiley, 1969), pp. 39–40.

age in the total population. Childbearing age ranges from 15 to 44. A *death rate* for a population is calculated just like the birth rate. Using the figures above to represent deaths, the death rate would be 40 deaths per 1000 persons.

The *growth rate* of a population is expressed by its increase or decrease in size for a specified time period, usually over the period of a year. Obviously, the birth and death rates within a population are central to changes in its size. If the birth rate within a population exceeds the death rate, then an increase in its numbers can be expected. This, however, may not be true in any concrete case because another factor is at work—that is, the gains or losses due to the difference between the numbers of people leaving and entering the population. It is possible for a population to decline even with a surplus of births over deaths if those leaving exceed those entering.

The movement of persons across a political line with the establishment of residence in the new area is called migration. Migration may take the form of population movement into a political unit (in-migration) or out of a political domain (out-migration). When the change of politically defined residence is from one country to another, in-migration is referred to as immigration and out-migration is termed emigration. The growth rate of a population, then, is determined by the rate of *reproductive* change (births minus deaths) and the net rate of *migration* (in-migrants minus out-migrants).

Of course, when the world population growth rate is calculated, there is no migration factor. Whatever the future of human settlement on other planets may be, so far neither the Russian nor the United States space programs affect the world's population size. Cosmonauts and astronauts either return or die. The absence of the migration factor makes calculation of the world population growth rate less complicated than determining the growth rate of a particular region, country, or community. The first step in arriving at the world population growth rate is to subtract the total number of deaths from the total number of births within a given time period. The second step is to divide the total world's population into the difference between total births and deaths. If the world's population were 20,000 and total births exceeded deaths by 2000, then the population growth rate would be 10 percent. This percentage would then be multiplied by 1000, and, in this hypothetical case, the growth rate would be 10 persons for every 1000 persons in the total population.

Population growth

Rapid world population growth—now standing at about 2 percent each year —is a relatively recent event.[6] By estimate, only 200 to 300 million persons were on the earth in 1 A.D. And it was not until 1650 that the world's population doubled to reach half a billion. While it required 16 centuries for the world's population to double for the first time, subsequent doublings have taken less and less time. The second doubling occurred in 1850; after the passage of 200 years the world's population stood at approximately 1 billion. By 1930, only 80 years later, another doubling was observed. A mere 42 years later, in 1972, a fourth doubling was imminent as the world's total population had climbed to almost 4 billion. At the present rate of growth, the world's population is expected to reach 6.5 billion by the year 2000, an addition of nearly 3 billion persons in only 28 years. If this projection becomes reality, as many people will have been added to the world's population in that 28 years as it took nearly 2000 years to reach (the world's population totaled 3 billion only in 1960).

There is another trend in population growth (explored more fully later) that becomes evident when regions of the world are divided into "developed" (Europe, USSR, U.S., Canada, and Japan) and "developing" (Asia excluding Japan, Africa, Latin America, and Oceania). Up to 1920, developed regions exhibited a faster population growth rate than did developing ones; after 1920, the trend was reversed, with the faster growth rate appearing among developing regions.

The ideas of Thomas Malthus provide a theoretical backdrop for a look at future population growth, especially as it is contrasted in developing and developed regions of the world.[7]

• MALTHUS' PESSIMISTIC VISION. For Malthus, man was destined to exist on the very margin of survival. In an essay first published in 1798 Malthus predicted subsistence living on the basis of his conception of the nature of population growth—man's capability to produce food would not keep pace with his tendency to produce children. Whereas human population, when unchecked, grows at a geometric rate of increase (2, 4, 8, 16, 32, 64), the human capacity for creating food and other means of subsistence progresses at an arithmetic rate (1, 2, 3, 4, 5, 6). If true, at some point population would outrun the means to support it. What Malthus called the "positive" checks on population growth were supposed to be constantly operating to keep population size on a level with the means sufficient for bare survival. Positive checks on population growth encompassed all those factors shortening human life, including diseases, epidemics, wars, famines, and insufficient shelter and clothing.

Malthus saw little hope for man to exist above the subsistence level. If one or more positive checks—a famine or epidemic—whittled population size down to a point that a surplus in the means of living existed, Malthus contended, the condition of surplus would simply cause people to have more children. Soon the surplus would evaporate under the crush of added numbers.

But what about man's ability to limit population growth by his own efforts? Given his observation of the human sex drive, Malthus had scant faith in the "preventive" check on population growth that he labeled "moral restraint"—that is, postponing or avoiding marriage while abstaining from sexual intercourse, or having an inactive sex life in marriage. Other preventive checks, such as prostitution or homosexuality, Malthus could not condone. Being among other things a minister, Malthus also reflected his times in absolutely ruling out the use of any birth control methods except moral restraint.

    • PROJECTED POPULATION GROWTH IN DEVELOPED AND DEVELOPING REGIONS. According to Malthus' geometric rate of growth, the population was to double every 25 years. It is only in the most recent times that this prediction has had any correspondence with reality. Partly because his pessimistic vision did not come true, Malthus' theory fell on very hard times. However, the current rate of population growth has led to the resurrection of some of his arguments. Still, their validity seems to be limited only to developing regions of the world, for it is in those areas that the rate of population growth raises the specter of the Malthusian bad dream.

As stated earlier, since 1920 the growth rate in developing regions has been greater than in industrialized areas. More important, if the tide is not turned, the next 28 years promise a near doubling of the population in developing countries. The top part of Table 13.3 contains, in millions, the population in various regions of the world as of 1972, along with the projected populations for the year 2000 in these same regions. Column 3 of Table 13.3 shows the percentage increase in populations now expected between 1972 and 2000. Consider the projected percentage population increases in the developing countries: Asia, 43 percent; Africa, 55.5 percent; Latin America, 54 percent; Oceania, 42.9 percent. Among the developed regions, the highest percentage population increase is 30.6 percent (United States and Canada). When the developed and developing regions are categorized separately, as they are in the bottom part of Table 13.3, two things are clear. Not only is the population projected to almost double in developing regions between 1972 and 2000, their rate of increase is twice that of developed regions.

Concentration of the bulk of the world's population in developing regions in 1972 and 2000 is equally apparent from columns 4 and 5 of Table 13.3. Seventy-two percent of all people lived in the developing regions of the world in 1972, and 78.9 percent is projected to do so by 2000, with massive concentration in Asia.

If unchecked, then, the population of the developing regions will double in the next 28 years and bring in its wake some of the dire consequences Malthus foresaw. Yet Malthus' prophecy appears to remain invalid for developed regions, which brings up the debate between those who believe the population to be exploding beyond control and those who are convinced that the so-called population explosion will be defused in the near future.[8] Those predicting the abatement of the rapid population growth often do so on grounds that modern birth-control methods are gaining widespread acceptance around the globe. This debate is more easily understood when viewed within the context of the process known as the demographic transition and the process of economic development.

• THE DEMOGRAPHIC TRANSITION. If developed nations have confounded Malthus' theory, they have done so by making what is called the *demographic transition*—they have lowered their death rates by successfully combating disease and have subsequently controlled their birth rates. This achieved balance between the birth and death rates at a low level leads to slower population growth. This process of attaining low birth and death rates is part of a "transition" because of the two stages of population growth that theoretically precede it. Prior to industrialization, the birth rate is high, but the population increases slowly because of a matching high death rate. Economic development ushers in the medical technology for reducing the death rate. However, the check on the death rate operates while the birth rate remains at its previously high level. The result is a rapid population growth rate. It is only in the third stage of the demographic transition that a low death rate is accompanied by a comparably low birth rate, returning a population to a slower pace of expansion. The three stages of the demographic transition may be summarized in this way: (1) high death rate + high birth rate = slow population growth; (2) low death rate + high birth rate = rapid population growth; (3) low death rate + low birth rate = slow population growth.

Various developing regions of the world are at different points in the first two stages of the demographic transition. Developed regions are in the third stage, but few have completed the transition entirely.

Lower birth rates must occur in developing areas if they are to curb their runaway population growth. While modern medicine and sanitation have reduced death rates in developing regions, birth control practices have not as yet been widely enough accepted to affect their high birth rates. Of course, the birth control technology exists, and great efforts are being made to distribute it throughout the developing world. Whether or not these efforts will be successful in moving developing countries into the third stage of the demographic transition is open for debate, for it is not

TABLE 13.3 Population projections by regions of the world (in millions)

Regions	(1) Population in 1972	(2) Projection for 2000	(3) Percent Population Increase Between 1972 and 2000	(4) Percent of World Population in 1972	(5) Percent of World Population in 2000
Asia	2154	3777	43.0	56.9	58.0
Africa	364	818	55.5	9.6	12.6
Latin America	300	652	54.0	7.9	10.0
Oceania	20	35	42.9	0.5	0.5
Europe	469	568	17.4	12.4	8.7
USSR	248	330	24.8	6.6	5.1
U.S. & Canada	231	333	30.6	6.1	5.1
WORLD	3786	6513	41.9	100.0	100.0*
Developing Regions (Asia excluding Japan, Africa, Latin America and Oceania)	2732	5137	46.8	72.2	78.9
Developed regions (Europe, USSR, U.S., Canada, Japan)	1054	1376	23.4	27.8	21.1
WORLD	3786	6513	41.9	100.0	100.0

*Percentages for the developed and developing countries in columns 4 and 5 in the top half of the table are not equal to those in the bottom half because Japan is included as part of Asia in the top half.
SOURCE: Adapted from "1972 World Population Data Sheet" (Washington, D.C.: Population Reference Bureau, 1972).

just a matter of the availability of birth control methods. People have to do more than know about birth control; they have to practice it. And practicing birth control seems to hinge partly on economic development. Fertility rates are clearly related to the level of economic development—people in poorer regions of the world have children at a much higher rate than those in richer areas. What is it about economic development that promotes the widespread practice of limiting the number of children born?

• ECONOMIC DEVELOPMENT AND POPULATION GROWTH. There are several factors associated with economic development, aside from the sheer availability of birth control technology, that appear to encourage family size limitation. For one thing, urbanization, which has accompanied industrialization in developed regions, has made land and housing scarce and, therefore, expensive. There is money to be saved if a smaller house or apartment can accommodate the family. In the second place, industrialized societies have laws prohibiting the employment of children. Children were economic assets in an agricultural society because of the labor they provided; however, in a society that makes them entirely dependent on their family for financial support while giving them no productive functions, children become expensive liabilities. Finally, because of rising educational requirements for employment in an industrialized economy, young people stay out of the labor force even longer than the law requires in order to become qualified for more desirable occupations. Consequently, even industrialized societies whose religious ideals forbid mechanical birth control have much lower birth rates than do developing countries.

It was stated above that lowering the birth rate by practicing birth control seems to depend on a high level of economic development. Certainly this was the case for those regions that are already economically developed. However, the pattern may be just the opposite for the developing world regions. A convincing argument can be made that rapid economic and social progress in developing regions must be preceded by a reduction in the birth rate. Otherwise, consistent with Malthus' theory, attempts to generate economic surpluses are often frustrated by an expanding population. It is not that a lower birth rate ensures economic growth. Rather, the high birth rate and low death rate characteristic of developing regions severely retard economic and social advancement. If marked economic development does not necessarily occur *with* a deflation in the birth rate, it is not likely to occur *without* it. Significant economic advancement is most promising when a successful birth control program is combined with a real agenda for economic development.[9]

Currently, the question of whether the so-called developing regions can overcome their population crush will easily draw a crowd and a heated argument. Optimists and pessimists, often nonsociologists, square off with little provocation, each dragging out the evidence of doom or salvation that he believes to be compelling. At this point, only one thing is certain—the humane solution is for population control to become a feature of societies in developing areas. Much of the debate centers on the probability of this happening before it is too late, before a rising death rate accomplishes what people have refused to do themselves. The specter raised by Thomas Malthus still appears to haunt peoples in developing regions of the world.

What a difference a child makes

The importance of limiting family size, even by only one child, can be illustrated by population projections for the United States, a country already in the third stage of the demographic transition. Figure 13.1 contrasts

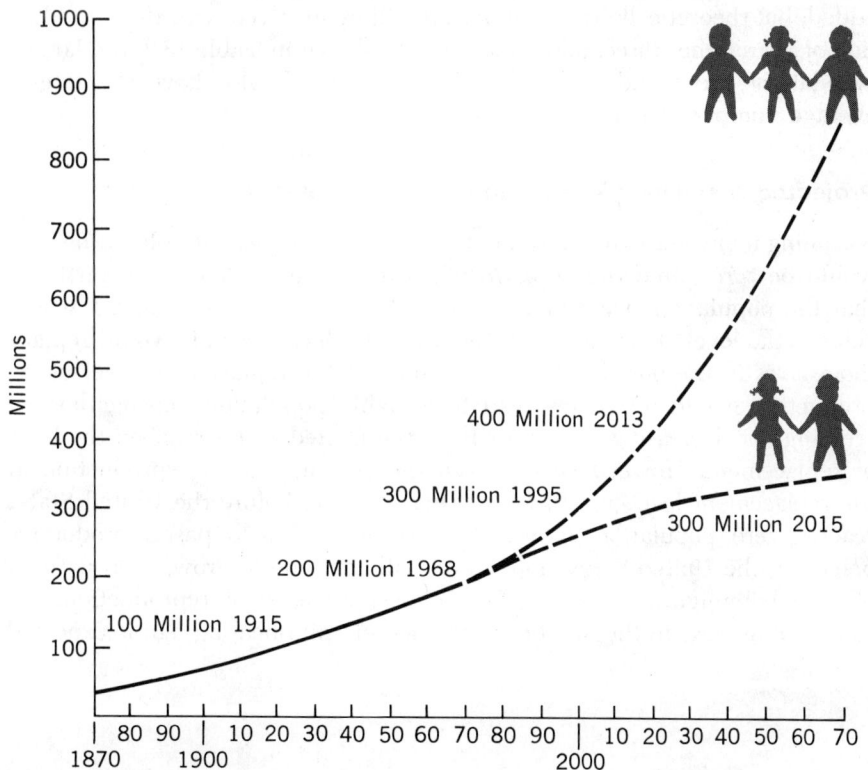

Figure 13.1 Projected population of the United States: 2- versus 3-child family
SOURCE: Adapted from **Population and the American Future. The Report of the Commission on Population Growth and the American Future** (Washington, D.C.: U.S. Government Printing Office, 1972), p. 23.

the projected population of the United States to the year 2070 for an average family size of two children and an average family size of three children. Assuming small decreases in the death rate and immigration at the present level, the two-child average family size would result in a population of 300 million in 2015. Should the average family size be three children, 400 million would be reached by 2013. And as times passes, the difference of only one extra child per family assumes added significance. By 2070, the two-child family would produce a population of 350 million, while the three-child family would push the population to almost a billion. To say it another way, with an average family of two children the United States population will not quite double itself in the 100 years between 1970 and 2070. Should the three-child family be the average, the population would double itself twice in this same period.

The population problem of developing regions becomes clearer with the recognition of the effect of even one child added to the average number of children in a family. The addition of one child per family has a greater impact as the population base gets larger; not only is one extra person added, but theoretically that one person will be involved with the reproduction of yet another three, and on it goes. As shown in Table 13.3, the largest populations are found in developing areas, which also have the largest average number of children per family.

Projected population growth in the United States

Assuming no increase in immigration, the end of the demographic transition would be *zero population growth*—when deaths are balanced by births so that the population size remains stable. A total fertility rate of 2.1 would achieve the level of replacement, the level at which a couple would replace themselves in the population. Maintenance of the replacement level of reproduction would ultimately lead to a stable population, one neither increasing nor decreasing in size. In 1972, the United States reached the level of replacement. However, even given the current rate of reproduction at the replacement level, it will be another 70 years before the United States reaches zero population growth. This delay is due to past reproductive behavior—the United States population will continue to grow, even without increased immigration and at the replacement level of reproduction, because an increase in the number of women of child-bearing age is expected in the next few years.[10] In other words, because the part of the population that reproduces will be larger as a result of past reproductive behavior, the total population is expected to increase even if the fertility rate remains constant. Therefore, according to the average two-child family population projection in Figure 13.1, the United States population will reach 350 million in 2070.

Demographic change and social structure

Changes in population size, composition, and distribution do not qualify as alterations in social structure as such, for total populations or their subpopulations, as studied by demographers, are merely social categories. But demographic changes are very relevant to the study of social structure, partly because of their implications for the nature of social relationships. That the worldwide shift in population known as urbanization carries with it many consequences for social structure was shown in Chapter 8 ("Community Structure: Urbanism"). The current trend toward small families in industrial societies, a trend affecting population size, alters the nature of family life. Many married couples are deliberately choosing to have no children at all; others are having fewer children so that, among other things, the mother will be freer to work outside the home. Occupational careers for mothers, in turn, may dramatically modify family social relationships—with the father sharing in the "psychological fulfillment" of preparing meals, taking his turn in the school car pool, or changing diapers.

SOCIAL MOVEMENTS

Collective behavior, social movements, and social change

Because sociologists are interested in social structure, they spend most of their time probing predictability and recurrence in social life. Yet not all human behavior is predictable and recurrent. America in the 1960s, for example, witnessed a kaleidoscope of events that defied social convention, that ran counter to the culturally defined ways in which people were supposed to behave. Ghettos were burned and looted. College and university administrators temporarily lost their offices to ransacking student rebels. Razor blades, scissors, and lipstick lost out to beards, long hair, and the "natural" look among many of the young. Opponents of the Vietnam war burned their draft cards, while bra-burning females displayed their contempt for the male chauvinism they saw everywhere. Civil disobedience became a method of operation within both the civil rights movement and the peace movement.

Each of these types of behavior—whether involving a crowd, craze, fad, or a social movement—is a type of collective behavior. *Collective behavior* occurs when large numbers of people behave for a relatively short period of time in ways that are not part of an existing social structure. Collective behavior is of relatively short duration because the form of behavior either disappears from the social scene (where have all the flower children gone?) or is incorporated into one or more existing social structures. An illustration of the absorption of collective behavior into existing social structures is provided by the civil rights movement. Keep in mind that the goals of the civil rights movement were incorporated, not the means used for attempting to reach them. So, while integration and equal opportunity are more fully operative with respect to Blacks in American society than they were prior to the sixties, riots, violence of other kinds, and disregard for the law remain unacceptable.

Forms of collective behavior range from the most unstructured, temporary, and inconsequential to the comparatively structured, lasting, and impact-producing. Panic behavior is on the unstructured, temporary, and inconsequential end, whereas social movements tend to be on the structured, enduring, and consequential extreme of the collective behavior scale. Of all types of collective behavior, a social movement is the most structured, has the greatest likelihood of becoming part of existing social structures, and has the highest probability of producing social change. Formally defined, a *social movement* describes a large number of people acting together over a period of time in order to promote or prevent a change in a social structure of which they are a part.[11] Most social movements are mounted to bring about a change in social structure. This was as much the case for Nazism and the American Revolution as it is for the Gay Liberation movement. Still, as the definition indicates, social movements may take a stand *against* social change. The movement that brought Prohibition to early twentieth-century America and the Ku Klux Klan, which still lives and breathes fire, are cases in point.

Social conditions promoting social movements

Sociologists are not certain about the causes of social movements. There is some agreement, however, on the social conditions that are most likely to breed collective action for the alteration or preservation of social structure. First, there must be some frustration and discontent with things as they are. Second, the frustration and discontent must be communicated to, and be shared by, reasonably large numbers of people. Third, the frustrated and discontented must believe that something should and can be done to alter their situation. Finally, those involved in the movement must evolve a social structure.[12]

• SOURCES OF FRUSTRATION AND DISCONTENT. Satisfaction with present conditions does not fire the hearts of men to push and shove for change. It is the frustrated and discontented who desire alteration in social structure and who are the most willing to fight for it. There are at least three sources of frustration and discontent that make a time ripe for the emergence of one or more social movements. If a relatively large number of people perceive social injustice, relative deprivation, or unfulfilled rising expectations, the seedbed for a social movement exists. Because they are interrelated, these three social conditions very often are experienced at the same time.

Few conditions allow people to become angry enough to strike out against the existing order more than a sense of *social injustice*, the conviction that the status quo is unfair. It is not just children who get red-faced when convinced that the tide of events going against them is unfair. Why, women's liberationists ask, should men hold all the dominant social positions, perform the most meaningful work, and receive higher pay than women when both are doing exactly the same tasks? Why, Cesar Chavez wants to know, should migrant farm workers labor so long and hard for so little when farm owners are turning healthy profits and other American workers are receiving high union wages?

Although it is not always the case, both Chavez's migrant farm laborer movement and the women's liberation movement get much of their fuel from a strong sense of perceived relative deprivation. *Relative deprivation* is felt when people compare themselves with others and believe that they should have as much as those others have. Women's liberationists compare the situation of females to males and Chavez's workers contrast their condition to that of farm owners and members of other unions. Because a comparison is made between one's situation and the situation of others, deprivation of this type is purely relative. There is no absolute standard for comparison, only the conviction among persons that they have less than some specific others possess. Consequently, relative deprivation is not reserved for the poor alone. In fact, well-educated or affluent (or both) middle- and upper-class females have been at the forefront of the women's liberation movement. And they have found their most active and vocal following among the educated women of America. These facts highlight the lack of an absolute standard for comparison in the phenomenon of relative deprivation, for it is lower-class women and the very poor who are in reality at the greatest disadvantage compared to the middle- and upper-class males used as a reference point by women's liberationists. One difference may be that most lower-class women do not use middle- and upper-class males as a point of comparison; moreover, they do not as yet see their own blue-collar or unemployed husbands as enjoying any particular advantage over them. Like social injustice (discussed above) and unfulfilled rising expectations (to be treated next), the feeling of relative deprivation hinges on the perception and definition of numbers of people. "Objective reality"—something impossible to agree upon when values and norms are involved—has little importance compared with people's interpretations of the way things are.

A third social condition creating fertile ground for the growth of social movements is that of *unfulfilled rising expectations*—when newly raised hopes for betterment either are not fulfilled at all or are not fulfilled rapidly enough. Social movements are not generally spearheaded by the oppressed until they have experienced some improvement in their situation. When people have tasted advancement, expectations of, and demands for, a still larger share of a social structure's "good things" swell to new heights. The momentum of rising expectations has been observed in the American civil rights movement in the 1960s and among the poor people in developing countries of the Third World.

• THE COMMUNICATION OF SHARED FRUSTRATIONS AND DISCONTENT. So long as personal frustration and discontent remain locked in the minds of individuals, collective action for the change or preservation of a social structure cannot be mounted. To promote a social movement, frustration and discontent must be shared, and those who share in it must know that they are in it together. Revolutions are not made of individuals. Lenin, Martin Luther King, Jr., and Betty Friedan could not have been leaders in social movements if in each case relatively large numbers of people had not been aware of their common frustrations grounded in perceived social injustice, relative deprivation, or unfulfilled rising expectations.

• BELIEF THAT CHANGE SHOULD AND CAN OCCUR. Frustrated and discontented individuals can know how they think and feel, realize that they share those thoughts and feelings with many others, but still not constitute a social movement. In addition, a social movement must have definite goals to be achieved, reasons why they should be reached, and means that will supposedly allow the members to realize them. At least in the early years, the civil rights movement sought equality and integration partly on the grounds that since all people are created equal, it is socially unjust to deny equality to any people whatsoever. Large numbers of Blacks and Whites were pulled into the movement not only because they believed that something should be done, but because they were convinced that nonviolent means could achieve the movement's goals. Among other things, they had seen an organized boycott defeat the Montgomery, Alabama, law requiring Blacks to sit at the back of public buses.

• DEVELOPMENT OF SOCIAL STRUCTURE. If a would-be social movement is not to evaporate, it must become socially structured. Like any social structure, the interaction of movement adherents must produce and sustain relevant values, norms, and social positions, or they will disband after a short-lived period of activity.

Values are broad cultural principles embodying standards for thinking, feeling, and behaving that evoke deep emotional commitment. In the case of social movements, values relate to the change or preservation of the existing order of things. Values specify what the movement should accomplish; some of these values are made public while others are more confined to expression among movement members. One reason for attempting to keep some values hidden from outsiders is that they may clash with values in the larger society. When social movement values are not linked with at least certain values held by members of the larger society, the outside resistance to the movement is greatly intensified. Particularly in its early years, the civil rights movement, for example, carried high the banner of equality, a central value of American society. It was when "black power," black separatism, and violent revolution surfaced that public hostility reached a new level.

An essential aspect of maintaining a set of values associated with a social movement (or any socially structured activity) is an *ideology*, a set of ideas designed to justify values. An ideology is generally accepted as ultimate truth that is unchallengable either by insiders or outsiders. If people believe that they have a corner on truth, then it follows that their values must have been etched in the heavens. An ideology is a complex and integrated set of ideas. The nature of ideology can be seen by choosing only isolated aspects of the Nazi ideology. For one thing, world domination and the maltreatment of Jews was defended partly on the grounds of racial superiority. To take another dimension, one aim of the Nazi ideology was to convince the German people that only the party stood between them and a world controlled by Jews and Communists.

Values are very general principles and are not specific about acceptable ways of thinking, feeling, and behaving. As a result, more specific rules based on values must be developed. These rules, called norms, arise from social interaction among social movement members just as they do in all instances of social structuring. Norms associated with social movements are of two broad types—norms guiding social interaction among movement members and norms regulating social relationships with outsiders.

Since members of a social movement are in conflict with outsiders, norms related to internal affairs are the most important because conformity to them demonstrates member loyalty, intensifies identification with the movement, and may serve to distinguish members from nonmembers. Norms in social movements are wide-ranging. A "party line" emerges so that members have a programmed and unified response to particular issues and events. John Birchers know they must condemn the opening of trade relations with China or the Soviet Union, and ecologists are suspicious of almost anything industrialists propose. Other norms may regulate a variety of activities. Consider the campus radicals of the 1960s. Norms defined ways of dressing (T-shirts, blue jeans, no shoes, lots of hair wherever it might grow), speaking (conventionally foul language came equally from the mouths of males and females), spending leisure time (drugs and acid rock were preferred to beer and Johnny Mathis), and eating (devotion to organic foods). Special words are normally created: "Pigs" were not pork, "grass" was not Kentucky blue, and a "trip" was not a vacation.

Of course, the degree of actual conformity to norms will vary with a member's commitment to the movement, and may change from hot to cold or vice versa as time passes. Also, the members of some social movements require strict conformity to norms, while others are more relaxed. Although there was considerable pressure for conformity among campus radicals, the very fact that they were opposed to the conformity they associated with middle-class society led them to accept the idea of "doing your own thing." At the other extreme are Black Muslims, whose normative code is clearly specified, rigid, and strictly enforced.

Social positions are present within the social movements that are able to get off the ground. A primary distinction in this regard is made between leaders and followers. It is especially among those at the forefront of the movement that duties are divided and role prescriptions are attached to social positions. Evidence of this is found in the observation of three general types of positions of leadership within social movements—charismatic, administrative, and intellectual.

A social movement nearly always has a fire-eater, the person who is most clearly identified with the movement both within the movement and outside it, who agitates, oversimplifies, and makes grandiose gestures and speeches. To outsiders, the *charismatic* leader may appear courageous to a fault, impractical, and hopelessly idealistic, but, as the label "charismatic" indicates, followers are drawn to him or her because of attractive and magnetic personality characteristics. Look to Hitler, Lenin, Ho Chi Minh, Jesus, and Martin Luther King for models of the charismatic leader.

Administrative leaders attend to the many tasks that must be handled if the movement is to persist. If the charismatic leader is to deliver a speech to inspire and gain followers, it is the administrative leaders who see to the details, including transportation, money, living accommodations, food, and having a crowd on hand. Administrative leaders balance the idealism of the charismatic figure with their bent toward practicality. Because administrative leaders do not see the values of the movement in the same rigid and absolute mold as does the charismatic leader, they are more willing to compromise such values in order to achieve the movement's objectives.

A shorthand description of the positions of charismatic and administrative leaders might read like this—the charismatic leader reduces the values of the movement to their most simplified form and comes to symbolize them, while the administrative leader makes efforts to promote achievement of the values. The *intellectual* leader is supposed to justify these values. In short, his duties revolve around the creation and elaboration of the movement's ideology. Intellectual leaders are important to a social movement not only because they supply a justification for its values, but also because their knowledgeable, reasonable, and logical image draws public respect for the movement.

Each of these leadership positions is an ideal type. In any concrete social movement, one person may fulfill two or even all three of them. Combining them, however, requires an extremely talented and versatile individual. And even versatility and talent do not erase the sometimes conflicting demands of the three social positions. How can a person be the picture of logic and sweet reason one moment, stir the souls of men the next, all the while coping with the details of running the show? Some rare individuals, going against the odds, have pulled it off. Stalin did it in Russia, as did Mao Tse-tung in China.

Social movements and social change

Do social movements really alter social structures? Some social movements come and go without making much of a lasting impact. But short of wholesale revolution, successful social movements contribute to change by causing the incorporation of some of their values and norms into existing social structures. And this may occur without conscious realization on the part of nonmovement members, even those who voice their opposition to the movement. Conservative Republican women active in state politics may shudder over bra-less women and the possible loss of such male gallantries as carrying packages and opening doors, while at the same time asking why there are not more women in positions of political leadership. Change brought about by social movements is normally a compromise between the movement's values and norms and those of the established order. This sort of change is helped along by the fact that at least some movement values and norms are framed so that they fit in with those of the social structures with which they are in conflict.

Even successful revolutions fail to tear down the old order and bring in an entirely new one. After the victory celebrations are over, social structures operate with a great deal of continuity with the past. In an important sense, things return to "normal" sometime after the revolution has been pronounced a success.[13] This is not to say that revolutions do not bring about social change. They do alter social structures. But the new order is generally a compromise between the new and the old. Many of the effects of revolution are long range.

Social movements contribute to the sociological study of social change by underscoring the fact that social structures are modified as the result of the interaction of human beings. Through collective action, people can and do mold and change the social structures in which they participate; people are not merely passive responders to some inevitable consequences flowing from forces such as technology. These forces may set limits to the directions that social structures can be pushed, but they do not totally *determine* the nature of social structures. That different social structures may be accommodated to a similar technological base is suggested from the observation of marked social structural variations among communist nations, capitalistic societies, and the developing countries of the Third World. There is a current controversy on this matter among sociologists, some arguing that industrialized nations tend to evolve similar social structures as time passes, others contending that sociocultural variations among societies are retained in spite of their common technological foundation.[14]

OVERVIEW AND PREVIEW

The central theme of the first twelve chapters of this text has been the existing social structure. This emphasis may have given the impression that the present order of social life has always existed and will endure forever. As indicated at various points throughout the earlier chapters, any such impression is false. Social structures, particularly large and complex ones, are constantly undergoing modification. The final three chapters of the text will explore alteration in social structures—social change.

In the first part of the present chapter you were introduced to theories and processes of social change. Theories of social change may be classified in one of four categories—evolutionary, cyclical, functional, and conflict. The latter two theories, which are in direct opposition to each other and which currently dominate sociological thought on change, have caused sharp disagreement among sociologists. Functionalists assume that a society is an integrated whole, consists of elements that contribute to its welfare and survival, tends to remain stable, and rests on the consensus of its members. In contrast, adherents of the conflict view contend that inconsistency and conflict exist throughout a society, elements of a society contribute to its change, a society is subjected to change at every moment, and a society rests on the constraint of some of its members by others. Functionalists have reinterpreted their assumptions to meet some of the telling criticisms made by many sociologists. And while a synthesis of functionalism and the conflict perspective seems to be the solution closest to the real nature of things, points of contention currently remain. A most important source of heat among sociologists of both of these schools of social change is whether consensus or constraint is the best description of why social change takes place. Emphasizing consensus, functionalists tend to see change occurring as new elements are incorporated into a society that maintains a "dynamic equilibrium." Placing constraint at the heart of the matter, conflict proponents see change as the result of shifts in power.

Social change occurs through two basic processes: invention, the creation of something new from the combination of two or more old elements; and diffusion, the borrowing of elements from one society by members of another society. The overwhelming bulk of the elements in a complex society are borrowed rather than invented.

Demographic change, fluctuations in population size in particular, was treated in the second major section of this chapter. Some basic measures used by demographers in the study of change in population size are expressed as rates. They include the birth rate, fertility rate, death rate, rate of reproductive change, net rate of migration, and population growth rate.

Thomas Malthus predicted at the beginning of the nineteenth century that humans were destined to live at a mere survival level because their rate of reproduction was so much greater than their capacity for generating a food supply. It now appears that Malthus' dire prophecy will not hold true for developed countries but may be descriptive of developing nations of the Third World. Whether developing nations will enter the final stage of the so-called demographic transition—in which a low death rate is balanced by a low birth rate to produce slow or stable population growth—seems to depend in large part on the success of birth control programs. And the widespread use of birth control techniques is highly correlated with the level of economic development.

The conclusion of the demographic transition is zero population growth, when, assuming no increase in immigration, deaths and births balance each other to keep the population size constant. As of 1972 the United States reached the level of replacement—an average of two children per family to replace the parents—but given the higher fertility rate in the past, its population is expected to continue growing for the next 70 years.

Not all human behavior is predictable and recurrent, as is evidenced from the study of collective behavior—short-lived behavior that falls outside any existing social structure. Although all forms of collective behavior —crowds, mobs, crazes, and fads—may lead to social change, a social movement is most likely to effect such change. Compared with other types of collective behavior, social movements are the most structured, enduring, and consequential. Most social movements involve the efforts of large numbers of people to bring about social structural change, although some take the preservation of social structure as their goal. The causes of social movements are not precisely known. But there are some social conditions that provide fertile ground for the appearance of a successful social movement. These conditions include the presence of frustration and discontent among large numbers of people, communication of this frustration and discontent among those who share it, the conviction that something can and should be done to change the situation, and the development of a social structure complete with social positions and role prescriptions. If a social movement does not take the form of a successful revolution, its impact will probably consist of having some of its values and norms become part of the established social structure. Even successful revolutions do not appear to destroy the former social fabric completely.

In the following chapter, urbanization, a major trend all over the world, is explored. Central to urbanization are changes in the distribution of population and urban spatial arrangements of services, population, and facilities.

REFERENCES

1. Alvin Toffler, *Future Shock* (New York: Random House, 1970).
2. Julian H. Steward, *Theory of Culture Change* (Urbana: University of Illinois Press, 1959).
3. Robert K. Merton, *Social Theory and Social Structure*, rev. ed. (New York: Free Press, 1957), pp. 19–84.
4. Ralf Dahrendorf, "Toward a Theory of Social Conflict," *Journal of Conflict Resolution*, 2 (June 1958), 174–179.
5. T. B. Bottomore and Maximilien Rubel, *Karl Marx: Selected Readings in Sociology and Social Philosophy* (New York: McGraw-Hill, 1964).
6. Donald J. Bogue, *Principles of Demography* (New York: Wiley, 1969), pp. 47–51.
7. Thomas R. Malthus, *An Essay on the Principle of Population* (Homewood, Ill.: Dorsey, 1963).
8. Kingsley Davis, "Population Policy: Will Current Programs Succeed?" *Science*, 158 (November 1967), 730–739 and Donald J. Bogue, "The Prospects for World Population Control," in Bogue, op. cit., pp. 11–20.
9. Bogue, ibid., pp. 78–79.

10. *Family Planning Digest*, 2 (May 1973), 2.
11. Ralph H. Turner and Lewis M. Killian, *Collective Behavior*, 2nd ed. (Englewood Cliffs, N.J.: Prentice-Hall, 1972), pp. 246.
12. The following treatment of social movements takes its framework from Lewis M. Killian, "Social Movements," in Robert E. L. Farris, ed., *Handbook of Modern Sociology* (Skokie, Ill.: Rand McNally, 1964), pp. 432–454.
13. Crane Brinton, *The Anatomy of Revolution* (New York: Vintage: 1960).
14. Jon M. Shepard, ed. *Organizational Issues in Industrial Society* (Englewood Cliffs, N.J.: Prentice-Hall, 1972), pp. 1–61.

ADDITIONAL SOURCES AND READINGS

Social change

Allen, Francis R. *Socio-Cultural Dynamics: An Introduction to Social Change* (New York: Macmillan, 1971).
Appelbaum, Richard P. *Theories of Social Change* (Chicago: Markham, 1970).
Chambliss, William J., ed. *Sociological Readings in the Conflict Perspective* (Reading, Mass.: Addison-Wesley, 1972).
Lauer, Robert H. *Perspectives on Social Change* (Boston: Allyn & Bacon, 1973).
Moore, Wilbert E. *Social Change* (Englewood Cliffs, N.J.: Prentice-Hall, 1963).

Demographic change

Ehrlich, Paul R. *The Population Bomb* (New York: Ballantine, 1968).
Freeman, Ronald, ed. *Population: The Vital Revolution* (Garden City, N.Y.: Doubleday, 1964).
Hauser, Philip, ed. *The Population Dilemma* (Englewood Cliffs, N.J.: Prentice-Hall, 1969).
Peterson, William. *Population*, 2nd ed. (New York: Macmillan, 1969).
Wrong, Dennis H. *Population and Society* (New York: Random House, 1967).

Social movements

Blumer, Herbert. "Social Movements," in Alfred M. Lee, ed. *Principles of Sociology* (New York: Barnes & Noble, 1969).
Cameron, William Bruce. *Modern Social Movements: A Sociological Outline* (New York: Random House, 1966).
Cantril, Hadley. *The Psychology of Social Movements* (New York: Wiley, 1963).
Gusfield, Joseph R., ed. *Protest, Reform, and Revolt: A Reader in Social Movements* (New York: Wiley, 1970).
McLaughlin, Barry, ed. *Studies in Social Movements: A Psychological Perspective* (New York: Free Press, 1969).
Smelser, Neil J. *Theory of Collective Behavior* (New York: Free Press, 1963).
Toch, Hans. *The Social Psychology of Social Movements* (Indianapolis: Bobbs-Merrill, 1965).

{14}

Urbanization

DEMOGRAPHIC ASPECTS OF URBANIZATION • Urban places • Rate and extent of world urbanization • Urban growth and urbanization in the third world • Urbanization in the United States • Metropolitan dispersal • The future • Convergence of rural and urban **ECOLOGICAL ASPECTS OF URBANIZATION** • Spatial aspects of city growth • Ecological processes

Drawing by W. Miller; © 1971 The New Yorker Magazine, Inc.

A coast-to-coast hamburger chain carrying his name directly contradicts what Thoreau envisioned when he called for a return to nature. Nature, in Thoreau's mind, was tough enough without adding the digestive and health hazards associated with assembly-line sandwiches. Opening a "Thoreau-Burgers" stand in the wilderness turns Thoreau on his head, conflicting, as it does, with the social isolation and intellectual growth he sought at Walden Pond. Yet the irony of the cartoon that introduces this chapter highlights a central fact of modern community life—highly industrialized societies are highly urbanized societies. Let us take the United States as an example. In 1790, a mere 5 percent of the American population lived in "urban" areas (places of 2500 people or more). Today, America is not only an urban society, it is a metropolitan society. Approximately 70 percent of the American people live in areas defined as metropolitan (that is, cities of 50,000 or more in combination with the surrounding population economically and socially linked to the central city itself). It is becoming more and more difficult to find areas where the economic equivalent of Thoreau-Burger establishments are not popping up to serve the needs and desires of our expanding and concentrated population.

This chapter is devoted to an analysis of urban community structure through the concept of urbanization. Without defining it precisely at this point, it is worthwhile to note that urbanization pertains to the physical dimensions of community structure. Particularly important approaches are the *demographic*—alterations in the size, composition, and distribution of population within some territorial limits—and the *ecological*—growth and distribution patterns of services, people, and physical attributes such as highways and buildings, along with the processes involved in community growth and distribution.

Urbanization encompasses the physical dimensions of community structure within which the social aspects of community life are carried out. Urbanism, as you will recall from Chapter 8, captures the idea of the existence of distinctive social relationships within urban populations.

DEMOGRAPHIC ASPECTS OF URBANIZATION

It is easy to confuse urbanization with the growth of cities because the two processes tend to occur at the same time. Urbanization does involve the growth of cities but goes beyond it. *Urbanization* is the process by which an increasingly larger proportion of a society's population resides in urban areas. A society's total population lives in either rural or urban areas; as urban areas gain population relative to rural areas, urbanization is said to occur. Urbanization is broader than the growth of cities: If the rural population were to grow as fast as, or faster than, the urban population, urbanization would not be operating, even if cities themselves continued to gain in population. Urbanization, then, is a process that is meaningful only when applied to changes in the *ratio* of rural to urban population growth.

The distinction between the growth of cities and urbanization is important because one of these processes theoretically has a termination point whereas the other does not. When the urban population is no longer able to grow faster than the rural population, the process of urbanization is at an end. This contention would remain true even if the urban areas in which nearly all of the population lives were to continue to experience population expansion. In fact, urbanization in most highly advanced societies is slowing down considerably; that is, while the urban population continues to grow, there is too little rural population left to reflect a very significant rural to urban change in population.[1]

Urban places

Urban places are relatively high concentrations of people living within comparatively small geographic areas. For some time the United States Census Bureau defined as urban those incorporated places of 2500 persons or more. The growth of large cities made this long-standing census definition a limited one. It is hardly accurate to lump together places of approximately 2500 persons or even 250,000 inhabitants with those cities containing millions of people either stacked into high-rise apartment buildings or located in the suburban areas branching out from the city proper. For this reason, further definitions have been added in the last twenty years.

Urbanized areas contain one or two central cities with a total population of 50,000 plus the population of the nearby suburban areas. *Standard Metropolitan Statistical Areas* (SMSAs) refer to one or two central cities with a total population of 50,000 persons or more plus the population of counties in which the cities are located as well as the people of adjacent counties that meet certain criteria of economic and social integration with the central city or cities. Another designation covers the metropolitan complexes found in New York City and Chicago: *Standard Consolidated Areas* (SCAs) include those contiguous SMSAs and additional counties that have strong economic and social ties with the central city. While this designation will be used more extensively in the future, only the New York City and Chicago SCAs now exist in the United States.

These community size distinctions are important not because of their universal usage. In fact, the simple demarcation line for rural versus urban in countries over the world varies as dramatically as 2000 persons in France to 30,000 persons in Japan. Rather, the significance of urban community size lies in its implications for discussion of the ecological and social nature of urban community structure. For example, it should be kept in mind that differences can be observed among an urban community of 5000, an urbanized area of 80,000, an SMSA of 500,000, and an SCA of several million, even though each of these types of areas falls under the umbrella "urban place." These distinctions are also essential in comparing societies—a comparison of urban places of 2500 persons or more in America with urban places of 30,000 persons or more in Japan introduces some biases that should not be overlooked.

Rate and extent of world urbanization

Although the first cities appeared in the neighborhood of 5000 years ago, extensive urbanization had to wait until the industrial and agricultural revolutions of the last two centuries. Not only is extensive urbanization a relatively recent occurrence, its growth in the last century and a half is only slightly less astounding than its projected heights. Table 14.1 shows the percentage of the world's population living in cities of 20,000 or more and 100,000 or more from 1800 to 1970. It is clear that the proportion of the world's population living in either of these categories more than doubled each half-century from 1850 to 1950. Moreover, the pace of urbanization has not slackened since 1950. Since there is reason to believe that the 1900–1950 figures are too high, it may be that the pace of urbanization has actually picked up speed slightly.

How long can the present rate of world urbanization continue? Since urbanization is defined as the ratio of urban to rural population, it is certain that it cannot exceed 100 percent. This means that the process of urbanization would end in about 60 years when, according to the above projections, there will be no more rural residents. It is expected, however, that the

TABLE 14.1 Rate of world urbanization

	PERCENTAGE OF WORLD'S POPULATION	
Year(s)	In Cities 20,000 +	In Cities 100,000 +
1800	2.4%	1.7%
1850	4.3	2.3
1900	9.2	5.5
1950	22.7	16.2
1970*	32.2	23.8

*Estimated.
SOURCE: Adapted by permission from Kingsley Davis, **World Urbanization 1950–1970. Volume II: Analysis of Trends, Relationships, and Development** (Berkeley: Institute of International Studies, University of California, 1972), p. 51.

pace of world urbanization is currently at its peak, and projections indicate that it will decline in the future. Even if projections based solely on the 1950–1970 rate of urbanization do prove to be inflated above the reality of the future, human beings are unmistakably becoming urban creatures.

The figures in Table 14.1 refer to the total world population and do not reflect the differential extent and rate of urbanization in various regions of the world. Since urbanization is so closely associated with industrialization and economic development, it is predictable that urbanization would reach its highest level in countries affected by the culture of northwestern Europe, where the Industrial Revolution began. This is reflected in Table 14.2, which reveals that the highest levels of urbanization as of 1970 are found on the continents of Australia-New Zealand, North America, Europe, and in the USSR. Latin America is not far behind Europe and the USSR, but the enormous gap between Asia and Africa, on the one hand, and all other continents, on the other hand, has increased in the past 20 years. Since Asia alone contains over half of the world's population, its low population concentration in urban places severely depresses the worldwide level of urbanization discussed above. Urbanization in the less economically developed countries deserves some special attention.

Urban growth and urbanization in the third world

For the most part, the preceding discussion of urbanization has focused on the so-called *First World*—the Western countries—and the *Second World*—the Soviet Union and its associated countries. Yet the countries outside the

TABLE 14.2   Estimated degree of urbanization in continental areas: 1970

Continental Area	Rural	Total Urban	Places Less Than 100,000	Cities 100,000 +
Australia-New Zealand	15.7%	84.3%	23.1%	61.1%
Northern America	24.9	75.1	17.7	57.4
Europe	37.0	63.0	24.1	38.9
USSR	37.7	62.3	30.9	31.4
Latin America	45.6	54.4	20.9	33.5
Asia	74.6	25.4	9.7	15.7
Africa	78.2	21.8	10.6	11.2
Oceania	92.2	7.8	7.8	—

SOURCE: Adapted by permission from Kingsley Davis, **World Urbanization 1950–1970. Volume II: Analysis of Trends, Relationships, and Development** (Berkeley: Institute of International Studies, University of California, 1972), p. 170.

East-West axis hold three-fourths of the world's population; it is in this *Third World*, which includes Africa, Asia, and Latin America, that the most rapid growth of urban population is currently found. There are some marked differences between Third World countries and other countries that make the nature of urbanization in the former unique.

Although there are some highly economically developed countries in the Third World (Japan, South Africa, and Argentina) and some relatively undeveloped areas in the First World (eastern and southern Europe), Third World countries are those normally referred to as "developing" countries. It is the comparatively low level of economic development along with an unmistakable population explosion, in both urban and rural areas, that contribute most to the unique pattern of urbanization in the Third World.

In the Western and Soviet-bloc countries, industrialization preceded urbanization. Rural residents in these countries were drawn to cities to escape rural poverty and to take advantage of occupational and economic opportunities. With industrial development, the cities not only could absorb vast numbers of people, they needed them to satisfy the demand for an expanded labor force. Rural inhabitants in Third World countries have been even more willing to migrate to cities for the same advantages and opportunities sought by those before them in Western countries. Here the similarity ends. Because urbanization has preceded industrialization in Third World countries, the economic base of their cities is neither deep nor wide enough to absorb the heavy influx of rural migrants. Consequently, vast numbers of unemployed rural migrants settle into fast-growing city slum areas. Like slum dwellers everywhere, they are without jobs, adequate housing, public services, or health care.

This pattern of excessive urban growth in relation to economic development, which is characteristic of Third World countries, is heightened by an exploding population. Population growth in developing nations has doubled that of developed countries ever since 1940, a rate of growth that outstrips by a wide margin the rate experienced by industrialized countries during their nineteenth-century period of expansion. This phenomenal population growth rate, due largely to a dramatic decrease in the death rate without a sufficiently compensating reduction in the birth rate, pushes people off the land and into the cities, while simultaneously increasing the population already living in the urban areas. Third World countries thus find themselves in a double bind—they are unable to absorb urban residents successfully, and the strain of overpopulation further retards economic development.

Urban growth—a population increase within the confines of urban places —has been the point of this discussion thus far. Urbanization, you will recall, refers to an increase in the ratio of urban to rural population. Urban growth, then, can proceed either without urbanization or faster than urbanization. And in Third World countries, urban growth is taking place faster than urbanization. While the rate of urbanization in developing countries is slightly higher than it was for those industrializing in the nineteenth century,

Bob West

it is held in check because urban and rural segments of the total population are increasing simultaneously at a devastating rate.

Urbanization in the United States

At the time of the first census in the United States in 1790, no American city had more than 50,000 inhabitants. As noted at the beginning of this chapter, three-fourths of all Americans now live in cities of more than 50,000. In fact, more than half reside in cities of 100,000 or more. Given these proportions of our total population in metropolitan areas and the knowledge that as of 1970 the rural population itself began to decrease, it can only be concluded that our population growth is overwhelmingly reflected in metropolitan expansion. Metropolitan growth requires land, and almost all metropolitanization in the United States has involved the conversion of rural areas into suburbs. It is impossible, then, to consider population growth in the United States without reference to metropolitan dispersal or suburbanization.

• METROPOLITAN DISPERSAL. Standard Metropolitan Statistical Areas, you will recall, are comprised of one or two central cities with a total population of 50,000 persons or more plus the population in economically and socially integrated counties. *Metropolitan dispersal*—which occurs when central cities lose population relative to the area surrounding them—is a hallmark of contemporary American urban growth. By 1970, 15 of the 21 central cities that had a population of one-half million or more in 1960 showed losses in population. In the country as a whole, the population outside central cities is expanding several times as fast as are the central cities themselves. As of 1970, more than half the American metropolitan population lived outside central cities. Most of the metropolitan growth in the decade between 1960 and 1970 was due to suburbanization. Moreover, the rate of population growth appears to rise as distance from the central city increases.

Metropolitan dispersal is possible primarily because of developments in communication (notably the telephone) and transportation (especially highways, automobiles, and trucks). People can live outside central cities either because they can manage daily commuting to work or because businesses that have left the central city are now located near suburban residences. Technological developments encouraging metropolitan growth are constantly being marketed; part of the clerical staff of a large insurance company, for example, can be located far from the home office in Manhattan and still perform their jobs because of computer terminals that provide them ready access to data stored in the home office computer facility. Or, to take a more recent example, the Xerox Corporation's Telecopier enables a Bangor, Maine, architect to transmit, with the aid of the telephone, copies of blueprints to a San Diego, California, customer in just a few minutes.

• THE FUTURE. The past has seen urbanization in the United States evolve from small towns to cities to metropolitan areas. If the present character of urbanization lies in the growth of metropolitan areas, the future promises the integration of originally separate metropolitan areas. The population concentrations formed through the spatial meeting of formerly distinct metropolitan areas are called urban regions. Technically, *urban regions* are places containing population concentrations of one million or more people residing in a continuous belt of metropolitan areas. It is for the largest of such urban units that the U.S. Bureau of the Census devised the label Standard Consolidated Areas, more popularly known as "megalopolises."

If the present national population projections hold, the year 2000 will see 54 percent of our people living in two megalopolises. Forty-one percent will be contained in the converged metropolitan areas stretching south from southern New Hampshire to northern Virginia and extending westward to Chicago and beyond. The remaining 13 percent will live in the megalopolis that will have developed between San Francisco and San Diego. And this is not to mention those smaller urban regions developing around such city combinations as Detroit-Toledo, St. Louis-Kansas City, Houston-Dallas, and Miami-Tampa. It is projected that by the year 2000 five-sixths of our total population will live in fused metropolitan areas known as urban regions.

• CONVERGENCE OF RURAL AND URBAN. The process of metropolitanization and the creation of urban regions has an important impact on the physical nature of American community structure—the increased blurring of the distinction between rural and urban areas. In the first place, urban regions are formed from the physical meeting of two or more formerly separate metropolitan areas. This means that the rural areas between converging metropolitan areas continuously diminish. However, one need not necessarily envision wall-to-wall concrete, since it is projected that by the year 2000 five-sixths of the total United States population will be concentrated on one-sixth of its continental land area. Second, as of 1970 only 26 percent of the American population lived in rural areas. Rural areas have experienced a continual decline in the ratio of rural to urban proportion of the population—this is precisely what urbanization means. However, it was only in 1960 that the rural population displayed a decrease in its absolute size. While its growth rate in the past had always been slower than the urban population's, its number had always increased. Thus, the end of urbanization in America cannot be far away because the rural population continues to evaporate.

If the process of urbanization is nearly over, it must be recognized that, barring physical destruction through war or natural catastrophe, urban living itself will be a most constant feature of the American landscape. Although the percentage of the population in places of 10,000 or more has increased between 1940 and 1970—suggesting that small-town life is not completely disappearing—these places tend to be urban in life style because of their economic, social, and political ties with nearby metropolitan areas or urban regions. Communities, then, that appear to be spatially distinct, and therefore more rural in character, are actually heavily influenced by the urban way of life. The term "rural" has very nearly become nondescriptive of American community structure, both physically and socially.

ECOLOGICAL ASPECTS OF URBANIZATION

Thus far, the community as a physical entity has been discussed in terms of its demographic aspects. The sociological study of urban community structure goes beyond the size, composition, and distribution of people. In the biological sciences, ecology is the study of the relationships and adjustments of plants and animals to each other and to their environment. A familiar example of successful ecological adaptation among animals is the chameleon, which alters its coloration to blend with the physical surroundings when threatened by an enemy. The dinosaur, of course, is an example of unsuccessful adaptation. Human beings, like lower animals and plants, adjust to each other, other species, and their natural environment. *Human ecology* is the approach to community structure that deals with the growth and distribution patterns of services, people, and physical attributes such as highways and buildings, as well as the processes involved in community growth and distribution. According to the ecological approach, social structure is the product of human efforts to cope with natural environment. In the following discussion this broader idea of human ecology is primarily confined to the ecology of the city.

Spatial aspects of city growth

Let us look first at the growth and distribution patterns of services, people, and physical attributes within cities. Starting with the "Chicago School" in the 1920s, sociologists have attempted to establish the existence of uniformities in the spatial development of cities. Rather than establishing a single pattern, sociologists have evolved three competing theories of spatial growth, each of which must be considered as an ideal type. Like all ideal types, these three theories of city growth must be viewed not as detailed characterizations but as approximations when tested against actual cases.

The first theory of city growth was proposed by the University of

Chicago's Ernest W. Burgess, one of the early investigators of human ecology.[2] Burgess saw city growth as the gradual emergence of circles within circles of development from the central city outward—like ripples from a stone thrown into water: the *concentric zone theory* (see Figure 14.1). Each circle of development is said to be unique in terms of its population, land use, and other characteristics. Five concentric zones are especially emphasized. The central business district is characterized by firms engaged in retail trade, wholesale trade, commercial recreation, and light industry. Surrounding the downtown area is what Burgess labels the zone in transition, so called because it is a slum area that is being penetrated by industrial and business expansion. Next comes the zone of workingmen's homes, a residential area populated by industrial workers, many of whom are second-generation immigrants who have escaped the deteriorating zone in transition. A further rise in social class comes in the next zone, which is a residential area containing high-rent apartment buildings and "restricted" districts of single-family dwellings whose occupants include professionals, managers, office workers, and some extremely well-paid factory workers. Finally, near or beyond the city limits is the commuters' zone, the higher-class suburban residential area surrounding the city.

Burgess' theory has attracted considerable criticism, the thrust of which says that the concentric zone pattern is primarily descriptive of Chicago, the source of its inspiration. Most other cities, American and otherwise, it is contended, do not conform to this pattern of growth. Consequently, other theories have been developed to explain city growth. Two prominent ones are the sector theory and the multiple nuclei theory.[3]

Figure 14.1 contains a graphic illustration of the pattern of city growth captured in the sector theory. The sector theory depicts the city as a circle, as does the concentric zone concept, but with an important difference. The concentric zone theory describes the city as a series of ever-widening circles of growth, each containing a distinct type of land use and population. However, in the *sector theory*, land use and population distribution from the central business district outward do not uniformly change as distance from the central city increases. Rather, similarity in land use and population distribution within a given area of a city is said to be the result of growth along one or more major transportation routes into and out of the city. A particular type of land use begins at the center of the city and radiates out toward the city limits. For example, the hypothetical pattern in Figure 14.1 shows low-class residential areas extending outward from two sides of the central business district. Since land use is said to be basically the same within any

Districts

1. Central business district
2. Zone in transition
3. Zone of workingmen's homes
4. Residential zone
5. Commuters' zone

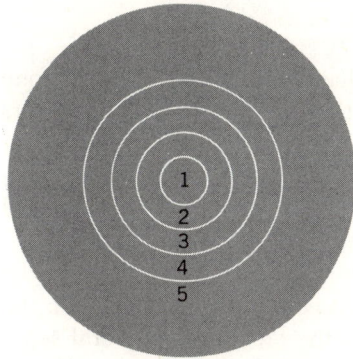

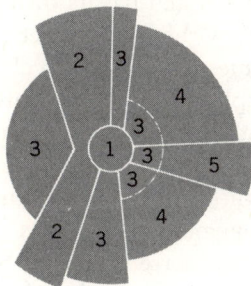

CONCENTRIC ZONE THEORY

Districts

1. Central business district
2. Wholesale, light manufacturing
3. Lower-class residential
4. Middle-class residential
5. Upper-class residential

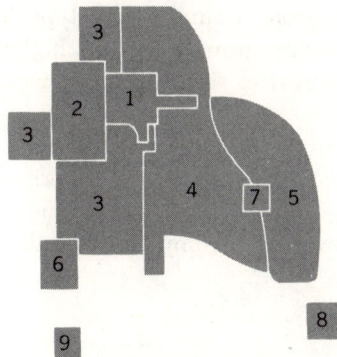

SECTOR THEORY

Districts

1. Central business district
2. Wholesale, light manufacturing
3. Lower-class residential
4. Middle-class residential
5. Upper-class residential
6. Heavy manufacturing
7. Outlying business district
8. Residential suburb
9. Industrial suburb

MULTIPLE NUCLEI

Figure 14.1   Theories of city growth

SOURCE: Reprinted from "The Nature of Cities" by Chauncy D. Harris and Edward L. Ullman, in Volume 242 of **The Annals** of the The American Academy of Political and Social Science. © 1945 by The American Academy of Political and Social Science.

given sector, a city conforming to this pattern of growth has somewhat of a star-shaped appearance. The starlike pattern is only a rough approximation because, as you can see from Figure 14.1, the sector theory allows for sectors of city growth that assume a wide, semicircular shape rather than a relatively narrow, long one. Keep in mind that while the concentric zone theory proposed an invariant pattern of growth, the arrangement of sectors in Figure 14.1 is merely hypothetical. It is unimportant whether any actual cities have their sectors arranged in this particular order or in the proportions drawn in this figure. It is the general pattern of growth that should retain your interest.

If the sector theory is a modification of the concentric zone theory, the multiple nuclei pattern is a radical departure. As the term itself implies, the *multiple nuclei theory* portrays city growth as the creation of several separate centers. Rather than cities developing from the central business district outward, this theory contends that numerous distinct districts emerge without much reference to the central business district. Each has its own unique land-use emphasis that tends to dominate activity within the district.

Because of the lay of the land, property values, historical development, and other localized forces, each city will display a different pattern of nuclei location. Districts for heavy manufacturing, light manufacturing, and wholesaling, to cite a few illustrations, develop in unpredictable locations within a given city. Therefore, the diagram for the multiple nuclei theory in Figure 14.1 is merely one of many possible arrangements of districts.

Which of these theories of city growth is the correct one? It appears that each is correct; each pattern of growth has been found. This also means that no single pattern holds universally, either within American culture or in other cultures. In fact, in countries outside the United States a certain type of city (for example, a commercial city with a large seaport) may exhibit a pattern of development quite different from a similar city type in America. The validity of these three theories of city growth, then, is higher for American cities. This should come as no surprise, since all three were formulated in the United States.

As Jessie Bernard points out, it is not so crucial to know which of these three patterns of city growth has been the most descriptive of American cities. It is more important to realize that city growth has assumed one of several logical paths—that cities have not grown in a completely random manner.[4]

Ecological processes

These theories of city growth provide approximations to various spatial patterns cities may assume. But human ecology goes beyond seeking pictures of the distribution of services, people, and physical facilities to ask this question: By what processes do cities develop their observable spatial patterns? Ecologists have come up with several "ecological processes" that go a long distance in answering this question.

Ecological processes make the most sense when they are linked to particular social and economic units of the city like districts and natural areas. Some of the most important types of city districts appear in Figure 14.1. *Natural areas* are geographic areas within a city containing one or a few distinctive types of people, land use, and activities bound together by mutual dependence. A Harlem, a Chinatown, a skid row, a rooming-house district, and a Greenwich Village are all natural areas. Natural areas are not restricted to lower-class areas but include the "gold coasts" as well. The label "natural" comes from their generally unplanned nature. It is usually not decided by some administrative or governmental unit to create an area in which certain types of people and activities will be located. Rather, people sharing a similar characteristic (social class, ethnicity, race, culture) or having a common need (cheap temporary housing, a life style centered around wine, prestige housing) congregate within a delimited geographic area in which their desires or needs can be most readily served.

Now to the ecological processes themselves. It is through these processes —centralization, decentralization, segregation, invasion, and succession—that city districts and natural areas are created, altered, and destroyed.

As a variety of economic and social services become consolidated into one geographic area, the process of *centralization* is occurring. The central business district is the most clear-cut case of centralization, for in that district appears a composite of retail businesses, financial organizations, and entertainment facilities, as well as many other social and economic services.

Congestion, crime, pollution, and land values have generated the desire among people, industry, commerce, and other services to move away from the central business districts in American metropolitan areas. This desire to leave the city has been made realizable as a result of the transportation and communication capabilities already noted. The effects of the process of *decentralization* are there for anyone to see: the mushrooming of shopping centers; the locating of theaters and night clubs outside the central city; the flight of industry, business and the middle class to the suburbs; and the deterioration of central cities due to their dwindling tax base. Metropolitan dispersal takes place through the process of decentralization.

Centralization and decentralization are most relevant for understanding the formation and change of city districts. When natural areas are the point of interest, segregation, invasion, and succession are the most useful ecological processes to consider. *Segregation* has occurred when an area of a city is occupied by one or a few types of people, land use, and services. Thus, natural areas are the product of the process of segregation.

If natural areas are formed through segregation, they are altered or dissolved via the processes of invasion and succession. *Invasion* is the movement of a different type of people, land use, or service into a natural area.

An area of entertainment may be invaded by a new type of entertainment, as in the widespread introduction of flagrant prostitution and pornography to New York City's theatrical area. A racial or ethnic minority may move into a formerly all-white neighborhood. A residential suburb may be on its way to becoming an industrial center. When applied to ethnic and racial minorities, social classes, and religions, this process nearly always involves the invasion of a higher status area by persons and activities of lower status. A particularly outstanding contradiction to this normal pattern is the construction of high-rent apartment buildings in formerly deteriorated areas in the central city. If an invasion leads to the departure of the people and services originally there, and to the dominance of the new types of people or services, then *succession* has taken place.

OVERVIEW AND PREVIEW

When the proportion of a society's population is increasingly living in cities and when the urban population is increasing faster than the rural population, the process of urbanization is occurring. City growth is not the same as urbanization, since cities can develop within a society while its rural population continues to grow faster than its urban population.

There are two basic approaches to the study of the physical dimensions of community structure, the demographic and the ecological. In the demographic approach, emphasis is on changes in the size, composition, and distribution of population within a given geographic area. Over the years the U.S. Census definition of an urban place has evolved from the simple classification of 2500 persons or more to include urbanized areas, Standard Metropolitan Statistical Areas, and Standard Consolidated Areas.

While urbanization is not a new phenomenon, its modern rate and extent are unprecedented. The world's population living in cities of 20,000 persons or more and 100,000 persons or more has exceeded a doubling every 50 years since 1850. Moreover, there is no indication that the pace of urbanization has slackened since 1950, although it is expected to taper off before the entire world becomes urbanized.

Urbanization in those countries outside the East-West axis is as unique as it is swift. Not only is urban growth in so-called developing nations currently the most rapid, it is occurring without the industrial base on which urbanization in the East and West has taken place. Also, urban growth in

Third World countries is increasing at a faster rate than is the ratio of urban to rural population growth.

Urbanization in America is metropolitan growth. Population growth in metropolitan areas takes the form of metropolitan dispersal or suburbanization, a process made possible by developments in communication and transportation. The future of urbanization in America lies with megalopolises or urban regions, with places comprised of a continuous string of metropolitan areas containing one million or more persons.

The ecological approach to community structure is concerned with the growth and distribution patterns of services, people, and the physical attributes and the processes involved in these patterns. Three theories of the spatial growth of cities have been developed—concentric zone, sector, and multiple nuclei.

How do cities assume spatial patterns? Ecologists generally start with natural areas that contain one or a few distinctive types of people, land use, and activities. Natural areas are altered and destroyed by several ecological processes, including centralization, decentralization, segregation, invasion, and succession.

The next chapter covers three basic institutional structures present in all complex societies—family, religious, and political institutional structures. Although other aspects of these institutions will be included, emphasis will be placed on social change.

REFERENCES

1. This view of urbanization is elaborated in Kingsley Davis, "The Urbanization of the Human Population," *Scientific American*, 213 (September 1964), 40–53.
2. Ernest W. Burgess, "The Growth of the City," in Robert E. Park, Ernest W. Burgess, and Roderick D. McKenzie, eds., *The City* (Chicago: University of Chicago Press, 1925), pp. 47–62.
3. Homer Hoyt, "The Structure of Cities in the Post-War Era," *American Journal of Sociology*, 48 (January 1943), 475–492; Chauncy D. Harris and Edward L. Ullman, "The Nature of Cities," *Annals of the American Academy of Political and Social Science*, 242 (November 1945), especially 244–246.
4. Jesse Bernard, *The Sociology of Community* (Glenview, Ill.: Scott, Foresman, 1973), p. 38.

ADDITIONAL SOURCES AND READINGS

Adams, Robert M. "The Origin of Cities," *Scientific American*, 203 (September 1960), 153–168.

Duncan, Otis Dudley. *Metropolis and Region* (Baltimore: Johns Hopkins Press, 1960).

Ford, Thomas R., and Gordon F. DeJong, eds. *Social Demography* (Englewood Cliffs, N.J.: Prentice-Hall, 1970).

Gist, Noel P., and Sylvia F. Fava. *Urban Society*, 5th ed. (New York: T. Y. Crowell, 1964).

Hadden, Jeffery K., Louis M. Masotti, and Calvin J. Larson, eds. *Metropolis in Crisis* (Itasca, Ill.: Peacock, 1967).

Hauser, Philip M., and Leo F. Schnore, eds. *The Study of Urbanization* (New York: Wiley, 1967).

Hawley, Amos H. *Human Ecology: A Theory of Community Structure* (New York: Ronald, 1950).

Hawley, Amos H. *Urban Society: An Ecological Approach* (New York: Ronald, 1967).

Morris, R. N. *Urban Sociology* (New York: Praeger, 1968).

Schnore, Leo F. *The Urban Scene: Human Ecology and Demography* (New York: Free Press, 1965).

Theodorson, George, ed. *Studies in Human Ecology* (New York: Harper & Row, 1961).

Thomlinson, Ralph. *Urban Structure: The Social and Spatial Character of Cities* (New York: Random House, 1967).

Changing Institutional Structures

SOCIAL STRUCTURE IS SLOW TO CHANGE

Another break with the past in Barnstable Village has to do with the treasury of the local amateur theatrical society, the Barnstable Comedy Club. The Club has a treasurer who, once a month for thirty years, angrily refused to say what the balance was, for fear that the club would spend it foolishly. He resigned last year. The new treasurer announced a balance of four hundred dollars and some odd cents, and the membership blew it all on a new curtain the color of spoiled salmon. This ptomaine curtain, incidentally, made its debut during a production of THE CAINE MUTINY COURT MARTIAL in which Captain Queeg did NOT nervously rattle steel balls in his hand. The balls were eliminated on the theory that they were suggestive.

Kurt Vonnegut, Jr., **Welcome to the Monkey House** (New York: Dell, 1970), p. 3.

RAPID SOCIAL CHANGE

In the three short decades between now and the twenty-first century, millions of ordinary, psychologically normal people will face an abrupt collision with the future. Citizens of the world's richest and most technologically advanced nations, many of them will find it increasingly painful to keep up with the incessant demand for change that characterizes our time. For them the future will have arrived too soon.

Alvin Toffler, **Future Shock** (New York: Bantam, 1970), p. 9.

All social structures change. But the pace of change seems to be quickening. The two quotes opening this chapter provide a contrast in the pace of social change. Developing a "theory" on the meaning of Captain Queeg's steel balls may be time well spent in all of the Barnstable Villages of this world. But, if Alvin Toffler is right, such concerns may be an unaffordable luxury for those persons in the most technologically advanced societies who must cope with "future shock." And as you saw in the last chapter, the Barn-

litical institutional structure? • Who has the power
in American society? •
Pluralism • Elitism • Colonialism and nationalism

stable Villages of this world are vanishing under the onslaught of urbanization; taking their place are large cities and megalopolises in which the
speed of change is considerably greater. This is partly because the social
and cultural base of economically developed societies promotes the process
of invention. It is also because the increased contact among nations—
including developing ones—leads to a great deal of borrowing.

In this chapter the focus will be on change in institutional structures.
It should be kept in mind throughout the following pages that social change
—even when it occurs at a rapid clip—does not blot out the basic continuity
between the social structures of one generation and those of subsequent
ones.

INSTITUTIONAL STRUCTURES

What are institutional structures?

Institutions are social structures because, like stratification, community, formal organizational, and group structures, the social positions associated with
them carry role prescriptions defining expected behavior. An *institutional
structure*, then, can be defined as an interrelated set of social relationships based on man-made patterns for thinking, feeling, and behaving that
is directed at taking care of one or more activities considered to be important for a society's perpetuation.

Consider the economic institution whose social relationships and material culture are directed toward providing goods and services. Role prescriptions exist within an industrialized economy indicating what is expected
of the occupants of a countless number of social positions including farmer,
assembly-line worker, salesman, company president, consumer, credit manager, and collection agent. Naturally, definitions of expected behavior will
vary from society to society as well as within one economy, depending on
the culture and the specific job description. Consistent with the approach
of this text, the emphasis will be on the analysis of social positions, role
prescriptions, and role behavior.

As indicated, the basic institutional structures are family, religion,
polity, economy, and education. Of these, only three need to be covered
in this chapter—the family, religious, and political institutional structures.
Various aspects of the economic institution were dealt with in Chapters 9
and 10 on formal organizational structure. For sociologists the most im-

portant dimension of the institution of education is the relationship between education and social stratification in general, and racial and ethnic minorities in particular. Chapters 6 and 7 on social stratification structure touch on this topic.

THE FAMILY INSTITUTIONAL STRUCTURE

What is a family?

A *family* is a social structure based on kinship. It is a culturally defined set of social relationships existing among relatives who either live together or interact frequently enough to be considered an operating social unit. Thus, kinship structure is not the same as a family. A *kinship structure* is a broader concept encompassing the social relationships among all relatives, including those who do not function together as an ongoing social structure. The families of two sisters separated by several miles may, if they engage in social relationships, be within a common kinship structure, but they are not part of the same family structure unless they arrange to live together or function as a recognizable social unit. The *family institutional structure* encompasses both kinship and family structures. Nevertheless, the concept of family structure alone will be used here, both because it is less cumbersome and because it is the family per se that is of most interest to sociologists.

The first section of the present chapter examines the functions of the family, some basic concepts that reflect variations in family structure, current trends in family structure, some of the changing role prescriptions associated with the social positions of wife and husband in the American family, and the future of the family.

The functions of the family

The family is the most basic institutional structure. It is the cradle of human nature, for it is within the family that infants are transformed from raw biological material to socialized human beings. Without the activities or services performed by the family, the other institutions could not exist— there would be no people to create them. Thus, in the simplest societies the family is the only institutional structure. In such societies the family can fulfill the educational, religious, and economic requirements all by itself: It can teach children about their culture and social positions, inform new members of their relationship to the gods, and supply its own goods and services. Only with social and economic development are separate institutions needed to structure religious, educational, economic, and political activities outside the family. Of course, removing these functions from the family changes its nature, as do the technological and other social changes accompanying industrialization.

Variations in family structure

Variations in family structure are reflected in the norms defining the composition of a family, who marries whom, who owns what, who controls whom, and who lives where.

• FAMILY COMPOSITION. Families may be composed in one of two basic ways. If the family consists only of the parents and their children, it is a *nuclear* family. While the nuclear family contains two generations, the *extended* family is composed of three or more generations. An extended family, for example, might contain one or both grandparents, their unmarried children, and their married children with their spouses and children. Extended families may or may not be structured around blood relatives. Those families that place blood relatives at the center while nonblood relatives are considered to be on the fringe are *consanguine* families. Consanguine families, which may be considered a subtype of the extended family pattern, emphasize the relationships between brothers and sisters, parents and children. They are the dominant social positions in the family whereas non-blood-related mates are subordinate, defined as being outside the inner circle of blood relatives. The strongest family ties of nonblood relatives in a consanguine family structure are normally with the family into which they were born. In contrast, in nuclear and nonconsanguine extended families, husbands and wives form the heart of the family structure.

• WHO MARRIES WHOM? *Marriage*—that complex of norms and social relationships involved in the formation and maintenance of a family—may assume several patterns. If they are to remain within the law and be approved by the church, marriages in American society must be *monogamous* —they must involve two persons only. While a person in American society who is married to more than one mate at the same time is a bigamist, in other societies he or she may be engaging in the expected marriage pattern. *Polygamous* marriages are those in which one spouse has two or more mates simultaneously. In theory as well as practice, polygamous marriages may appear in three forms. Polygamy typically takes the form of a husband with several wives (*polygyny*), although there have been a few societies sanctioning a wife marrying several husbands at the same time. Such a marriage pattern is called *polyandry*. Isolated instances of *group marriage*

—marriage of several males and females each to the other—have also been documented but not on a society-wide basis.

The question of who marries whom also involves norms specifying certain limitations on the choice of a mate. Norms of *endogamy* require that one must select a mate from within certain social structures of which he is a member. Prohibitions against marrying someone, say, from another race, religion, social class, or society would qualify as norms of endogamy.

On the other hand, norms of *exogamy* prohibit marriage among fellow members of a social category or social structure. The most widely accepted norm of exogamy is the incest taboo, the prohibition on marriage or sexual intercourse among relatives. As a rule, the severity of punishment for violation of the incest taboo varies with the closeness of the relatives involved. Thus, except for very special cases (royalty for example), societies attempt to keep a tight lid on sexual intercourse or marriage between a son and mother, a daughter and father, or a brother and sister.

• WHO OWNS WHAT? Different family structures exist for determining descent and inheritance. If the structure is *patrilineal*, descent and inheritance are passed from the father to his male descendents. Should they be transmitted from the mother and her female ancestors to descendents, the structure is a *matrilineal* one. In American society, inheritance and descent are *bilineal*—they are passed equally through both parents. Although it is true that children in American families are given the father's name, the father's and mother's relatives are accepted equally as part of the kinship structure.

• WHO CONTROLS WHOM? A *patriarchal* family is one in which the oldest male living in the household controls the rest of the family members. In its purest form, the father is the absolute ruler. Normally, patriarchal families are extended families structured along blood lines (consanguine). So rare is the *matriarchal* family, in which the oldest female living in the household calls the shots, that controversy exists over whether any society has ever had a genuinely matriarchal family structure.

Despite its patriarchal origins, the family in American society tends to be a *democratic* structure, with authority theoretically split evenly between husband and wife. There are two instances in American society where females appear to exercise more than half of the control. Because middle-class fathers living in the suburbs of large cities spend so much time away from home, wives are forced to make many independent decisions. Mothers also hold the authority in those lower-class homes in which the father is frequently absent, always absent, or unable to generate any income. Keep in mind that these two exceptions exist by default; they fall outside the general cultural definition of where authority rests in the American family.

• WHO LIVES WHERE? In the case of the nuclear family as it exists in American society, a married couple generally lives with neither set of parents. Such a residential arrangement is a *neolocal* one. Extended families, of course, involve residence norms of a different nature. A *patrilocal* arrangement calls for living with the husband's parents. Residing with the wife's parents is expected under a *matrilocal* arrangement.

Using the American family as an example for the application of these concepts of variations in family structure, you can observe a nuclear, monogamous, bilineal, democratic, and neolocal family structure. One of the most significant changes in traditional family institutional structure has been the trend away from the extended family.

The current trend in family structure

As societies move from agricultural economies to industrialized ones, the extended family tends to be replaced by the nuclear family structure. It is doubtful that industrialization alone *causes* the shift toward the nuclear family. Industrialization, however, does create certain conditions that are more compatible with the nuclear family than with the extended family.[1]

• INDUSTRIALIZATION AND FAMILY STRUCTURE. One reason for the association between industrialization and nuclear family structure is the increase in the amount of geographic mobility. People in rural areas must leave their relatives in order to secure employment in cities. Furthermore, those already living in urban areas have almost come to accept as a way of life the frequent changes in residence made for occupational reasons. In either event, geographic mobility makes the maintenance of close ties with numbers of relatives very difficult, since usually only the most immediate kin can be taken along.

In industrialized societies, social class level is not merely ascribed, that is, not determined solely by the social class of one's parents. Rather, a person's own achievements may influence social class level, and as a result, upward social mobility is more frequent. Upward social mobility, because it entails changes in life styles and may require geographic mobility, serves to weaken extended family ties.

A final condition created by industrialization that is more compatible with nuclear family structure is the loss of some services formerly performed by the extended family. Prior to industrialization, for example, family members were expected to take care of the sick and the old. Actually, they scarcely had a choice because there were few outside sources on which they could rely. With the growth of special purpose organizations and governmental programs, however, the sick can be cared for in hospitals (often paid for by insurance companies) and the old can be placed in homes for the elderly on their social security payments. In short, because outsiders have taken over many of the services formerly performed by the family, relatives do not have to depend on each other as they once did.

Associated with industrialization, then, are certain conditions that are more compatible with nuclear family structure. This was certainly true for currently developed countries in both the East and the West. Indications are that developing nations of the world will also eventually adopt a nuclear family structure.

• HOW ISOLATED IS THE MODERN NUCLEAR FAMILY? While families in industrialized societies tend to have a nuclear structure and maintain separate residence, there is some evidence that they are not as isolated from their relatives as was once believed. Early research depicting an isolated nuclear family in American society was conducted prior to some recent changes, changes occurring in other industrialized societies as well. For one thing, modern transportation and communication—limited access expressways, fast cars, airplanes, airmail, long-distance telephoning—make it easier for relatives to maintain family ties even though separated geographically. Second, with the trend toward metropolitanization, it is no longer as necessary as it used to be for children to leave their parents and other relatives in order to go to college or to pursue their occupations.

Among other researchers, Marvin Sussman has observed considerable cooperative effort and mutual aid between urban nuclear families and their parents in American society.[2] In particular he found parents offering a variety of services to their married children, including sporadic financial aid, home repair and maintenance, baby-sitting, and help during illnesses. At the very least it must be concluded that the modern family is a "modified nuclear structure," one located somewhere between the isolated nuclear family and the classical extended family.

Changing role prescriptions in the American nuclear family

• SUBCULTURAL VARIATIONS IN AMERICAN FAMILY STRUCTURE. Does *the* American family really exist? Because of the diversity of subcultures in American society (based on racial, ethnic, or social class differences), no single set of role prescriptions can be attached to each of the social positions of its nuclear family structure. As was shown in Chapter 7, social classes have quite different family life styles. Or, to take another illustration, research has shown that the nuclear family with the father missing is more characteristic of lower-class Blacks and Whites in the city. A catalogue of family dissimilarities could easily be extended—the rural Protestant family is different from the urban Jewish family, and the urban Catholic family is not identical with the urban Jewish family. Moreover, not all rural Protes-

Thomas Hopker, Woodfin Camp & Associates

tant, urban Jewish, and urban Catholic families are alike, because of variations in ethnic background and social class.

Despite the presence of subcultural variations in family structure in America, it is still possible to portray the American family as a distinct type if it is understood that such a portrayal has the most meaning when contrasted with families in other societies. While reading the following discussion of the changing role prescriptions of the husband and wife in the American family, it should not be forgotten that the portrayal is stereotypical, glossing over many dissimilarities among American families due to subcultural variations.

• CHANGING SOCIAL POSITIONS OF THE SEXES. Like other social structures, the family is composed of a set of social positions tied together by mutually understood role prescriptions. In the nuclear family structure there are several social positions—husband, wife, child, mother, father, sister, and brother. Alterations in the positions of husband, wife, mother, and father have captured the most attention in recent times.

The assignment of certain tasks to women and others to men comes not from a male-chauvinist-pig plot but from something as unexciting as the division of labor. All societies on record have different tasks and role prescriptions associated with the sexes. Although variations can be easily cited, the general pattern of the sexual division of labor within the family is for men to deal with matters outside of the home (whether it be hunting, fishing, or operating a computer), while women handle home-related tasks. To say it another way, mothers tend to perform *expressive* duties—offering emotional comfort or caring for the sick. Men, on the other hand, take care of *instrumental* matters such as obtaining food, providing protection from physical harm, or generating money.

Inspiration for the charge of a male-chauvinist conspiracy comes from the fact that in most societies the social positions of husband and father are defined as superior to those of wife and mother. Definitions of male superiority and dominance are derived in large part because placement on the stratification structure is based on social position outside the home. And, until very recently, men have virtually monopolized such positions. Very rare are those societies in which women have the powerful and prestigeful social positions either within or outside the home. And, in most societies, when women do work outside the home, they do not have an equal share of the most highly ranked occupations, nor do they always receive equal pay for equal work. These are some of the reasons that women's liberationists seek a revolution in the cultural definitions of the sexual division of labor.

There are some signs of change in American society. For one thing, the employment of women outside the home has become the expected pattern. As of 1970, approximately one-third of the American labor force is female. Forty percent of all American women are employed, and of these, about 80 percent are married. Compared to the beginning of the twentieth century, this represents a dramatic change in the role prescriptions associated with the social positions of wife and mother. And while American women still suffer tremendous discrimination in employment and pay, social trends seem to be in their favor.

Potential changes in the positions of mother, wife, husband, and father do not appear to be limited to the economic sphere. Even though male dominance persists and the traditional sexual division of labor in the family endures—working wives still do nearly all of the housework—there seems to be a trend toward greater equality between the sexes. So far, this trend of sexual equality is reflected less in role prescriptions linked with family social positions than in other areas of social life. Especially among the young, males can wear their hair to shoulder length, cry, and openly read poetry. Females can wear pant-suits and ties, attend formerly all-male colleges and universities, read *Playgirl* magazine, and even sit at the bar in what used to be exclusive male sanctuaries.

The cultural definitions surrounding sexual relations also appear to be undergoing modification. While the evidence shows no increase in the frequency of premarital and extramarital sexual intercourse, the social norms have changed; if sexual action is no more frequent, open discussion of sex is. Further, the more educated young people in America are now challenging the ideas that women are sex objects, that women merely service men without themselves experiencing pleasure, that only males can be aggressive in courtship and marriage, and that men may have premarital and extramarital affairs but women may not. As noted, these are signs of potential change. Whether they will actually alter family social positions permanently remains to be seen.

The future of the family

The family has received few good words lately. Some critics are even forecasting the end of the family as we know it, challenging the argument that the nuclear family is the structure best suited to industrialized and urbanized living.[3] As evidence of the decline of the family, these critics often cite the generation gap, the popularity of communes among the young, and the high divorce rate (one of every four American marriages now ends in divorce).

Is the nuclear family that is characteristic of industrialized and urbanized countries destined to go the way of the dinosaurs? Of course, predicting the future of the family, American or otherwise, comes under the heading of speculation. Nevertheless, given knowledge of the nature of social change, it seems likely that the nuclear family will not be replaced by another type of family structure such as the extended family of the commune. Rather, the nuclear family will in all probability be retained and will change in line with some of the directions already discussed. Among other things, the nuclear family of the future may be expected to emphasize extended family ties while maintaining the pattern of separate households, to reflect greater sexual equality both with respect to the home and the world of work, and to involve men more in household duties as women become less exclusively responsible for them. In brief, while experimentation with alternative family structures—communes and group marriages—will probably increase, the nuclear family structure is expected to survive, albeit with some important alterations.

RELIGIOUS INSTITUTIONAL STRUCTURE

What is religion?

As an institutional structure, *religion* is a set of social relationships based on ways of thinking, feeling, and behaving related to the sacred aspects of ultimate meaning. By now you are quite familiar with the first part of this definition of religion as an institutional structure. The terms "sacred" and "ultimate meaning," on the other hand, may be hazy concepts.

Questions of *ultimate meaning* are the "big" questions, those pertaining to why we are here, why things happen as they do, and what happens when life ends. Social or cultural elements may be considered *sacred* when they evoke intense emotional commitment, are believed to be above criticism, are thought to be universally valid, and are held to be beyond alteration at any given point in time. Sacredness may be imparted to material objects (Christian cross, national flag) or nonmaterial things such as supernatural beings. According to Emile Durkheim, sacredness is not intrinsic to material objects or nonmaterial things but exists in the minds of those who define them as sacred.[4] What is sacred to the followers of one religion may be valuable to those of another religion merely because the object tastes good or is very expensive. Such is the case with the Hindu sacred cow.

The religious institutional structure has no absolute monopoly on concern with either ultimate meaning or the sacred. Science, for example, wants to know the reasons why both physical and social events occur. Each brand of communism has its definition of reality and ultimate meaning. Yet neither science nor communism is considered a religion. As noted above, a national flag may be considered sacred. It was partly because of this definition of sacredness that burning the American flag or hoisting the flag of North Vietnam in the late 1960s touched off so much hostility among so many Americans.

How, then, is a religious institutional structure to be distinguished from other social structures? A primary difference between religion and other social structures is the relative stress placed on ultimate meaning and the sacred in religious structures. Although the sacred may appear in non-religious contexts (national flags) and religions may involve the nonsacred (rock bands playing in church services), it is only the religious institutional structure that is so heavily preoccupied with the sacred and with the meaning of life and death.

Religion as a social structure

That religion usually involves some dimensions of social structure is reflected in several areas. One such area is participation in church activities, which encompasses both the extent of church membership and the conduct of church-related business by parishioners and pastors. A second aspect of religious social structure to be covered here is the structural forms that religions may assume.

• PARTICIPATION IN CHURCH-RELATED ACTIVITIES. Figures on church membership are best viewed with some caution, for these reasons: Churches may tend to overestimate their numbers; all churches do not have the same system of counting their members; and care is not always taken to keep accurate records. According to available records, there has been a steady increase in church membership in the United States over the last 100 years, a trend that appears to have reached its peak. In 1850, 16 percent of the total population were church members. By 1968 this had increased to 68 percent, with 126 million Americans belonging to 241 religious faiths. Of these numbers, 70 million are Protestant, 48 million are Catholic, and nearly 7 million are Jews. Catholics, because they have no separate denominations, outnumber each of the Protestant denominations taken alone. There are, for example, twice as many Roman Catholics as Baptists, the largest Protestant denomination.[5]

Of course, membership figures are not the same as the number of active church members who participate in church-related activities on a relatively regular basis. It is among active church members and their leaders that an important aspect of the social structure of religious bodies is reflected. An obvious side of the social structure of religion can be observed in the formal religious rituals and ceremonies that are carried out in a particular order, on a given day, and at a set time. In addition, each religious body has its own beliefs, values, and norms, which structure the thoughts, feelings, and behavior of its adherents. Some religions are satisfied that sprinkling with water constitutes baptism, whereas others believe that anything short of total immersion is a waste of time. Some religions define makeup, women's shaved legs, and commercial motion pictures as sinful, but others permit their members to smoke tobacco and drink alcoholic beverages with a clear conscience.

As religious bodies increase in size, the need for formal leaders arises. Initially a single leader, the clergyman, may suffice; but if the body continues to grow, a number of other formal social positions—secretary, choir-leader, administrator of religious education—are added. At the same time that a formal church hierarchy of social positions is developing, a division of labor appears among church members—some teach religious classes, others help in the handling of business affairs.

The social relationships between clergymen and their church members are a vital aspect of the social structure of religion. Given the definition of religion, it follows that the social position of clergyman would be defined by role prescriptions pertaining to the sacred aspects of ultimate meaning, including the relationship between man and God, and man's relationship to man. Ministering to the sick and the old, and delivering messages that teach and reinforce the beliefs, norms, and values of the church, are two traditional role prescriptions.

However, the 1960s witnessed a challenge to the traditional definition of clergyman. Some of the more liberal American clergymen attempted to redefine their social position, adding some new role prescriptions related to such nonsacred matters as civil rights, poverty, peace, and the urban crisis. This led to conflict between church members and liberal clergymen, even within churches in the more liberal denominations. Why? Because even within relatively liberal denominations, it is the more religiously conservative members who are the most active in church-related activities. It is they who regularly attend services, financially support the church, and hire and fire the pastor. Evidence has been gathered recently to show that the bulk of the church membership disapproves of this redefinition of the clerical social position to include nonsacred areas of social life. It also appears that this reaction has not been lost on clergymen, the majority of whom now seem to be backing away from broader social concerns.[6]

• TYPES OF RELIGIOUS STRUCTURE. There are four basic types of religious structure: ecclesia, denomination, sect, and cult. They are listed in the rough order of the size, degree of structure, and extent of societal influence. A religious structure that claims most of the society's population and that is closely linked with the political authorities is called an *ecclesia*. The perfect illustration was the Catholic church in medieval Europe. Existing approximations to this ideal type are the Catholic church in Italy and the Orthodox church in Greece.

When several organized and well-established religions are present in a society without control on the part of any single one of them, *denominations* are said to exist. Religion in American society, with its explicit separation of church and state, is characterized by the presence of many denominations. The Catholic church, the various Protestant and Jewish denominations, as well as other religions are content to coexist and are tolerant of each other's presence. Both ecclesia and denominations are formally organized and accept the existing social order.

Sects, on the other hand, are religious bodies that are not highly organized in a formal sense and that reject certain aspects of the prevailing order of things. Often sects are splinters from a church or a denomination of a church whose values or beliefs no longer satisfy certain church members. The Methodists and Baptists are examples of sects that became denominations after the Protestant Reformation.

The type of religious structure that is the least formally organized and the least influential in a society is called a *cult*. Cults are the most temporary type of religious structures and are usually built around a leader whose ideas conflict with those of an ecclesia, denomination, or sect. Followers of the ideas of Father Divine constitute a cult.

Denominations and sects are the most important types of religious structures. In the first place, they appear the most often; ecclesia and cults are rare compared to denominations and sects. A second reason for emphasizing denominations and sects is their relevance for the study of social change in religious institutional structures. Table 15.1 contrasts the nature of denominations and sects.

Denominations, sects, and religious change

From the study of Protestant religious history, theologian H. Richard Niebuhr offered a theory of religious change based on the interplay between denominations and sects.[7] According to Niebuhr, a sect is composed of those whose established church no longer adequately represents their religious beliefs, norms, and values. These alienated people, generally recruited from the lower class, form a new religious body in accordance with their desires and conceptions of what the "truth" really is. As Table 15.1 indicates, members of sects are not only in conflict with their parent church; their "war" extends to other religious faiths and even to the existing culture and social structures. But, like real wars, sects do not last forever. If a sect

TABLE 15.1 Differences between sect and denomination

CHARACTERISTIC	SECT	DENOMINATION
Size	Small	Large
Relationship with other religious groups	Rejects—feels that the sect alone has the "truth"	Accepts other denominations and is able to work in harmony with them
Wealth (church property, buildings, salary of clergy, income of members)	Limited	Extensive
Religious services	Emotional emphasis— tries to recapture conversion thrill; informal; extensive congregational participation	Intellectual emphasis; concern with teaching; formal; limited congregational participation
Clergy	Unspecialized; little if any professional training; frequently part-time	Specialized; professionally trained; full-time
Doctrines	Literal interpretation of scriptures; emphasis upon other-worldly rewards	Liberal interpretations of scripture; emphasis on this-worldly rewards
Membership requirements	Conversion experience; emotional commitment	Born into group or ritualistic requirements; intellectual commitment
Relationship with secular world	"At war" with the secular world, which is defined as "evil"	Endorses prevailing culture and social structures
Social class of members	Mainly lower class	Mainly middle class

SOURCE: Adapted by permission from Glenn M. Vernon, **Sociology of Religion** (New York: McGraw-Hill, 1962), p. 174.

survives at all, it is in the form of a newly established church or denomination.

There are several reasons for the shift from sect to established church, a change that comes with the second generation of members. Since children born into the sect must be educated in the ways of the faith, formal mechanisms, which were not needed for the original converts who joined because of their prior convictions, must be instituted. Because the second generation does not share the religious fervor of its parents, it is more accepting of other religions as well as of the broader culture and social structures. Both as children and later as religious leaders and laymen, members of the second generation are willing to make compromises with the outside world unthinkable to their parents. The acquisition of power, wealth, and prestige by sect members who have been upwardly mobile in the society also contributes to the weakening of rigid sect boundaries. With power, wealth, and prestige comes greater involvement in the social and economic life of the society. There are many illustrations within Protestantism of this movement from sect to established church, including the Baptist and Methodist denominations.

Once a sect has traveled the route to established church, it is then obviously possible for the process to start again. Some of its members may become sufficiently dissatisfied with the church to form a new sect, either for the same reasons that sparked the original sect or for entirely new ones.

Religious change through secularization

The dominant religious trend in modern society is the separation of culture and social life from the influence of religion, a process known as *seculariza-tion*. This process is easily illustrated by looking at the evolution of religion in the Western world. Prior to the Middle Ages the degree of distinction among the economic, political, religious, educational, and family spheres was slight. Only the family constituted an identifiable institutional structure. It was within the family that these other major aspects of social life were enacted. Because religion was not a separate dimension, because all aspects of culture and social structure were saturated with religion, concern with the sacred was ever present.

Gradually, however, social and economic development resulted in the creation of separate economic, political, educational, familial, and religious institutional structures. This relative isolation of activities was accompanied by a decline in the influence of religion on other aspects of culture and social structure. With the rise of science, industrialization, and urbanization, religion has lost ground, especially to the political and economic institutions. In modern societies, for example, it is generally accepted that wars are waged for political and/or economic reasons and not because the gods or the devil made us. Nor do people in industrialized societies hang themselves because they are convinced that the end of the world is at hand, as did the African tribesmen during the seven-minute total eclipse of the sun in 1973.

The declining impact of religion on social life in American society is reflected in the weakening of religiously inspired beliefs, norms, and values, and in the increasingly nonsacred nature of religious holidays. Much of the moral tone regarding divorce and premarital intercourse, for example, is disappearing. And for most Americans the sacred qualities of Christmas and Hanukkah are obscured in the shuffle of commercialism and social activities that now surrounds these Christian and Jewish "holy days."

• IS THE ROLE BEHAVIOR OF THE CLERGYMAN CHANGING? As indicated, there has been some effort to redefine the role prescriptions attached to the social position of clergymen. Such redefinition, of course, would lead to a change in role behavior. If the role behavior of the American clergyman is changing, it is in the direction of increased involvement in secular affairs. Increasing involvement of the clergy in secular spheres can be seen both in and out of the pulpit. Many clergymen are taking stands on social issues in their messages to parishioners, a trend not welcomed by many church members. Outside the pulpit, clergymen now engage in such nonsacred activities as offering psychotherapy, serving on school boards, teaching school, and engaging in social work activities. In short, contemporary clergymen are becoming more secular in their outlook and behavior while continuing their traditional functions of attempting to influence the secular world with sacred beliefs, values, and norms.

The effort by liberal ministers to meet the trend of secularization at least halfway seems to be successfully resisted by conservative laymen and pastors alike. Such resistance may simply mean that conservatives are behind the times. It may be that liberal clergymen and church members are slightly ahead of their time, showing the pattern of religion in the American future. Or, it may be that the effort to maintain a strong accent on sacred matters will continue to be successful. One reason for taking the latter position is that conservative ministers and laymen are overwhelmingly in charge of administrative positions and local churches, while many liberal clergymen are becoming disillusioned and are abandoning the ministry altogether or filling positions in already liberal churches.[8]

In addition, there are some signs of a renewed search for ultimate meaning in contemporary America. The Jesus movement, the attraction of Eastern religions for the young, and the interest in fundamentalist religious sects among people of all ages reflect a counterpoint to secularization. All of this is guesswork, of course. We can only wait to see if the current trend toward secularization will be successfully retarded by these and other religious forces.

In any event, it seems unlikely that the secularization of religion will reach its logical concluding point even in highly industrialized and urbanized societies, of which America is only one. That is, it is unlikely that the role behavior of clergy and laymen will become so devoid of the sacred aspects of ultimate meaning that the institutional structure of religion will disappear. It is equally improbable that religion will ever regain the degree of influence it exerted in earlier times.

POLITICAL INSTITUTIONAL STRUCTURE

Social change has been the central theme in the preceding analysis of family and religion, an emphasis that will be continued in the treatment of political institutional structure. Following an introduction to the nature of political institutional structure, major emphasis will be on the structure of power in American society: Is power becoming more concentrated in the hands of a powerful and unified elite, or are far-reaching decisions the product of pressures from nonunified interest blocs, each of which seeks its

own unique ends? A second topic of interest is that of social change evident
in the rise of nationalism in Third World countries, reflecting the worldwide
trend away from colonialism.

What is political institutional structure?

According to T. H. White's novel *The Once and Future King*, the con-
temporaries of King Arthur saw force and physical strength as the accepted
means of settling disputes and righting wrongs.[9] Arthur was continually
frustrated in his quest to replace private coercion with publicly administered law based on authority. According to White's interpretation of the
legend of Arthur, this king of England was ahead of his time. Arthur is
portrayed as having the insight to see that a society with a political structure based totally on coercion and physical force is unstable and laden with
open, often violent conflict. Arthur knew the importance of power in social
life, for he attempted to attract the mightiest knights to sit at the Round
Table. But in place of sheer coercive power exercised by one political unit
in England over another, he envisioned a unified political structure founded
on authority, the type of power that the governed accept as legitimate.

Political institutional structure is that complex of culturally based social
relationships revolving around the acquisition and exercise of authority in
the coordination and administration of a society. A political institutional
structure involves power of all types, including coercion—and a good bit
of it in totalitarian societies—but ultimately such a structure rests on the
acceptance of the legitimacy of political power by those who are subject
to it. The need for legitimacy holds even for those political institutional
structures grounded in force, if they are to survive for very long.

The administration and coordination of society under the jurisdiction
of those with political authority encompass protection from foreign enemies;
making, changing, and enforcing a system of laws; and a variety of activities—so numerous that they defy description—designed to promote the
general welfare. In the United States, such activities include financial support of agriculture, aid for disaster areas, construction and maintenance of
highways, and matters related to ecology—to mention only a very few.

Authority in the political institutional structure resides in the occupants
of certain social positions. The role prescriptions of these social positions
specify the limits of authority and coercive power. A jailer is not supposed
to execute his prisoners, a judge in a criminal case cannot declare a man

guilty if the jury has voted for acquittal, and a United States president cannot declare war without the formal approval of Congress.

As you know, some controversy surrounds the authority of the president of the United States in the making of war. In fact, both the Korean and Vietnam wars are sometimes referred to as "conflicts" because they were waged in the absence of a formal declaration of war. This is merely one example of the fuzziness and flexibility that often surrounds the exercise of authority. There have been strong American presidents who have expanded the limits of the power of that position and there have been presidents operating as caretakers of the status quo. And, like persons in positions of authority throughout the political institutional structure, there have been American presidents who have conducted the affairs of state via means that lay outside definitions of legitimate authority. Those American presidents accused of exercising illegitimate power include Franklin D. Roosevelt (the attempt to stack the Supreme Court in his favor), Lyndon Johnson (the waging of war in Vietnam), and Richard Nixon (the Watergate affair and related matters).

The latter situation has led to what some label a "confrontation" in the American political institution, revolving around the question: Where does political power reside—in the Congress, in the executive branch, or in the judiciary? A much larger question is: Who has the power in American society?

Who has the power in American society?

Although those in political positions may have the authority to coordinate and administer a society, political institutional structures are not run on authority alone. Within the political institutional structure there is much more at work than mere legitimate authority. Those in positions of political authority do not make decisions in a vacuum. Any lobbyist is testimony to this, and any candid business leader could reveal the presence of influence-peddling, buying of political favors, and cooperative efforts profitable to those in and out of positions of political authority. It does not take a Watergate scandal to reveal this, although the course of events following the break-in of the Democratic national headquarters brought it to public attention in a forceful way. We looked on with fascinated horror at the mounting revelations of governmental activities that were either clearly illegal or at least rested on weak ethical grounds.

Although the negative example of Watergate has been used, it should not be concluded that most of the relationships between those in and out of political positions are questionable or illegal. Even basic civics textbooks detail the existence and operation of lobbyists whose function it is to persuade congressmen to vote in a manner beneficial to those who are paying the lobbyists. It does mean, however, that the coordination and administration of society by those in political positions are influenced by many persons who do not hold political authority. Around this fact has been raised the question of who really runs America, who really has the power to determine the course of events in the United States. The debate on the nature and distribution of power in American society has been long and hot. *Pluralists* see decision making on the national level as the outcome of conflicting and shifting power blocs. *Elitists*, on the other hand, portray American society as being controlled from the top by a unified and enduring few.

• PLURALISM. America is popularly depicted as a pluralistic society, one in which power is said to be distributed among a variety of interest blocs, including political parties, so that societal control is not continually in the hands of the same few people. Liberals in American society have typically subscribed to this picture of diffused power distribution. One advocate of the pluralistic theory of power distribution, David Riesman, argues that power in American society is exercised through "veto groups."[10] According to this formulation, decisions on a given issue are made as a result of certain interest blocs (each of which has its own stake in the issue) having exerted power to prevent an outcome contrary to their own interests. In addition to initiating actions to attain their own special ends, veto groups also maneuver to garner sufficient power to protect themselves from other interest blocs that may attempt to do them harm. Examples of veto groups would be the oil industry fighting to maintain its depletion allowance and the National Rifle Association lobbying for the right of private citizens to own guns. In all of this, national political leaders are depicted as referees, as those charged with the responsibility of balancing the public welfare with the self-centered desires of special interest blocs.

• ELITISM. The question of who has the power was not new when Riesman attempted to answer it for American society early in the 1950s, but it became more prominent when C. Wright Mills' theory of monolithic power appeared a few years later.[11] Those who view power in American society within the context of manipulation and coercion find that the monolithic, conspiratorial theory of Mills' "power elite" carries great appeal. Those on the left, particularly radical intellectuals, believe Mills' theory to be quite descriptive of the "military-industrial complex." According to Mills' view, we no longer have separate economic, political, and military spheres. This outdated conception of power, he contends, must be replaced by the reality of a triumvirate: The top men in military, economic, and political positions have coalesced to form the power elite.[12] Whereas Riesman sees two levels

of power—interest blocs operating in a political context, and the masses—
Mills outlines three levels. Overshadowing the interest blocs and the masses,
says Mills, is the power elite, a unified power bloc comprised of top military,
corporate, and government leaders (the executive branch in particular).
Mills thus places congressmen at the middle levels of power rather than at
the high levels where decisions are made regarding national policy, foreign
policy, war, and the direction of domestic affairs.

The base for the exercise of power within the power elite is the common interests they share. In addition to sharing similar material interests,
persons in high military, economic, and political positions come from similar
socioeconomic backgrounds. Because of similarity in background—they tend
to be educated in military academies or Ivy League schools, belong to
Episcopalian and Presbyterian churches, and come from upper-class families
—members of the power elite have either known each other for some time
or have mutual acquaintances of long standing and have many nonmaterial
values in common. All of this makes it easier for them to coordinate their
actions toward common goals. Pluralists, as represented by Riesman, concede the existence of no such coincidence of interests.

Both Mills and Riesman see World War II and the events that followed
it as a significant turning point, but their interpretations are directly opposite. While Mills contends that power is increasingly concentrated in the
hands of a few, Riesman argues that there is an increasing dispersal of
power among conflicting interest blocs. A summary of Riesman's and Mills'
respective conceptions of power in American society appears in Table 15.2.

Now that we have examined the elitist and pluralistic conceptions of
power in American society, as expressed in the specific ideas of C. Wright
Mills and David Riesman, the question remains: Who has the power?

TABLE 15.2 Elitist and pluralist conceptions of the American power structure

	MILLS	RIESMAN
1. Levels	a. Unified power elite b. Diversified and balanced plurality of interest blocs c. Mass of unorganized people who have practically no power over elite	a. No dominant power elite b. Diversified and balanced plurality of interest blocs c. Mass of unorganized people who have some power over interest blocs
2. Operation	a. One group determines all major policies b. Manipulation of people at the bottom by bloc at the top	a. Who determines policy shifts with the issue b. Monopolistic competition among organized blocs
3. Bases	a. Coincidence of interests among major institutions (economic, military, governmental)	a. Diversity of interests among major organized blocs b. Sense of weakness and depend-ence among those in higher as well as lower status
4. Changes	a. Increasing concentration of power	a. Increasing dispersion of power

SOURCE: Adapted from William Kornhauser, " 'Power Elite' or 'Veto Groups'?" in S. M. Lipset
and Leo Lowenthal, eds., **Culture and Social Character** (New York: Free Press, 1961), p. 261.

There is no doubt that interconnections exist among the occupants of top military, economic, and political positions. Robert McNamara, for example, left the presidency of Ford Motor Company to become secretary of defense in the Kennedy administration. And Washington is a virtual turntable of influential and wealthy persons who go from business (much of it related to the military) to high political appointments and back again to high corporate levels. Although the truth regarding the nature of power in American society probably lies somewhere between elitism and pluralism, the fact remains that the question of whether there is a unified power elite is as yet unanswered by definitive sociological research.[13]

Up to this point, the discussion of political institutions has focused exclusively on the American scene. But what of other nations of the world and the effect of the winds of change on political structure? One of the strongest political currents in the modern world is nationalism, a force now being felt in the Third World.

Colonialism and nationalism

The rise of nationalism in Third World countries is traceable in large measure to the impact of colonialism. Nationalism dates to the beginning of the sixteenth century, when nation-states had been established in the West (England, Spain, France, Portugal) and in the East (Russia). While other nations were established shortly thereafter in the East and West, it was not until after centuries of colonialism that peoples in the Third World began to transform local political units such as tribal jurisdictions into relatively unified nation-states. And, in fact, it was colonialism that created many of the conditions favorable to the rise of nationalism both within and outside the Third World. America as well as Malaysia emerged from colonialism as independent political units known as nation-states.

An inherent part of colonialism seems to have been a tendency toward self-destruction, accomplished in several ways.[14] In the first place, colonial powers created a "country" where none had existed before by establishing geographic boundaries and naming the newly created political unit. This was an important piece of groundwork, for it was then possible for the colonial country to stand as an identifiable and independent political unit at a later time. Second, colonial rulers set up a variety of social structures that served to unify the country and that could be converted to the ends of the national leaders when independence came. Even though the specific educational, economic, and political institutional structures that helped tie a country together could be rejected by the new leaders, they represented a starting point for the establishment of new ones. These various social structures provided a framework that could either be partially continued after independence or used to evolve a different social order. A third way that colonialism promoted nationalism was its forging of a sense of national identity among colonial subjects. This creation of nationalistic feeling was not an intentional act but came partly from the colonizer's view of the colonial country as an identifiable unit. Finally, not only were colonial subjects provided with a point of reference for national pride and loyalty, they were often given a target for hatred by the actions of their colonial rulers. Rejection of colonial rulers fired further the desire for independence, the desire for the establishment of a nation-state apart from the colonial power.

OVERVIEW AND PREVIEW

Change in the family, religious, and political institutional structures has been the focus of this chapter, with a particular emphasis on American society. An institutional structure was defined as an interrelated set of social relationships based on man-made patterns for thinking, feeling, and behaving that is directed at taking care of one or more activities considered to be important for a society's perpetuation. It was noted that institutional structures are the most general and complex social structures because of their interrelationships with each other and with other types of social structures.

The family institutional structure—a culturally defined set of social relationships existing among relatives who either live together or interact frequently enough to be an operating social unit—is the most fundamental of the institutions because it is the cradle of human nature. The manifold variations in family structure are reflected in the norms defining the composition of a family, who marries whom, who owns what, who controls whom, and who lives where. In spite of the variety of family structures that has been observed, as societies become industrialized there is a shift from the extended to the nuclear family structure.

While recognizing that variations in family structure exist in American society, it is still possible to consider changing social positions of the American family in general, particularly when the American family is contrasted with those in other societies. One of the most pronounced changes in the American family is the increasing percentage of working wives and mothers. If the current thrust of the women's liberation movement becomes an established part of American society, many other alterations—presently only potentialities—in the social positions of wife, mother, husband, and father will occur. Even if such potential changes are realized, the nuclear family structure is expected to survive.

The religious institutional structure is a set of social relationships based on ways of thinking, feeling, and behaving related to the sacred aspects of ultimate meaning. Social structural aspects of religion are reflected in participation in church-related activities, on the part of both parishioners and pastors, and in the various types of religious structures. Church membership in America has increased steadily over the last 100 years, and the 1960s saw an attempt by liberal American clergymen to become involved in such nonsacred concerns as civil rights and poverty. Types of religious structure range from the ecclesia, which encompasses nearly all members of a society, to the cult, which claims relatively few members. Between these two extremes lie the denomination and the sect. The latter two types of religious structure are the most important because they are the most prevalent and because they are the most relevant for change in religious institutional structures.

Secularization is the dominant religious trend in modern society. This process involves the declining influence of religion on culture and social life. Religion has gradually lost its former widespread impact in the course of becoming differentiated from other institutional structures. Secularization is reflected in the changing role behavior of American clergymen, who seem to be more involved in nonsacred affairs.

The future of religion is not predictable at this time. Although there are signs of a revival of interest in the sacred aspects of ultimate meaning, it is unlikely that religion in America will ever exercise the influence it does in nonindustrialized societies. At the same time, it is not probable that the religious institutional structure in America, or in other highly industrialized societies, will ever fade away completely.

The political institutional structure is that complex of culturally based social relationships revolving around the acquisition and exercise of authority in the coordination and administration of a society. Although those in social positions within the political institutional structure may at times exercise physical force and attempt to manipulate others, the political institutional structure ultimately rests on legitimate power or authority. In spite of the fact that authority for the coordination and administration of a society rests with those in official political positions, it is recognized that their actions are influenced by people not in positions of political authority. Among sociologists there is disagreement about the distribution of power in American society. Elitists contend that American society is controlled by a unified and enduring elite. In contrast, pluralists depict decision making on the national level as the product of conflicting and shifting power blocs. Conclusive evidence does not exist as yet to settle this controversy.

Nationalism, now being experienced in the Third World, is one of the most prominent political trends in the modern world. Colonialism contributes to the rise of nationalism in several ways.

Nothing has been said up to this point about the research methods used by sociologists in the scientific study of social structure. The next chapter is devoted to this topic. Care will be taken to avoid coverage of particular research techniques such as sampling design or the correlation statistic. More important than a detailed elaboration of the range and variety of research procedures is an introduction to the basic orientations that guide sociologists in the shaping of their research questions and the testing of their theories and predictions. Chapter 16 will cover the inadequacy of nonscientific knowledge and selected aspects of the language of science.

REFERENCES

1. William J. Goode, *World Revolution and Family Patterns* (New York: Free Press, 1963).
2. Marvin B. Sussman, "The Help Pattern in the Middle Class Family," *American Sociological Review*, 15 (February 1953), 22–23.
3. David A. Schulz, *The Changing Family: Its Function and Future* (Englewood Cliffs, N.J.: Prentice-Hall, 1972), pp. 417–423.
4. Emile Durkheim, *The Elementary Forms of the Religious Life*, trans. by J. W. Swain (New York: Free Press, 1947).
5. Lauris B. Whitman, ed., *Yearbook of American Churches* (New York: Council Press, 1968); and Lauris B. Whitman, ed., *Yearbook of American Churches* (New York: Council Press, 1969).
6. Jeffery Hadden, *The Gathering Storm in the Churches* (Garden City, N.Y.: Doubleday, 1969); and Rodney Stark, Bruce O. Foster, Charles Y. Glock, and Harold Quinley, *Wayward Shepherds: Prejudice and the Protestant Clergy* (New York: Harper & Row, 1971).
7. H. Richard Niebuhr, *The Social Sources of Denominationalism* (New York: Holt, Rinehart and Winston, 1929).
8. Stark et al., op. cit.
9. T. H. White, *The Once and Future King* (New York: Berkley Medallion Books, 1969).
10. David Riesman, *The Lonely Crowd* (Garden City, N.Y.: Doubleday, 1953).
11. C. Wright Mills, *The Power Elite* (New York: Oxford University Press, 1956).
12. An excellent comparison of Riesman's and Mills' conceptions of power in American society can be found in William Kornhauser, " 'Power Elite' or 'Veto Groups'?" in S. M. Lipset and Leo Lowenthal, eds., *Culture and Social Character* (New York: Free Press, 1961), pp. 252–267.
13. Thomas Dye and Harmon Ziegler, *The Irony of Democracy* (Belmont, Calif.: Wadsworth, 1970), p. 6.
14. Leonard Broom and Philip Selznick, *Sociology: A Text with Adapted Readings*, 5th ed. (New York: Harper & Row, 1973), pp. 588–589.

ADDITIONAL SOURCES AND READINGS

General sources

Turner, Jonathan H. *Patterns of Social Organization: A Survey of Social Institutions* (New York: McGraw-Hill, 1972).

Wells, Alan. *Social Institutions* (New York: Basic Books, 1971).

Williams, Robin M. *American Society: A Sociological Interpretation*, 3rd ed. (New York: Knopf, 1970).

Family institutional structure

Burgess, E. W., Harvey J. Locke, and Mary Margaret Thomes. *The Family*, 4th ed. (New York: Van Nostrand Reinhold, 1971).

Cavan, Ruth Shonle. *The American Family* (New York: T. Y. Crowell, 1969).

Farber, Bernard. *Family and Kinship in Modern Society* (Glenview, Ill.: Scott, Foresman, 1973).

Ferriss, Abbott L. *Indicators of Change in the American Family* (New York: Russell Sage, 1970).

Kenkel, William F. *The Family in Perspective*, 3rd ed. (New York: Appleton, 1973).

Kephart, William M. *The Family, Society and the Individual*, 3rd ed. (Boston: Houghton Mifflin, 1972).

Skolnick, Arlene S., and Jerome H. Skolnick. *Family in Transition* (Boston: Little, Brown, 1971).

Religious institutional structure

Berger, Peter L. *A Rumor of Angels: Modern Society and the Rediscovery of the Supernatural* (Garden City, N.Y.: Doubleday, 1970).

Berger, Peter L. *The Sacred Canopy: Elements of a Sociological Theory of Religion* (Garden City, N.Y.: Doubleday, 1967).

Cox, Harvey. *The Secular City*, rev. ed. (New York: Macmillan, 1966).

Glock, Charles Y., and Rodney Stark. *Religion and Society in Tension* (Skokie, Ill.: Rand McNally, 1965).

O'Dea, Thomas F. *The Sociology of Religion* (Englewood Cliffs, N.J.: Prentice-Hall, 1966).

O'Dea, Thomas F., and Janet K. O'Dea. *Readings on the Sociology of Religion* (Englewood Cliffs, N.J.: Prentice-Hall, 1973).

Schneider, Louis. *Sociological Approach to Religion* (New York: Wiley, 1970).

Yinger, J. Milton. *The Scientific Study of Religion* (New York: Macmillan, 1970).

Political institutional structure

Bendix, Reinhard. *State and Society* (Boston: Little, Brown, 1968).

Bendix, Reinhard. *Nation-Building and Citizenship: Studies in a Changing Social Order* (New York: Wiley, 1964).

Coser, Lewis A., ed. *Political Sociology: Selected Essays* (New York: Harper & Row, 1966).

Eisenstadt, S. N., ed. *Political Sociology: A Reader* (New York: Basic Books, 1971).

Gillam, Richard, ed. *Power in Postwar America* (Boston: Little, Brown, 1971).

Horowitz, Irving Louis. *Foundations of Political Sociology* (New York: Harper & Row, 1972).

Horowitz, Irving Louis. *Three Worlds of Development: The Theory and Practice of International Stratification* (New York: Oxford University Press, 1966).

Kornhauser, William. *The Politics of Mass Society* (New York: Free Press, 1959).

Lipset, S. M. *Political Man: The Social Bases of Politics* (Garden City, N.Y.: Doubleday, 1960).

Nisbet, Robert A. *Community and Power* (New York: Oxford University Press, 1962).

Shepard, Jon M., ed. *Spectrum on Social Problems: Society, Economy and Man* (Columbus, Ohio: Merrill, 1973), pp. 19–50.

part [VI]

SOCIOLOGY AS A SOCIAL SCIENCE

The Science of Social Structure

The word "sociologist" evokes different images in different individuals—depending on their age, sex, and social class. Some may think of a sociologist as a person unsuited for any kind of "useful" work, by which they mean manual labor or similar down-to-earth, practical occupations. Others may think of a sociologist as an ivory-tower isolate, social worker, socialist, or social engineer with solutions to pressing social problems. In individual cases, any one of these stereotypes might be quite accurately applied to a particular sociologist. However, sociologists in general would vehemently reject these images (except possibly that of social engineer, which has gained some acceptance in sociological circles in recent times), preferring to think of themselves as *social scientists*. In common with all scientists, sociologists seek understanding, explanation, and prediction of phenomena through the interplay of theory and research. The present chapter is directed toward an elaboration of this conception of the sociologist's role. It will be devoted to a discussion of the inadequacy of nonscientifically generated knowledge and to an outline of some basic aspects of the language of science.

THE NEED FOR A SCIENTIFIC APPROACH

The emphasis in sociology on *scientific* inquiry has had a long history. In the 1950s particularly, there was heated debate (some of it public) on whether or not sociology could accurately be called a science. This debate has subsided considerably in recent years as sociology has made gains in both societal approval and acceptance by the broader scientific community. Ironically enough, however, at the very moment that sociology has gained significant acceptance as a science, the old debate has been reopened—this time by sociologists themselves. The so-called radical sociologists, and radicals in general, have recently labeled sociology a two-time loser. They charge that sociology either informs us of what we already know or tells us things that we don't know but that are not worth knowing anyway. This would appear to leave sociology with no redeeming value. Do these charges have merit?

Sociological knowledge as useless

Behind the assertion that sociology informs us of nothing worthwhile lurks the wish of the social activist to alter American society, to upend the Establishment, to eradicate social inequities, and to solve all social problems. Because of his activist frame of mind, he is quite impatient with the "trivial" work being done by sociologists. However, the precision sought in scientific research requires that all theories be subjected to empirical testing, and thus the results may appear useless for purposes of immediate or sweeping societal transformations. Such testing can seem needlessly time-consuming and is therefore frustrating to the activist, who ignores the potential harm inherent in the alternative of basing public policies and programs on ideas that have never been adequately tested.[1] Further, if the sociologist-as-scientist permits his research to be influenced by his personal values—which he almost invariably does—it would be disastrous to abandon scientific standards that at least establish rules for the minimization of bias and vested interest. Therefore, if sociology is to "save" society, as the activist demands, its practitioners must not abandon science but must become even better theorists and researchers. Otherwise, invalid information that happens to coincide with some sociologists' viewpoints may become the basis for social policies and programs.

However, the fact that careful scientific methods of research are far from speedy should not be taken as a denial of the potential of sociology in the realm of social affairs. Sociologists are increasingly receiving requests from government and business to act as researchers and consultants, and have made many contributions in that role.[2]

Caution is in order, however, for two reasons: the danger that more will be expected of sociology in this respect than can be delivered, and the willingness of some to make socially relevant recommendations on a nonscientific basis.

Policy decisions, it should be noted, are not usually simply based on the best scientific evidence, even when it is readily available. For one thing, decisions are more likely to be made by those who, in conflict with other interest blocs, are able to exercise enough power to gain their ends. And if scientific evidence is used to support a decision, that evidence may not be the best available but may be chosen because it buttresses the viewpoint of the bloc in the position to make the decision. It also happens that sociologists as well as other social scientists find themselves obligated to produce findings to support the decisions of those who are paying them. This "buying-off" of researchers need not be a conscious process on the part of those involved. In addition, a researcher's ideas on what is good or bad affect the research he undertakes, the manner in which he conducts the research, and the interpretation he places on the findings. Prowar scientists, for example, are more likely to take jobs with companies making tanks, airplanes, or bombs than are antiwar scientists. The probability is also high that their research will be selected, conducted, and presented in a manner favorable to their employers. The fact is that one does not normally remain employed for long by those who are hurt by his work, or in other words, "he who pays the piper calls the tune."

Sociological knowledge as obvious

What about the second indictment, the charge that sociology is the pursuit of what everyone already knows? This criticism is a long-standing one, and while it has lost some of its earlier punch, it remains part of the public stereotype of sociology.

If iron and steel had mind and voice, they would undoubtedly inform the physicist, "Of course, we rust when exposed to air and moisture for long periods of time without preventive protection." Obviously, the subject matter of sociology—humanity—does have mind and voice. Partly because humans have either observed, heard, or read about various aspects of social structure, they are quick to respond to social scientific findings with a blasé "so what—everybody knows that." A vague familiarity with a dimension of human life, which perhaps has never been previously raised to the point of consciousness, is suddenly transformed in the human mind into an "obvious" truth when it appears in print as a sociological finding. And it is true that sociologists do sometimes spend a lot of money and time "discovering" what common sense would dictate. Consider the statements below:

1. Exposure to pornography promotes criminal or antisocial behavior.
2. Alcohol is less harmful than most currently illegal drugs.
3. Homosexuals can be easily identified because of their highly effeminate characteristics.
4. Women are by their biological nature "weaker" than men.
5. Militant college students perform poorly academically and drop out of college more often than their classmates.

The public may ask: Why spend time and money on such obviously accurate statements? Are there not less well established matters to absorb the sociologists' attention? Actually, as you undoubtedly know, research

Bob Combs

has shown that each of these statements is too simplified to be accepted at face value. A link between exposure to pornography and criminal or anti-social behavior has not been established; alcohol may be even more harmful than heroin; homosexuals can be supermasculine; in some respects women are "stronger" than men; militant college students fare well academically and have a lower dropout rate than their nonactivist classmates.

These findings may now seem obvious to you, but at one time all five statements above were regarded as true. The point is, the "obvious" may be shown to be false when it is scientifically probed. Moreover, what may seem common sense to one person may seem false to another, depending on his personal knowledge and experience. Finally, sociologists study some aspects of social structure that are never entertained by the layman.

Changing social conditions alter relationships

An important function of research is to discover the *conditions* under which a given event will or will not occur. In a study of American soldiers during World War II, this proposition was tested: White privates are more eager than their black counterparts for noncommissioned status. The basis of this proposition was the widely held belief that Blacks have less ambition than Whites. In fact, the evidence showed Blacks to be more interested in military promotion than were Whites.[3] It has been suggested that during the 1940s and 1950s Blacks were more ambitious in the military than in civilian life because they perceived a greater opportunity for upward mobility within the military hierarchy. If this were actually the case, then it would mean that the comparative desire for upward mobility in the military between Blacks and Whites was conditioned by the perceived opportunities of each race for upward mobility in civilian life.

From the foregoing discussion, it must now be clear that a scientific approach in sociology is necessary. This can be further reinforced by an examination of the alternatives to science.

Inadequacies of nonscientific knowledge

By what methods do people generally form and alter their beliefs? What are some means that enable people to raise false statements, such as those just cited, to the level of truth? Involved in this process are three standard methods: habit, intuition, and appeal to authority.

To cling to a viewpoint because one has always held it is to rely on *habit* as a source of knowledge. Of course, it is difficult to jettison a long-standing belief. An old shoe is more comfortable than a new one.

A second source of knowledge is *intuition*, by which a belief is thought to be correct because alternatives are incomprehensible: "It simply could not be any other way. It seems so right." Few things are as satisfying as subscribing to a belief because it appears to be so self-evident. One can appreciate the dismay that ensued when men first voiced their conviction that the "end" of the ocean is not the edge of the world, or when Copernicus stated that the sun, not the earth, is at the center of our solar system.

Citing an authority—someone who should know—is a third method for the verification of knowledge. This source of knowledge may be extremely unreliable. Acceptance of a statement by a political candidate that transit fares will not be raised, or a statement by a real estate broker that property values always decline when Blacks move into a neighborhood, are cases in point. On the other hand, appeal to authority may be a valid source of knowledge. Experts can be trusted to give us the best current estimate of the distance between the earth and the moon, and we can put faith in the statistics linking emotional stress with heart attacks.

Of these three sources of knowledge, then, habit is the least desirable. Intuition and appeal to authority, on the other hand, in certain or even many instances, yield valid and reliable knowledge. Indeed, the intuitive powers of philosophic and literary figures (not to mention scientists) have produced innumerable significant insights. And, since being an expert in one or more fields is hardly a realistic prospect for more than a few, authorities must necessarily be one of our most important sources of knowledge. Of course, we must be open to the fact that expert opinions may conflict at any point in time and are likely to change with the passage of time. Moreover, the validity of relying on authority as a source of knowledge rests on the trustworthiness of the means by which experts arrive at their conclusions. That is, reliance on authority is "safe" only if we can evaluate the methods employed by those experts in obtaining such knowledge.

The unique advantage of science

In areas of natural and social sciences, then, it is important to know if a scientific approach has been followed by the reporter of knowledge. Why? Because a scientific approach—whatever the specific research techniques used—has an important feature that gives it a unique advantage in generating valid and reliable knowledge. This feature is *self-correction*, which occurs because scientists are trained to maintain constant doubt about their findings. Of course, being human they do so with varying degrees of success. Maintaining doubt works in two ways. First, the scientist is encouraged to examine his evidence with sufficient skepticism to minimize the intrusion of his personal values into interpretation of data; the descriptive term most often used for this aspect of the scientific attitude is *objectivity*. Second, once evidence has been made public, it will be critically evaluated and subjected to further scrutiny by one or more different scientists.

• SCIENTISTS AND THEIR VALUES. A norm of long standing among scientists states that their mission is to study what *is*, not what *should be*. In the course of their work, scientists are supposed to avoid making judgments based on their values, on their ideas of what is good or bad. Attempting to be value-free remains a role prescription of the social scientist. However, its interpretation has been altered under the attack of those who question the possibility of human beings actually remaining neutral. Since people, even as scientists, cannot realistically be expected to divorce themselves completely from their learned standards of good and bad despite their constant efforts, they should make their values known so that readers of their research —as well as they, themselves—can be aware of their biases.

A viewpoint that has led to fierce debate among sociologists in the past few years is that social scientists should not even attempt to keep their values out of their work. Rather, it is now being argued, social scientists *should* conduct their research from a definite value standpoint. The logical extension of this stance is that social scientists should conduct their research with an eye to affecting social structures. Instead of merely being "objective and impartial" investigators of social life, social scientists have the moral obligation to be in the thick of things, to call attention to shortcomings in existing social structures and offer guidelines for improvement and change. The social action position rests on the assumption that social scientists are among the best qualified to offer knowledge and advice for human betterment.[4] This position is closely tied to the sociological imagination (see Chapter 1) as defined by C. Wright Mills, a prominent intellectual forerunner of contemporary social actionism.[5] Whether social scientists are prone to social actionism or not, they are still constrained to maintain some level of objectivity. This is so partly because the public nature of scientific research contrains even the most socially committed scientists to base their conclusions and recommendations on solid evidence rather than on the mere echoes of their minds. Objectivity is also promoted by the expectation that scientists be aware of and make known their biases.*

• PUBLIC NATURE OF SCIENCE. Self-correction operates in science, then, not only because scientists may make known their assumptions and biases. The self-correction tendency exists also because researchers report the steps they took and the methods they used, as well as the relevant information they collected and the logic they employed. Thus, all pertinent factors are "public," that is, open to scrutiny. Consequently, other scientists can evaluate and challenge the findings and conclusions either by revealing errors in the research or by conducting further study of their own on the matter. It is

---

*Some of my biases may be found in the Preface to this text.

difficult for a scientist to hide behind a falsely reached finding, conclusion, or theory because other scientists will be questioning and probing further. Sigmund Freud is credited with making significant breakthroughs in the study of the mind. To do so, he had to weather the storm of ridicule that comes with bucking convention, for scientists, like all human beings, have values that are not easily put aside. Further, Freud's ideas have been severely criticized by other scientists after further testing and research.

Thus, because science is geared to the detection and correction of errors and false conclusions, the knowledge that science yields is the most trustworthy and the most rapidly changing body of information extant. Naturally, the process of built-in doubt that promotes self-correction must be based on appropriate research techniques. What follows is an introduction to some aspects of the language of science.

THE LANGUAGE OF SCIENCE

Scientists attempt to explain a given event or process by first formulating a theory about it. This is in line with the basic goal of science: the development of broad explanations for events and processes. In these two deceptively simple statements are implied several key aspects of the language of science. What is scientific explanation? What is scientific theory? What is the relationship between theory and explanation?

Scientific theory

The overarching goal of science is *explanation*—accounting for a given event or process by specifying factors that cause such an event or process to occur. The scientist arrives at this by first developing a *theory*—a set of logically interrelated concepts and propositions that provides a systematic view of selected aspects of a specified event or process. A theory does not burst from the head of a brilliant scientist like a lightning bolt from the heavens. A great deal of painstaking, even agonizing, work by many other scientists usually precedes the ultimate construction of a theory. A rather slow accretion of concepts and single propositions is a normal prelude to any theory.

• CONCEPTS. As a language form, scientific theory must take concepts as its basic building blocks. It is with concepts that any eventually developed theory gets its start. A *concept* is one or a series of words that serves as a shorthand description of an object, event, or process. An essential aspect of the acquisition of language is the gradually developed ability to deal with the general and the abstract. To a small child, a truck is a truck, a doll is a doll, and a ball is a ball. After a time, a child gains the capacity mentally to classify all these objects under the more general and abstract concept, "toy."

Although obviously on a higher plane, the scientist too attempts to move from the particular and concrete to the general and abstract. The scientist looks for commonality among apparently dissimilar events or processes. For example, what do the Russian Revolution, the women's liberation movement, and the civil rights movement have in common? To the sociologist, each of these phenomena, while vastly different in countless details, shares a vital characteristic: Each attempts to arouse widespread public support in favor of the particular forms of social change it is advocating. Sociologists find sufficient similarity among these social currents to incorporate them under the general and more abstract concept (or shorthand description) labeled "social movement."

Concepts in science tend to be more abstract than terms in nonscientific language. Moreover, scientific concepts must be defined in language more precise than our everyday language. Only by attempting to define their concepts clearly can scientists hope to measure them accurately—which brings us to the term "variable," a word you will encounter often in reading any sociological literature.

• VARIABLES. Scientific concepts are not only labels for a class of events or processes; if concepts are to be measured and used in research, the phenomenon to which they refer must occur in varying degrees. Thus, the phenomenon described by a concept actually varies in the real world; the scientist must work toward detecting and demonstrating this variation with some measuring device. The resulting classified variation is a *variable*. One of the most difficult tasks of the scientist is to translate concepts from definitions to variables. Only upon demonstrating that individual cases can be reasonably accurately classified, either within a category or at some point along a range of magnitude, have scientists made the step from conceptual definition to scientific variable.

The nature of the measuring device employed to translate a concept into a usable scientific variable partly depends on whether the variable is considered to be qualitative or quantitative. *Qualitative variables* are measured by categories that differ in kind rather than in numerical degree. A person is either male or female, and if a person is a member of a religious denomination he or she can be appropriately classified as Catholic, Protestant, Jewish, Buddhist, or whatever. Sex and religion are frequently used qualitative sociological variables.

Qualitative variables, then, are characterized by categories that differ in kind. *Quantitative variables* in sociology carry a range of values that reflect the various degrees to which persons or groups possess the characteristic defined by the concept. Age and income are quantitative variables that are fairly easily measured because a standard numerical system already exists. However, most concepts occupying sociologists (as well as other scientists) require considerable labor and ingenuity before they can be measured quantitatively. Concepts such as alienation, social class, or white-collar crime present problems of measurement much too complex for treatment here. The history of most scientific concepts, as already implied, is a movement from a qualitative to a quantitative level of measurement. As examples, gravity can now be expressed in *g* units; and numerical scales have been developed for measuring different aspects of alienation.

• PROPOSITIONS. Concepts are a mere beginning in science. The reason for formulating concepts and developing appropriate measurement devices for them is the use to which they can be put in stating and testing the validity of propositions. A scientific *proposition* is any statement of a relationship among things that can be shown to be valid or invalid. Consider this proposition: Left-wing students tend disproportionately to be the children of left-wing or liberal parents. Assuming that the concepts "left-wing," "student," and "liberal" have been clearly defined and can be measured in some acceptable manner, the validity of this proposition can be tested against reality. Prior to a test of its validity, this or any scientific proposition is called a *hypothesis*—a tentative proposition intended for empirical testing so that it can be either accepted or rejected. If, for example, it can be demonstrated (as it has been) that left-wing students do tend to come disproportionately from homes headed by left-wing or liberal parents, then this proposition may be termed a fact. A *fact*, then, is a hypothesis that has been empirically verified. Of course, scientific facts are by their nature tentative; they should not be considered with the sense of finality normally involved when something is labeled a "fact." Further empirical observations or tests of a scientific fact may cast doubt on its validity. Scientific facts tend to be tested repeatedly, and those facts that withstand this continuous scrutiny are called scientific *laws*.

• THEORY. The definition of scientific theory stated at the beginning of this section on the language of science should be clearer now. *Theory* was defined as a set of logically interrelated concepts and propositions that provides a systematic view of selected aspects of a specified event or process. Concepts are the building blocks of the scientific propositions contained in a theory. Theoretical propositions may be one of three types: a hypothesis, if it is virtually untested; a fact, if it has been verified; a law, if repeated verification has led to the belief that it is valid. Each of these types of propositions shares a common characteristic—each can be tested against reality. Because science is dynamic, theoretical propositions constantly undergo examination and revision. And further tests can change the nature of a proposition. A hypothesis can become a fact or even a law; a law or a fact can either be rejected as false or changed from its original form into a somewhat different hypothesis, and so on.

So far, two characteristics of a scientific theory have been described. First, the concepts of a theory must be defined. Second, once defined, theoretical concepts must be linked together in propositional form. A third characteristic—that propositions must be logically interrelated—has not yet been touched upon. The requirement that propositions in a theory be logically interrelated is merely another way of saying that a theory is a deductive system. A set of propositions forms a *deductive system* when the lowest-level proposition logically follows from higher-level propositions.[6]

The deductive property of theory can be illustrated by returning to Durkheim's study of suicide.[7] It had been observed before Durkheim's work that, as a category, Catholics exhibited a lower suicide rate than Protestants. However, this fact was merely an isolated empirical generalization. From Durkheim's effort the following set of logically interrelated propositions can be stated, thus placing this observed relationship between religion and the suicide rate within a deductive system:

1. Suicide rates are functions of *unrelieved* anxieties and stresses to which persons are subjected.
2. Social cohesion provides psychic support to group members subjected to acute stresses and anxieties.
3. Catholics have greater social cohesion than Protestants.
4. Therefore, lower suicide rates should be anticipated among Catholics than among Protestants.

That proposition four is deduced from the logical progression of the first three propositions is obvious.

But the question remains: What is the advantage of theory over isolated hypotheses and facts? An answer to this question is best offered within the context of the link between theory and explanation.

Theory and explanation

One important advantage of theory is quite clear—the ultimate goal of science is the explanation of events or processes. That is, the success with which a scientific discipline pursues its area of study depends on the extent to which it can transform isolated facts and hypotheses into testable theories and thus into an explanation of an event or process. An explanation for an event or process exists when the factors causing that event or process can be specified. *Causation*, a concept central to explanation, assumes that a given event is the effect or result of one or more antecedent factors. For example, according to Durkheim's theory, the existence of a higher rate of suicide among Protestants than among Catholics is traceable to three inter-related factors antecedent to suicide. That is, propositions one, two, and three in Durkheim's theory of suicide precede suicide in time and therefore cause the variation. This example should clarify the relationship between theory and explanation—Durkheim's *theory* purports to *explain* variation in suicide rates.

Before Durkheim, the fact that Catholics had a lower suicide rate than Protestants was without a sociological explanation. A second advantage of theory over single propositions—an advantage that has just been implied—is its recognition of *multiple causation:* Any particular social phenomenon may be the result of the interaction of several causal factors. If, in Durkheim's theory of suicide, we were satisfied with the proposition that the suicide rate is a function of social cohesion, then we would remain ignorant of the manner in which social cohesion leads to variation in suicide rates. That is, we would remain uninformed about the role of social cohesion in providing psychic support for group members under acute stress and anxiety, and the role of unrelieved stresses and anxieties in the promotion of acts of suicide.

In addition to providing an explanation for an event or process and emphasizing multiple causation, a theory may lead to new hypotheses and/or incorporate already existing but yet unexplained facts. Durkheim's theory of suicide, as we saw in Chapter 1, involves more than an explanation of differences in the suicide rate between Catholics and Protestants. Among other things, his theory also attempted to account for variations in the suicide rate among the military, the old and sick, and the divorced and separated, as well as fluctuations in the suicide rate according to educational level and the state of the economy.[8]

A formula for scientific research

The so-called scientific method is a general formula designed to generate valid and reliable knowledge. "Scientific method" is a misleading label partly because it is easily confused with specific scientific methods such as those involved in sampling and statistics. Actually, the *scientific method* is a series of abstract steps intended to guide the conduct of research. These steps include identification and definition of a problem, formulation of empirically testable propositions, and determination and activation of an appropriate research design.

• PROBLEM IDENTIFICATION AND DEFINITION. Problems for scientific study come from a variety of sources, including personal observation, intuition, reading research reports of other social scientists, or classroom preparation or discussion. Nonscientific sources also attract the attention of scientists. If an apple really did fall on Isaac Newton's head, raising his curiosity about what came to be called gravity, it would be an ideal example of significant scientific problems coming from the most unlikely source.

Problems are not generally chosen on the basis of convenience, although it is true that availability is a reason for problem selection at times. A scientific problem is more likely to be chosen for study because it promises to contribute to knowledge, to have practical application, or both. It should be obvious from the earlier discussion that problem identification is influenced, consciously or not, by the standards of goodness and evil held by individual scientists.

Whatever the source of a problem that attracts a scientist's interest, he must identify and define it as a first step in the research process. This step normally involves developing the problem in the light of relevant theory and previous research findings, if they exist.

• FORMULATION OF TESTABLE PROPOSITIONS. From scrutiny of relevant theory and previous research findings, the scientist formulates one or more propositions that can be tested against empirical observation. They may be hypotheses stating previously untested relationships, or they may be a mixture of hypotheses and facts (propositions with prior empirical verification). Ideally, these propositions are part of a deductively constructed theory. In reality, sociologists generally have to settle for less, because few deductive sociological theories have as yet been evolved. It is in the nature of science to formulate and test isolated propositions under the long-range goal of cultivating deductive theories. Theories are eventually shaped after the long-term cumulation of what may be seemingly unrelated facts. As with any science, the cumulation period for sociology is glacial in movement.

Whatever the precise nature or source of the propositions, they must be testable. As already acknowledged, making propositions testable demands considerable labor in precisely defining concepts and transforming concepts into either qualitative or quantitative variables. The formulation of testable propositions is intimately intertwined with the research design aspect of the scientific formula for research.

• DETERMINATION AND ACTIVATION OF AN APPROPRIATE RESEARCH DESIGN. A *research design* is the product of a series of decisions regarding the most appropriate procedures for pitting propositions against empirical observation. Decisions have to be made as to the variables to be used in the study, including variables that although not directly involved in the propositions to be tested, may alter the observed relationship appearing between any two variables. The manner in which these variables are to be measured is, of course, a crucial dimension of research design. A sample of cases must be selected among which the propositions can be tested. The researcher has to make decisions designed to ensure that the findings and conclusions based on the data collected can be generalized to the larger population from which the sample was taken. Another area of decision making involves the techniques for analyzing the data after they have been collected. For this, sociologists must look to the growing body of available procedures. Although the areas of decision making in shaping a research design have not been exhausted, you should at least be sensitized to the complexities involved in translating a vague idea for research into results that have been subjected to scientific safeguards.

The best-laid research plans must confront the real world. Consequently, almost any research design, regardless of the care given it, will be modified. Contingencies alter the research design after the data collection, data analysis, and data evaluation subphases have been activated.

Thus, the determination of an appropriate research design is at the heart of the scientific method because it is involved in both the problem identification and definition phase as well as the proposition formulation phase. Moreover, the research design part of the scientific method entails several additional subphases that must be executed after the design has been fashioned. These subphases include data collection, data analysis, and the reflection of the results back on their theoretical origin. From this reflection comes either confirmation or alteration of the theory from which the propositions were generated.

Serendipity and science

One problem with any discussion of the "scientific method" is that it presents an incomplete, and therefore partially false, picture of research. Outlining these phases presents the conduct of research as a more rigid and programmed process than it really is. The last section was deliberately labeled "a formula for scientific research" rather than something like "*the* scientific method." While strict adherence to the steps indentified with the scientific method is the predominant model for research, it is not the only way to reach scientific goals of understanding, explanation, and prediction.

Serendipity, a term that sounds like a product of Walt Disney's mouse factory, is enlightening in this context. *Serendipity* refers to the observation, during the course of research, of an unanticipated event that catches the scientist's eye because it clashes with accepted theory and established facts.[9] To be considered a serendipitous finding, an unanticipated and surprising observation must either lead to the extension of an existing theory or spark an entirely new line of theoretical and empirical inquiry. Examples of serendipity in science are many, including the chance discovery of penicillin and Freud's use of such apparently insignificant behavior as forgetfulness and verbal errors for the extension of his theory of repression.

OVERVIEW

Vestiges of the charge that sociology cannot be scientific remain with us. Radicals, some of them sociologists, have brought the issue to the forefront once again. Sociology, they allege, is a failure as a science because its findings are either useless or painfully obvious. Even if these indictments were accurate (which they are not), sociologists would be ill-advised to abandon scientific principles; the alternative sources of knowledge (including habit, intuition, and appeal to authority) generate uncontested and unexamined information. Scientifically derived findings and conclusions, on the other hand, are exposed to the very important principle of self-correction. Because of the operation of this principle, scientific knowledge is constantly undergoing challenge and change. Knowledge sifted objectively through the testing and retesting of findings is the most reliable and valid we can hope to get.

Formulating and testing explanations for events and processes is the business of science. Explanation—specifying the factors causing an event or process—is accomplished through the logical interrelationship of propositions (theory). A deductive system of propositions is the ideal. Much hard labor precedes the formulation of a theory. Concepts and propositions usually have been worked and reworked by various scientists before they are combined into a theory. Once a theory has been constructed, the propositions derived from it will be tested and retested, leading to the confirmation, modification, or abandonment of the theory. The so-called scientific method is the general formula for research used in the process of testing either isolated propositions or propositions derived from theories.

REFERENCES

1. For a concrete example of this possibility, see Daniel P. Moynihan, *Maximum Feasible Misunderstanding* (New York: Free Press, 1969).
2. Lewis M. Killian, "The Social Scientist's Role in the Preparation of the Florida Desegregation Brief," *Social Problems*, 3 (April 1956), 211–214.
3. Paul F. Lazarsfeld, "The American Soldier—An Expository Review," *Public Opinion Quarterly*, 13 (Fall 1949), 378–380.

4. Thomas Ford Hoult, ". . . Who Shall Prepare Himself to the Battle?" *The American Sociologist*, 3 (February 1968), 3–7.
5. C. Wright Mills, *The Sociological Imagination* (New York: Oxford University Press, 1959).
6. For a criticism of the failure of sociology to generate deductive theories, see George C. Homans, "Bringing Men Back In," *American Sociological Review*, 29 (December 1964), 809–818.
7. Elaboration of this illustration is contained in Robert K. Merton, *Social Theory and Social Structure*, rev. ed. (New York: Free Press, 1957), pp. 96–99.
8. For additional advantages of theory, see *ibid.*, pp. 97–99; and William J. Goode and Paul K. Hatt, *Methods in Social Research* (New York: McGraw-Hill, 1952), pp. 9–12.
9. For an elaboration of the serendipity pattern, see Merton, op. cit., pp. 103–108. An interesting illustration of serendipity appears in Bernard Barber and R. C. Fox, "The Case of the Floppy-Eared Rabbits: An Instance of Serendipity Gained and Serendipity Lost," *American Journal of Sociology*, 64 (September 1958), 128–136.

ADDITIONAL SOURCES AND READINGS

Blalock, Hubert M., Jr. *Theory Construction* (Englewood Cliffs, N.J.: Prentice-Hall, 1969).
Douglas, Jack R., ed. *The Relevance of Sociology* (Appleton, 1970).
Filstead, William J., ed. *Qualitative Methodology: Firsthand Involvement With the Social World* (Chicago: Markham, 1970).
Freeman, Howard E., and Robert Hagedorn. *Social Research and Social Policy* (Englewood Cliffs, N.J.: Prentice-Hall, 1970).
Kaplan, Abraham. *The Conduct of Inquiry* (San Francisco: Chandler, 1964).
Kerlinger, Fred N. *Foundations of Behavioral Research* (New York: Holt, Rinehart and Winston, 1964).
Labovitz, Sanford, and Robert Hagedorn. *Introduction to Social Research* (New York: McGraw-Hill, 1971).
Lofland, John. *Analyzing Social Settings* (Belmont, Calif.: Wadsworth, 1971).
Mueller, John H., Karl F. Schuessler, and Herbert L. Costner. *Statistical Reasoning in Sociology*, rev. ed. (Boston: Houghton Mifflin, 1970).
Shepard, Jon M., ed. *Kaleidoscope: Adapted Readings for Introductory Sociology* (New York: Harper & Row, 1973), pp. 314–337.
Webb, Eugene, Donald T. Campbell, Richard D. Schwartz, and Lee Sechrest. *Unobtrusive Measures* (Skokie, Ill.: Rand McNally, 1966).
Zetterberg, Hans L. *On Theory and Verification in Sociology*, 3rd ed. (Totowa, N.J.: Bedminister Press, 1965).

Index

Donne, John, 245
Duncan, Otis Dudley, 112, 113, 142
Durkheim, Emile, 5, 6, 246, 311
  and structural perspective, 7, 9
  study of suicide, 12–14, 341, 342

Ecclesia, 313
Ecology and urbanization, 293–298
Economic development and population
    growth, 270–271
Education
  occupation, income, and, 142
  race, occupational status, and, 112–113
  and upward mobility, 141–143
Ego, 221
Elites, ideology, and stratification,
    104–105
Elitism, political, 320–322
Ellsberg, Daniel, 225
Emotional support in primary groups, 246
Endogamy, 305
Environment, geographic, and social
    structure, 27–28
Equal Pay Act of 1963, 110
Erikson, Erik, 223
Ethnic villagers in inner city, 167
Ethnicity and race as changing master
    position, 110–116
Ethnocentrism, 63–66
Evolutionary theories of social change,
    257
Exogamy, 305
Expectations, rising, and social
    movements, 276
Expertise and power, 179

Family
  defined, 303
  descent and inheritance, 305
  functions, 303–306
  future of, 310–311
  and industrialization, 306–307
  isolation of, 307
  marriage patterns, 304–305
  nuclear vs. extended, 304
  patriarchal vs. matriarchal, 305
  patrilineal vs. matrilineal, 305
  patrilocal vs. matrilocal, 305–306
  social position of sexes, 309–310
  and stratification, 105
  subcultural variations, 307, 309
Fertility rate and population size,
    264–265
Folkways, defined, 22, 50
Formal organization
  and bureaucracy, 178–179
  implications of informal organizations
    in, 199–200
  as social structure, 177–178
  stratification in, 127

Fox, Robin, 222
Freud, Sigmund, 338
  personality theory, 221
Friedan, Betty, 276
Frustration, sources of, 275–276
Functional theory of stratification,
    102–103
Functionalism and social change,
    257–260
Future Shock (Toffler), 254

Gans, Herbert, view of urbanism,
    166–169
Generalized others, 219
Geography, heredity, and social life,
    28–29
Goal displacement in bureaucracy, 187
Group. See also Informal organization;
    Primary group
  defined, 235–236
  and individuals, 236–237
  reference, and self-concept, 216
  size, and growth of primary
    relationships, 242
  stratification in, 127
Growth rate and population size, 265

Habit, as source of knowledge, 235
Harris, Chauncy, D., 295
Hatt, Paul K., 139
Hawthorne effect, 196
Heredity, social life, and geography,
    28–29
Heritage, biological, and social
    structure, 27
Herzberg, Frederick, job enrichment
    concept, 203
Hierarchy of authority in bureaucracy,
    179–181
Hodge, Robert W., 131
Human ecology and urbanization,
    293–298

Id, 221
Ideology
  elites, stratification, and, 104–105
  market, 195
  and social movements, 277
Imagination, sociological, 5–6
Incapacity, trained, in bureaucracy,
    186–187
Income
  Blacks vs. Whites, 113–114
  occupation, education, and, 142
  women vs. men, 109
Individuals. See also Man; Self
  conflict with social structure, 10–11
  and group structure, 236–237
  lack of conflict with social structure,
    11–14

Primary group (*Continued*)
  and socialization of individuals, 245,
    246–247
Primary relationships
  characteristics, 239–241
  growth factors, 241–245
  and primary groups, 237–238
Proletariat vs. bourgeoisie, 122
Proposition, formulation of, 343

Race
  education, occupational status, and
    112–113
  and ethnicity, as changing master
    positions, 110–116
Ranking
  vs. differentiation, 99–101
  and stratification, 98, 116–117,
    125–132
Reagan, Ronald, 124
Reification fallacy, 43–44
Relativity and deviance, 223, 225
Religion
  and class, 148
  defined, 311–312
  and participation in church-related
    activities, 312–313
  types, 313–314
Religious change
  denominations, sects, and, 314–316
  through secularization, 316–317
Repercussions and stratification, 99,
  117–118, 143–153
Research, scientific, formula for,
  342–345
Resources
  rewards as, 135–136
  and stratification, 98, 117
Retention and stratification, 99, 117,
  136–143
Retreatism and deviance, 227
Rewards
  distribution of, 133–135
  as resources, 135–136
  and stratification, 98, 117, 133–136
  types, 133
Riesman, David, and political
  pluralism, 320
Rights vs. obligations, 85–86
Ritualism and deviance, 227

Role behavior, 87–88. *See also* Behavior
  of clergymen, 316–317
  defined, 23
  and social structure, 77
Role expectations
  defined, 23
  and social structure, 78–79
Role prescriptions, 84–85
  defined, 23
  and social position, 85–87
  and social structure, 77
Role taking, self, and social structure,
  217–219
Roosevelt, Franklin D., 261, 319
Rose, Arnold, 29
Ross, Al, 121, 122
Rossi, Peter H., 131
Ruesch, Hans, 56
Rules and procedures in bureaucracy,
  183–185
Rural-urban convergence, 162–163,
  292–293
Russo, Anthony, 225

Sanctioning and socialization, 48
Sanctions and norms, 48–52
Scammon, Richard, 113, 114, 115
Science
  advantages of, 336–338
  concepts, 338–339
  propositions, 340
  public nature of, 337–338
  research formula, 342–345
  and serendipity, 344–345
  theory and explanation, 340–342
  variables, 339–340
Secondary relationships and secondary
  groups, 238–239
Sect, denomination, and religious
  change, 314–316
Sector theory of city growth, 293–296
Secularization, religious change
  through, 316–317
Segregation and urbanization, 297
Self
  looking-glass, 215
  mind, social interaction, and, 216–220
  socialization, symbolic interactionism,
    and, 214–220
  and society, 5–6